Tangled Routes

Tangled Routes

Women, Work, and Globalization
on the Tomato Trail

Second Edition

DEBORAH BARNDT

ROWMAN & LITTLEFIELD PUBLISHERS, INC.
Lanham • Boulder • New York • Toronto • Plymouth, UK

ROWMAN & LITTLEFIELD PUBLISHERS, INC.

Published in the United States of America
by Rowman & Littlefield Publishers, Inc.
A wholly owned subsidiary of The Rowman & Littlefield Publishing Group, Inc.
4501 Forbes Boulevard, Suite 200, Lanham, Maryland 20706
www.rowmanlittlefield.com

Estover Road, Plymouth PL6 7PY, United Kingdom

British Library Cataloguing in Publication Information Available

Library of Congress Cataloging-in-Publication Data
Barndt, Deborah.
  Tangled routes : women, work, and globalization on the tomato trail / Deborah Barndt. —
2nd ed.
     p. cm.
  Includes bibliographical references and index.
  ISBN-13: 978-0-7425-5556-3 (cloth : alk. paper)
  ISBN-10: 0-7425-5556-9 (cloth : alk. paper)
  ISBN-13: 978-0-7425-5557-0 (pbk. : alk. paper)
  ISBN-10: 0-7425-5557-7 (pbk. : alk. paper)
  1. Women in the food industry—Mexico. 2. Women agricultural laborers—Mexico. 3. For-
eign trade and employment—North America. 4. Tomatoes—North America. I. Title.
HD6073.F72.M493 2008
331.4'816648056420972—dc22

                                                                    2007029540

Printed in the United States of America

∞™The paper used in this publication meets the minimum requirements of American
National Standard for Information Sciences—Permanence of Paper for Printed Library
Materials, ANSI/NISO Z39.48-1992.

Contents

Preface to the Second Edition

More Signs of Hope

Spring has finally arrived in Canada, and everyone is in their gardens, hungry for the precious few months of growing we enjoy in a northern clime. I take breaks from writing to dig into my own backyard, clearing the way for a new spiral garden I have designed, as both a spiritual refuge and a source of nourishment. Grabbing hold of a particularly tenacious root, I examine it and am reminded of the metaphor that frames this book; tangled roots/routes still represent for me the complexity, mobility, and historical grounding of the current global food system, and the challenge of pulling apart the entwined roots of colonialism, capitalism, racism, and sexism that conspire to keep it going. At the same time, in uprooting this plant, I have made space for the heritage tomatoes, which I have just purchased from Erin, coordinator of Community Shared Agriculture (CSA) at an eco-village northwest of Toronto, and partner of Amanda, who has been my major collaborator on this revised edition. In his greenhouse, Erin has seeded seventy-eight varieties of heritage tomato plants!

The first edition of *Tangled Routes* ended with a chapter subtitled "Signs of Hope." In many ways, the preface to the second edition could bear a similar title. In the decade since I embarked on the twisty journey of following a tomato from a Mexican field to a Canadian fast-food restaurant, there have been major shifts in public consciousness around the issues I raised in the 2002 edition. While it's true that the forces that maintain the global food system have, in some ways, become more deeply entrenched, the critical questioning of its consequences and the crafting of alternatives, such as Erin's CSA, have become more widespread, and, in some cases, even mainstream.

Who could have predicted, for example, the mad-cow scares, the threat of avian flu, or the spinach recalls—all of which were catalysts for unsolicited consumer education about how globalized and disconnected the processes of production and consumption have become? They have revealed, as I attempt to do in my never finished detective work on the tomato, that the "emperor has no clothes," that, in fact, nobody knows the full story of how food gets to our table.

Who would have imagined that climate change would dramatically and viscerally awaken people's innate sense of our interdependence with the rest of nature? And that in Canada, the four major political parties would be vying to be seen as the "greenest of them all"? Who could have predicted that Wal-Mart, as the world's largest retailer, would be promoting organic produce, and that Mc-Donald's would be paying Mexican day laborers in Florida more for the grape tomatoes featured in their healthy salads? Or that those undocumented Mexican migrant workers would be the instigators of a major new civil rights movement and Alliance for Fair Food in the United States?

I am pleased that *Tangled Routes: Women, Work, and Globalization on the Tomato Trail* has resonated with so many, and in particular, that it is being used in diverse university classrooms, from international relations to gender and labor studies, from anthropology to political economy, from Latin American studies to qualitative research methods, and, of course, the burgeoning new field of food studies. A Spanish edition, *Rutas Enmarañadas*, translated by Martha Gonzalez, a popular Argentine educator, financed by royalties from the first edition, and shepherded through production by the activist/scholar Rafael Reygadas, was published in the summer of 2007 by the Universidad Autónoma Metropolitana–Xochimilco in Mexico City.

I am more convinced than ever that a transnational and interdisciplinary perspective is critical if we are going to both understand and transform unjust social systems that are simultaneously economic, political, and cultural. Food has become a powerful code for many who see, as I do, that it can offer an intimate starting point for a critical education about globalization, the environment, equity, and health, among other issues. Part of the problem we are confronting is, in fact, a fragmentation in our thinking and in our acting that limits our view to disciplinary frames and single-issue organizing.

Several professors have shared with me the creative ways in which they have used this book to engage students in actively examining their own practices and in making connections between personal and collective actions. When I have spoken to classes in the United States and Canada, students who work in retail or food services have immediately connected with the stories told here, helping me to decode, for example, the homogenized script that their employers require they repeat endlessly. Some are finding their own voices in campus organizing around these issues. At York University, where I teach, students created guerrilla theater protesting the exclusive rights of Pepsi on campus, for example. There is a new coalition, Healthy Food Initiatives @ York, as well as a sustainable purchasing coalition.

In the early 1990s, I felt alone in this project, but now I feel part of an expanding network of activist-scholars whose books have contributed to the rising public consciousness, such as Naomi Klein's *No Logo*, Marion Nestle's *Food Politics*, Eric Schossler's *Fast Food Nation*, Michael Pollan's *The Omnivore's Dilemma*, Barbara Kingsolver's *Animal, Vegetable, Miracle*, Brewster Kneen's *Farmageddon*, Gerardo Otero's *Mexico in Transition: Globalization, Neoliberalism, State, and Civil Society*, and Annette Aurelie Desmarais' *Vía Campesina*, to name a few. As an educator, I also appreciate more popular efforts to reach a broader public through documentaries such as *Super Size Me* and *The Corporation* and the feature film

Fast Food Nation, which cover many of the issues raised here, from the role of Mexican labor to the organizing efforts of young environmentalists.

When I was asked to update *Tangled Routes*, I was supported by my publisher, Rowman & Littlefield, as well as by my Faculty of Environmental Studies at York to contract experts in the various sectors featured in the chapters. Lauren Baker, Antonieta Barrón, Leigh Binford, Angelo DiCaro, Amanda Henderson, Brewster Kneen, Wendy Rogers, and Gabriel Torres all offered invaluable advice and research material about the new developments to be inserted. I found, however, that I had to revisit everything, eliminating material that was no longer so relevant and making new sense of shifts and changes.

Deepening Integration, Growing Resistance

Since the North American Free Trade Agreement (NAFTA) was implemented in 1994, there has been a deepening economic integration of the Americas, its most recent manifestation being the Security and Prosperity Partnership between Mexico, the United States, and Canada reflecting the post-9/11 mentality and paving the way for an ever-rising flood of Mexican workers into both the United States and Canada. Merger mania has continued into the new millennium with corporate concentration and global competition intensified; McDonald's, for example, has spread throughout Mexico, while Wal-Mart owns the biggest supermarkets in Mexico and has moved aggressively into Canadian food retail, threatening Loblaws, as predicted.

The impact on the Mexican countryside has been devastating, as Indigenous and subsistence farmers have lost access to land and been forced to migrate both within their country as well *al norte*, to the wealthier NAFTA countries. Mexico has gone from being self-sufficient in corn to being totally dependent on cheap imports from the subsidized U.S. producers, resulting in contamination by genetically engineered corn of land race maize plants in their centers of origin in Oaxaca, and, most recently, in rising costs of tortillas, due to big-business investment in converting corn to ethanol as a fuel alternative.

The neoliberal policies reigning in Mexico have contributed directly to increasing violence and repression in the countryside; brutal attacks by the military on Indigenous and peasant populations claiming land in Atenco, Oaxaca, and Chiapas in 2006 have bred an atmosphere of fear. The political situation mirrors this instability, with PAN candidate and new president Felipe Calderón following in the neoliberal footsteps of Vicente Fox, while PRD candidate Manuel Lopez Obrador proclaims a more progressive parallel government, and the Zapatista movement mounts "The Other Campaign," outside of the electoral system.

A growing consciousness of the unhealthy aspects of chemical industrial agriculture in the agroexport sector in Mexico has led local environmentalists to denounce the indiscriminate use of pesticides and the inhuman treatment of poor Indigenous migrant workers. Economic motives still overrode environmental consciousness in 2005, however, when the tomato companies in the region featured here failed to adhere to a ban on planting and thus unleashed an infestation of the white mosquito that forced all of them to move their production sites to another part of Jalisco state. The major technological development in agribusiness across the NAFTA countries has been the shift to greenhouse production, allowing greater control, longer growing seasons, increasing agroexports, and more stable employment, mainly for male workers.

Tomato sorting and packing, however, remains the domain of very young females, between the ages of fifteen and twenty-four, such as Ana Maria, who appears on the cover of this second edition. She is the granddaughter of Tomasa, the field worker featured in chapter 6, who is retiring just as Ana Maria carries on the family trajectory of working in foreign-owned companies to contribute to the shrinking family wage. In December 2006, I returned to Mexico to visit with this family, as well as local environmentalists. I also reconnected with Irena, the migrant farmworker who continues to come to Canada for our harvest season, and with Marissa, the Loblaws' cashier featured in chapter 4, who offered her own critical assessment of the labor concessions made by UFCW in negotiation with Loblaws. The feminization of labor and the proliferation of part-time work continues unabated, with the only hopeful signs being groups such as the Toronto-based Workers' Action Centre organizing around contingent labor and an incipient Continental Minimum Wage Campaign initiated by labor and social justice activists in Canada.

One of the major developments in the north, at the consumption end of the tomato chain, has been a growing public consciousness around the relationship between environment and health in general and, in particular, between fast food and child obesity. Consumer demand has caused McDonald's to offer healthier fare and, most recently, to pay suppliers more for the tomatoes they use in their salads, effectively increasing the wages of Mexican migrant workers in Florida. The challenge to fast-food culture has taken many forms: in Canada, where schools have come to depend on corporate funding in exchange for being branded a Coke or Pepsi school, young activists have advocated for transparency and healthy alternatives, following the example of celebrity chef Jamie Oliver, who convinced the United Kingdom to ban fast food in schools.

Supermarkets such as Loblaws have led the healthier trend toward organics, which contributes to their green image but still only supports large organic producers, who often reproduce all the other dynamics of large-scale production, without addressing environmental standards or workers' rights. They have been most threatened by Wal-Mart's move into food retail and recent incursion into Canada, also promoting organics while controlling supply chains notorious for cheap labor costs. Loblaws' new Real Canadian Superstores mimic Wal-Mart not only in integrating merchandise with food but also in offering lower wages. Labor organizers such as the United Food and Commercial Workers claim that this global competition has forced them into wage concessions in exchange for saving jobs. Flexible part-time labor has become entrenched, especially in the case of female supermarket cashiers, but gender issues seem to have dropped off the table of bargaining concerns. Women working on the front line are also threatened by technological developments such as the smart box, a self-scanning supermarket checkout option. After thirty years Marissa, the Loblaws cashier featured in chapter 4, has been promoted from part-time cashier to full-time inventory analyst, also a highly technologized task.

On a more hopeful note, the most interesting labor development in recent years has been the effort to organize the migrant farmworkers from Mexico and the Caribbean brought to Canada through the Seasonal Agricultural Workers Program. Chapter 5, focusing on truckers and migrant workers, has been greatly expanded because of this activity; labor-community coalitions are working with the growing migrant labor force, and some workers are risking their jobs to speak out about their working conditions. Films such as *El Contrato* have helped to raise public consciousness around the temporary worker labor force, whose numbers are swelling through the Security and Prosperity Partnership.

Chapter 8, "Signs of Hope," has been the most dramatically revamped. This is understandable, on the one hand, because actions are always conjunctural, responding to particular circumstances. Forces and priorities shift, and so actors and strategies must also change. From Mexico I have integrated recent campaigns organized by peasants such as El Campo No Aguanta Más (The Countryside Won't Take It Anymore!) and La Otra Campaña (The Other Campaign) mounted by the Zapatistas parallel to, but outside of, the 2006 Mexican federal elections; it prioritizes Indigenous rights while creating a coalition of diverse marginalized groups, building a new form of politics from the ground up. For the first time, I have included actions of new coalitions in the United States, focusing on the Alliance for Fair Food, which supported the Coalition of Immokalee Workers in getting McDonald's to concede more money for suppliers and thus for tomato workers in the Florida fields.

The new signs of hope in Canada include Food Secure Canada, a national advocacy body formed in 2005, and Common Frontiers, the Canadian arm of the Social Hemispheric Alliance, which has promoted cross-border coalitional actions with civil society groups in the United States and Mexico, and has crafted an alternative platform in response to the neoliberal trade model. Finally, Vía Campesina, with leadership from Canada, represents farmers and Indigenous peasants from around the world in reclaiming their rights to land and their seeds, to sustainable agricultural practices, and to diverse cultural knowledges. They represent an important shift toward self-advocacy, through which those most marginalized by corporate globalization are organizing themselves and providing leadership to broader transnational alliances.

Once again, this last chapter could have easily turned into a book of its own. This is probably the greatest sign of hope, but I will leave it to the reader and to fellow scholars and activists to make many other stories known, to share their own critical analyses, to dream their own visions of alternatives, and to actualize their dreams.

Acknowledgments

Thanks to Collaborators of Many Kinds

I start my thanks from the most intimate core of my circle of collaborators and work my way out, reversing the conventional order of acknowledgments. Like ripples in a moving lake, there have been different levels and kinds of collaboration throughout this multiyear project. I move from family and friends as collaborators, to student researchers, faculty advisers, community collaborators, and, finally, the collaboration of managers and workers whose stories are the heart of this book.

FAMILY AND FRIENDS AS COLLABORATORS

Thanks first to my son, Joshua, who accompanied me on many stages of this long journey. When I began the project in the mid-1990s, he joined me on the first forays into the Mexican tomato fields as my youngest research assistant at age ten. At that point, he most relished the periodic "research" visits to McDonald's. By 2002, he had developed a more critical perspective: two weeks before the first edition of *Tangled Routes* was launched, he and his teenage friends stood in front of a McDonald's distributing their own production—a zine raising critical questions about the fast-food industry's environmental, health, and labor practices.

The process transformed our household in other ways: my critical study of the current food system stimulated us to grow tomatoes in our backyard (a project started by our housemate, Sandy Gillians) and to protect even more tenaciously the family dinner as a sacred space. Antonio Savone, Joshua's father, first taught me that both healthy eating and educating on the political economy of food could happen at the kitchen table.

Many friends ate and talked with me about food and nourished my body, mind, and spirit through these years of research and writing: Mary Corkery, Leesa Fawcett, Edmee Franssen, Harriet Friedmann, Jorge Garcia, Lanie Melamed, Valerie Miller, Larry Olds, Harry Smaller, Kari Dehli, and John Vainstein. In particular, six of them offered me writing retreats, from the sunshine coast in British Columbia to the Vermont hills and Berkshire mountains, from Ontario's Algonquin lakes to its Bruce Peninsula and Beaver Valley. Through their generosity, I found the perfect formula for writing: beautiful natural settings and delectable meals with the good company of my best friends.

ACADEMICS AND ACTIVISTS AS COLLABORATORS

While I accept responsibility for the selection of stories and elaboration of positions within these pages, the gathering of stories as well as the wrestling with frameworks and analyses involved many other people. The photos on the following page honor some of them and make visible processes often hidden from the final write-up of any research.

At the bottom right of the collage are fifteen women activists and academics from Mexico, the United States, and Canada who contributed their expertise, passion, time, and energy to the project at different points. In May 1998, we spent three days together, critiquing essays and creating a collective anthology as a tasty stew, each one's flavor adding to the others. Our collaboration culminated in the book, *Women Working the NAFTA Food Chain: Women, Food, and Globalization.*[1]

The cross-border research process was facilitated greatly by funding from the Canadian Social Science and Humanities Research Council (SSHRC) as well as support from my own Faculty of Environmental Studies at York University in Toronto. Three kinds of research collaborators that deserve special attention are student researchers, academic advisers, and community collaborators.

Student Researchers

Thirteen extraordinary graduate students from York University's Faculty of Environmental Studies offered me the most intimate kind of collaboration over the years, helping to frame and focus the study, to draft funding proposals and organize seminars, to do corporate research and search Internet sites, to interview workers and managers, to transcribe tapes and organize negatives, to photograph and videotape actors in the tomato's journey, to write and edit articles, to produce videos and educational kits, to mount Web sites and photo exhibits, to facilitate workshops and animate community festivals, to translate data and check references, to scan photos and design pages. They have accompanied me on visits in three countries: to corporate offices and wholesale markets, tomato fields and packing plants, campesino village homes and migrant worker camps, fast-food restaurants and supermarkets, food terminals and border inspection complexes.

The outcomes of our collaborative research in this book are, in many ways, the work of these fellow travelers. In 1994–1995, Deborah Moffett and Emily Levitt helped set the original parameters for the project. Lauren Baker helped secure the research grant in 1995, joined me in 1996 for the first two Mexican trips in search of women tomato workers, and helped chart a three-year strategic plan for the project. Her own commitment to bioregional alternatives[2] led her to work with FoodShare, where she grew heritage tomatoes on Toronto rooftops; she is now completing a PhD in agroecology and biodiversity.

In 1996 and 1997, Stephanie Conway and Ann Eyerman took on major chunks of corporate research and primary interview activity, Stephanie with Loblaws and Ann with McDonald's. Stephanie helped with photo documentation,[3] and Ann contributed to the anthology and later published her own book.[4] We met biweekly to discuss emerging themes and problems growing out of the complex interdisciplinary research. Egla Martinez-Salazar and Karen Serwonka joined the project in 1997–1998. Karen did further work on McDonald's and helped with the supermarket cashier story, while Egla worked with the Mexican interviews (especially Indigenous workers), helped develop links with Mexican migrant workers in Canada, and set up a Tomasita Web site as well as published relevant articles.

In 1998, Anuja Mendiratta helped develop Tomasita's popular education work with local immigrant workers,[5] school classes, and international conferences; she also coedited (with Mark Haslam) a video based on local alternatives.

Melissa Tkayschk organized data and filled in research gaps, with interviews and Internet searches. Four master's in environmental studies (MES) students—Sheelagh Davis, Anuja Mendiratta, Joanna Shaw, and John Vainstein—joined me in early 1999 to document the tomato's movement across the U.S.–Mexico border at Nogales, Arizona. While in Mexico in 1999–2000, Sheelagh Davis updated the manuscript and liaised with the Mexican Institute for Community Development (IMDEC), our Mexican project collaborator. Finally, Michelle Doncaster helped in the final editing and production phases in 2000 and contributed photos, while Christina Lessels helped in the final editing and layout process.

When I agreed to produce an updated edition of this book in 2006–2007, Amanda Henderson became my key student research assistant. Besides undertaking specific research, she helped me to connect with consultants, organized and categorized all the new research material, suggested changes and additions, reviewed and edited the new drafts, and renumbered all the endnotes. She was meticulous and insightful, and I could not have undertaken this new project without her.

Academic Advisers

While these students provided the most constant kind of collaboration, shaping the project on a daily basis, a team of academic coresearchers helped focus the research, brought their own specific expertise to the study, contributed essays to our anthology, and provided valuable feedback on this manuscript. SSHRC funding allowed us to meet annually, and we mounted several conference panels (Canadian Latin American Studies Association [CALACS], Toronto, 1996; Latin American Studies Association [LASA], Guadalajara, 1997, and Miami, 2000; and the Agriculture, Food, and Human Values Society [AFHVS], Toronto, 1999).

Two Mexican economists offered their intimate knowledge from long-term studies on rural women workers. Maria Antonieta Barrón, of the Universidad Autonoma Mexicana (UNAM) in Mexico City, is a pioneer in gender dynamics in the rural sector and Mexican migrant labor patterns. Antonieta created new paths for the project, interviewing Mexican migrant workers in Ontario. Kirsten Appendini, of the Colegio de México in Mexico City and from 1997 to 1999 with the Food and Agricultural Organization (FAO) in Rome, brought substantial understanding of Mexican agriculture, food policy, and the shifting roles of women workers in agribusiness.

Fran Ansley, the only U.S. academic collaborator, is a Tennessee law professor who has been active in research, education, and advocacy around the impacts of global restructuring on workers in the Appalachian region, the poorest region of the United States. She joined us for visits with migrant workers in both Ontario and Jalisco, as well as at academic conferences.

The consumption end of the food chain was well represented by Ester Reiter, York University sociologist and author of the classic *Making Fast Food*. Ester helped shape the McDonald's study and brought an analysis of consumerism and citizenship to our anthology.[6] York sociologist Jan Kainer provided a much-needed gender analysis of labor union activity and collective bargaining in the food retail sector. University of Toronto sociologist Harriet Friedmann was a key academic collaborator and project consultant. As a global agriculture scholar as well as a local food policy activist, Harriet contributed to the historical and global frame[7] for my analysis, helping me think through complex issues.

My positions on agricultural ethics; popular environmental education; feminist ecological economics; women's health, gender, and diversity; ecofeminism; and women and social movements have been stimulated by the work of colleagues Mora Campbell, Leesa Fawcett, Ellie Perkins, Becky Peterson, Barbara Rahder, Cate Sandilands, and Gerda Wekerle, respectively. The interdisciplinary philosophy of the Faculty of Environmental Studies (FES) has provided a nurturing intellectual space for this work. Two other important institutional bases for support of this project were the Centre for Research on Latin America and the Caribbean at York University and the Toronto Food Research Network, headquartered at Ryerson University.

Two FES colleagues, Barbara Rahder and Gene Desfor, were partners in a three-year trinational consortium on Sustainable Community Development and Planning funded by the North American Mobility Program. It deepened research links with Mexican professors and students at the Centro de Investigaciones y Estudios Superiores de Anthropología Social (CIESAS), the Universidad de Guadalajara (UDG), and Universidad Autónoma Agraria Antonio Narro (UAAAN). UAAAN's Gilberto Aboites, UDG's Ofelia Perez Peña,[8] and CIESAS's Gabriel Torres have been key advisers for this study in the Mexican context. Drawing from his own doctoral research on Jalisco tomato workers,[9] Gabriel helped us identify the agribusiness case; his creative methodological advice has challenged me during both the fieldwork and writing. Another Mexican collaborator, Maria Dolores Villagomez,[10] helped gather interviews from Del Monte management and workers in Irapuato.

When it came to the writing stage, many of these collaborators provided critical feedback. Chapter 1 on the tomato's journey was enriched by careful reading by Elizabeth Abergel and Francisco Martinez. Dean Birkenkamp, Stephanie Conway, Michele Doncaster, Harriet Friedmann, and Egla Martinez-Salazar helped me organize and rewrite chapter 2 on theories and methods. Ann Eyerman and Ester Reiter offered useful comments on McDonald's for chapter 3. Chapter 4 on Loblaws supermarket cashiers benefited from the insightful comments of Stephanie Conway, Jorge Garcia, Jan Kainer, and Wendy Rogers. Gilberto Aboites, Kirsten Appendini, Lauren Baker, Antonieta Barron, Harriet Friedmann, Egla Martinez-Salazar, and Gabriel Torres all helped me sharpen the analysis and organization of chapter 6 on women working for Empaque Santa Rosa.

Margie Adams, graphic artist and longtime collaborator, contributed book design ideas and is responsible for the original drawings. I am indebted to the staff at Rowman & Littlefield for ongoing support and advice and, in particular, to Dean Birkenkamp and Gretchen Hanisch in the editorial division, copyeditor Laura Larson, and April Leo of editorial production.

Consultants for the Second Edition

Susan McEachern of Rowman & Littlefield invited me to produce a second edition of *Tangled Routes* and sought feedback from instructors who had used the book in their classes. I was able to contract experts in the various sectors of the food system to read specific chapters and offer suggestions. Brewster Kneen offered invaluable advice and material for an elaborated section on biotechnology in chapter 1. The updating of chapter 4, on supermarkets, was enriched by the careful reading and additions proposed by Angelo DiCaro and Wendy Rogers. Chapter 5 was greatly expanded thanks to the suggestions from Leigh Binford. Both Antonieta Barrón and Gabriel Torres offered fresh information and analysis in chapter 6 on Mexican agribusiness workers; Pedro and Teresa Sintero de la Torre provided updates on their own stories as salaried farmworkers. Finally, Lauren Baker provided important suggestions of new developments in organizing at both local and transnational levels in chapter 8. Collaboration thus continued to be a hallmark of this process and product in its latest form.

Community Collaborators

While this project is global in scope, we have consistently worked with local organizations exploring food alternatives, a kind of counterpoint to the corporate tomato. Our home base has been FoodShare Metro Toronto, an organization that since 1985 has promoted access for low-income communities to nutritious, affordable, and culturally appropriate food. Between 1995 and 1999, along with several graduate students, I collaborated with their Focus on Food training program. FoodShare's executive director, Debbie Field, helped link students to relevant community research, Field to Table director Mary Lou Morgan opened up opportunities for exchange and documentation of the training program, and Zahra Parvinian coordinated the Focus on Food/FES collaborative projects.

The former Doris Marshall Institute for Education and Action (Chris Cavanagh, Jorge Garcia, Sandy Macintosh, and Manuel Pinto) in Toronto and the Highlander Research and Education Center (Jim Sessions and Susan Williams) in Tennessee offered advice initially. This project helped Canadian and U.S. popular educators develop a strong link with the Mexican Institute for Community Development (IMDEC) in Guadalajara, which served as an institutional base for the Mexican research. IMDEC offered research collaborators (Catalina Gonzalez and Sara San Martin), video documenters (Luis Fernando Arana Gutierrez and Juan Jose Esquivel Ballesteros), student interns (Francisco Armenta, Jose Modesto Barros, and Roberto Ernesto Antillon Mena), and transcribers. Two community groups in Sirena, Amigos de la Naturaleza and Grupo de Salud Popular Nueva Vida, were critical activist links in Mexico; in particular, Leonardo Lamas, Maria Isabel Muñiz, Maria de Jesus Aguilar, Horacia Fajardo Santana, and Ana Isabel Gaetán. Both groups have been using royalties from our collective book to mount workshops on sustainable development and to improve working and living conditions of Indigenous migrant workers.

Managers and Workers as Collaborators

Perhaps I have left the best until last after all. In recognizing the tremendous generosity of managers, technicians, and women workers in Mexico, the United States, and Canada, I acknowledge that they were not intimately involved in defining the research or in writing it up. The key women actors in this story—Tomasa,

Marissa, and Irena—did carefully review their stories and suggest changes. It is their lives and their voices that provide the core of the stories told here, even though I take responsibility for their framing. I thank all those who let us interview them, listed here by company (workers' names are pseudonyms; the name of managers and technicians are not):

Empaque Santa Rosa: Managers Conrado Lomeli, Howard Kelsey, Cesar Gil, and Yves Gomez; fieldworkers Pedro and Teresa Sintero de la Torre, Reynalda Ursurio Atanacio, Jesus Casslez Hernandez, Reyna Gomez, Luz Maria Ramon Jacobo, Guadalupe Ramon Jacobo, and Gladis Ortega; packers Maria Elena Mazo, Mirna Melendea, Yoshira Soto Ceceña, and Alma Berenice Diaz; and greenhouse workers Ana Marta Lopez Diaz, Enrique Dao Flores, Soledad Mendez Silva, Marcela Barba, Socorro Ramirez Garcia, Leticia Lopez Aguilar, and Gabriela Silva Perez

Del Monte: Vice President Jorge Betherton, training manager Juanita Ullua, former worker Alfredo Badajoz Navarro, and Antonio Velazquez of the Frente Auténtico del Trabajo (FAT)

Loblaws: Environmental affairs officers Ken Mulhall and Marcela Diaz-Granados; trainers Sandra Lot and Kim Scharnowski; local manager Andrew Stock; environmental consultant Vive Wark; cashiers Karen Botello, Lily Defide, Corinne Muccilli, Marissa Ronen, and Rosina Villella; and deli worker Noriko Grasso

McDonald's: Julie Hamilton, Cathy Cacioppo, and Anna DiMarco

National Grocers: Gary Lloyd

Ontario Food Terminal: Angelo Vento

Joyce Foods: Dominique Stillo

Pacific Produce (Vancouver): Larry Tenelia

U.S./Mexican border officials: Jonathon Barnes and Jesus Cruz

Canadian customs: Greg Hummell

UTTSA Trucking: Heriberto Castillo

GAPCO (Nogales, Arizona): Luis Palafox and Ana Maria Martinez

Ontario FARMS program: Irena Gonzalez

Mexican independent producer: Benjamin Segura

I am thankful to Stephanie Conway for allowing me to use the photos on pages 30 and 31; to Socorro Ramirez Garcia, who supplied the photos on pages 234 and 268. All other photographs are mine. All drawings are by Margie Adams of Art Work—chapter 1: pages 10, 11, 22, 26, 28; chapter 2: pages 70 and 73; chapter 6: page 221.

Finally, I acknowledge the land, and especially the tomato, both represented here by my own particular framing but central to the story as well as to our very survival.

Notes

1. Deborah Barndt, ed., *Women Working the NAFTA Food Chain: Women, Food, and Globalization* (Toronto: Second Story Press, 1999). The anthology received the top award in the category of women's issues at the 2000 Independent Publisher Book Awards.

2. Lauren Baker, "A Different Tomato: Creating Vernacular Foodscapes," in *Women Working the NAFTA Food Chain*, 249–60.

3. Stephanie Conway, "Scanning the Future: Towards an Exposé of Flexibilization and Automation in the Supermarket Industry," unpublished manuscript, 1996.

4. Ann Eyerman, "Serving Up Service: Fast Food and Office Women Workers Doing It with a Smile," in *Women Working the NAFTA Food Chain*, 161–74; see also Ann Eyerman, *Women in the Office: Transitions in a Global Economy* (Toronto: Sumach, 2000).

5. Deborah Barndt and Anuja Mendiratta, "Eating Stories and Telling Food: Immigrant Women Tap the Power of Food," in *Women and Food: An Interdisciplinary Exploration*, ed. Arlene Voski Avakian and Barbara Haber (Berkeley: University of California Press, 2002).

6. Ester Reiter, "Serving the McCustomer: Fast Food Is Not about Food," in *Women Working the NAFTA Food Chain*, 81–96.

7. Harriet Friedmann, "Remaking 'Traditions': How We Eat, What We Eat, and the Changing Political Economy of Food," in *Women Working the NAFTA Food Chain*, 35–60.

8. Ofelia Perez Peña, "A Day in the Life of Maria: Women, Food, Ecology, and the Will to Live," in *Women Working the NAFTA Food Chain*, 237–48.

9. Gabriel Torres, *The Force of Irony: Power in the Everyday Life of Mexican Tomato Workers* (New York: Berg, 1997).

10. Maria Dolores Villagomez, "Grassroots Responses to Globalization: Mexican Rural and Urban Women's Collective Alternatives," in *Women Working the NAFTA Food Chain*, 209–19.

Introduction:
ROOTS AND ROUTES

Where Does Our Food Come From?

This book starts with that seemingly simple question. But the question itself raises many other questions.

To start with, why are we even asking the question now? A century ago, our great-grandparents had little reason to wonder where their food came from; if they didn't grow their own, at least they usually knew the people who did. To ask the question today is to admit, in fact, a shared ignorance; very few of us have much sense at all of the processes that have brought food to our table, nor can we envision the many people who have moved it along the way. Our disconnection from both the earth and its fruits is not only physical and social but also mental and spiritual.

When we explore the disconnection, however, we open a Pandora's box. A whole array of other questions comes tumbling out: What soil and climate have nurtured the food we eat? Whose hands have planted, cultivated, picked, packed, processed, transported, inspected, sold, and cooked it? What production practices have transformed it from seed to fruit, from fresh to processed form? Who decides what is grown and how? What is the effect of those decisions on our health and the health of the planet? The questions are, indeed, endless.

The Tomasita Project

As an educator, I am deeply interested in the ways we learn, how we come to understand more fully our own daily experiences and the broader forces shaping them. In 1994, I found a popular education tool, "A Whirlwind Tour of Economic Integration with Your Guide, Tomasito the Tomato,"[1] that addressed some of the aforementioned questions by tracing the journey of a tomato from Mexico to Canada. The tomato story helped demystify globalization, revealing the role of corporations in creating and maintaining a global food system dependent on genetically modified seeds, pesticide packages, expropriated Indigenous land, cheap peasant labor, and environmental racism.

The tomato seemed a perfect "entrée" to a process of cross-border research and popular education around the complex phenomenon and often confusing concept of globalization. "Entrée" is used in two senses: it could be the content, or main course, of an educational process, as well as an entry point into both the personal experience of eating and the globalized process of food production, as one slice of the globalization pie. That is, as an "intimate commodity,"[2] food (or the tomato) touches our bodies as well as our minds and hearts and finds its way into our stomachs as well as our stories; as a border-crossing market commodity, it leaves a trail that offers clues to broader economic, ecological, political, and cultural processes.

I briefly toyed with the idea of following a blouse instead of food or corn instead of a tomato. The fact that we ingest food, and become what we eat, made it more compelling; food shapes us physically as well as emotionally and culturally. The tomato was ripe with many possibilities: though it originated in Mexico, it has become central to the diets of all three North American countries; it can be grown in all three, at least seasonally. As a fruit of the earth, the tomato needs the elements (land, water, air, sun) to grow; as a many-seeded fruit, it has been the object of diverse technological interventions, from hybridization to bio-

genetic engineering. Finally, it is a food that can stimulate our growing awareness about the impact of long-distance production: almost any northern consumer can tell you the difference in taste between an imported winter tomato
and a local summer one!

In adapting the idea of the tomato's journey, I decided to focus on the dynamic relationship between the tomato and the women workers who are most
involved in both its production and consumption; so Tomasito became Tomasita,
representing both. The Spanish name, too, reminds us that, within the NAFTA
(North American Free Trade Agreement) food system, the most marginalized
workers are Mexican. Thus began a five-year collaborative adventure in research, education, and action called the Tomasita Project.

Little did I realize, however, that I was embarking on a journey that would
send me along very twisty trails and into deep and complex histories. The path the
tomato takes is certainly not a straight line, nor do the stories of women who pick
and pack, scan and sell tomatoes fit a linear notion of history. The *roots* and *routes*
of these women workers, as well as the tomatoes they bring us, are indeed tangled.

Tangled Roots and Routes

My search for the roots of this tomato story took me to Mexico. There I also
found trees that expose their gnarled roots, crawling along the ground, wrapped
around each other. "Tangled roots and routes" seemed a perfect metaphor for the
process of analysis framing this book. The stories of women workers and the
tomatoes they move from field to table, from Mexico to Canada, are tenaciously
intertwined, making it next to impossible to examine one alone, without considering how it is connected to, and often embedded in, another.

The exploration itself has challenged my deeper understandings of both
roots and routes, of time and space, raising questions about the complex dialectical relations of production and consumption, work and technology, health and
environment, biodiversity and cultural diversity. The routes of the tomato as
well as the movements of women workers reflect broader social practices guided
primarily by corporations, nation-states, and financial institutions. Each
woman's experience is shaped by her own tangled roots, influenced by where
(and when) she was born, her ethnic and/or racial identity, her economic situation and status, her age, and her family status. Many of these factors are not only
dynamically interrelated but also constantly shifting.

I realize that I run the risk of simplifying a multilayered and contextually
shaped global food system by focusing on just one commodity (the tomato), in
one context (North America), and highlighting one particular social group
(women food workers). These are only concrete entry points for exploring
broader processes that move beyond the particularity of the tomato. The
metaphor of tangled roots and routes reminds us that these stories are neither
simple nor one-dimensional but rather complex, messy, and very rich.

Recovering Personal Roots

Whenever I drive to visit my parents in Ohio, I pass by the small village where I lived as a child in the 1950s. As I approach the exit on the divided super-highway, I encounter a cluster of gas stations and fast-food restaurants, almost identical to any highway stop in North America. The town itself lies one mile south, its main intersection surrounded by the abandoned shells of what used to be the general store, the local tavern, and the sole gas station. I grew up play-ing with my friends on their families' farms, which provided not only their livelihood but also our sustenance. The farms, too, are now shells, and towns-people can be found among the travelers who stop for a quick fill-up of fuel and food by the highway.

Five years ago, I did not realize that one of the routes this project would take would be into my own history. As I dug into the roots of the continental food system, I reconnected with my own roots, revisiting my own more inti-mate experiences with food production in that rural community. In exchange for his duties as the minister of the local church, for example, my father was sometimes paid in produce; I have memories of bushels of vegetables dropped on the doorstep or half a frozen pig left on the table. We tended our own large garden, and my mother canned food for the winter. In the fall, townswomen gathered in the churchyard around a fire to stir an immense cauldron of apple butter, which was then distributed to each of their kitchens. There was little distance between production and consumption; we knew intimately how our food was grown and prepared.

As I was growing up in the 1950s and eating fresh tomatoes from our garden, the globalized food system was also in its formative years. My lifetime parallels major transformations in global agriculture, mostly originating in the nation of my birth. They were spurred on by post–World War II notions of economic growth and development, an increasing industrialization of agriculture, and other interrelated processes (chapter 1) reflected in the divided highway and roadside restaurants that turned my rural community into a ghost town by the 1990s.[3] Born in 1945 in the "belly of the beast"—or the country that was on the road to global hegemonic control of many economic, political, and cultural processes—I was profoundly shaped by this transformation of food.

For the past thirty years, however, I have lived in Canada and have spent more time in Mexico than in the United States. Moving outside my own coun-try of origin and viewing it from the other side of both its northern and its southern borders have opened up the fertile space of the margins for rethink-ing the systems often created and propagated by U.S. initiatives. Canada's am-biguous historical identity as colonized and colonizer has helped me rethink my own ambivalent and mixed identity; most particularly, the multicultural-ism of Toronto has offered me encounters with many diasporic histories that have fertilized my postmodern imagination. My regular forays into Latin America over the last twenty-five years, have exposed me to yet other cultural forces shaping my political perspectives and educational work. Living and working in Peru in the 1970s, in Nicaragua in the 1980s, and in Mexico in the 1990s has helped me put the tomato story in a hemispheric perspective. It is that journey that I invite you to join now.

Zooming Out/In/Out: Tracing the Trail of This Book

As a photographer, I think about the stories unfolding in this book like a camera lens, zooming out and zooming in. Chapters are organized into three sections.

In the first section, chapters 1 and 2, I zoom out, laying the broader ground for the women's stories and framing them conceptually. In chapter 1, "Across Space and through Time: Tomatl Meets the Corporate Tomato," I trace the tomato trail from the Mexican field to a Canadian fast-food restaurant. In two intertwining stories, we follow both "Tomatl," the indigenous tomato that is rooted in traditional practices and today being re-created for local consumption, and the "Corporate Tomato," the tomato that has been commodified and chemicalized through industrial agriculture in Mexico and then exported, scanned, and sliced for northern consumption. The chapter offers a wide-angle view of the tomato story not only through space but also through time, as we excavate its roots in key scientific, industrial, chemical, and genetic moments. Chapter 2 introduces the theoretical frames and methodological approaches used in tracing the tomato's journey and in gathering the stories of women workers along the trail. I introduce key frames (globalization from above and from below, interlocking analysis of power, and four key axes of investigation) as well as methodologies (popular education and methods, corporate and qualitative research, and photographic tools) applied.

To get to the heart of this story, we zoom in on specific food companies and women workers. Chapters 3, 4, 5, and 6 offer close-ups, or case studies, of key stops along the tomato trail, from a Mexican agribusiness to a Canadian supermarket and a U.S.-owned fast-food restaurant, with a pause along the highway to consider truckers and migrant workers. While the tomato story in chapter 1 follows Tomasita's movements from south to north, these chapters reverse the order, beginning with our consumption of tomatoes in the north and working our way back to the roots of tomato production in the south. Each chapter is framed by the globalization-from-above and globalization-from-below dynamic, so corporate stories are told as well as the daily work and home lives of the women workers. Woven into these stories and concluding each chapter are examples of "the other globalization," or resistance at both individual and collective levels.

In chapter 3, "Arch Deluxe with a Smile: Women Never Stop at McDonald's," we examine the meteoric rise and global dominance of McDonald's fast-food restaurants as a model for both economic restructuring as well as cultural hegemony. The stories feature primarily younger workers reflecting on their working conditions and how their own eating practices are affected by constantly changing shift work and quick, convenient food. As an example of the other globalization, an elementary school class undertakes participatory research on fast food, deconstructing ads and making their own images. We also consider the growing public consciousness about child obesity traced to fast food.

The Canadian retail giant, Loblaws supermarkets, owned by the conglomerate George Weston Ltd., is featured in chapter 4, "You Can Count on Us: Scanning Cashiers at Loblaws Supermarkets." First we probe the secrets of their success as a company—particularly through corporate brand development, designer supermarkets, and labor restructuring. Their increasing vulnerability as Wal-Mart moves into Canada is also examined. Then we move to the stories of the women workers on the front line, the cashiers. They represent two major trends in global workplaces: the phenomenon of part-time "flexible" labor and the intensification of work through technology; in particular, the scanners symbolize the pressure on them to be both "fast and friendly," while also affecting their health and sense of themselves. The other globalization is represented by the growing debate around the labeling of genetically modified foods.

Chapter 5, "On the Move for Food: Truckers and Transnational Migrants," provides a brief interlude between consumption in the north and production in the south, by introducing two different kinds of workers who must migrate in order to feed themselves while serving the global food system. The story of Humberto, a truck driver for Mexican agribusinesses who moves the tomatoes across the Mexico–U.S. border, and of Jim, who brings them to Canada, reveals the centrality of transportation to this system. And a little-known story of Mexican migrant workers coming to Canada is told by Irena, who has spent four months every summer for the past thirteen years picking our summer tomatoes in Ontario. A budding movement for migrant worker rights is stimulating cross-sectoral actions.

Finally, we reach the roots of the corporate tomato story in chapter 6, "Picking and Packing for the North: Agricultural Workers at Empaque Santa Rosa." For northern consumers, I offer a rich and complex history of agriculture in Mexico; the current push for agroexport production is epitomized by the story of Empaque Santa Rosa, the second-largest domestic producer of tomatoes with 85 percent now being exported. I peel away the layers of the stories of women workers in this agribusiness, from the poorest Indigenous women brought for the harvests to the more privileged mestizo packers offered higher wages and better working and living conditions. The other globalization is represented by recent mobilizations by human rights groups to expose the unjust treatment of Indigenous migrant workers housed in horrific camps on the edge of the fields.

In the third section (chapters 7 and 8), we zoom out again, comparing the stories of the women workers across borders and companies, and using an even wider lens to reflect on different forms of resistance in both Canada and Mexico, which I am calling the "other globalization."

Chapter 7, "Crossing Sectors and Borders: Weaving a Holistic Analysis," compares the experiences of women workers in the different sectors of the tomato chain, following the key axes of the study. The analysis evolves around the corresponding concepts of *distancing* (production/consumption), *fragmentation and uniformity* (biodiversity/cultural diversity), *flexibility of labor* (work/technology), and *holistic health* (health/environment).

Chapter 8, "Signs of Hope: Taking Action for Justice and Sustainability," leaves us with a sense of possibilities and alternatives to the global food system. I introduce a framework for examining "the other globalization" through four levels or forms of resistance: individual critical thoughts and actions, local/global education, collective action, and transnational coalitions. There are examples of each, from both the Mexican context and the Canadian context.

Notes

1. Ecumenical Coalition for Economic Justice, "A Whirlwind Tour of Economic Integration with Your Guide, Tomasito the Tomato," *Economic Integration in the Americas Kit*, Toronto (1994).

2. Anthony Winson, *The Intimate Commodity: Food and the Development of the Agro-Industrial Complex in Canada* (Toronto: Garamond, 1993).

3. Alexander Wilson, *The Culture of Nature: North American Landscape from Disney to the Exxon Valdez* (Toronto: Between the Lines, 1991).

CHAPTER 1

Across Space and through Time:

TOMATL MEETS THE CORPORATE TOMATO

The history of the tomato can reveal the unfolding global food system and the shifting role of women workers within it.

In excavating the tangled roots and following the tangled routes of the tomato, two main characters introduce the contrasting approaches to growing food: Tomatl is the homegrown tomato, named with the Indigenous name it was given in Aztec times; the corporate tomato is the fruit in its more familiar com-modified form, produced in large quantities through multiple technological in-terventions. While the focus will be on the journey of the corporate tomato, we will periodically refer to the contrasting and shorter journey of Tomatl, from pre-colonial to postcolonial times.

In tracing the trail from Mexican field to Canadian fast-food restaurant, we move through the three NAFTA countries, from south to north, on a journey that is clearly not a straight line. To simplify the story, I am dividing the process into three major stages following the trip north:

- the production of tomatoes in Mexico;
- their transport, trade, and distribution into the United States and Canada; and
- their commercialization and consumption in Canada.

While the linear south-north trajectory suggested here reflects a predominant dynamic of the south producing for the north,[1] all three phases—production, dis-tribution, and consumption of tomatoes—take place in each of these three coun-tries, as well as in others around the planet. This journey could, in fact, have many other starting and ending points, the processes described here playing out differently in other contexts.[2]

I am building on the tradition of global commodity chain (GCC) analysis, an approach developed by Gary Gereffi and others to understand the current forms of capitalism in which production and consumption not only have crossed na-tional boundaries but have been reorganized under a "structure of dense net-worked firms or enterprises."[3] While my framing of the tomato story does not follow a classic commodity chain analysis,[4] it does try to link the particular and general, the local and global aspects of tomato production and consumption.

Gereffi distinguishes between producer-driven commodity chains, in which transnational corporations control production networks, and buyer-driven com-modity chains, in which large retailers and brand-named merchandisers shape and coordinate decentralized production networks while controlling design and marketing themselves. Because the corporate tomato moves from globalizing Mexican agribusiness and processing plants to Canadian supermarkets and restaurants that are also globalized, we will see both types of chains in their over-lapping complexity.

This chapter foregrounds the story of the tomato, leaving the workers who move the tomato along this chain in the background for now. As the stories of women workers unfold in subsequent chapters, we will also see what com-modity chain analysis suggests are the two primary factors in the restructuring of the global economy: the search for low-wage labor and the pursuit of orga-nizational flexibility. What I bring to the commodity chain approach is an eco-logical perspective and a gendered analysis, integrating as well race, age, and regional differences.

In a popular education workshop with immigrant women in Toronto, Neema, a Trinidadian woman, described the global food system like this: "It seems like one big puzzle and we don't have all the pieces. So we've got to see if we can fit all the pieces together and get a clearer picture of what's going on."[5] This is no easy task. In my particular telling of the tomato tale, the overall impression is of a long and twisty trail, a many-staged journey that no one understands in its entirety. We were most struck by this fact as we interviewed campesino and company vice president, cashier and chief buyer alike: no one person has the whole picture; each actor in this complex chain perhaps has some sense of the steps that come just before and after his or hers, but sometimes not even that much.

Of course, each stage is perceived differently by each person engaged in it; these multiple subjectivities, in fact, make the story not only contradictory but also more human. It is a daunting task to piece together the puzzle. I have confronted roadblocks and detours, discovered diversions and surprising openings. In this telling, I have chosen to follow certain tangential paths and not others. This is a constantly changing process that I personally can't hope to unveil fully.

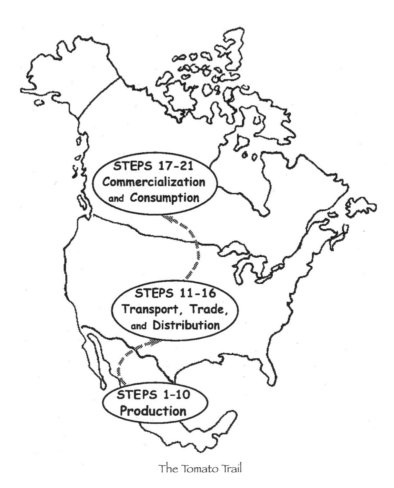

The Tomato Trail

I am arbitrarily dividing the journey into twenty-one steps (for the corporate tomato's journey) and five stages (for Tomatl and alternative practices); each step or stage introduces a key issue to be explored later through the case studies of Mexican agribusiness and Canadian food retail and service industries. The tangled journeys make us realize we cannot separate our survival in the north from the survival of people in the south, nor the fate of human beings from the fate of the earth. The corporate journey is described in steps (numbers 1, 2, 3), while we can follow Tomatl's story (designated as stages and marked by Roman numerals—I, II, III) from the margins: the survival of more sustainable locally controlled growing practices.

Tomatl's Story from the Margins

STAGE I: TOMATO'S BEGINNINGS IN PREHISPANIC AMERICA

The tomato originated as a wild plant in the Andean region (what is now northwest Peru), its seeds then probably carried north by birds to what is now Mexico, centuries before the time of Christ. First domesticated by the Mayas and the Aztecs, the fruit was named *tomatl*, which in Nahuatl, the language of the Aztecs, means "something round and plump." For centuries the tomato was a native crop grown by Indigenous peoples in Mexico to feed their families. Using traditional agricultural practices (chapter 6), they grew tomatoes in great variety,

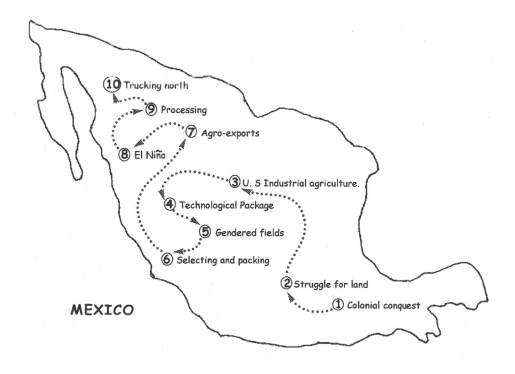

interplanted them with other crops, and rotated crops from year to year, in the context of complex local ecosystems. Wild tomato species, for example, supplied other varieties of tomatoes with resistance to nineteen major plant diseases.

The Journey of the Corporate Tomato

Step 1: Colonial Conquest of the "Love Apple"

In the sixteenth century, the Spanish conquistadores received tomatoes as part of tributes from Indigenous peoples in the Americas and eventually took the plant back to Europe along with other natural riches they had "discovered." There it was initially feared as poisonous and primarily considered decorative as a "love apple," until Italians began to embrace it in their cuisine. French settlers carried tomatoes to Quebec and Louisiana in the eighteenth century, and it was soon proclaimed medicinal and promoted by agricultural innovators such as Thomas Jefferson. Since then the tomato has been central to diets in the Americas and considered rich in vitamins (A and C) and minerals (calcium and potassium), especially when ripe. It has been bred into hundreds of hybrid forms; the most common big round red version, *Solanum lycopersicon* in Latin, is known in Mexico as *jitomate*.[6] The tomato is now the most widely grown fruit in the Americas as well as the most heavily traded.

Step 2: The Struggle for Land (Campo)

In recent decades, many Mexican *campesinos* (which means literally "of the land," or *campo*) have lost access to lands for cultivating the plant, either individually or collectively in peasant communities. Indigenous peoples have struggled for land for centuries, especially after the Spaniards arrived and sent them to work as peons in the mines and plantations. Mestizo and Indigenous campesinos gained greater access to land through the Mexican Revolution (whose battle cry was "Land and liberty!") and through agrarian reforms under President Lázaro Cardenas in the 1930s (chapter 6). In the 1980s, Mexican neoliberal policies privatized *ejidos* (communal lands) and encouraged foreign investment, and in the 1990s and 2000s, NAFTA increased agroexports. Since then, more and more campesinos from the southern states of Mexico have migrated to richer northern states to work as salaried labor for large agribusinesses. If they still own plots in their home regions, much of the land has been degraded through endless cycles of fertilizer and pesticide use.

Land, or the *campo*, is thus central to the story of the corporate tomato, particularly as it has become viewed as a natural resource and as private property by Western science and industrial capitalist interests, both national and global.

Step 3: Monocultures Led by U.S. Industrial Agriculture

Tomatoes were the first fruit produced for export in Mexico, beginning in the late 1880s, but their production intensified with the development of capitalist production in Sinaloa in the 1920s. Often financed by U.S. capital and inputs, Mexican companies adopted American industrial practices such as Taylorization, the assembly line production and standardization developed after World War I. The work was divided into small manageable units, and technology was introduced that didn't depend on physical force, opening up jobs for women. In the late 1920s, U.S. surplus and protectionist policies forced Mexican producers to standardize packing tomatoes in wooden crates[7] to compete with U.S. producers. In the 1950s, two technologies revolutionized tomato cultivation: the use of plastic covering "mulch" that kept the plants from direct contact with the earth[8] and the growth of seedlings in greenhouses.[9] By 2004, tomatoes accounted for 11.98 percent of the fruit and vegetable production in Mexico, even though they took up only 0.5 percent of the arable land.[10]

Monocultural and cash crop production is a central feature of the global food system today. It has, however, eliminated many types of tomatoes; 80 percent of the varieties have been lost in this century alone.[11] Now Indigenous and mestizo campesinos tend tomatoes as salaried workers in agribusinesses built on a Western scientific logic and rationalism. Each worker is relegated to a specific routinized

task, in large monocrop fields or more recently in greenhouses (called "factories in the fields"), where the goal is to harvest thousands of tomatoes at the same time and in identical form primarily destined for export.

The industrialization of agriculture has, in fact, been accompanied by a feminization of agricultural labor, particularly in greenhouses and packing plants.

[ogbop]

STAGE II: COMBINING SALARIED WORK WITH SUBSISTENCE AGRICULTURE

While large monocultural agribusinesses dominate tomato production in Mexico, the campesinos who work seasonally for them cannot survive without also cultivating their own staple crops. As the case study of Empaque Santa Rosa, the Mexican agribusiness, shows, the low wages of industrial agriculture are based on the assumption that workers will combine salaried work with subsistence agriculture. For the poorer Indigenous migrant farmworkers, this is becoming less possible as they must migrate to more and more harvests to survive and as they lose access to arable land in their home states. But many peasants maintain their subsistence knowledge and more environmentally sustainable practices by growing basic foods in plots on hillsides outside their village, working in their *milpa* (cornfield) after returning from picking tomatoes in large plantations. This double day not only assures their survival but keeps traditional knowledges alive alongside more industrialized practices. The interplanting of corn, squash, and beans (called the "three sisters" by North American Aboriginal people) uses the advantages of each crop to improve the growth of the others while maintaining the fertility of the soil.[12]

Step 4: Multinationals Control the Technological Package

Even though many tomato seeds originated in Mexico, they have now become the "intellectual property" of multinational companies, which claim patents on genetically modified forms of the seeds. They have been re-created in thousands of varieties, hybridized and more recently genetically engineered by multinational agribusinesses such as Monsanto and its counterparts such as Western Seed of Mexico. In 1996, Western Seed produced, for example, a seed that is immune to the whitefly that destroyed thousands of tons of tomato production in Autlán, Jalisco, in the early 1990s.[13] These seeds sell for $20,000 a kilogram and are geared entirely to the export market.

For many Indigenous peoples and campesinos, this has meant not only a loss of ownership and control of the seeds but also a loss of their own knowledge about how to grow tomatoes in endless varieties. Ironically, Mexican producers such as Empaque Santa Rosa must now buy tomato seeds from foreign companies in the United States, Israel, and France; they also hire French and Israeli engineers who bring a whole technological package that must be used with the seeds, as well as an entire production process adopting European and North American management and work practices.[14]

Agrochemicals are central components of the "technological package," and their origins in the Green Revolution are examined later in this chapter. Long before tomato seedlings are planted in the ground, for example, the soil has been treated with fertilizers to enrich the soil for growth. As the tomatoes grow, there is a constant barrage of a variety of agrochemicals—pesticides, herbicides, and fungicides—

aimed at killing pests, bacteria, and fungi. Under the mantra of efficiency and productivity, they are heralded as making the plants grow faster, stronger, more uniform, and in greater quantity; they are also critical to the production of the blemish-free tomatoes demanded by the export market.[15] The agrochemicals themselves are primarily imported from U.S. multinationals: Bayer, DuPont, Monsanto, and Cargill. There is neither training in their use, however, nor protective gear provided for workers in fields where pesticides are sprayed by hand, combine, or small plane. Every year an estimated three million people are poisoned by pesticides.[16]

⌐⌐⌐⌐⌐

STAGE III: ZAPATISTAS, NAFTA, AND FOOD

It is no coincidence that the poorest field-workers are Indigenous families from the south, forced away from their land for the myriad of reasons named earlier. Nor was it an accident that the Zapatistas chose 1 January 1994, the inaugural day of the North American Free Trade Agreement, as the moment for an uprising of Indigenous communities who had lost their land and livelihoods through colonial practices and neoliberal policies. The Zapatista struggle, for bread and dignity, has been transformed into an international movement that is reclaiming Indigenous rights and knowledges as critical not only for the survival of poor campesino communities but also for the survival of the planet (chapter 8). Food is a political centerpiece of this initiative, reflecting the continuing struggle for the land (campo) as well as for cultural identity of campesinos and Indigenous peoples.

⌐⌐⌐⌐⌐

Step 5: Gendered Fields: Women Workers Plant and Pick

Primarily young women plant the seeds in Empaque Santa Rosa's large greenhouses in Sinaloa and nurture them into seedlings, ready to be distributed to production sites in other parts of the country. Once shipped to Sirena, they are transplanted in the surrounding fields by the few full-time workers hired by Santa Rosa from neighboring villages. The young plants are watched carefully over the first few weeks, pruned by campesino women who pluck off the shoots so the stems will grow thicker, faster, and straighter. If tomatoes grow from a main stalk, they take up less space, are less vulnerable to pests on the ground, and are easier to pick. When the plants reach a certain height, women workers tie the vines to strings that hold them up, so they can grow without being crushed on the ground.[17]

As one of the most labor-intensive crops, tomato picking requires many more person hours and careful work than does picking bananas, for example. While most agribusinesses in the United States now have mechanical harvesters that pick tomatoes very fast and in massive amounts, in most Mexican monocultural plantations, tomatoes are still handpicked by campesinos. Hired by the companies, many of them are Indigenous families who have been brought on a one- to two-day journey from the poorer southern states for the harvest season, and they live precariously in migrant labor camps near the fields.

At Empaque Santa Rosa, the tomato workers usually start picking tomatoes at 7:30 A.M., stop for a lunch at 10:30 A.M., and are finished by 2:30 P.M., by which

time the sun has become unbearably hot. They pluck them fast, too, so that they can fill the quota of forty pails a day to earn their twenty-eight pesos (approximately U.S. $5 in 1997).[18] Both men and women (as well as children) pick tomatoes, but women pickers are considered more gentle, so there is less damage to the crop. Men, on the other hand, are the ones who stack crates on flatbed trailers that they pull by tractor from the field to the packing plant. This gender dynamic needs to be understood in the context of a *machista* culture perpetuated by an international sexual division of labor (chapter 6).

Step 6: Selecting and Packing the Perfect Tomato

Men unload the tomatoes in crates from the trucks and dump them into chutes that send them sailing into an agitated sea of 90 percent chlorinated water, a bath to remove the dirt, bacteria, and pesticide residue from their oversprayed skins. They are dried by blasts of warm air, then moved along on conveyor belts through another chute that coats them with wax. It keeps the moisture in and the bacteria out, protecting the tomatoes from further breakdown during their long journey, but it also gives them a special shine that makes them more attractive to wholesalers and shoppers in the north.[19]

Not all tomatoes will make the longer trip north, as only the "best" are selected for export. To be chosen, they must be large, well shaped, firm, and free of any cracks, scars, or blemishes. The "nimble fingers" that decide which tomato goes where belong to young women, many of them brought by Santa Rosa from its larger production site in Sinaloa to handle this delicate task. They sort the fruit according to grades and destinations but also by size (determined by how many fit into a box— e.g., 5 × 5s or 6 × 7s) and by color (from shades of green to red), because this is how the importers order them.[20] In Santa Rosa's packing plants, tomatoes are sorted by hand, while in the greenhouses, they are sorted partially by a computerized system that weighs and scans them by laser, then sends them down specific chutes for packing by size and color.

As the tomatoes move along the conveyor belt, primarily women sorters determine their destiny. If they are perfect by international standards, they are deemed "export quality" and divided into second and first grades.[21] If they are regular sized, they go to belts for national consumption and are again categorized as second and first grade. The domestic tomatoes are sent to the big food terminals in Guadalajara and Mexico City, where they may be sold at one-third the price that they will draw internationally.

Women packers have even more responsibility with the tomatoes. They pick them up from depositories that have divided them by color but often have to re-sort them, checking on the sorters' work. Then they put them gently but quickly into boxes. It's a contradictory tension for these women because they are paid by the box and not by the day (as the sorters are); so they try to put several tomatoes into boxes at the same time, while also being careful not to damage the fruit. The contents are inspected before being closed. In the past few years, as Empaque Santa Rosa has more fully entered the global export market, little round stickers are pasted on the skin of the tomatoes before they are packed up and

sent off. Also delicately applied by women, these stickers indicate the particular variety of tomato, according to an international numbering system (e.g., Roma tomatoes are #4064, while cherry tomatoes are #4796).[22]

Step 7: Tomatoes, Trade, and Agroexports

It is easy to tell the difference between those destined for local or export markets: if they're going north, they're packed in cardboard boxes with "Mexican tomatoes" written in English on the outside, often with Styrofoam or plastic dividers that hold each tomato in place; those chosen for domestic consumption are packed, without separators, in wooden crates marked with the company's Mexican label, Empaque Santa Rosa. The real rejects are dropped unceremoniously through a big chute into a truck outside the packing plant and sold to local farmers as animal feed.

Once packed and stickered, the boxes that will carry the tomatoes north are sealed, stacked, wrapped, and moved by men working in the packing plant. They are stacked into skids of 108 boxes and wrapped with a plastic netting that keeps them intact en route. Bar codes are also stuck on the skids by ticketers (usually men); when scanned, the lines on the bar code identify the company, tomato variety, the field they were grown in, the day they were packed, and so forth, allowing inventory to be recorded and problems to be traced.[23] An additional sticker bears a number identifying the worker who packed and inspected the boxes at the point of origin. Men driving motorized forklifts deposit most skids directly onto big trailer trucks, while leaving others in temporary storage.

Structural adjustment programs and neoliberal policies in Mexico in the 1980s encouraged agroexports, and NAFTA in the 1990s opened the doors for competition with northern producers. As we will see in chapter 6, tomatoes are one of the few Mexican crops to really "win" with NAFTA, because Mexico maintains the comparative advantage with more intense and consistent sun, easier access to land, and cheaper labor than the United States and Canada. Empaque Santa Rosa, for example, used to produce tomatoes as much for domestic production as for export, but by 2000, it sent 85 percent of its harvest north across the border; an ever-increasing number of greenhouse operations produce cherry tomatoes entirely for export. Mexico ships almost nine hundred thousand tons of tomatoes annually to the United States and Canada.[24] Prices are better in the north, and with the asymmetry of currencies and wages, companies like Santa Rosa can make much more money in the export market.

Tomatoes are ordered by international brokers who request them not only in specific sizes, but also in different shades, from green to red (1 = green, 6 = red).[25] Their journey north may be delayed while the company owners wait for the prices in the United States to rise so they can be sold for more profit. Thus, they might be stored away in refrigerated rooms at the packing plants or near the food terminals, at a temperature that keeps them from ripening too fast, remaining there for a few days up to a week, until the market is more favorable. When the producers decide to fill an order, then, depending on the color requested as well as the destination, the tomatoes may be gassed with ethylene, the same substance that naturally causes ripening, so that the ripening process, temporarily slowed down, is now speeded up. The doors of the storage rooms are closed for twenty-four hours, while the tomatoes are gassed, as the ethylene is dangerous for humans to inhale.

Step 8: Erratic Weathers: El Niño or Climate Change?

Besides being sprayed incessantly with chemicals, tomatoes have been subjected recently to intense rains and even freak snowstorms. If a premature freeze occurs in the fields, the juice and pulp of the tomato freeze like ice, as though they had been put in a refrigerator. The journey for some tomatoes dead-ends here, causing the company economic losses and ending the work season prematurely for thousands of poor campesinos.

These erratic weather conditions are often blamed on El Niño, which originates in Peru and is caused by the clashing of hot and cold currents off the Pacific coast. But many contend that human intervention is also affecting global weather patterns, and crops have suffered from their erratic nature in recent years. Global warming is particularly accelerated by the emission of greenhouse gases into the atmosphere, slowly depleting the ozone layer. Among the greatest culprits of this process are the large trucks that transport food over long distances, the focus of step 10.

Step 9: Detour to Del Monte Processing Adds "Value"

Second-rate tomatoes are sent in wooden crates to the major food terminals (in Guadalajara, Mexico City, and Monterrey), to local markets, and sometimes to food-processing plants. Santa Rosa, for example, supplies Del Monte with tomatoes for processing into canned tomatoes, ketchup, or salsa at its plant in Irapuato, Guanajuato. Tomatoes received at Del Monte are dumped into an assembly production line that moves them along to be weighed and washed, sorted and mashed, then processed through cooking tanks, evaporating tanks, and pasteurizing tanks. Again, primarily women workers fill the bottles through tubes, and the bottles are capped, cooled, labeled, and packed into boxes.[26]

While one might think Del Monte would prefer overripe tomatoes for processing, they actually prefer firmer varieties, so that the tomatoes won't get caught in the automated conveyor systems and mess up the technology for transporting them into the plant.[27] More and more, however, ketchup producers like Del Monte are buying tomato paste rather than whole tomatoes, because the paste-making business draws on cheap labor and facilitates the process for the manufacturer. In bottled form, tomatoes join many other processed and frozen foods that are increasingly replacing fresh food in North America; known as "value-added" products, they increase the price more than the quality.

Step 10: Trucking: A Nonstop Dash North with Perishable Goods

Empaque Santa Rosa owns a few of its own trailer trucks to transport tomatoes to both domestic and northern markets; they guzzle fossil fuel and also contribute to the depletion of the ozone layer. More often, however, Santa Rosa contracts independent truckers to deliver tomatoes to the Mexico–U.S. border at Nogales. It often hires UTTSA, for example, a trucking company whose refrigerated units can carry fifty thousand–pound shipments of fresh produce. The tomatoes are sometimes precooled in a hydrocooling machine that brings their core temperature from 75 degrees down to 34 degrees, because if the temperature drops from 75 to 34 during the two-day journey north, the fruit might deteriorate.

Trucking is a male job, further described in chapter 5. Truckers often work in pairs, so that one can sleep in the back of the cab while the other takes over the driving. The trip to Nogales from Sirena may take thirty to forty hours, depending how many drivers there are; time is of the essence, because tomatoes are highly perishable and preferred at a certain ripeness, but not overripe. Their average life span, in fact, is 4.7 days, so the faster the drive, the quicker they arrive, and the more market days remain for the critical activity of selling them.

We now enter the second phase of the journey of the corporate tomato from Mexico to Canada, highlighting issues of trade and transport, inspection and distribution. While it involves processes in all three NAFTA countries, this phase is clearly controlled by U.S. regulatory agencies, political interests, and multinational corporate needs. Contending political, economic, and legal interests converge in activities around the borders, especially the highly charged U.S.–Mexico line.

Step 11: Controlling the Gates: Dumping, Drugs, and Deportees

To better control and facilitate the border inspection process, the U.S. Department of Agriculture (USDA) has installed its own inspectors within many Mexican agroexport plants to check the tomatoes before they're even loaded onto the trailer trucks. Mexican environmental laws are not as strict as those in the United States and Canada, though NAFTA has provided some pressure to "harmonize." U.S.-based companies, however, sometimes "dump" pesticides in Mexico after they have been banned in their own country. The problem comes back to haunt them when tomatoes are exported back to the United States, carrying higher concentrations of agrochemicals and threatening the health of U.S. consumers.

The USDA hopes to eventually complete all inspections at the point of origin, in the Mexican plants where the tomatoes are packed. Nonetheless, loads of tomatoes are inspected again and again along the route to the border, and the trucks carrying them are stopped regularly by inspectors at four checkpoints. Usually it is not the tomatoes that interest them as much as other possible cargo

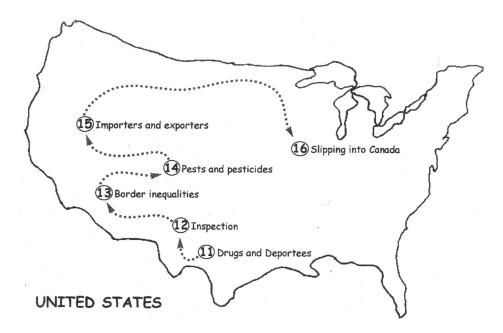

15 Importers and exporters

16 Slipping into Canada

14 Pests and pesticides

13 Border inequalities

12 Inspection

11 Drugs and Deportees

UNITED STATES

that could be smuggled within the trucks, such as narcotics or Mexicans seeking illegal entry into the United States. Narcotraffic is actually a much more lucrative (and volatile) enterprise than tomato production, and a lot of the border activity centers on attempts to control or eradicate it.

The border patrol complex in Nogales is located in a sandy ravine with desert brush competing with enormous spotlights and police cruisers on the hillside, a veritable militarized zone.[28] U.S. Customs officials, guns bulging at their hips, check for truck fraud and narcotics; the work of sniffing dogs has recently been complemented by high-tech X-ray equipment that can scan entire truckloads for suspicious objects. The increasing drug trade is just one more sign of deepening despair and uncontrollable violence in both

countries, but particularly Mexico.[29] The U.S. government and the Mexican government have joined forces to address this matter.

Second to drugs is concern for the growing number of desperate Mexicans who try to escape poverty and unemployment by illegally crossing the border, securing jobs in the United States where they earn in one hour what they would make in a day at home. Horror stories abound about the ways they try to smuggle themselves in, under truck cabs, amid produce, or across rivers at night, and about how they are often captured, mistreated, and sent back to Mexico. Surveillance of the border area has intensified since September 11, 2001, and in 2006, U.S. President George W. Bush mandated the construction of a 1,125-kilometer wall along the notorious border, further inhibiting the movement of Mexicans seeking work in the north.

Tomatoes account for 56 percent of the cargo of the nine hundred to thirteen hundred big trailer trucks that cross the Nogales border daily. Truck traffic has been increasing at such a dramatic pace since NAFTA (in peak season in 1998, over twenty-seven thousand trucks crossed here in one month) that new lanes are being added to the highway to ease the congestion.

Step 12: Checking for Quality: Appearance Matters

Most food inspection actually takes place on the Mexican side of the border. At the complex of the Confederation of Agricultural Associations (CAADES), in Nogales, Sonora, six kilometers south of the U.S. border,[30] tomatoes are run through a series of checks by the USDA officials. First they weigh the trucks, to be sure they don't surpass the total limit of eighty-eight thousand pounds; if the loaded trucks are overweight, they must unload and reload the tomatoes in smaller trucks. Then a USDA inspector goes through a truckload and randomly stamps boxes of tomatoes at the top, middle, and bottom of a skid. Ten boxes are opened and inspected at a time.

Some tomatoes get their temperature taken to be sure that the refrigeration of the truck has not failed; if they were packed pink and register higher than 50 degrees, they may be deteriorating too fast and are turned back. Of the long list of potential "quality defects" and "condition defects" used to check the tomatoes, most (such as "smoothness" and "color") relate primarily to the appearance of the fruit.[31] To be deemed suitable as a U.S. No. 1 grade, no more than 10 percent of a load can have either quality defects or condition defects.

Step 13: The Line Is Drawn: Border of Inequalities

There is a stark contrast at the border between the huts dotting the hillsides on the Mexican side and the more elegant homes on the U.S. side; just as the price of tomatoes rises the minute they cross the line, the wages and standard of living also rise. The way business is organized on both sides of the border area also reflects this asymmetry between nations. A growing number of maquiladora plants, set up since the 1960s on the northern Mexican border by multinational companies, employ thousands of young women in assembling electronics, in piecing together garments, and, in lesser quantity, in food processing. On the U.S. side, on the other hand, an immense infrastructure of administrative offices and warehouses has been established to facilitate the speedy movement of tomatoes

beyond the border to northern consumers. The border thus also separates the workers in the south (Mexico) from the managers in the north (the United States).

Step 14: Keeping Pests and Pesticides at Bay

Truckers who have passed the inspection in Nogales, Sonora, on the Mexican side, and are transporting tomatoes from a reputable agribusiness, can pass through the rapid transit lane, merely handing in the paperwork and moving quickly north. Others, however, may be directed into the U.S. Customs complex on the Arizona side of the border, for further inspections by the FDA and USDA. The Food and Drug Administration officials randomly select a box from a truck and cut a chunk out of a sample tomato to send to an FDA lab in Phoenix, Arizona. About 1 percent of the produce is tested for pesticide residues. This is one way of-

ficials can check to see whether Mexican tomato producers are following the standards regarding the acceptable levels of pesticide residue permitted in the United States. The lab testing may take a few weeks, by which time the chemically suspect tomatoes may have already been unwittingly digested by U.S. or Canadian consumers. Growers whose produce is proven to have certain chemicals[32] above the legal limit are warned that enforcement action might be taken if the problem continues.

What can be detected more immediately, however, are the pests or plant life that may be carried inadvertently in the trucks or boxes in which the tomatoes are packed. USDA botanists don rubber gloves and check the fruit for microbes or markings (a hard scar may be evidence of a pest). If found defective, they may be sent back to Mexico for domestic consumption, sent on to Canada "in bond" (quarantined and wrapped with unbreakable metal straps), or sprayed by a Nogales fumigation company, with USDA officials monitoring the process.[33]

Step 15: Exporting/Importing: Brokers and Wholesalers

When a Mexican trucker is not certified to cross the border, he will pay an American trucker $20 to drive the truck through customs and to a warehouse a few miles north of the border. The warehouses are owned by exporters as well as brokers; Empaque Santa Rosa, for example, has its own office on the U.S. side to manage international sales and distribution within the United States and into Canada. The skids are unloaded in thirty to sixty minutes and stored temporarily in the warehouse. Throughout the day, brokers arrange sales by phone, fax, and e-mail. This is clearly a man's world, and tomatoes are constantly repacked and reloaded on the trucks of brokers or distributors for U.S. and Canadian wholesalers and retailers.

The Blue Book lists hundreds of wholesalers and retailers in the United States and Canada who purchase tomatoes, especially during peak season. Loblaws supermarkets in Ontario, for example, brings up three truckloads of tomatoes daily from the Nogales border. Like other wholesalers and retailers in Canada, they deal with brokers or shippers in Nogales who receive their orders and seek out the best deal from warehouses in the area.

It takes about three days in refrigerated trucks (kept at 48 degrees Fahrenheit) for the tomatoes to reach Ontario from the Mexican border; if coming from Florida it's only two days, while from California it may be four. Three National Grocers trucks leave Nogales daily filled with three key varieties of tomatoes: the extra large Romas, vine ripes, and Gas Greens. Loblaws has its own warehouse, National Grocers, near the Toronto airport, open seven days a week, twenty-four hours a day, and employing one thousand people (mainly men). Supplying Loblaws, Zehrs, Valu-Mart, No Frills, and some Atlantic chains, National Grocers also brings tomatoes in by air daily from around the world (France, Morocco, the Canary Islands, and Israel), especially between December and February when local hothouse production is closed down because of cold weather.

STAGE IV: CHALLENGING GLOBALIZED PRODUCTION:
ECOLOGICAL FOOTPRINT

Activists and academics concerned about the often hidden ecological costs of production and distribution in a global food system that depends on moving tomatoes long distances have developed tools for measuring the impact of such practices. Neither transportation, which is heavily subsidized by government, nor environmental degradation (exacerbated both by the burning of fossil fuels and by the hydrofluorocarbons in refrigerated units of trucks) appears either in the balance sheet of the companies or in the price we pay as consumers. One such tool, the ecological footprint, developed by William Rees,[34] calculates both primary energy consumption and carbon dioxide emissions.

The footprints below represent the contrasting energy costs of producing tomatoes in Mexico and in Ontario greenhouses for Canadian consumption. Of the tomatoes imported annually into Ontario, 74 percent were from the United States, 25 percent were from Mexico, and 1 percent were from other countries.[35] In Canada, imported tomatoes travel an average distance of 4,692 km from sixty-three states and countries.[36] A recent study[37] estimates that most tomatoes enter Toronto by truck but that North American imports emit 221 tons of carbon dioxide into the atmosphere while the transportation of Ontario greenhouse tomatoes only emits 67 tons. Air transport is even more damaging to the environment;

THE ECOLOGICAL FOOTPRINT

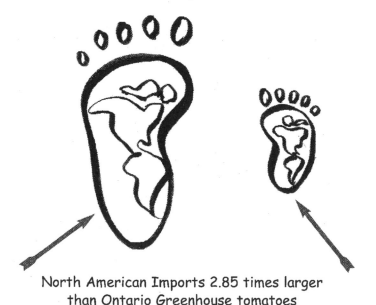

North American Imports 2.85 times larger
than Ontario Greenhouse tomatoes

according to a 2005 study, tomatoes arriving by air contributed 1,101 grams per ton-kilometer, compared to 269 for truck, 130 for marine, and 21 for rail travel.[38]

Step 16: A More Permeable Border: Slipping into Canada

It's difficult to know how many Mexican tomatoes actually make it into Canada. One-quarter of the tomatoes sold in Ontario come directly from Mexico, but this doesn't include those that are shipped from Mexico to border states, then repacked under new U.S. trademarks and sent on to Canada.[39] While the journey from Nogales to Sarnia may take as long as the Sirena–Nogales trip within Mexico, tomatoes have a much easier time at the Canadian border. Fortunately, the prolonged inspection at the Mexico–U.S. border is not repeated, because the standards in the United States and Canada are pretty much the same. If the tomatoes pass as U.S. No. 1 grade tomatoes in Nogales, they're considered certified and won't be inspected again at the Canadian border.[40]

Truckers who, since the deregulation of transportation in the late 1980s and NAFTA in the early 1990s, cross the border more regularly merely present a "confirmation of sale," which has often been previously faxed or sent electronically to both Canadian Customs and the Canadian Food Inspection Agency (CFIA). A small number (about 4 percent) of the shipments are inspected by customs officials (and dogs), usually initiated as a search for contraband (drugs, weapons, liquor, tobacco), and secondarily as a check on the quality of the tomatoes. If the fresh produce smells or appears spoiled, a CFIA inspector will be called in.[41]

Tomatoes are the subject of intense communications between the brokers (shippers) at the U.S.–Mexico border, and U.S. and Canadian buyers (wholesalers), and then again between the brokers at the Canadian border and the buyers awaiting the arrival of fresh tomatoes. Ontario Produce, one of the key wholesalers at the Ontario Food Terminal, for example, has its own brokers negotiating the crossing of tomato shipments at Sarnia, Ontario. Ontario Produce faxes its record of the load, and its broker helps shepherd it across the Sarnia border. Customs officials check the shipper's manifest and the buyer's manifest, and if there are no problems, the tomatoes are allowed to enter Canada.[42]

Finally, we move on to the third phase of the corporate tomato's journey north, as it is received, inspected, and distributed in Canada to terminals and then to supermarkets and fast-food restaurants.

Step 17: The Morning Zoo: Food Terminals Work While We Sleep

Tomatoes are delivered (by truck via Sarnia) to the Ontario Food Terminal, often in the middle of the night, to be ready for sale when wholesalers and retailers arrive from 4 A.M. on.[43] Ontario Produce,[44] one of largest of the twenty companies in the terminal, has eight buyers who order tomatoes from all over the world (Belgium, Spain, Italy, Mexico); while most are beefsteak tomatoes from Florida, they also buy tear drops, cherry, hothouse, and Roma (demanded by the ethnic market), and sell eleven truckloads a day. If they arrive too early, the trucks may have to wait for hours before unloading, while wholesalers

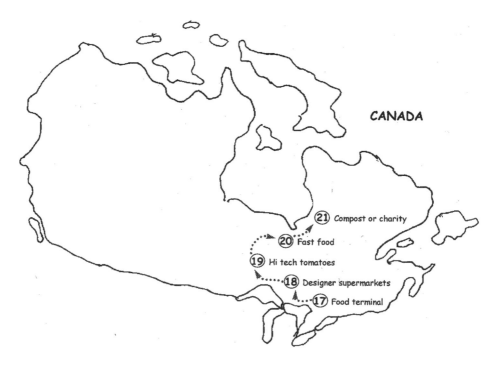

close down for a couple of hours to clean up and prepare displays of the best samples for the following day.

Once unloaded at the terminal, the tomatoes may be returned to refrigerated storage units, similar to the ones in Sirena, but with computerized temperature control, where they're kept at a temperature of 36 to 40 degrees Fahrenheit. These units are also equipped with catalytic generators to produce ethylene, which accelerates the ripening of the fruit. Signs around the heavily locked door warn of the gas's highly flammable nature, indicating that smoking around it could cause an explosion.

Wholesalers like Joyce Foods arrive in the early morning to buy for fast-food restaurants, the primary customers for tomatoes. They prefer the firmer Florida tomatoes (without any markings) because they are more sliceable (e.g., for McDonald's Big Xtra or for pizzas). While importers and wholesalers have noted an increase in Mexican tomatoes since NAFTA, some claim they are too watery for fast-food use. Tomatoes that have been traveling several days from Mexico ripen at different times and, to different degrees, suffer from stem puncture or deteriorate. Importers can claim for damages, but this involves lengthy court procedures, so they may just send them to be repacked. Women workers at Bell City Packers near Toronto, for example, eliminate the decayed tomatoes, wash them again, and re-sort them into six different colors through a computerized laser system and a mechanized assembly line similar to the one in the Santa Rosa greenhouse in Mexico.

◨◧◪◩◨◩

STAGE V: LOCAL TOMATOES PICKED BY MEXICAN HANDS

In the summertime, fewer tomatoes are imported from Mexico, since Canadians can get them fresh from local farmers. Even the sales manager at Ontario Produce recognizes the difference: "Anything that is grown locally has a better taste than the imported merchandise. If you compare it with the local stuff, it is totally different, just like night and day."[45]

There is also a growing greenhouse production of hothouse tomatoes in Ontario year-round. The climate can be carefully controlled in these sophisticated glass greenhouses, and the production is more predictable. Many people also prefer them, because they can ripen on the vine and thus are tastier than tomatoes picked green and sent on the long journey north from Mexico. With a growing demand for organic tomatoes, biological methods of pest control are being used in greenhouses as well.

National Grocers buys tomatoes for Loblaws from Mennonite farmers in western and southern Ontario. Ironically, many of the locally produced tomatoes are harvested by Mexican migrant farmworkers, men and women, who come north every summer through the Seasonal Agricultural Workers Program. Irena Gonzalez, for example, has been coming for twenty years from April–June to October.

While she is still only paid slightly above minimum wage, she makes in an hour in Canada what she would make in a day in Mexico picking tomatoes (chapter 5).

Step 18: Designer Supermarkets and Multicultural Labels

A mixture of corporate tomatoes and (in season) locally grown tomatoes is delivered to Loblaws supermarkets, where they become part of a simulated village market within megastores, which now combine selling groceries with gourmet takeout, dry cleaning, pharmacy, photo processing, plant nurseries, art galleries, and even banking (see chapter 4). The produce section has been moved to the front of stores to create the illusion of being closer to the source of food. The walls surrounding the tomatoes are brightly colored and well lit. With their waxed shiny surfaces,[46] tomatoes are arranged artfully on carts, under umbrellas and a sign that says "Fresh from the Fields."

As part of a global retail market, Loblaws now proclaims that "Food Means the World to Us." Having come from Mexico, tomatoes are part of its global reach, either in fresh form or processed into one of Loblaws' corporate brand President's Choice sauces, Italian style plum tomatoes, or salsas and tacos being promoted in colorful Latino-style aisles, introducing Canada and its multicultural population not only to new tastes but to new ways of being. The seduction of consumers into lifestyle foods and an illusion of diversity is a key theme in the story of Loblaws that unfolds in chapter 4.

Step 19: High-Tech Tomatoes and Computerized Cashiers

Corporate tomatoes can be purchased in fresh or processed form, and they are either punched in or scanned at the supermarket checkout lane. Fresh tomatoes are given PLU (product look-up) codes[47] either on tickets or on stickers.[48] Because they are of variable weight, they must first be weighed and their PLU numbers punched in to calculate their price. If a cashier is not sure of the type of tomato (nine different varieties are sold by Loblaws), she may check the visual inventory on her computer screen. Canned tomatoes or bottled salsa, on the

other hand, can be quickly swiped through the scanner; their bar codes are read by a laser beam, and the type and price appear immediately on a printed receipt.

Global food production has become highly technologized in recent decades, and work practices have been transformed by the information revolution. The high-tech corporate tomato mediates a complex relationship between the worker and the technology; the electronic devices that control pricing and inventory, for example, can also monitor the productivity of cashiers such as Marissa, featured in chapter 4.

Step 20: Fast Food: Homogenized Tomatoes and Toys

McDonald's, which traditionally has targeted a young market, doesn't include tomatoes in the Big Mac, since many children don't like them.[49] In 1996, however, when the fast-food giant's domestic sales were slipping, it created the Arch Deluxe[50] for grown-ups, adding tomatoes; in 1999, it was replaced by the Big Xtra. McDonald's prefers to buy Florida beefsteak tomatoes that are pulpier, firmer, and easier to slice for a hamburger bun, while the tastier Mexican produce is juicier and more likely to fall apart.[51] It is clearly a question of appearance and not of taste. The draw of McDonald's is often more the lifestyle, reflected in the glossy ads, billboards, TV commercials, toys, and videos that promote dominant popular culture. At the final destination of the corporate tomato, it becomes clear that tomatoes and hamburgers are not just food, nor even mere commodities, but symbols of a way of life. The cultural experience of food consumption is examined in depth in chapter 3.

Perfectly sliced tomatoes on a cookie cutter hamburger and bun are part of a global trend toward homogenized diets. In fact, the term *McDonaldization* is now equated with this rationalizing and homogenizing process, which is built on principles of efficiency, calculability, predictability, and control; other businesses and social institutions are increasingly modeled on practices similar to the fast-food restaurant. The resulting loss of both biodiversity and cultural diversity are key themes explored in the case studies (chapters 3, 4, and 6).

The standardization of meals also fits a frantic lifestyle that devalues the preparation or savoring of food such as tomatoes, and the experience of commensality, or enjoying sharing a meal as an intimate social act. Homogenized consumption patterns in Canada parallel the monocultural production of tomatoes in the Mexican fields, both representing dominant practices at either end of the current global food system.

Step 21: Waste or Surplus: Compost or Charity?

There is a "paradox of hunger"[52] reflected by a deepening poverty in the context of a relatively affluent Canada. Food retail giants such as Loblaws are by far the largest donors to a burgeoning network of food banks. Besides getting a tax write-off for its contribution, Loblaws also invites customers to buy goods, such as canned tomatoes, and add them to a donation box in the store. There are critics of this practice, and food bank organizers complain that the kinds of items donated aren't always the most needed. Organic produce such as tomatoes, however, is disposed of in a different way; in collaboration with Organic Resources, Loblaws uses a system of underground holding tanks where wasted tomatoes are stored until they can be recycled as compost on experimental farms outside of Toronto. McDonald's takes a "total life cycle" approach to solid waste where possible, trying to recycle and/or compost solid waste such as corrugated paper.

STAGE VI: FULL CIRCLE: SEEDS IN THE MULTICULTURAL CITY

Tomatl is well and alive and living in Toronto. One sunny day in May 2000, I made my way to Field to Table, the warehouse where FoodShare Metro Toronto is promoting a variety of food alternatives for low-income communities (chapter 8). Lauren Baker, who helped me trace the corporate tomato journey for two years, sells me heritage tomato seedlings that she has grown in the first certified organic rooftop garden in Canada. There she has transformed organic waste into rich composting soil, which is then recycled in diverse urban agricultural projects. Between 1999 and 2002, Lauren coordinated FoodShare's Seeds of Our City project (chapter 8), involving eight ethnically diverse community gardeners in researching and exchanging seeds and agricultural practices they have brought with them to Canada.

After taking my new seeds and native plants home to my backyard garden, I attended an afternoon cultural event at the Native Canadian Centre, also in downtown Toronto. A concert releasing a CD, *Food for Chiapas,* offered music, drumming, poetry, and comedy by Latin American and native artists of diverse origins but all now living in Toronto. The benefit was also an educational event, reminding us of the struggles of Indigenous campesinos in Chiapas, whose access to land and to traditional practices has been threatened over centuries by the production of the corporate tomato (chapter 6) and of the Zapatista movement, which has strengthened the resistance of these people fighting for food, for land, and for dignity (chapter 8). They envision a more just and sustainable relationship to the earth, recovering the practices of Tomatl in the twenty-first century.

These two events embodied the struggle and the hope of Indigenous Mexican campesinos and Canadian natives and immigrants alike, joined by others who question the impact of the journey of the corporate tomato, and who are reclaiming traditions and creating new alternatives.

Untangling Roots: The Tomato across Time

The two intertwining journeys provide stark contrasts between producing tomatoes for local consumption, a relatively short trail, and the corporate production of tomatoes in the south for massive consumption in the north, a much longer and more convoluted trail. We are compelled to ask, How did we get to this place? In other words, What historical processes created this complex global food system that now feeds us? In this section, we examine more deeply the roots of the current food system. First, I question how we conceive of the tomato: as a commodity or living entity. These two perceptions are at the source of the conflict between Tomatl and the corporate tomato. Second, I trace what I call five key "moments" in Western history that have transformed Tomatl and shaped the corporate production of tomatoes.

COMMODITY OR LIVING ENTITY?

Most northern consumers are very conscious of the difference between the taste of a winter, imported tomato and of a fresh, local summer tomato. A friend offered an oft-repeated lament about the hard, pulpy, juiceless tomato she is forced to eat when she cannot buy locally or grow her own, bemoaning that the "soul had been bled out of it."[53] While in Western culture we are not accustomed to talking about food having "soul," we can understand what she means, we can *taste* the difference. It is not uncommon, however, among Indigenous peoples and campesinos in many parts of the world to talk about plants and animals, and even seemingly inanimate elements, such as rocks and water, as living, as imbued with spirit.

It has only been since the Industrial Revolution and more recently with the pervasiveness of a monetarist trading system and a rising consumer culture that objects we buy and even those we ingest, such as food, have become so commodified. This is the dominant view of the tomato perpetrated by those with a "globalization from above" perspective (chapter 2)—in other words, those who benefit from the buying and selling of this commodity. It fits well into the logic of Western capitalism and also with a reductionist science, which reduces the value of all things to a price. This notion of value has become so pervasive that we rarely question it, and are easily seduced into many forms of consumer activity, accepting standards of living that define economies and cultures alike in purely monetarist terms.

Expanding on Marx's notion of *commodity fetishism*, Leah Cohen argues that any value ascribed to an object such as a tomato is constructed both culturally and personally; in capitalism, the fetish of the commodity is built on the notion of land as property, to be bought and sold, and the related conception of all of nature as a resource to be exploited for the accumulation of wealth. Commodification is related to control; as Western cultures began to commodify all of the elements (land, air, fire, water), they assumed that they could control nature. While foodstuffs and raw materials have been exchanged among peoples for millennia, the more recent abstraction of money as the medium of exchange (and in its most extreme and more ephemeral form, futures trading through electronic communications) has come to dominate our understanding of the value of food, among other things.

Underlying the journey of the corporate tomato is this logic of capital accumulation and profit making, based on the commodification of food, the fruit of the earth. Food has been incorporated into the marketplace. According to the bottom-line mentality of capitalist corporate businesses, growing tomatoes in Mexico (where labor is cheaper) and transporting them long distances to Canadian consumers makes (financial) sense; neither Mexican agribusinesses, nor Canadian supermarkets, nor multinational fast-food restaurants such as McDonald's are particularly interested in food per se but rather in its business potential.[54] Food is primarily a medium for their production practices and accumulative motivations. Even we as consumers may feel uncomfortable talking about tomatoes as living beings rather than objects to be consumed. It challenges a deep schism between human and nonhuman nature that underlies Western capitalist forms of production as well as our dominant cultural values and ways of understanding ourselves in and of the world.

In conceptualizing commodity fetishism, Marx was concerned not only with the invisibility of the labor behind products we consume but also with the alienation between the worker and the production process, with the broader and deeper separation of us all, producers and consumers alike, from the social dynamics, context, and conditions that bring things into being. With capitalist industrial production, not only products but also labor and time became commodified and monetarized. For Marx, the value of an object had to take into account its "surplus value," created by the labor that went into it; he was, however, mainly focused on industrial proletariat labor and didn't value in the same light the agricultural work of peasants.

As Cohen elaborates this process, she implies that in obscuring the work that went into the product, "we erase the singularity of both the object and the worker. Money is the fetish that swoops in and supplants the story of real human hands; this was Marx's concern." The stories of the human beings behind products must also move beyond the particular role of producers, she suggests: "Each of the items has hands behind it, and shoulders and backs and brains and souls, and there must live in each one tales of breakfast and blood and soil and toothache and laughter and nightmare and boredom and prayer."[55] Revealing the limits of Marx, she argues that "there are other stories in things that are not the stories of labor."[56] These more layered stories, hinted at in the blending of "blood and soil," require other voices. The story of the tomato, for example, reveals an ecological dimension to production and consumption; it invites a critical reflection on how we construct or understand nature and engage with it.

Such a reflection would question the underlying forces that move the corporate tomato through the twenty-one steps, across borders and through multiple transformations, from seed to box, from truck to Arch Deluxe sandwich. The end of the line is a cash register or a company's annual report; a bottom-line mentality drives the global economy. The tomato as commodity is moved through its complex journey by market forces and ultimately benefits certain people more than others; its value in the corporate food system is best expressed in the profits of the domestic agroexport companies, the brokers and truckers, wholesalers and retailers, owners and managers of supermarkets and restaurants, and the investors and bankers who support these globalized capitalist corporations at both ends of the tomato chain.

TANGLED ROOTS: FIVE MOMENTS SHAPING GLOBAL AGRICULTURE

"The seeds came with the genetic code of the society that produced them. They produced not just crops but replicas of agricultural systems that produced them. They came as a package deal, and part of the package was a major change in traditional cultures, values, and power relationships both within villages and between them and the outside world."[57] Challenging a narrow scientific view of the Green Revolution, Cary Fowler and Pat Mooney, pioneer seed analysts/activists concerned with the loss of biodiversity in seeds, frame the story of industrialized global agriculture as a social and cultural process. Canadian food analyst Brewster Kneen has charted the "agenda of the seed" as determined by four major social institutions: corporate or commercial companies, governments, universities, and industry organizations; he suggests they not only shape the structure, policy, and financial underpinnings of agriculture but also culture, ideology, and politics.[58]

While the journey of the corporate tomato from Mexican field to Canadian table may have seemed endless, digging into the histories underlying this journey feels even more daunting. With a postmodern caution,[59] I'd like to explore the tangled roots of contemporary agriculture through five key historical processes that I am calling "moments": the scientific moment and colonialism (sixteenth and seventeenth centuries), the industrial moment and capitalism (eighteenth and nineteenth centuries), the chemical moment and development (mid-twentieth century), the genetic moment and neoliberalism, and the computer moment and globalization (late twentieth and twenty-first centuries).

I am borrowing from Antonio Gramsci's notion of the "moment," not as a short period of time but rather as a convergence of various economic, political, and ideological forces that make possible the emergence of specific kinds of practices. The five "moments" elaborated in this section unfold over five centuries, but they are very much interrelated and have shaped each other. Like roots, they reach so deeply and are so intertwined that it is almost impossible to separate them.

The Scientific Moment and Colonialism

Two seventeenth-century European philosophers, René Descartes of France and Francis Bacon of England, laid the foundation for a reductionist Western science. Descartes's coordinate system separated out a narrow set of causal factors to explain phenomena, thus denying the complexity of ecosystems and agrosystems; his famous mind/body dichotomy ("I think, therefore I am") reinforced a growing sense of superiority (among primarily white European male aristocrats) based on a conception of nature as separate from culture and spirit as separate from matter. Bacon, considered the father of modern science, framed nature not only as separate but as wild, to be conquered and subdued. Judith Soule and Jon Piper suggest that certain values of this reductionist science have shaped modern agriculture—simplification, quantification, and objectivity as well as the conquering of nature.[60] Such an approach, they argue, along with the economic values of efficiency, productivity, and short-term return, has contributed to a destruction of ecosystems, which, to survive, require ecological or holistic perspectives and a longtime frame of reference.

The Indian physicist and feminist Vandana Shiva suggests that the worldview of most Indigenous peoples incorporates an ecological perspective that considers human beings as part of nature and all of nature as self-generative and self-organizing.[61] The colonization by Europe of much of the Americas, Asia, and Africa framed land as *terra nullius* (land that is unowned and so is open to exploitation) rather than *terra mater* (mother earth), denying the rights of original inhabitants. Paradoxically, though, the colonial enterprise in the Americas, initiated by Christopher Columbus, began partially as a search for food (spices) from the East; and it was colonialism that eventually created export agriculture. The economic and military motives of the European colonizers converged with their religious mission to "civilize the savages" (also considered soulless) and with an emerging scientific vision of nature, a worldview that underlies the twenty-one steps of the journey of the corporate tomato.

Offering an ecofeminist analysis, Carolyn Merchant points out that "this transformation of nature from a living, nurturing mother to inert, dead, and manipulable matter was eminently suited to the exploitation imperative of growing capitalism."[62] Ecofeminists critique as well the patriarchal beginnings of this science, which not only aimed to "master" nature but, associating women with nature, devalued their ways of knowing and justified their domination (chapter 2). An antiracist analysis of this science also critiques its development in the context of colonialism, which denigrated nonwhite non-Western peoples and their traditional agricultural practices; in fact, a science of eugenics built on these assumptions emerged to rationalize racism (as well as sexism, ableism, speciesism, etc.).

Shiva argues that both a rich biodiversity as well as an immense cultural diversity of Indigenous knowledges (and thus understandings of nature) are being denied and destroyed by the kind of global agricultural system that has resulted from this dominant Western science. As a paradigm that fragments our very understanding of the world and of life itself, she suggests it is based on three separations: separation of mind and body; the gendered separation of male activity as intellectual and female activity as biological; and the separation of the knower from the known (the assumption of objectivity).[63]

Our difficulty in seeing the tomato as a living entity, then, is rooted in a reductionist and fragmented science. Ironically, in denying the self-generating qualities of nature, this science has also been used to deny the natural processes of birth and death of human beings. In asserting the superiority of humans (a kind of "speciesism"), it has denied us a sense of reciprocity with living things, such as plants, which in their own life cycles sustain us, their energy transformed with ours. Many Indigenous peoples speak of this reciprocity and relationships of respect they hold with animals as they are killed for the purpose of sustaining life. The Judeo-Christian tradition of saying grace before eating at least hints as well at a recognition of our dependence on plant and animal life, and a gratitude for their existence that makes possible our own.

The Industrial Moment and Capitalism

The transformation of nature in the European mind from a self-generating living system to mere raw material also provided the base for the continued exploitation of the natural resources of the colonies and for the ensuing Industrial Revolution in the eighteenth and nineteenth centuries. Ironically, the roots of the word *resource* mean "to rise again," reflecting the self-generating quality of nature more than the dominant notion of "natural resources" that "became inputs for industrial commodity production and colonial trade."[64]

I earlier warned that this historical telling of the tomato story would not follow a linear chronology, and so I double-back to the process of colonization by Europe that began in the late fifteenth century and that shaped the development of Western science as well as capitalism. While the Indigenous campesinos in Mexico "conquered" by the Spaniards may have been forced to produce food for local landlords in precolonial times, they always maintained their own subsistence farming and traditional practices, even after colonization. Colonial rulers, however, initiated both monocultural production as well as export agriculture. Often building on already existing agrarian hierarchies, they forced Indigenous campesinos to work as local hires or indentured labor on large single-crop plantations, producing for European cuisines. Eventually slave labor was brought from Africa to the Americas to replace Indigenous campesinos, reflecting yet another level of exploitation and racism. Harriet Friedmann asserts that the colonial process that birthed export agriculture broke patterns of diet and cultivation that had existed for thousands of years, creating an entirely new dynamic of production and consumption that we take for granted today, in which "what was grown became disconnected from what was eaten, and for the first time in history, money determined what people ate and even if they ate."[65]

While tomatoes, already "native" to Mexico, got carried back by the colonizers in the form of seeds, planted in European gardens, and transformed into the famous sauces of Italian cuisine, they did not make good export crops at that stage of history; due to their perishability, they could not survive the long boat trips back to Europe, as could coffee or corn, for example. This was before the development of the steam engine or fossil fuel forms of transport and refrigeration. But the massive movement of plants, animals, and peoples stimulated by the colonial process did create a dependency of nonproducing European countries on rich tropical environments for food. At the same time, the central colonial practice of monocultural production through plantation agriculture (as well as the introduction of grazing animals) initiated a slow but steady destruction of the biodiversity that made those environments so fertile in the first place.

The Industrial Revolution in Europe only intensified and extended the practice of monocultural cash crop production and facilitated export agriculture. Soule and Piper suggest that the key components of the agricultural industrialization process were mechanization, chemicalization, and new crop-breeding priorities and that while each solved certain problems that previously limited agricultural production (e.g., labor inefficiency and yield), each one also created new ecological and economic problems.[66] Because both crop breeding and agrochemicals figure prominently in the chemical moment (Green Revolution) and the genetic moment (discussed later), I focus here on the initial mechanization of agriculture that pushed it squarely into the industrial mind-set.

The mechanical philosophy that dominated Western scientific thought (in which even the body was conceived of as a machine) also made possible the development of tools and processes that set out to dominate and control nature, usually aimed at purposes of producing higher yields, not only to feed an increasing population but also to gain ever higher profits. Thus the values of efficiency and productivity reflected the primarily economic motives of those who controlled the industry, in this case agriculture, within the context of a Western capitalist economy.

There were two phases in the mechanization of agriculture: the replacement of human power by animal power in the mid-1800s and the replacement of draft animals by the gasoline engine. As less labor was now required, farms could be bigger; yet as machinery was expensive, fewer farmers could afford it. This development was well suited to monocultural production, as fields were redesigned geometrically to conform to the use of the large equipment rather than to follow the land's contours. The specialization of a single crop was reinforced by the expensive machinery that had to be used frequently to justify costs. Small-scale farmers were either squeezed out or got caught on an "agricultural treadmill," pressured to buy the ever more efficient equipment of their competitors in order to survive in the marketplace.

The economic and ecological impacts of this mechanization, however, were innumerable, though not initially understood or acknowledged. Larger fields were more vulnerable to wind erosion, and the heavy machinery compacted the soil, reducing its moisture-holding capacity. When work animals were replaced, their manure was lost as organic matter to help reduce erosion. And the cultivation of single crops with specialized machinery led to the end of crop-rotational practice, which was a traditional method for replenishing the soil and reducing erosion. Thus, these mechanized practices contributed to a loss of biodiversity.

The manufacturing, operating, and maintaining of farm machinery accounted, by 1973, for 60 percent of the energy expended on agriculture in North America, and contributed greatly to the depletion of fossil fuel supplies. Economically, the costs of farming and debt load rose astronomically with machinery such as the four-wheel-drive tractor, eliminating many small farmers and favoring the growth of agribusiness simply on the basis of economies of scale. Thus, while mechanization addressed the issue of labor inefficiency, it created new problems of erosion, energy dependency, capital expenses, interest payments, larger farms, and fewer farmers; ironically, it eventually robbed many farmers of their livelihood.

This process evolved first with U.S. agriculture[67] and then was exported, with both similar and different results, to the Third World. Perhaps the biggest difference was related to the cheap labor that sometimes didn't justify large capital investments in highly labor-intensive crops, such as tomatoes. Empaque Santa Rosa, the Mexican agribusiness featured in chapter 6, has been increasingly drawn into the industrial model of North American agriculture. Certainly the plowing of the monocultural fields and the application of pesticides depend on expensive machinery, and the packing plant uses the conveyor belt system of assembly line production to sort and move tomatoes along to the boxes.

In fact, most "inputs" (a term for all tools and technologies used in production, echoing its industrialized nature) involved industrial processes and products: the greenhouses that produce the seedlings, fertilizers that prepare the ground and pesticides that control the destruction of plants, the irrigation systems that provide the vast amounts of water needed for tomato growth, the plastic sheets that keep the moisture in the ground while keeping pests out, the pails and boxes that carry the tomatoes from field to plant to truck, the netting that turns a stack of boxes into a skid, the forklifts that carry the skids to refrigerated rooms, and so forth.

With each new tool, there are also new work processes and organization of workers (both in agriculture per se as well as in the manufacturing of industrial inputs for farming). The move toward greenhouse production epitomized in the Santa Rosa operation is by far the most automated and reflects the high-tech approach to tomato production that is also being heavily adopted in the north: total climate control, drip irrigation that incorporates water, fertilizer, and pest control, mobile carts for picking tomatoes extended to the ceiling, packing processes that are computerized to measure weight and sort by color, foam dividers that protect the boxed tomatoes during their long journey north, and so on.

While these new technologies have in many ways simplified the labor processes, they also constantly reshape the work (and the gendered division of labor) as well as dictate the production processes. At the Del Monte processing plant, for example, firm tomatoes are preferred as raw materials for making ketchup, rather than the ripe or overripe tomatoes that would seem more logical. This is because the conveyor belt system that carries the tomatoes from the place they are dumped into the cauldrons where they are cooked can better handle firm tomatoes; the machinery is too harsh for soft tomatoes, which get caught in the belt system and create a mess that must be cleaned up. Ketchup production is designed as an even more industrialized process than cultivating and picking fresh tomatoes, following a Fordist-style assembly line process in which much of the work (e.g., filling, capping, and labeling bottles) is almost fully automated.

The political economic dynamic underlying the tomato story—that food is produced in the south for consumption in the north—is premised on the industrialization of transport. The steam-driven train system that carried Mexican tomatoes to the United States and Canada in the early part of the last century has been replaced in recent decades by a massive network of trucking companies, all dependent on mammoth gas-guzzling trucks, complete with refrigeration. Subsidized by government-built highways, this transport system is a major contributor to the depletion of the ozone layer (the trailer tanks emitting carbon dioxide and the refrigeration units emitting hydrofluorocarbons). Industrial agriculture is, in fact, a major cause of global warming. The asymmetry among the three NAFTA countries is reflected in the fact that industrial processes and equipment are more sophisticated in the United States and Canada than in Mexico, though foreign multinationals and agroexport markets are bringing Mexican companies quickly up to speed.

Finally, the movement of the tomato across the checkout counter in a supermarket (in the north and increasingly in the south) requires electronic devices: the laser scanner and computerized inventory and pricing system (chapter 4). If it makes its way into an Arch Deluxe sandwich, the tomato may be sliced by machine to join a hamburger that has been cooked on a moving grill that requires a human hand only to feed the patty and bun at one end and grab them as they drop from the other end. At the retail end of the tomato chain, we also find the highly standardized production of megastores and restaurant chains, displays and tables, that make our buying and eating experiences very predictable. In fact, one important characteristic of a globalized and industrialized agriculture and food system is its homogenization at every level. The uniformity at the consumption end only mimics the uniformity promoted at the production end—in the name of simplicity, quantifiability, efficiency, and productivity—merging Western scientific, industrial capitalist, and consumer cultural values.

The Chemical Moment and Development

When Mexican farmers speak of the *paquete tecnológico,* or "technological package,"[68] that has been strongly influenced by the North American model of industrial agriculture, they usually are referring to the combination of hybrid seeds and agrochemicals, as well as the water systems and machinery necessary to their use in monocultural production. The industrialization of agriculture became entrenched in Mexico in 1941, when U.S. vice president Henry Wallace convinced Mexican president Manuel Avila Camacho to set up an agricultural educational and research program in Mexico (and another in the Philippines). Funded by the Rockefeller Foundation and staffed by U.S. scientists, this program not only dramatically shaped the future of Mexican agriculture[69] but was exported to countries around the world as the Green Revolution, a somewhat deceptive title for the period that I'm calling the "chemical moment."

The American scientists and agronomists who came to Mexico and established the program were very much influenced by a worldview that glorified

Western science, technology, and industrialization; it became part and parcel of the post–World War II "development" era heralded by President Harry Truman, in which the "civilizing mission" of European colonizers was replaced by an equally self-righteous notion of "modernization." It was also shaped by the Cold War; U.S. politician Robert McNamara affirmed the naming of the Green Revolution with the comment, "So that it won't be red, it should be green!"[70] The "green" descriptor may more accurately refer to the profits in dollars generated by highly capital-intensive agriculture dominated by foreign interests.

This was the era that birthed the Bretton Woods institutions (the World Bank and International Monetary Fund [IMF]) and created the concept of "foreign aid" through these multilateral as well as bilateral agencies. Often equated with economic growth and progress within a very linear conception of history, this model has further deepened U.S. hegemony and reshaped the agricultural policies of countries such as Mexico. The development of hybrid seeds, for example, was very much tied to their commercial potential and the rise of large U.S.-based agribusinesses.

Agrochemicals were central to the technological package developed and promoted by the Green Revolution, and their origins were certainly neither economically nor politically neutral. During and following World War II, military petrochemical industries were converted from wartime production to other uses. It was found that DDT, for example, could kill insects in crops, and parathion, created originally for chemical warfare in concentration camps, became a major competitor for DDT as an insecticide. And so when explosives were no longer needed, cheap fertilizers became available. Nelson offers a deeper cultural analysis of how American farmers were sold this more "scientific" practice, in which chemical farming was socially constructed as "clean," while the use of natural processes and materials, such as manure, was now considered "dirty."[71] We in the Western world have certainly internalized this attitude toward nature, by preferring unblemished and hyperreal tomatoes to those that may be healthier but bear the marks or dirt of a more organic growth.

Mexican campesinos were pushed into modernizing their agricultural practices because of shifting markets as well. A U.S. policy of subsidizing American farmers had resulted in food surpluses that, beginning in the 1950s, were exported to the newly emerging Third World countries as "food aid." They also served to undermine local prices and eventually contributed to Mexico's shift from food self-sufficiency to food dependency.

Scientists working in the Green Revolution research and development centers, such as CIMMYT[72] in Mexico, developed hybrid or cross-pollinated (as opposed to open-pollinating) seeds that were aimed at increasing crop yields and uniformity, critical for the American industrialized agricultural model that was being imported. Standardization improved both production and efficiency, which were the dominant values. The hybrid seeds were produced to grow at uniform heights and to arrive at common ripening dates, making mechanical harvesting easier.

The hybrid plants, however, did not produce seeds similar to the seeds from which they grew; Shiva calls the hybridization "an invasion into the seed itself."[73] The commodified seed, she suggests, was "ecologically incomplete," because it could not regenerate itself and could not produce by itself but required purchased inputs. So farmers were forced to purchase new seed each year, increasing their costs and dependency on purchasing what previously had been regenerated naturally. The ecological effects were multiple: the so-called "miracle seeds" actually reduced genetic diversity and allowed pests to more easily exploit a crop, because there were no natural resistors or diversity among plants that would allow some to survive if others did not.

Most insidious was the need created by the seeds for chemical fertilizers and pesticides, designed to respond to the very problems created by mechanized and monocultural production. The cheap inorganic nitrogenous fertilizers promoted after the war replaced soil fertility but also promoted processes that further reduced soil fertility. Pesticides often created worse problems as pests became resistant to certain chemicals or as new seeds invited new pests, weeds, or fungi. In the U.S. context where agrochemicals were first developed as central to the emerging "scientific agriculture," they represented 30 percent of the energy use on a farm, while the ongoing purchase of fuel, fertilizer, and pesticides (all of which fluctuated with oil prices) drained 52 percent of farm income.[74] A heavy dependency on irrigation, particularly voluminous in tomato production, also disrupted ecological systems by the diversion of rivers and construction of dams. The longer term ecological costs of this industrial agricultural production are also becoming clearer now, as this chemical dependency contributes to the greenhouse effect and global warming.

In the Mexican context, the whole *paquete tecnológico* adopted included hybrid seeds, a diverse range of agrochemicals (fertilizers, pesticides, insecticides, fungicides), applicators (from backpack sprays to tractor-drawn spray rigs and airplanes), as well as more water and the irrigation systems and pumps to deliver it. Often labeled the "chemical treadmill," this package quickly became a very costly venture for campesinos, requiring them to buy seeds every year, try every new pesticide created to attack the pests increased by the last, and invest in pesticide pumps and motorized water pumps.[75]

Most Green Revolution scientists and technicians proceeded to transform Mexico (and other Third World economies) disregarding these structural inequalities (between the north and south, and within countries of the south) and assuming that the economic model was applicable everywhere and that the technology was socially and ecologically neutral. There were some early critics, however, who recognized that the economic model deepened existing inequalities. Carl Sauer, an American geographer who had studied Mexican agriculture for decades, maintained that its problems "had far more to do with economic exploitation than with Mexican agricultural practices."[76] He was concerned that intervention could destroy Indigenous economy, ecology, and culture. Along with Green Revolution scientist Paul Manglesdorf, he praised the beans-squash-maize complex as productive, nutritious, and ecologically healthy, recognizing how central these crops were to Indigenous religious and political practices as well.

Vandana Shiva, from the vantage point of India in the 1990s, makes a passionate indictment of the legacy of the Green Revolution, which was "essentially based on miracle seeds that needed chemical fertilizers and did not produce plant outputs for returning to the soil." It broke the mutual relationship between the seed and the earth, and nature's process of regeneration and renewal. As a paradigm of agriculture, then, it "substituted the regenerative nutrient cycle with linear flows of purchased inputs of chemical fertilizers from factories and marketed outputs of agricultural commodities."[77] It clearly built on the Western scientific vision of nature and the commodification further entrenched by industrializing agriculture. Shiva suggests that its impact was even more far-reaching: "This shift from ecological processes of production through regeneration to technological processes of nonregenerative production underlies the dispossession of farmers and the drastic reduction of biological diversity; and is at the root of the creation of poverty and of nonsustainability in agriculture."[78] In any case, the Green Revolution laid the ground for the next level of intervention—into the genetic material of the seeds themselves.

The Genetic Moment and Neoliberalism

"Transgenic organisms are indicator species, or perhaps canaries in the gold mines of the New World Order, Inc."[79] With this pronouncement, feminist scientist Donna Haraway enters the current debate about genetic engineering by historically locating this revolution within the particular political economic context shaping it. She calls this the New World Order, one in which the technoscientific agenda is increasingly globalized but still set by the economically dominant power, the United States, and multinational corporations often headquartered in the United States, Europe, or Japan. The fact that the genetic revolution is unfolding within a neoliberal era driven by global trade agendas very much shapes its direction and issues. Global food and agriculture offer one of its major sites of potential development and contention. Neoliberalism, or the free rein of market forces, has made it easier for multinational corporate interests to get access to and control over natural and genetic resources.

It is always harder to grapple with historical shifts when we are in the middle of them and have neither the value of hindsight nor the luxury of simplifying the debates in our memories. This is the case of the genetic revolution, as battles are being fought daily around the questions of the production, labeling, and sales of genetically modified foods, the uncertain ecological impact of their cultivation, their potential health dangers, and the political and ethical issues of their ultimate application. I synthesize some of the underlying issues by considering genetically engineered foods from several vantage points: scientifically, politically, economically, ecologically, and epistemologically. The interrelationship of these perspectives is illustrated through the case of the Flavr Savr tomato.

In *technoscientific* terms, genetic engineering (also referred to as *genetic modification* or *genetic manipulation*) involves taking genes and segments of DNA that are coded for certain characteristics from one species and inserting them into another species. While hybridization, cross-pollination, and the crop-breeding central to the Green Revolution are considered biotechnology by some, others argue that only genetic manipulation constitutes biotech. The difference in the current genetic moment is the creation of transgenic organisms that cross species (as opposed to hybridization within species); a tomato, for example, can be inserted with the antifreeze gene from a fish so that the plant can survive colder weather.

Intense debates have been waging within the scientific community about the risks in the process of genetic engineering. Nine European and North American experts recently agreed that much more research is necessary before GMOs are commercially released. "Genes are ambivalent and dynamic, and epigenetic regulation mechanisms are more complex than had been assumed for a long time"; "they follow network rules not specified by DNA . . . and we do not fully understand these rules."[80] Swiss scientist Cesare Gessler charges that current GE products are "still at the level of dinosaur technology."[81] Gilles-Eric Seralini proposed that GMOs, like pesticides, should be tested for toxicity using long-term feeding trials with animals (which raise other ethical issues).

Belinda Martineau, who worked with Calgene on GE experiments with tomatoes, is even more adamant about the lack of scientific support for GMOs, suggesting that "no scientific evidence to the contrary" means "no scientific evidence, period."[82] She contends there is only opinion, and no fact, on the matter of food safety or environmental impact, though studies published in *Nature* have raised concerns about superweeds, pollen that can kill monarch butterfly larvae, and taco shells that became contaminated with animal feed corn.

GE proponents, on the other hand, tout its many advantages. Specific characteristics can be added to a plant to address specific deficiencies or problems; tomatoes have been engineered not only to withstand cold but also to have longer shelf life and to pack better (i.e., square rather than round). The time needed to produce new varieties of plants can be cut in half and the breeding time can be reduced by years; in other words, all processes have been speeded up and purport to be more efficient and to result in higher yields.

Politically, the crucial questions are who is controlling these processes and who ultimately owns the genetically engineered plants. Multinational corporations have received protection through U.S. patent laws[83] as well as from recent multilateral agreements (such as the Biodiversity Convention and the Trade Related Intellectual Property Measures [TRIPs] that came out of the Uruguay round of the General Agreement on Tariffs and Trade [GATT][84]) that apply a very narrow definition of intellectual property rights (IPRs). Thus, state and multilateral bodies have supported this increasing control by corporations, putting regulations in place that favor the growth of multinationals. Companies that finance biogenetic research and development often use the natural resources of Third World countries (which are the greatest sources of biodiversity), but by isolating one element in their genetic makeup, they can claim a patent on the new material (or on the innovative processes used to engineer the new product). In denouncing the neocolonial and capitalist logic underlying the TRIPs agreement, Shiva points to two aspects of the definition of IPRs it uses: intellectual property rights are recognized only as private rights, thus excluding the collective nature of ideas shared in an "intellectual commons" among campesinos and Indigenous peoples;[85] and only innovations that are capable of industrial application are considered IPRs, thus denying other uses aimed more at the social good than at maximizing profits.

Shiva accuses multinational corporations (and governments that support them through research money and patent laws) of "biopiracy," not only robbing the Third World of its rich biodiversity but destroying also its intellectual diversity. Mexico, for example, has no international patents on agricultural material.[86] Shiva sees biopiracy as an extension of capitalist logic, an "enclosure of the intellectual commons," drawing a parallel to the "enclosure of the commons" that intensified in England in the 1500s and led to the privatization of property and the commodification of land. Other critics agree that the deeper motives are primarily *economic*. As Haraway reminds us, even though biogenetics raises complex issues, "power, profit and bodily rearrangements are at the heart of biotechnology as a global practice."[87]

In a globalized economy, those corporations investing in biogenetic engineering of food are the same ones that have controlled the seed market, and are linked both horizontally (across borders) as well as vertically, with connections to tomato growers, agrochemical producers, wholesalers, and distributors. While the 1990s saw a flurry of mergers, corporate concentration intensified even further beginning in 2004, with the top ten seed companies controlling one-half of the global seed trade, the top ten biotech companies controlling three-quarters of world sales, and the top ten pesticide manufacturers up to 85 percent of market share; similarly, the dominant food processors and food retailers controlled a quarter of their multitrillion dollar markets.[88]

There is an increasing monopoly control by a few key multinationals, as well as the penetration of foreign multinationals into the Mexican corporate structure. Leading producers of genetically modified food, such as Monsanto, have used the argument that genetically engineered seeds are green products, decreasing the use of pesticides; ironically, in emphasizing this point, they also acknowledge the harmful effects of decades of use of their own toxic agrochemical products. But, in fact, corporations like Monsanto often insert genes into their seeds that will impart resistance to their own herbicides or pesticides, forcing agribusinesses and farmers once again to buy the whole package as well as increasing the power of these transnational companies.[89] Recent studies show that 71 percent of all GE crops are herbicide resistant while only 22 percent have been developed specifically to reduce the dependency of farmers on agrochemicals.[90] In some cases, pesticides such as Bt toxin (*Bacillus thuringiensis*) are inserted into GE plants, but with regulatory implications: as pesticides are exempt from FDA regulation, so, too, are GE Bt foods.[91] Scientist Gilles-Eric Seralini notes that almost all GEs "tolerate or produce pesticides and 75–80 percent of all GEs are made resistant to only one herbicide—Monsanto's Roundup."[92] Seralini's lab studies showed that human placental cells were very sensitive to Roundup and might account for miscarriages and premature births among North American farm families.

One potential problem of GE crops is that weeds bordering the fields, wild relatives of those being cultivated, can become cross-pollinated by wind and develop a similar herbicide resistance, resulting in superweeds. In *environmental* terms, the greatest dangers lie in the unknown consequences of the airborne spread of transgenic material to other crops[93] as well as the loss of genetic diversity perpetrated by the new crops that replace traditional varieties.[94]

The real interests of multinationals engaged in this enterprise became dramatically clear in 1998, when Delta & Pine Land Company patented the production of sterile seeds which would make it impossible for farmers to save any seeds from one year to the next and force them to buy new seeds (and new agrochemicals) every year. Although the annual purchase of seeds was already a reality created by the chemical treadmill, this "terminator technology" reflected a complete disrespect for the self-generating qualities of nature. Bad press as well as strong advice from the Rockefeller Foundation made companies back down on this development in 1999. Research on the so-called suicide seeds, however, reappeared in early 2000 in the midst of mergers among Monsanto, Astra Zeneca, and Pharmacia & Upjohn. Despite the FAO's (the United Nations' Food and Agriculture Organization) opposition to terminator technology, the USDA defended Delta & Pine Land's antifarmer patent, research, and efforts to commercialize terminator seeds.[95]

In UN meetings in February 2005, the Canadian government took the lead in trying to overturn the international moratorium on terminator seeds, pushing for field trials and commercialization. Although delegates from the Canadian Food Inspection Agency (CFIA) to the Biosafety Protocol meetings in Montreal in May 2005 claimed they were neutral on the issue, their proposal nonetheless would have allowed companies to apply to government regulatory bodies to approve crops using terminator technology. For Canadian activists,[96] this lobbying effort only confirmed the government's commitment to corporate agriculture and genetic engineering.[97] At the international level, the United Nations Convention on Biological Diversity preserved the moratorium on terminator technology, delaying its commercialization, but stopping short of an outright ban. The Convention expressed concern about the potential impact on small-scale and indigenous farmers and on crop genetic diversity.

Biotech companies promoting the technology argued that it could solve the problem of airborne pollen of GE crops contaminating neighboring fields. This had become a major issue in 1999 when Canadian farmer Percy Schmeiser sued Monsanto for contaminating his Saskatchewan field with genetically modified canola seeds. Monsanto countersued, charging Schmeiser with using its seeds without paying for the patent rights. The case went all the way to the Supeme Court of Canada, which ruled in 2004 that Monsanto's patent was valid, but Schmeiser did not have to pay Monsanto since he did not profit from the canola in his fields.[98]

At the root of the debate around genetically modified food are two compet-ing views of life and of the relationships between human and nonhuman nature. As Kneen asserts, "genetic engineering in its very conception requires the isola-tion and identification of fragments of life for purposes of appropriation, ma-nipulation, and ownership."[99] Shiva critiques the worldview of dominant West-ern technoscientific and capitalist economic models based on a linear paradigm assuming total certainty and control, and geared toward centralization and uni-formity. She advocates diversity as a worldview rather than the one-dimensional instrumental worldview underlying much biotechnology: "The recognition of the diverse roles and interdependence of each part puts limits on our exploita-tion of other species and limits human arrogance."[100] This *epistemological* battle (between knowledges) is also a political one: "The seed has become the site and symbol of freedom in the age of manipulation and monopoly of its diversity."[101]

The Flavr Savr Tomato   The interaction of the technoscientific, political, economic, ecological, and epistemological aspects of genetic engineering can be illustrated through the case of the Flavr Savr tomato, one of the first and most celebrated and contentious genetically modified foods.[102] In the late 1980s, Cal-gene, a company based in Davis, California (and fed by researchers from the Uni-versity of California), developed a tomato engineered precisely for the demands of a global food system: in response to complaints about the tastelessness of tomatoes picked green and gassed, the Flavr Savr tomato would purportedly stay on the vine longer, thus maintaining taste, but without rotting; it would then be picked fresh but firm enough to withstand the long journeys to northern mar-kets and have a shelf life of three weeks, increasing its marketable period. Ac-cording to its public relations director, Calgene Fresh would provide tomatoes with "the summer taste" all year round.[103]

Technically, Calgene scientists extracted from a tomato cell the promoter gene responsible for turning on the production of the enzyme (polygalactur-onase) that produces ethylene (which causes ripening and rotting); they reversed the elements on the gene to slow both processes; and they reinserted the mirror-image version into the tomato plant, along with a marker gene from the antibi-otic kanamycin.[104] This process of inserting the copy backward is called *antisense*, as it effectively silences the promoter gene, so that ethylene production isn't turned on, and the walls of the tomato cells don't break down.

Politically, by 1990 Calgene received a U.S. patent on its improved tomato and on the antisense technology involved, and by 1992, it had secured a ruling from the USDA that allowed it to grow genetically engineered (GE) tomatoes commercially without USDA permits. In 1994, the FDA gave Calgene notice that the new tomato had satisfied its food safety requirements. By 1995, it was faced, however, with a federal court lawsuit launched by Enzo Biochem, alleging in-fringement of its antisense technology patents.

The initial agreements among the companies involved gave Calgene exclu-sive global rights to produce and sell fresh tomato products using this biotech-nology and gave its partners, Zeneca A.V.P. and Campbell's Soup Company, exclusive rights to produce and sell processed products with these tomatoes.[105] As the initial backer of the project, Campbell's had selected a variety of tomatoes that were intended to be processed rather than sold fresh and hand-eaten. When Campbell's backed out of the deal in 1995 because of customers' nervousness about the genetically modified foods, Calgene was left with a tomato better suited for processing and not totally appropriate for the fresh market. Financially, Calgene had suffered some $161 million in losses since its founding in 1981[106] and had invested $4.2 million in developing the Flavr Savr and in buying the marketing rights for fresh tomatoes from Campbell's. Perhaps desperate for new investors as well as for consumers, it launched a major media campaign in 1995; because of such hype, everyone awaited the miracle tomato. But there were further obstacles: three of the tomato packers Calgene had arranged to grow and distribute the Flavr Savr also backed out, concerned about the control the company was exerting over all aspects of production and distribution.

The first Flavr Savr tomatoes didn't live up to the hard sell; in fact, they were too soft for the technologies of industrial agriculture. The first shipments did not withstand the handling and traveling and arrived at markets bruised and battered. Attempting to salvage the product, Calgene got packing companies to devise gentler handling procedures, and then it further invested in its own processing facilities closer to the growing areas. High-tech "soft-touch" machines (initially created for peaches) were adapted for tomatoes, using optical sensors to distinguish the weight, shape, and color of the tomatoes. But these new technologies also created the need for more labor and thus increased production costs. There were reports that Calgene planned to grow its tomatoes in Mexico because of the cheap labor. What's more, it admitted by 1996 that its Flavr Savr tomatoes did not have acceptable yield and disease resistance performance and that it would have to improve them through further research.

Eventually, the tomato did Calgene in. Monsanto began rescuing the company in 1995 and by the end of 1996 had bought it out completely. While the Flavr Savr tomato has faded from view, Monsanto has benefited from the research on genetics that it is now applying to other foods. As the "first bioengineered whole food," the Flavr Savr tomato "opened the door for the use of biotechnology to spread like weeds on the global market."[107]

It also served to bring the issue to the public consciousness and to promote efforts such as the Pure Food Campaign (PFC), which named the Flavr Savr one of the "frankenfoods," and raised concerns about the health hazards hidden in these transgenic experiments. For example, another biotech company, DNA Plant Technology, spliced an antifreeze gene from an Arctic flounder to create a tomato that can withstand the cold in the field or refrigerator and that can have a potential shelf life of three months.[108] PFC activists contend that people with fish allergies could unknowingly become sick eating these tomatoes.[109]

Around the turn of the millennium, a growing resistance to GE crops and food was evident in public demonstrations at three meetings of the Food and Drug Administration, at the World Trade Organization meeting in Seattle, at the

Montreal summit to forge a biodiversity safety protocol, and at annual share-holder meetings for various companies.[110] According to Haraway, activists challenge biotechnological practices of the New World Order with a variety of arguments, which include and synthesize many of the concerns raised in this chapter:

- increasing capital concentration and the monopolization of the means of life, reproduction, and labor;
- appropriation of the commons of biological inheritance as the private preserve of corporations;
- the global deepening of inequality by region, nation, race, gender, and class;
- erosion of Indigenous peoples' self-determination and sovereignty in regions designated as biodiverse while Indigenous lands and bodies become the object of intense gene prospecting and proprietary development;
- inadequately assessed and potentially dire environmental health consequences;
- misplaced priorities for technoscientific investment funds;
- propagation of distorted and simplistic scientific explanations, such as genetic determinism;
- intensified cruelty to and domination over animals;
- depletion of biodiversity;
- undermining established practices of human and nonhuman life, culture and production, not engaging those affected in democratic decision making.[111]

Free Trade and the Tomato War   If it isn't clear by now that tomatoes are much more than fruits of the earth but are codes for broader social processes and debates, then the story of the "Tomato War" will reveal how they can become political footballs as well. One of the key developments of the new era of globalization has been the impact of free trade on production, imports, and exports. The North American Free Trade Agreement, which was implemented on 1 January 1994, offered great promise for Mexican tomato producers because of their comparative advantage. Besides the favorable climatic conditions and accessibility of land, the big difference, of course, was labor costs. Mexican wages, for example, averaged $3 to $4.50 *a day* in 1994, while U.S. wages were between $5 and $6 *an hour*. Mexico's major competitors for the winter production of tomatoes are Florida producers, who share the growing season. Production costs in Florida are double those in Mexico but the yields are also double, due to the use of more advanced technology.[112]

When devaluation and the ensuing peso crisis spurred a recession in Mexico at the end of 1994, Mexican tomato producers were able to sell their tomatoes in the United States at lower prices and still do well with the exchange rate. They were nonetheless constrained by the safeguards provided in the NAFTA agreement, which limited their imports to the United States between certain key periods (15 November–29 February and 1 March–14 July). But in 1995, Florida growers were suffering; one producer declared, "What natural disasters couldn't do to us the good Mexican harvest is now doing: killing our industry."[113] They took their complaints to the International Trade Commission (ITC), seeking the imposition of punitive tariffs on Mexican tomatoes and charging the Mexicans with illegal competition, or dumping. These cases became the first tests of the dispute mechanisms established by NAFTA. In July 1996, the ITC ruled in Mexico's favor on the first issue and decided not to impose punitive tariffs.

By late October 1996, the U.S. government had reached an agreement with the Mexican producers that suspended the dumping charge and fixed the floor price at $5.17 for a twenty-five-pound box of tomatoes sold in the United States, which still allowed Mexican tomatoes to be sold at 17.56 percent below market prices.[114] The USDA also offered some Florida growers exemption from certain requirements that had favored the mature tomatoes produced primarily in Mexico, while in Florida, most tomatoes are picked green and gassed.

An irony of this cross-border dispute is that the losses suffered by Florida growers in the face of Mexican competition ended up most hurting the large number of Mexican migrant farmworkers picking tomatoes in Florida. Massieu summarizes this well: "It's a dramatic outcome of the principal comparative advantage of the Mexican producers, cheap labor, in the face of the technological superiority of the U.S. growers, that it's always the Mexican farmworkers who will lose: if they work in Mexican fields, they get paid low wages; and if they work in Florida fields, they get less work due to competition with the Mexican tomato."[115]

NAFTA and Transgenic Maize in Mexico   While Mexico had a comparative advantage over the United States with tomatoes, free trade privileged the U.S. corn market, which was highly subsidized. It became cheaper for Mexicans to import U.S. corn than to produce it; since NAFTA was implemented, Mexico has gone from being self-sufficient in corn production to being dependent on imports. In Mexico, corn is not only the basic staple of the diet but also deeply, culturally significant, especially for Indigenous populations. As a result, this dependency has generated great debates and struggles around the threats of imported GE crops to biodiversity and cultural diversity. In 2001, a highly controversial study by two University of California scientists found DNA from transgenic maize in locally planted fields in two states[116]; by 2003, the genes had spread to nine states.

The contamination of native land races in a center of origin for maize, which has thus far maintained tremendous genetic diversity, became an international issue for social movements and a major test case for the GE debate. Indigenous communities pushed NAFTA's Commission on Environmental Cooperation (CEC) to undertake a study of the effects of gene flow on the country. Their November 2004 report recommended that Mexico maintain its moratorium on planting GE maize; and while it could offer no proof of positive or negative effects on biodiversity or human health, it emphasized the significance of the sociocultural effects of the GE gene flow.

Jennifer Clapp reveals how neoliberal trade trumps environmental concerns, even in the response of the Mexican government to this threat. Even though the Mexican National Institute of Ecology confirmed the contamination of local land races, the Mexican government signed a trilateral agreement with the United States and Canada in 2003 with very weak requirements on labeling and documentation of GE grain shipments. A new biosafety law implemented in 2005 establishes a regulatory framework for assessing the risks of GE seeds and allows their limited release; opponents have dubbed this the "Monsanto Law" because it does not ban GE crops or require that local communities be informed when GE seeds are planted in their areas.[117]

Once again, it becomes clear that the GE issue cannot be considered as a purely technical challenge; the political interests underlying the scientific debates are being revealed and both government interventions as well as social movements challenging GE crops are the driving force.

The Computer Moment and Globalization

> The coming together of the computer revolution and the biotechnology revolution into a single technological complex foreshadows a new era of food production—one divorced from land, climate, and changing seasons, long the conditioning agents of agricultural input.
>
> —Jeremy Rifkin, *The End of Work*

One of the first radio broadcasts I listened to after 1 January 2000 featured a group of Canadian farmers making a public declaration that this would be the first millennium without farmers.[118] I found the apocalyptic announcement disturbing but not surprising, especially after witnessing the decline of family farms over the past two decades and the increasing control of food production by the retail sector (featured in chapter 4). Rifkin, in prophesying not only the end of farming but, more broadly, the end of work, argues that no sector has escaped the influence of the microchip, and that the new production processes in agriculture have been created by the combined forces of biotechnology and information technologies. In fact, genetic engineering would not be possible without the precise computerized manipulation of living matter.

Quoting Donald Holt, the administrator of an agricultural college, Rifkin asks us to imagine a future of totally automated farms:

> During the night, the farm computer automatically dialed several local and national databases to obtain information on current fertilizer, seed, fuel, and pesticide supplies and prices, weather, markets, insect and disease predictions, and buyer offers . . . information gathered and processed by the computer during the night appears on the bedroom monitor. . . .
>
> The computer has been scanning by telemetry a number of miniature portable weather stations placed in the fields. . . . On this particular day it anticipates low soil moisture in sands near the river and has activated the pivot irrigation system in that field. . . . [A] photo-activated herbicide . . . will be applied . . . by high-clearance ground equipment with precise micro-processors control and monitoring of steering, ground speed, pump pressure.

While this vision of roboticized farming may seem far-fetched, especially for the labor-intensive agroexport production of tomatoes in Mexico, the images are not that alien from what I witnessed in a new greenhouse packing plant in Jalisco. Tomatoes passed by in cups on conveyor belts, while laser sensors measured their color, weight, and size. Women workers were still needed to pack the fruit that had been sorted electronically. But even the harvesting of tomatoes has been mechanized in the north, displacing the work of many Mexican immigrant workers in the United States. A new robotic picker can identify tomatoes that are ripe by "smell," with sensors that measure ethylene levels.

The combination of the mechanical, biological, and chemical revolutions in agriculture has already put millions of farm laborers out of work, and scientists predict that within twenty years, virtually every aspect of farming will have come under the control of computers.[119] Not only production technologies are transforming global agriculture, however; computerized information technologies have become the new motor of all the aspects of the transnational economy. As we will see in the case studies to follow, just as the corporate tomato is monitored by agribusinesses, brokers, wholesalers, and retailers who control inventory for just-in-time production, so, too, is every movement of the workers who pack tomatoes in Mexico and scan tomatoes in Canada computer monitored. Fruit/commodity, worker, and technology are totally intertwined and controlled by the silicon chip.

Production, distribution, marketing, and consumption have been integrated through a management technique called *quick response* that connects manufacturers electronically with points of sale. As we will see in the supermarket case study (chapter 4), the consumption end of the food chain has been transformed by these technologies. Heather Menzies argues that two computer-linked technologies—the bar code and the scanner—have revolutionized the retail sector. Through what are called "automated management systems," stores use the data recorded by the scanner not only to trim inventories through just-in-time stock reordering but also to trim staff to just-in-time scheduling. Computerization has affected retail work in more ways than one: it has replaced certain tasks, has precipitated a shift from full-time to contingent employment, and has made monitoring workers such as cashiers even more insidious. Scanning data are used, for example, to check productivity levels, with high-scoring employees given more work hours and below-average scanners subjected to disciplinary action.[120]

As consumers, we are also (perhaps unknowingly) caught in this new web of surveillance, as companies use information about us to target particular markets; we may be offered discounts, for example, based on our (computer-monitored) shopping patterns. David Altheide notes that, while we may think the bar code allows us to see the price of an item we are purchasing, it serves at least eight functions, all allowing greater social control: (1) advertising, (2) recording a sale, (3) inventory, (4) personal history, (5) group history, (6) organizational surveillance, (7) rational decision making, and (8) self-monitoring.[121] Information about our personal practices can be shared across companies and sectors, with police officers stopping us on the highway, for example, having access to information about overdue bills.

This period of history has been dubbed the Information Age, and the use of information by new media technologies is a key component of the global food system. The so-called information- or knowledge-based economy is almost synonymous with globalization, distinguishing this period from other, earlier, periods of colonialism or capitalism. The most pervasive use is found in the marketing of goods, including food. As a system of scientific management, marketing consists of four elements: targeting, motivation research, product development, and sales communications.[122] The first two use computerized data to identify key consumers and gear product development toward them. But product management, illustrated in chapter 4 with the corporate branding of Loblaws products, involves manipulating the appearance of a product to stimulate buying. We have seen how tomatoes framed in produce sections as "Fresh from the Fields," for example, have been sprayed, washed with chlorine, waxed, and gassed before a four-day journey north from Mexico and how many are discarded and repacked before being selected as perfect, hyperreal specimens for display. For the more processed forms of tomatoes, such as salsas, packaging is key.

It is advertising, the best-known element of sales communications, that most distinguishes the marketing of the twenty-first century. Benjamin Barber contends that advertising has itself become big business on a global scale, with total world advertising revenues estimated to be between $150 and $250 billion, nearly half of which are American.[123] Advertising depends on the synergy of information and communications technologies. Using computer-analyzed data on consumer attitudes and behaviors, advertising artists manipulate our desires as magically as they manipulate images through increasingly sophisticated computer graphics technologies. We are bombarded daily—from more conventional billboards and newspaper and magazine ads to the ubiquitous television commercials, Internet advertising,[124] and brand labels on our clothes as well as on our food—with corporate images seducing us to buy not only products but a lifestyle. As we explore in chapters 3 and 4, the logos of multinationals such as the McDonald's golden arches and the representation of exotic places to promote Loblaws global cuisines play on our unconscious and invite us not only to eat their products but to become the people portrayed in their ads.[125]

The commodification of tomatoes, like the commodification of life, has been greatly facilitated by these information and communication technologies and strategies that have shaped our perceptions of the fruit and, therefore, our relationship to it, in more ways than we can imagine.

Clearly, the five moments reviewed in this journey are still all present in some form in the twenty-first century, as the genetic and computer moments are built on the earlier scientific, industrial, and chemical moments; and neoliberalism and globalization build on histories of colonialism, evolutions of capitalism, and reframings of development. But they have also undergone significant transformations, and, far from being monolithic, have taken different forms in different contexts. The historical processes that brought us to this moment will be revisited in the case studies to follow in chapters 3, 4, and 6, with more concrete

examples of these transformations and also with a sense of their fluidity and mu-
tability. This chapter has offered the tomato vine as a kind of spine for a journey
that is both geopolitical and historical, exploring routes and roots. The human
actors shaping (and being shaped by) the present moment along the tomato trail,
and particularly the women workers, are highlighted from now on.

Notes

1. Mexico predominates in tomato production, compared to the United States, Canada,
and Holland. While it is the only country that can produce all year round, it is in close
competition with Florida, where intense production occurs for nine months. Source: The
Blue Book for exporters and importers of fruit and vegetables, Carol Stream, Ill.: Producer
Reporter Company Blue Book Services, 1999.

2. While I agree with the postmodern contention that the dynamics of any particular
context are socially constructed and historically contingent and I guard against universalizing stories, this telling attempts to acknowledge both general structural and regulatory dynamics, while also grounding them in specific case studies. I run the risk of over-
generalizing but prefer to articulate this partial knowledge, owning my particular
framing of it, and hope that it generates diverse interpretations as well as moral and political debates.

3. Gary Gereffi, Miguel Korzeniewicz, and Roberto Korzeniewicz, "Introduction:
Global Commodity Chains," in *Commodity Chains and Global Capitalism,* ed. Gary Gereffi
and Miguel Korzeniewicz (Westport, Conn.: Praeger, 1994), 1.

4. Gereffi suggests that global commodity chains (GCCs) have three main dimensions:
an input-output structure (set of products and services), a territoriality (production/dis-
tribution networks), and a governance structure (authority and power relationships).

5. Quoted in "The Global Food Puzzle: Where Do You Fit into the Picture?" an educational video coproduced by Mark Haslam and Anuja Mendiratta, with Deborah Barndt,
Tomasita Project, 1998.

6. The historical information on the tomato is drawn from several sources: Sophie D.
Coe, *America's First Cuisines* (Austin: University of Texas Press, 1994), 46–50; Jennifer Ben-
nett, ed., *The Harrowsmith Tomato Handbook* (Camden East, Ontario: Camden House, n.d.),
6–13; Philip Hardgrave, *Growing Tomatoes* (New York: Avon, 1992), 7–9; World Resources
Institute, "Food Crops and Biodiversity" (Washington, D.C.: World Resources Institute,
1989), also on its Web site: http://www.wri.og/wri/biodiv/foodcrop.html.

7. The production of wooden crates, in fact, upset the ecosystem balance in rural Mexico and contributed to a plague of *la roña* (a whitefly), which destroyed tomato harvests
in Autlán in the early 1990s. The forests surrounding the plantations were cut down to
make crates, and the whitefly that had lived from the leaves of the trees was forced into
the tomato fields for sustenance. Personal communication with Antonieta Barrón, Miami,
Florida, 17 March 2000.

8. The plastic sheets have several functions: they keep the moisture in and the weeds
out, they maintain uniformity among the plants, and the shine on their surface repels
pests.

9. Sara Lara, "Feminización de los procesos de trabajo del sector fruti-horticola en el
estado de Sinaloa," *Cuicuilco* 21 (April–June 1988): 29–36.

10. FAOSTAT, http://faostat.fao.org/site/340/DesktopDefault.aspx?PageID=340.

11. A study by the Rural Advancement Foundation International (RAFI) of seventy-five types of vegetables found that 97 percent of the varieties on the old USDA lists are now extinct. Of the 408 varieties of the common tomato, *Lycopersicon exculentum*, existing in 1903, only 79 varieties are now held by the U.S. National Seed Storage Laboratory, perhaps the major seed bank in the world. Cary Fowler and Pat Mooney, *Shattering: Food, Politics, and the Loss of Genetic Diversity* (Tucson: University of Arizona Press, 1996), 51, 62–63, 67.

12. Sometimes called *polycropping*, this approach has multiple advantages. "The beans 'fix' organic nitrogen, thereby enhancing soil fertility and improving corn growth. The corn in turn provides a trellis for the bean vines, and the squash plants, with their wide shady leaves, help keep the weeds down." Scientists have proven that total yields of these three crops grown together are higher than if the same area were sown in monocultures. John Tuxill, "The Biodiversity That People Made," *World Watch* (May/June 2000): 27.

13. "Jalisco produce un jitomate libre del virus de la mosca blanca," *Economía*, 5 December 1996, and "Western Seed colocará 400 kilos de semilla de jitomate híbrido," 6 December 1996.

14. Interview by author and Sara San Martin with Yves Gomes, San Isidro Mazatepec, Jalisco, 24 July 1996.

15. The cosmetic standards that Mexican agroexport companies feel pressured to adhere to have been written under pressure from U.S. growers as one tactic to keep the competition down. Mexican agronomists admit that much higher amounts of pesticides are used to avoid blemishes and irregularities caused by pests. Entomologist Mayra Aviles Gonzales suggests that anxious growers who use an irrationally high quantity of pesticides could get the same production and cosmetic results with 50 percent the amount used. Angus Wright, *The Death of Ramón González: The Modern Agricultural Dilemma* (Austin: University of Texas Press, 1990), 33–35.

16. Tuxill, "The Biodiversity That People Made," 32.

17. Interview by Maria de Jesus Aguilar with Milagros Baltazar, Santa Rosa field-worker, Sayula, Jalisco, 23 August 1997.

18. Interview by author and Sara San Martin with Santa Rosa field-worker Gomez Farias, Jalisco, 26 April 1997.

19. Interview by author and Lauren Baker with Cesar Gil, plant manager, Santa Rosa packing plant, 7 December 1996. See also Wright, *The Death of Ramón Gonzalez,* 34.

20. Interview by author with Angelo Vento, Ontario Food Terminal, Toronto, January 1999.

21. Lara, "Feminización de los procesos de trabajo," 29–36.

22. Produce list used by Loblaws supermarkets, for the week of 28 July–3 August 1996. It identifies almost five hundred items by name and PLU number.

23. Interview by author and Lauren Baker with Enrique Padilla, greenhouse worker, San Isidro Mazatepec, Jalisco, 10 December 1996.

24. FAOSTAT, http://faostat.fao.org/site/343/DesktopDefault.aspx?PageID=343. Less than 1 percent comes to Canada, over 99 percent to the United States.

25. The Blue Book used by exporters and importers of tomatoes uses the following categories to classify the range of colors: Green—completely green, Breakers—not more than 10 percent turning, Turning—10 to 30 percent turning, Pink—30 to 60 percent pink or red, Light red—60 to 90 percent pink or red, and Red—more than 90 percent red. Tomatoes may be ordered in any of these categories. Those harvested for distant transport are of-

ten picked in the mature green state, are gassed, and ripen during transport if kept at temperatures between 55 and 70 degrees Fahrenheit.

26. Interview by author and Maria Dolores Villagomez with Alfredo Badajoz Navarro, Irapuato, Guanajuato, 28 April 1997. See also Lara, *Cuicuilco*, 35.

27. According to California producers, juicy and tasty tomatoes are not ideal for processing; rather, they prefer those that are "bred for thick walls and lots of 'meat' per tomato." While dry and flavorless when raw, such tomatoes apparently "provide just the right color and texture for prepared sauces, salsas, and paste." The major concern, however, seems to be for the transport, not the taste: "The thick walls are what allows a pretty red tomato to survive at the bottom of one of those big truck bins." Carlos Alcalá, "California Really Is the Big Tomato," *Sacramento Bee*, 10 August 1997, B6.

28. Somewhat naively, I crossed this border by foot with three graduate students, armed with video cameras and tape recorders. It wasn't until we had passed by several checkpoints that one of the customs officials stopped us. "Do you realize you are in a highly sensitive area?" he queried and then admonished us: "You really shouldn't be here; we would be liable if there was a shootout or if something happened to you."

29. In 1999, mass graves were discovered in what is being called a "narcocemetery" ten kilometers south of the border city Ciudad Juárez, where the city's ruthless drug cartel (topping tourism and sweatshops as the leading industry) allegedly killed more than one hundred people—mostly Mexicans but also Americans—since 1990. John Stackhouse, *Globe and Mail*, 1 December 1999, 1A.

30. By February 1999, a new CAADES complex had opened at a location thirteen kilometers south of the border and equipped so that all of the inspections could be done on the Mexican side of the border, facilitating quick passage through customs and easing the growing bottlenecks.

31. The "Quality Defects" listed in the Blue Book include maturity, cleanness, shape, smoothness, development, bacterial spot, bacterial speck, catfaces, puffiness, growth cracks, field scars, hail injury, insect injury, cuts or broken skins, and sun scald, while "Condition Defects" include color, sunken and discolored, sunburn, internal discoloration, freezing injury, chilling injury, alternaria rot, gray mold rot, and bacterial soft rot.

32. One problem with the FDA testing procedure is that it only tests for a limited number of chemicals and for single chemicals, while the impact of pesticides on humans comes from a cumulative or synergistic effect that results from being exposed to a variety of pesticides. Wright, *The Death of Ramón Gonzalez*, 196.

33. Personal interview with Jonathon Barnes, USDA inspector, Customs Complex, Nogales, Arizona, 17 February 1999.

34. William Rees and Mathis Wackernage, *Our Ecological Footprint: Reducing Human Impact on the Earth* (Gabriola Island, Canada: New Society, 1996).

35. FAO STATISTICS, 2005.

36. For every kilogram of tomatoes that you get locally rather than importing, you will be saving 952 grams or 95.2 percent of its weight in greenhouse gas emissions. Lifecycles Good Food Directory, http://www.lifecyclesproject.ca/initiatives/food_directory/?a=taxonomy/term/81.

37. Alex Murray (with Eric Krause), "The Ecological Footprint of Food Transportation," *Proceedings from Moving the Economy, An International Conference* (Toronto: Detour Publications, 1999), 84.

38. Marc Xuereb, "Food Miles: Environmental Implications of Food Imports to the Waterloo Region," Region of Waterloo Public Health, November 2005.

39. Linda Tons, *Toronto Star*, 16 March 1997, 5F.

40. Interview by author with Larry Tenelia, 8 August 1997.

41. Interview by author with Greg P. Hummell, customs superintendent, Blue Water Bridge, Sarnia, Ontario, 2 January 2000.

42. Interview with Angelo Vento, manager, Ontario Produce, Ontario Food Terminal, 26 January 1999.

43. *The Morning Zoo,* a documentary by Daisy Lee, takes an intimate look at the early morning operations of the Ontario Food Terminal, where the Chinese Canadian filmmaker went frequently as a child with her farm family. A Grindstone Films Inc. Production, 1989.

44. Most of the information in this section is drawn from an interview by author and Anuja Mendiratta with Angelo Vento, sales manager, Ontario Produce, and Dominique Stillo, Joyce Foods, Toronto, 26 January 1999.

45. Interview with Angelo Vento.

46. According to Gary Lloyd, chief buyer for National Grocers, importers sometimes won't accept the tomatoes if there is too much wax on them. "It's really just like body builders; they put oil on and they look bigger and better. But customers go crazy when they pick it up and their hands are all covered." Interview by author and Stephanie Conway with Gary Lloyd, Erin Mills, 7 May 1997.

47. According to Larry Tenelia, sales manager for Pacific Produce, Canadian importers of fresh fruit and vegetables in Vancouver, the PLU code is for products that have to be sold by weight and are not scannable, while the UPC bar code is for commodities that are fixed weight and can be scanned. An importer must first get a code for any new item from the Produce Electronic Identification Board, located in the United States, having proven that they are moving a significant number of items. Personal interview by author and Stephanie Conway with Larry Tenelia, Vancouver, 8 August 1997.

48. Stickers on other fresh produce, such as Chiquita bananas, have also become microadvertisements for other products such as computers.

49. While many North American children have an aversion to tomatoes, they are generally drawn to ketchup, a highly sweetened tomato-based sauce, often added to McDonald's sandwiches or french fries. Ketchup recipes, however, vary by country and cultural tastes; a Del Monte executive in the Mexican plant revealed that Mexicans prefer acidic to sweet ketchup, so a different formula is used there. Interview by author with Jorge Betherton, vice president, Del Monte, Irapuato, Guanajuato, Mexico, 19 July 1996.

50. The Arch Deluxe, however, lasted for less than five years, recently replaced by the Big Xtra. See chapter 3, note 18.

51. Interview by author and Lauren Baker with Dominique Stillo, Joyce Foods, 1996; interview by author and Stephanie Conway with Larry Tenelia, sales manager for Pacific Produce, 8 August 1997.

52. "The coincidence of hungry mouths with overflowing grain silos may seem to be a paradox, but it is a paradox not of our analysis, but of capitalist agribusiness itself." Fred Magdoff, Frederick H. Buttel, and John Bellamy Foster, "Hungry for Profit: Agriculture, Food, and Ecology," *Monthly Review* 50, no. 3 (July/August 1998): 3.

53. Conversation with Tesair Lauve, Cambridge, Massachusetts, 10 December 1999.

54. This is perhaps best illustrated by the curriculum of McDonald's Hamburger University outside Chicago, where management-level staff for restaurants throughout North America get trained in the operations of the business but don't get any courses related to the food per se that is central to their enterprise.

55. Leah Hager Cohen, *Glass, Paper, Beans: Revelations on the Nature and Value of Ordinary Things* (New York: Doubleday, 1997), 236.

56. Cohen, *Glass, Paper, Beans,* 251.

57. Fowler and Mooney, *Shattering*, 76.

58. Brewster Kneen, *The Rape of Canola* (Toronto: NC Press, 1992), 146.

59. Who tells the story and who re-creates the history is critical; my framing is influenced by various critics of the current system. In an intellectual era that recognizes multiple subjectivities and "regimes of truth" as socially constructed and historically specific, I recognize that today's dominant discourses (including the critical ones) will shape and limit the versions of history that I choose to name and frame.

60. Judith D. Soule and Jon K. Piper, *Farming in Nature's Image: An Ecological Approach to Agriculture* (Washington, D.C.: Island, 1992), 72–79.

61. Vandana Shiva, *Biopiracy: The Plunder of Nature and Knowledge* (Toronto: Between the Lines, 1997), 46–47.

62. Quoted in Shiva, *Biopiracy*, 47.

63. Shiva, *Biopiracy*, 60.

64. Shiva, *Biopiracy*, 104.

65. Harriet Friedmann, "Remaking 'Traditions': How We Eat, What We Eat, and the Changing Political Economy of Food," in *Women Working the NAFTA Food Chain: Women, Food, and Globalization*, ed. Deborah Barndt (Toronto: Second Story, 1999), 39.

66. Soule and Piper, *Farming in Nature's Image*, 52. Their analysis of these ecological and economic problems feeds the ensuing discussion.

67. Soule and Piper credit the development of industrial agriculture in the United States with the work of institutions such as the USDA, land grant colleges, and the U.S. Patent Office, all of which were established in the nineteenth century. Soule and Piper, *Farming in Nature's Image*, 59–62.

68. The commodification of nature and of food in general and of the tomato in particular is revealed in the expression often used in Mexico to describe all the "inputs" of the dominant system as the *paquete tecnológico*. The metaphor of the "package" reflects the industrialized nature of this imported agricultural model, and "technological" emphasizes a highly mediated practice. Any approach to agriculture involves certain technologies, which both shape and are shaped by the worldviews of those creating and using them. The tomato journey outlined here reflects only one agricultural practice, but it is the one that has dominated food production in the West for recent decades and increasingly in the Third World.

69. Mexican agriculture was already developing in this direction, and so the Green Revolution scientists found receptiveness and support, as well as competing approaches with state-supported institutions such as the IIA (Instituto de Investigaciones Agrícolas) or the Agricultural Research Institute. Gilberto Aboites, "Los Fitomejoradores Mexicanos: Ciencia, Nación, y Compromiso Social," Ph.D. diss., Universidad de Guadalajara—Centro de Investigaciones y Estudios Superiores en Antropología Social (CIESAS), 2000.

70. Francisco Martinez, Ph.D. diss., University of Guadalajara (CIESAS), 2002.

71. Joyce Nelson, "Culture and Agriculture: The Ultimate Simulacrum," in her *Sign Crimes/Road Kill: From Mediascape to Landscape* (Toronto: Between the Lines, 1992), 218.

72. CIMMYT, el Centro Internacional de Mejoramiento del Maiz y Trigo, or the International Center for the Improvement of Corn and Wheat.

73. Shiva, *Biopiracy*, 50.

74. Soule and Piper, *Farming in Nature's Image*, 56.

75. With the low cost of labor in Mexico and the increasing dependency on mechanical and chemical inputs, by 1993 the total costs of agricultural inputs accounted for 26.76 percent of production, while labor costs only accounted for 18.59 percent. Yolanda Cristina Massieu, "Comercio bilateral México–Estados Unidos y logros del TLC: 'La guerra del tomate,'" *El Cotidiano* 79 (octubre 1996): 115.

76. Wright, *The Death of Ramón Gonzalez*, 177.

77. Shiva, *Biopiracy*, 48.

78. Shiva, *Biopiracy*, 50–51.

79. Donna Haraway, *Modest_Witness@Second_Millennium. Female/Man©_Meets_Oncomouse™* (New York: Routledge, 1997), 57.

80. Florianne Koechlin, "Nine Interviews on Epigenetics and Transgenic Plants," in *Risk Underestimated* (Hamburg, Germany: Greenpeace, 2005), 8.

81. Ibid., 9.

82. Belinda Martineau, *First Fruit—The Creation of the Flavr Savr Tomato and the Birth of Biotech Food* (New York: McGraw-Hill, 2001), 233.

83. As another example of U.S. hegemony, the Special 301 clause of the U.S. Trade Act is being unilaterally imposed worldwide, universalizing the U.S. patent regime. Shiva, *Biopiracy*, 9.

84. Though the TRIPs agreement came out of a multilateral institution, the General Agreement on Tariffs and Trade, now replaced and superseded by the WTO, one of the three organizations that conceived and shaped it was the Intellectual Property Committee, which is a coalition of twelve major U.S. corporations, including Monsanto and DuPont. Shiva, *Biopiracy*, 81.

85. Fowler and Mooney note that IPR laws are like other laws in industrialized countries that are designed to recognize the achievements of individualized work, while the Third World system of innovation is more informal and communal in structure; this very informality contributes to their being unrewarded and even denigrated. Fowler and Mooney, *Shattering*, 145.

86. Personal communication with Gilberto Aboites, March 2000.

87. Haraway, *Modest_Witness*, 61.

88. ETC Group, "Oligopoly, Inc. 2005: Concentration in Corporate Power," *Communiqué* 91 (November/December 2005): 1–2.

89. It is cheaper for the seed-chemical multinationals to adapt the plant to the chemical than the chemical to the plant, comparing the cost of developing a new crop variety (about $2 million) to the cost of a new herbicide (over $40 million). Shiva, *Biopiracy*, 91.

90. James Cowan, "Hard to Swallow," *This Magazine* (May/June 2002): 8.

91. Martineau, *First Fruit*, 235.

92. Koechlin, "Nine Interviews," 9.

93. Biologist Mae-Wan Ho explains the depth of this danger: "To understand why genetic engineering biotechnology is so inherently hazardous, we have to appreciate the prodigious power of microbes to proliferate, the protean promiscuity of the genes they carry, and their ability to jump, spread, mutate, and recombine." Quoted in Brewster Kneen, *Farmageddon* (Gabriola Island, B.C.: New Society Publishers, 1999), 27.

94. Even before genetic engineering, the major cause of extinction of traditional plants was the introduction of new varieties produced by professional breeders. Fowler and Mooney, *Shattering*, 75.

95. "GMO Updates #9: Suicide Seeds on the Fast Track," www.globalvisionary@cybernaute.com, accessed 26 March 2000.

96. Two Canadian organizations fighting to protect farmers' rights to save seeds are the National Farmer's Union (www.nfu.ca) and Seeds of Diversity Canada (www.seeds.ca).

97. Lucy Sharratt, "Canadians Confront Government on Terminator Technology," *The Activist* (Spring 2006): 6–7.

98. "Monsanto vs. Schmeiser: The Classic David vs. Goliath Struggle," http://www.percyschmeiser.com/conflict.htm, accessed 23 May 2007.

99. Kneen, *Farmageddon*, 178.

100. Shiva, *Biopiracy*, 124.

101. Shiva, *Biopiracy*, 126.

102. Apparently Calgene claimed that the Flavr Savr tomato was not a transgenic organism, because the promoter gene was genetically engineered to be reversed and blocked, and thus not functioning. Haraway points out, however, that it still has been inserted with a marker gene that is there to verify the successful insertion of the reversed gene. *Modest_Witness*, 56.

103. Jeff Bergau, public relations director of Calgene Fresh, quoted by Massieu, "Comercio bilateral México," 116.

104. Kneen, *Farmageddon*, 96; "The Tomatoes Are Coming! The Tomatoes Are Coming! Calgene's High-Tech Fruits Are Set to Roll," *Restaurant Business*, 1 March 1994, 26; and U.S. Department of Agriculture, "The New Tomato: An Inside View," July 1994.

105. Massieu, "Comercio bilateral México," 118.

106. Ralph T. King, Jr., "Low-Tech Woe Slows Calgene Super Tomato," *Wall Street Journal*, 11 April 1995, B6.

107. Emily Fattore, "Public Awareness of Biotechnology in Agriculture," bachelor's thesis, York University, 1998, 50.

108. It is feared that, if commercialized massively, the DNAP tomato with its three-month shelf life could potentially eliminate the winter niche market that Mexican producers now hold. Massieu, "Comercio bilateral México," 118.

109. Allan Hepburn, "Genetically Engineered Food Gets Ready to Go to Market," *Healthwatch* 6, no. 4 (winter 1994): 12–13.

110. Martineau, *First Fruit*, 230.

111. Haraway, *Modest_Witness*, 60–61.

112. Massieu, "Comercio bilateral México," 115.

113. Teena Borek, tomato producer from Dade County, Florida, quoted by Massieu, "Comercio bilateral México," 119.

114. "La Secofi, inconforme con el pacto jitomatero de EU," *Siglo XXI*, 30 October 1996, 6.

115. Massieu, "Comercio bilateral México," 119.

116. Along with his graduate assistant David Quist, Mexican-born microbiologist Ignacio Chapela published the results of his study in the renowned journal *Nature*, which later retracted the article. The charge of transgenic contamination infuriated Mexican biotech advocates and the biotech industries that worked closely with the University of California, where Chapela was later denied tenure. John Ross, "The Sad Saga of Ignacio Chapela," *Anderson Valley Advertiser*, 18 February 2004, http://www.theava.com/04/0218-chapela.html, accessed 23 May 2007.

117. Jennifer Clapp, "Unplanned Exposure to Genetically Modified Organisms: Divergent Responses in the Global South," *The Journal of Environment & Development* 15, no. 1 (March 2006): 8–10.

118. The epigraph is taken from Jeremy Rifkin, *The End of Work: The Decline of the Global Labor Force and the Dawn of the Post-Market Era* (New York: Putnam, 1996), 123.

119. Rifkin, *The End of Work*, 115.

120. Heather Menzies, *Whose Brave New World? The Information Highway and the New Economy* (Toronto: Between the Lines, 1996), 70.

121. David Altheide, *An Ecology of Communication: Cultural Formats of Control* (New York: Aldine de Gruyter, 1995), 31.

122. Robert W. McChesney, Ellen Meiksins Wood, and John Bellamy Foster, eds., *Capitalism and the Information Age: The Political Economy of the Global Communication Revolution* (New York: Monthly Review, 1998).

123. Benjamin Barber, *Jihad vs. McWorld* (New York: Random House, 1996), 61.

124. "The main reason for corporate interest in the information highway lies in the fact that it is seen as opening up vast new markets," contend Michael Dawson and John Bellamy Foster, "Virtual Capitalism: Monopoly Capital, Marketing, and the Information Highway," in *Capitalism and the Information Age*, 58.

125. Indeed, a growing field within cultural studies analyzes the psychological, social, and political processes of consumer culture, through discourse analysis, deconstructing advertising images, texts, architectures, and performances. See *Representation: Cultural Representations and Signifying Practices*, ed. Stuart Hall (Thousand Oaks, Calif.: Sage, 1997).

CHAPTER 2

Frames and Filters:

THEORETICAL AND METHODOLOGICAL APPROACHES

How do we make sense of this twisted trail of the tomato, its journey through space and time? What can we learn from it about the seemingly abstract process of globalization? How will the stories of women workers along the tomato trail enlighten us about the dynamics of power?

This chapter offers frames and filters for the three case studies that form the body of this book. The first part of the chapter introduces key theoretical frames: globalization from above and from below, an interlocking analysis of power, and four axes for exploring the relationship between the tomato journey and the women's stories. In the second half, I highlight the methodological approaches of the Tomasita Project as a popular education process, integrating collaborative research methods and innovative photographic tools.

The Bigger Picture: Globalization from Above and from Below

For the past few years, I have been visiting three Mexican migrant women workers—Irena, Maria, and Carolina—who come to Canada every summer to pick tomatoes on a southern Ontario farm. In the summer of 1999, I invited them for their first visit to Toronto on a Friday afternoon, the only time they had off in their twelve-hours-a-day, six-and-a-half-days-a-week work schedule. As we had very little time for sightseeing, I offered them the quickest and most comprehensive tour: from the rotating lookout point of the Canadian National (CN) tower, the largest free-standing structure in the world, and Toronto's key logo as a "world-class city."

As we rocketed 1,815 feet up in the glass elevator to our vantage point in the clouds, I pointed out various landmarks in the Toronto cityscape. While the tower trip gave us a spectacular view, like most tourist activities, it offered little insight into the daily workings of the neighborhoods below or the people who inhabit them.

After an equally speedy and disorienting ride back to earth again, we traveled a few blocks east to the warehouse of Field to Table, a community-based project of FoodShare, an organization that has initiated a wide range of food alternatives for low-income communities. Urban agriculturalist Lauren Baker[1] showed us around the warehouse, introducing us to a sprouts-growing business, living machines, a community kitchen, composting projects, and an alternative food distribution project called the Good Food Box. I was struck by the contrasting views of the city, one from the tower and the other from this urban agriculture site. Although as migrant workers they are totally entrenched in the continental food system, the Mexican women showed keen interest in the community-based alternatives they witnessed.

The two stops on our whirlwind tour, from the clouds above the city to the land on which it stands, represent two contrasting notions of development, or its most recent incarnation, globalization. The CN tower offers the perspective of "globalization from above," not only because of its god's-eye view but because it symbolizes the priorities of Western economic growth. As a telecommunications tower, it also reflects the dominance of the so-called knowledge economy in the present information age. The Field to Table warehouse, on the other hand, represents "globalization from below," not only because it is closer to the ground but because it advocates a vision of development that emphasizes local community building and ecological sustainability.

At a 1993 international gathering critically assessing globalization from the perspectives of environmental and social justice, Richard Falk suggested,

> There is globalization from above, reflecting the collaboration between leading states and the main agents of capital formation. This type of globalization disseminates a consumerist ethos and draws into its domain international business and political elites.
>
> The second type of globalization is both reactive to these developments and responsive to different impulses and influences. . . . Identified as globalization from below, [it] consists of an array of transnational social forces animated by environmental concerns, human rights, hostility to patriarchy, and a vision of community based on the unity of diverse cultures seeking an end to poverty, oppression, humiliation, and collective violence.[2]

I find the naming of globalization from above and globalization from below both liberating and limiting. It is liberating because it shatters the aura often surrounding public discussions of globalization that imply it is monolithic, universal, inevitable, and basically good for everyone. Merely suggesting two perspectives, though somewhat simplistic, at least exposes a dominant discourse that represents certain interests, while revealing contesting interests, and thus the possibility of alternatives, of agency and change. As we crack open the globalization mystique, we begin to realize that globalization from above and globalization from below are, in fact, completely intertwined, like the tangled roots, each feeding and defining the other. The Field to Table warehouse, for example, has evolved in response to the failures of the dominant food system to provide sustenance to all people and in response to the resultant poverty and environmental degradation.

The limitations and weaknesses of Falk's frame, I think, are revealed by the Mexican migrant workers who went to the top of the tower and back. These women are forced by need to work for a dominant continental food system that removes them from their families for four months a year so they can provide low-wage labor for Canadian farms and ultimately offer Canadian consumers cheaper fresh tomatoes. We rarely hear their "from below" perspectives on the globalizing processes of the food system. These women workers, in fact, are often invisible not only to the architects of the dominant system but also to the critics of that system who propose more just alternatives. Not to be dismissed as mere victims, these women are also agents, courageously carving out their families' survival; while forced to work within a system that benefits but also exploits them, they constantly find ways, both individual and collective, to resist it. I will use globalization from below as a frame for their stories within the global food system.

The stories of the women workers told within these pages respond to a big gap in the discussion, by bringing the voices, knowledge, and wisdom of those most affected by globalization. These workers and their allies, social justice activists organizing with and for them, are also given space in the stories of what is sometimes called "the other globalization," a mobilization of civil society across borders and around common visions of social justice and environmental sustainability.

The case studies represent three different kinds of multinational corporations in the new global economy: McDonald's fast-food restaurants represent the epitome of the U.S.-based transnational, setting the standard for many other businesses and now making its profit from major expansion into the global market. Loblaws is Canada's largest supermarket chain, one of eighteen within George Weston Ltd., which controls the retail market in Canada and sells corporate brand products in the United States and beyond. Empaque Santa Rosa is a domestic company in Mexico, the second largest tomato agribusiness that now produces primarily for export, being pushed more and more into global trade. The women workers providing the globalization-from-below perspective are the lowest paid and least skilled (a notion we will challenge) in these three corporations: Mexican women picking and packing tomatoes, Canadian cashiers scanning tomatoes at Canadian supermarket checkouts, and women fast-food workers slicing tomatoes for the Arch Deluxe sandwich.

These cases will ground what is often a mystifying concept of globalization and reveal cracks within it. I agree with Maria Mies and Vandana Shiva that "the 'global' in the global order means simply the global domination of local and particular interests by means of subsuming the multiple diversities of economies, cultures, and/or nature under the control of a few multinational corporations, and the superpowers that assist them in their global reach through 'free' trade, structural adjustment programs, and, increasingly, conflicts, military or otherwise."[3] By taking the notion of globalization off a pedestal, they question why and how particular local interests have become globalized and who benefits.

Some suggest that the current economic restructuring associated with globalization is merely a continuation of deeply rooted colonial and imperialist practices and that the discourse itself obscures the power struggles within it. Edward Said reminds us of this international legacy: "Hardly any North American, African, European, Latin American, Indian, Caribbean, Australian individual—the list is very long—who is alive today has not been touched by the empires of the past. This pattern of domination or possessions laid the groundwork for what is in effect now a fully global world."[4]

Shiva further demystifies globalization in naming its architects, the G-8, or "the group of the seven [now eight] most powerful countries, [which] dictate global affairs, but remain narrow, local and parochial in terms of the interest of all of the world's communities."[5] She charges that "the 'global' exists only in offices of the World Bank and the IMF and the headquarters of multinational corporations."[6] It is no coincidence that thirty-three thousand of the more than thirty-seven thousand transnational companies operating today still have their home countries in Western Europe, North America, or Japan.[7]

This hegemonic control, or globalization from above, is also being challenged by countries excluded from the elite seven. Just prior to the 2000 meeting of the G-8 in Washington, D.C., the Group of 77 held their first summit, claiming that the process of globalization of recent years has only exacerbated problems. When the coalition of Third World nations formed in 1974, it called for a New International Economic Order (NIEO), essentially a reform of the world economic system to improve its position in international trade and its access to technological and financial resources.[8] But since then, the group has expanded to include 133 countries, and inequalities have deepened not only between but also within countries of the so-called north and south. The G-77 summit denounced the growing gap between the richest and poorest 20 percent of the world's people that has grown from 30 to 1 to 82 to 1.[9]

The late Jesuit scholar Xabier Gorostiaga starkly articulated this inequality: "The countries that form the Group of Seven, with their eight hundred million inhabitants, control more technological, economic, informatics, and military power than the rest of the approximately four billion people who live in Asia, Africa, Eastern Europe and Latin America."[10]

The companies whose women workers are featured in this book reflect the dominant globalizing tendencies of increasing decentralization of production and centralization of decision making. Mexican agribusinesses as well as Canadian food retail and U.S. fast-food businesses are being pressured to become ever bigger and further integrated into global systems of production and trade, transportation, finance, and telecommunications.

Mexican political leader Cuahtémoc Cárdenas dramatized the shifts: "[In the post–Cold War era] . . . competition has been moved from the military to the trade arena. [Third World Countries] have been assigned the role of providing labor and raw materials; serving as captive markets to complement those of the industrialized countries; supplying agricultural products that require mild climates; and providing new zones for the expansion of First World tourism. They are also replacing the North as a site for production that threatens the environment and for disposing of toxic wastes."[11] Cárdenas lays the ground, figuratively and literally, for our focus on food and agriculture as an intensely ecological undertaking deepening south-north interdependence.

As neoliberalism has risen, not only in the hemisphere but worldwide, the role of the nation-state has been downgraded to one of promoting privatization, deregulation, and removing the legal barriers for investment and the free trade of goods and services by corporations. International financial institutions such as the World Bank and the IMF have replaced governments as decision makers that transform economies and cultures through the conditionalities of their loan programs, commonly known as Structural Adjustment Programs (SAPs), which ironically have often only deepened debt crises. The World Trade Organization (WTO) has replaced the GATT as the international body coordinating these restructuring efforts in trade terms at a multilateral level.

GLOBALIZING FOOD

While the journey of the tomato from Mexican field to Canadian supermarket is framed, historically and geographically, by the North American Free Trade Agreement, NAFTA is merely a continuation of policies and practices that have long been shaping the global economy. When the WTO replaced the GATT in 1994, it further "institutionalized the rules of a neoliberal world order to match (and deepen) the corporate-led integration underway."[12] Agriculture has long been integrated into the advanced industrial capitalist model; food is in fact the largest industrial sector in the United States, and 95 percent of American food is manufactured and sold by corporations.

Global food production has been dominated by the agroexport model since the post–World War II period. But the organization of production in the south and consumption in the north has been spearheaded by transnational food companies that have expanded and merged into an ever smaller number of key conglomerates. The case studies in this book reflect this deepening corporate concentration, through both horizontal integration (expanding within the same level of the food system, such as Weston Ltd., which controls many different supermarket chains, including Loblaws) and vertical integration (increasing ownership and control within a number of stages, such as Santa Rosa, which grows, packs, distributes, and sells tomatoes).

At the end of the second millennium, key food analysts concluded that while this now globalized food system "does meet the needs of a limited group of large farmers and, of course, the sellers of agricultural inputs as well as the processors, distributors, and sellers of food, it is not beneficial for the masses or farmers or the environment, nor does it ensure a plentiful supply of food for all people."[13] In the case studies in chapters 3, 4, and 6, the voices of both those who benefit and those who do not are heard.

While I separate the corporate tales and the women workers' stories in each chapter, they must be seen as dynamically interrelated, one shaping the other, just as globalization from above and globalization from below define each other. In adapting the from-above and from-below frame, I hope not to oversimplify how power operates, as I share the critique of analyses that erase the contradictions within and between actors and institutions that keep globalization going from day to day. In trying to understand the complexities of women workers in the tomato chain, I draw on Gabriel Torres's appreciation for the "force of irony"[14] and on Anthony Giddens's notion that power relations in the workplace are "two-way . . . all human relations manifest autonomy and dependence in both directions."[15]

AN INTERDISCIPLINARY TOMATO

I bring an interdisciplinary perspective to issues of food and women workers, framing their stories with two principal axes—production/consumption and biodiversity/cultural diversity—and two secondary axes—health/environment and work/technology. These central dynamic tensions shape both the tomato's life cycle as well as the experiences of women workers within it.

Production/Consumption

In following Tomasita from Mexican field to Canadian fast-food restaurant, we explicitly explore the dynamic relationships between the production and consumption of food, and more particularly the agricultural production of tomatoes in the south for commercialization and consumption in the north. This axis raises questions about the evolution of the global food system, in which we have become increasingly alienated from the land and the people who provide our sustenance. Canadian food analyst Brewster Kneen's concept of *distancing* helps us understand this development not only in political economic terms but also in cultural and spiritual terms. According to Kneen, there are many dimensions to distancing, or the separation of raw-food production from the consumers of the final product, including breeding and engineering longer shelf life, processing and product differentiation, preservation techniques, and packaging technologies.[16]

While political economy and commodity chain analysis will contribute to the analysis of the tangled routes of the tomato, the field of cultural studies helps us

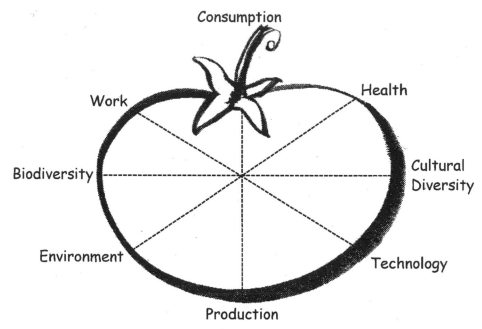

Tomasita: Four Axes

frame the experience from the consumption end, in which marketing and advertising produce not the food but its meaning and thus shape our experience of eating. Not surprisingly, the case studies of McDonald's and Loblaws both focus on the consumer's end of the production/consumption axis, even as both companies represent the growing phenomenon of control of production by the retail and fast-food service sectors. In a related vein, the restructuring of Mexican agribusiness for agroexport also reveals how food production has become increasingly consumer-driven, in the context of south-north inequalities.

Biodiversity/Cultural Diversity

The other principal axis shaping this investigation of tomatoes and women food workers brings together the concerns arising from a critical analysis of production and consumption. It integrates political economic and ecological frames with cultural and epistemological perspectives, by analyzing the impact of certain production and consumption practices not only on the physical environment but also on the knowledges and ways of knowing of the world's peoples. It builds on the critical analyses of development and globalization introduced earlier as well as social ecofeminist analyses of philosophies of Western science (which separate humans from the rest of nature and promote notions of progress and development that both fragment and homogenize cultures).

Shiva suggests that the *fragmentation and uniformity* promoted by the current global economic system "destroy(s) the living forces which arise from relationships within the 'web of life' and the diversity in the elements and patterns of these relationships."[17] She further contends that "uniformity and diversity are not just patterns of land use, they are ways of thinking and ways of living."[18] She calls this global mental homogenization "monocultures of the mind."

Both the monocultural production predominant in the agricultural production of the corporate tomato, as well as the homogenized production of highly processed Big Macs by McDonald's at the other end of the chain, threaten the Earth's biodiversity by destroying ecosystems and limiting the variety of plants grown. But this decrease in biodiversity is accompanied by a parallel loss of cultural diversity, as people who maintained biodiversity for millennia lose their knowledge and relationship to disappearing ecosystems. This study examines how women workers are experiencing this loss of diversity and knowledge in their jobs and, specifically, in relationship to the tomato.

The two secondary axes explored here help ground the principal axes: the intimate relationship between work and technology, and the dynamic relationship between health and environment. Again these tensions are like tangled roots, inseparable one from the other.

Work/Technology

The dramatic restructuring of work is central to globalization, and women workers in the tomato chain exemplify this in many ways. A combination of Fordist and post-Fordist practices[19] demand a new corporate *flexibility of labor* responding to just-in-time production, facilitated by the ever greater mobility of capital and the decentralization of production. Women workers in agribusinesses as well as in retail food businesses are seen as particularly compliant to the demands for flexibility,[20] and their numbers have increased, even as their work has intensified and their real wages have dropped, particularly through the proliferation of part-time work.

Changes in the nature of work in the food system have been largely shaped by the introduction of new technologies. In the agribusiness context, the dependency on the whole "technological package" (biotech seeds, pesticides, machinery, and production practices), usually dictated by foreign multinational interests, is deepening. The technologization of women's work in the food system is epitomized by the computerized sorting of tomatoes in Mexican greenhouses and the electronic scanning at Canadian supermarket checkout lanes, stories that are featured in these pages.

Health/Environment

This study advocates a broader definition of the environment, one that includes the land on which the tomato is grown in the south as well as the computers that record its sales in the north. In all cases, the natural world is mediated by technology as an extension of human intervention. So, we explore the health impacts of both chemical-dependent agriculture on Mexican women picking tomatoes as well as the speeded-up electronic scanning system on Canadian cashiers who weigh and punch in tomatoes in supermarkets. Both are examples of the human effects of current practices of the production and commercialization of food, and suggest the need for a broader definition of *holistic health*. In assessing the global food system, we then consider its impact on the health of the workers who produce food, the consumers who eat it, and all the elements of nature engaged in its production, distribution, and consumption.

The overall and long-term impact of the globalized food system on the physical environment is also considered in the case studies, as women workers offer their own perspectives on *ecological health*. Mexican campesino women, for example, reflect in their life stories the long-term impact of fertilizer use and fertilizer debt, which has forced thousands of poor Indigenous people to migrate from now barren land to seek employment in large agribusinesses. In the Canadian supermarket context, on the other hand, we explore not only the environmental impact of northern consumerism but also corporate responses to demands for more environmentally friendly products, packaging, and practices, as well as consumers' concerns about the safety of genetically modified food.

An Interlocking Analysis of Gender

Why focus on women workers? Women are at the center of the food system, both as producers and as consumers;[21] the only links in the tomato chain dominated by men, besides management, are shipping, transportation, and distribution (chapter 5).

In most cultural contexts, women take major responsibility for the provisioning and preparation of family meals and, in rural societies, growing food for subsistence and gathering fuel for cooking. It is a primarily female labor force in agribusinesses that plants, picks, and packs fresh produce such as tomatoes; again, at the consumption end of the food chain, women also predominate in the handling, sales, bagging of tomatoes in supermarkets, as well as the preparation and serving of meals in restaurants. This focus on women does not mean to obscure the many men who also work as low-paid salaried workers in the food system—for example, picking tomatoes alongside women field-workers in Mexico, or stocking the produce that Canadian cashiers scan. This study recognizes many kinds of oppressions and their complex interconnections.

Even if it is mainly women's hands who move the tomato from field to table, the case studies reveal great diversity among those women. An interlocking analysis of power[22] acknowledges that gender is differently constructed depending on many other contextual factors. The diagram on the following page identifies some of the other dimensions of power[23] that interact with gender to significantly shape the experience of women workers in the NAFTA food system.

CLASS

There are clearly different socioeconomic statuses among women in the food system, even among the lower waged workers in each sector that we are studying here. Each company constructs its own hierarchy of workers, sometimes though not always related to educational level but usually defined by skill levels, disparate wage levels, and working conditions. Some women entering the workforce gain economic status (Mexican packers), while many whose jobs are being downgraded and deskilled actually lose status (Canadian supermarket cashiers).

RACE/ETHNICITY

Also interacting with class and gender are race and ethnicity, shifting in meaning from one place and time to another. Ethnic differences are perhaps most pronounced in the Mexican context, between the Indigenous workers that the agribusiness brings by truck to pick tomatoes under the hot sun and the more skilled and privileged mestizo[24] women they bring in buses to pack tomatoes in

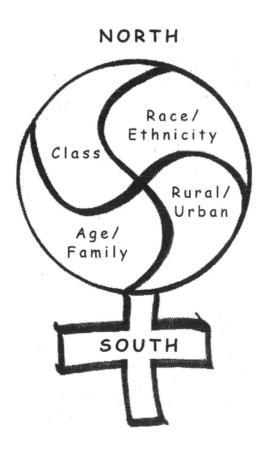

the more protected packing plant. In the Canadian retail and service sectors, race is constructed differently, particularly related to a wide range of immigrant workers and occupational hierarchies within the companies.

AGE AND FAMILY STATUS

The interrelated factors of age, marital status, and generational family roles are clearly significant in the Mexican agricultural context,[25] where the workforce is predominantly young and female. The family becomes critical, too, as family members combine wages to survive a deepening economic crisis. In the Canadian cases, supermarket cashiers are primarily either younger students or older mothers. Age is a defining yet shifting dimension of fast-food work, too, as more older women are finding it a last resort in a shrinking job market and replacing the predominantly young labor force.

RURAL/URBAN

In the context of food and agriculture, the rural-urban dynamic is central. Development strategies in both Mexico and Canada have favored urban dwellers but still depend on rural workers to feed populations of the burgeoning cities. In the stories of women workers shared here, we hear from rural women engaged in production activities in Mexico and urban women engaged in commercial and consumption activities in Canada. Mexican campesinos are migrating to both rural and urban areas in Mexico, and the survival of most families depends on the migration of some family member(s) to the United States or Canada.

SOUTH/NORTH

A key contradiction in the tomato story is that the corporate tomato comes north, while McDonald's hamburgers go south; in Canada and the United States, we depend on southern production for our food, while northern practices of production and consumption are exported to increasingly transform southern economies and cultures. The tomato's journey is built not only on inequities among standards and conditions in the three NAFTA countries but also on regional differences. This is especially true in the Mexican context, where dramatic north-south disparities exist within the country; the poorer southern states, for example, have been historically marginalized, while northern states have been favored for large agribusiness development. Such regional disparities are also defining this struggle in the Canadian context.[26]

ﾛｇﾘﾛﾛ

It is almost impossible to describe these dimensions of power in isolation. The tangled roots metaphor again helps us conceptualize their interrelationship. The experience of Soledad, a fifteen-year-old Mexican greenhouse packer, for example, contrasts sharply with that of Carol, a student cashier at a Canadian supermarket. They are both inexperienced workers with the lowest wages and least demanding jobs in their respective ends of the food chain. Yet while Soledad's earnings feed a family wage, to complement dollars sent by her parents working in the States, Carol uses her part-time salary (more than double Soledad's) to pay tuition for law school. The complex intersections of class, ethnicity, and age as well as region and rural-urban migration, conspire differently in each context to shape these two women both materially and socially. The stories that follow reveal the complex interaction between these categories of identity and thus enrich our understanding of gender and women's experience as plural, diverse, and constantly changing.

Feminist Theoretical Frames: Toward an Ecology of Women and Tomatoes

This study is by definition a feminist and an ecological project. First, it is a feminist act to make visible the women workers in the food system, redressing their invisibility in other studies as well as in the public consciousness. Beyond filling in the gaps left by male-dominated perspectives, this study benefits from the rich development of diverse feminist theories over the past decade. In introducing the frames and filters that resonate most with my own analysis and approach, I am drawing from a wide array of fields, ranging from political economic labor studies to feminist ecological economics, from socialist feminism to feminist environmentalism, from gender and sustainable development to social ecofeminism. My own positions have also been shaped by three decades of research and activism in the United States and Canada, as well as Peru, Nicaragua, and Mexico. They are still evolving as I am daily challenged both by colleagues as well as by new and different realities.

In the 1980s, streams of Western feminism were often categorized as liberal, radical, Marxist, or socialist.[27] The concerns of *socialist feminists* with the sexual division of labor and labor relations are particularly relevant to this study, as well as the perspective offered by Dorothy Smith and others on women's knowledge grounded in subsistence work as valuable for the transformation of patriarchal and capitalist relations.[28]

Political economic studies of gender and restructuring expose the neoliberal economic agenda as neither apolitical nor gender, race, or class neutral.[29] Critical feminist political economists such as Isabella Bakker, Marjorie Cohen Griffin, and Leah Vosko argue that analyses of globalization should be locally contextualized rather than based on universal abstracts. They ground their analyses in research on the feminization of labor, the reorganization of work, the impacts of trade, structural adjustment, a growing contingent labor force, and declining social welfare. Comparative analyses of wage structures in the north and the south suggest that agroexport countries such as Mexico are family wage economies while consumer wage economies such as Canada are still built on individual wage structures.

Labor studies feminists also challenge orthodox structural analyses, arguing that women are not mere victims but also potential agents for change. Feminists like Ester Reiter and Jan Kainer studying labor relations not only examine the push for equity issues in collective bargaining but also the failure of some unions to address the gendered aspects of restructuring.[30]

Feminists sociologists and economists[31] such as Swasti Mitter examine the phenomenon of the growing number of women employed by the new global economy, particularly within export processing zones (EPZs). Kathy Kopinak's work focuses on the Mexican *maquiladoras,* which depend on young female labor (cheap and often dispensable).[32] Maquilization as a gendered process is reflected in the Mexican case study in this book, but it is unfolding in the north as well, part and parcel of trade liberalization.

In critiquing neoclassical economics, *feminist economists* examine why women's domestic labor remains undervalued and unpaid and is not calculated in the gross national product. A relatively new network of *feminist ecological economists* such as Ellie Perkins adds the environmental costs of globalizing production practices to the balance sheet.[33] Both women's unpaid labor and the environment are part of the uncounted economy in the tomato story.

Women of color theorists within North America as well as *postcolonial scholars and activists* from countries of the south have critiqued second-wave feminism (shaped by events in the United States and Europe in the 1960s) for its exclusive focus on gender in isolation from other factors. Black feminist Patricia Collins emphasizes the interlocking nature of race, class, and gender oppression, and the historical specificity of their interconnections.[34] Chandra Mohanty charges that Western women have constructed the category of "Third World women" as a homogeneous and victimized group, negating the rich diversity of cultures, traditions, and practices outside of the West. Latin American feminists have contributed substantially to my analysis of campesina and Indigenous women workers.[35] In particular, the work of *Mexican feminist economists* Kirsten Appendini, Antonieta Barrón, and Sara Lara takes into account differences not only of gender but also race, age, and family status in interaction with different types of agricultural production.

Southern feminists have also challenged the ways of knowing and theories of knowledge (epistemologies) of Western feminisms. The very experience of oppression offers a unique perspective, a view from the margins that could be valuable in constructing alternatives to patriarchal society. Uma Narayan suggests that members of any oppressed group possess an "epistemic privilege"; a man cannot fully understand women's experience of sexism, nor can I as a white woman know what it means to experience racism.[36] The women who speak within these pages bring a perspective that could surely never be offered by their employers, nor by us academics studying them. I guard against the romanticization of women workers' knowledge, however, and the danger of merely reversing established hierarchies. Oppression is complex and multidimensional and can also be internalized as well as projected outward.

I find feminist scientist Donna Haraway's notion of "situated knowledges" a useful theoretical tool for dealing with this dilemma. She sees all knowledge as situated, embodied, embedded in the power relations of particular places, and therefore always partial.[37] Like anyone else, women tomato workers can offer unique and important but also contradictory and reactionary viewpoints. *Postmodern feminist analyses* offer important cautions for this undertaking, insisting on historically contingent analysis. Like Carolyn Sachs, I find this perspective useful as long as "the emphasis on difference and diversity is not devoid of analysis of power and oppression or political agendas," and I agree that the best way to counter that danger is to do "grounded and political analyses of difference."[38] I hope this study offers such grounded exploration.

Feminist critiques of science also feed this epistemological debate. In challenging the underlying assumptions of Western science, they question the whole package of modernity, including notions of progress and scientific rationality, deconstructing the nature/culture and mind/body splits. The environmental crisis perhaps best reveals the limits of the so-called objective perspective of modernism (chapter 1).

Ecological and feminist critiques of Western progress have converged within more critical strands of the field of Women in Development (WID). While early WID studies conceptualized the "feminization of poverty,"[39] critics of WID argued that the development model itself deepened that process. In the late 1980s, Gender and Development (GAD) emerged to reframe the goals of development as transforming unequal gender relations and not merely increasing women's participation in development projects. Antidevelopment or transformational advocates focus on the destructive impacts of Western development on women, the environment, and Third World peoples in general.

GAD proponents have contributed to the carving out of alternative notions of development through new networks such as Women, Environment, and Sustainable Development (WED). Largely shaped by the many international conferences organized by the UN, development agencies, and nongovernmental organizations (NGOs)—from the NGO Women's Forum in Nairobi in 1985 and in Beijing in 1995 to the flurry of global gatherings leading up to and surrounding the UN Conference on Environment and Development (UNCED) meetings at the Rio Summit on the Environment in 1992—these forums have provided spaces for debates about the deeper causes of the environmental crisis and have promoted women's activism in development projects aimed at protecting the environment.

A more cultural stream in this debate portrays women as "naturally" privileged environmental managers because their work within the sexual division of labor brings them closer to nature. Indian scientist and activist Vandana Shiva is often associated with this perspective in her attacks on the "dominant mode of development as Western, patriarchal, and based on a reductionist model of science and technology that serves the global market, but is destructive for women, nature, and all 'others.'"[40] She proposes the recovery of subsistence agriculture as a solution, around the Hindu "feminine principle" as the life-giving force.[41] Indian activist Bina Agarwal argues that poor women are important actors in environmental movements, not because of a special relationship with nature but because they have been marginalized by the economic system. Calling her perspective *feminist environmentalism,* Agarwal takes a more materialist rather than cultural approach: "the link between women and the environment can be seen as structured by a given gender and class (caste/race) organization of production, reproduction, and distribution."[42]

The rural sociologist Carolyn Sachs examines how global economic restructuring is changing rural women's connections to the natural world. Like Shiva, she agrees that through globalization women are losing their knowledge of local environments, which could offer insight into constructing a more harmonious and reciprocal relationship between humans and nature. But like Agarwal, she tries to understand men's and women's relations with the environment as rooted in their concrete, material realities.[43] Along Tomasita's trail, Mexican campesino women have been thrust into salaried work in industrial export-oriented agriculture, while many still maintain traditional practices of subsistence agriculture. I draw on both perspectives.

Conceptions of women and nature are perhaps most vociferously being debated within the field of *ecofeminism.* Initially an outgrowth of environmental and women's movements in North America and Europe, the field has increasingly been challenged as well as shaped by southern feminists like Shiva and Agarwal. While there are many positions within ecofeminism, what they share is an assumption that there is a critical connection between the domination of nature and the domination of women. Many root their critique of patriarchal frameworks in Western science and the socioeconomic systems that perpetuate dualisms and hierarchies, oppression of particular peoples, as well as exploitation of natural resources.

The contrasting positions within ecofeminism are sometimes distinguished as cultural ecofeminism and social ecofeminism, roughly corresponding to a key debate between essentialist and constructivist explanations of the women–nature relationship.[44] Cultural ecofeminists critique patriarchal power structures for oppressing both women and nature; they suggest that women's ways of knowing that are more relational can help develop a more caring and sustainable society. Those who claim that women's connection with nature is innate or biologically determined have been charged as essentialist;[45] they are critiqued, particularly, for not taking into account differences of race, class, and culture.

I identify more with *social ecofeminism,* which draws from the socialist feminist position, arguing that both gender and nature are socially constructed. Socialist ecofeminists believe that violences against both women and nature are linked to capitalism as well as patriarchy.[46] In contrast with the cultural ecofeminist emphasis on spirituality[47] and women-centered community (which sometimes reproduces dualisms and reverses hierarchies), they merge the critical and transformative potential of ecology and feminism, advocating radical change that moves beyond dualisms and hierarchies. A transformative ecofeminism, based on an understanding of the interwoven nature of oppression, also uses ecology as a model for understanding connections and diversity. I agree with

Catriona Sandilands that "what is necessary is a more thoroughly transgressive politics, one that shows the wielding of women and nature as part of systems of domination that show dualism to be an oppressive fiction rather than a fact of nature itself."[48]

At the same time, the investigation of the tomato story has made me question not only the commodification but also the objectification of nature. While cautious about falling into an anthropomorphic stance, I am very sympathetic to Indigenous as well as deep ecologist beliefs that all living entities (including tomatoes) are imbued with spirit, challenging a purely materialist analysis. Nonetheless, I recognize that my understanding of the other-than-human will always be socially constructed, viewed through a human lens.

This brief theoretical review cannot do justice to the wide range and rich diversity of feminist thought and practice being crafted all over the planet and with varying visions of that planet. The complexity of the work and home lives of the women workers in the tomato food chain can only be understood, I believe, by considering particular social constructions of their relationship with nature and, in Haraway's terms, their situated knowledges. These are inevitably contradictory given that the women workers featured here are immersed in diverse contexts where competing notions of development and globalization are at play.

Cross-border research demands a diversity of approaches and can help shape new configurations. This project is by definition multidisciplinary; I have sought more multilayered and holistic ways of exploring our relationship to food. Ellen O'Loughlin contends that "ecology" as a concept, in fact, suggests the interconnection between all elements—human and nonhuman—of an ecosystem and "helps explain the various oppressions women face as a network, as a web."[49] The analysis that unfolds within these pages attempts to weave, liked tangled roots and routes, an ecology of women and tomatoes that respects local contexts while acknowledging broader social and historical processes in constant interaction with them.

Methodological Lenses: From Popular Education to Border-Crossing Research

I was drawn to the device of the tomato's journey and women's stories because of their popular education potential, and many users of the first edition have used this book to generate their own popular education processes. Popular education (also called *transformative*, *liberatory*, or *anti-oppression education*) aims to unveil, analyze, and transform power relations, based on class, race/ethnicity, gender, sexuality, age, religion, or any social dimension of oppression. It promotes democratic practice through teaching/learning processes that are collective, critical, systematic, participatory, and creative. Motivated by principles of equality and justice, it integrates research, learning, and organizing for social change.[50]

Practices and theories of popular education developed greatest force and conceptual sophistication in Latin America, beginning in the 1960s, as an integral part of burgeoning social movements challenging poverty, U.S. hegemony, and military dictatorships. Powerfully articulated and massively diffused by Brazilian educator Paulo Freire's classic *Pedagogy of the Oppressed*, "educación popular" inspired practices worldwide, with networks forming across the hemisphere to further develop methodologies appropriate to diverse contexts. While there are precedents in North America,[51] many U.S. and Canadian educators and activists involved in Central American solidarity efforts in the 1970s and 1980s were influenced by this reframing of education as "praxis," and North American adaptations of popular education now abound.[52]

The study of the tomato's journey builds on this tradition, as it probes the contradictory historical origins of our food and gathers the stories of the most marginalized women workers in the food chain. Over recent decades, various streams of popular education have emerged, usually within social movements addressing specific inequities, among them labor education (addressing class), feminist pedagogy (confronting sexism and gender relations), antiracism education (challenging racism), development/global education (concerned with north-south inequities), and environmental education (critiquing human domination of nature). Each of these streams raises questions relevant to this study and can adapt this story as a catalyst for education and action.

Five "creative tensions" of popular education frame this project: personal/social-political, nature/culture, critical/creative, local/global, and reflection/action.[53] I'm suggesting that these classic dualisms—embedded in traditional education as well as western culture itself—can be challenged, transformed, and engaged as dialectical tensions in this study.

1. *Personal/social-political:* Popular education starts with people's daily experiences and promotes a deeper structural analysis that helps us understand the historical and social origins of their personal attitudes and actions. By starting with the work and home lives of women workers, this study hopes to bring a human face to the broader social process of globalization.
2. *Nature/culture:* The tangled roots of the tomato story lead us to question how the nature/culture dualism was constructed to begin with, and how this split is reproduced in our thinking as well as in global food systems; the women workers' connections to the tomato provide a starting point for this exploration.
3. *Critical/creative:* Popular education encourages both a critical analysis of unequal power relations, as well as the creative transformation of them. Woven into the stories of women workers in the corporate tomato chain are many tales of resistance, individual as well as collective responses.
4. *Local/global:* In analyzing the global food system, we come to understand how broader structures impact on local practices. Popular education engages the local-global tension not as a dichotomy but as a complex and dynamic relationship. This project attempts to craft a new concept of education that integrates the local and the global.[54]

5. *Reflection/action:* Central to popular education is the dialectic between analysis and action, what Freire calls "praxis." It is hoped that the stories and analyses within these pages will inspire action.

The use of the tomato as a "code" draws specifically on a popular education method and tool that Paulo Freire developed in Brazil in the 1960s.[55] Codes represent "generative themes" that can engage learners in a "problem-posing approach" to education, moving from practice to theory and back to practice. While starting with personal stories, a critical decoding of the world in the tomato can lead us to deeper social analyses.[56] Decoding[57] is at the heart of "conscientization,"[58] what Freire articulated as critical (and collective) reflection on the world in order to change it, a process that links the personal and the political.

As a code for a dominant generative theme of our era, globalization, the story of the tomato represents key contradictions reflected in opposing visions of the earth and of the development of human society in relationship to it, framed in this book as globalization from above and globalization from below. The tomato becomes a mirror (or prism) of the state of the world and our location within it.

The notion of following one commodity through its life cycle, and specifically the device of tracing food from south to north, has captured the imaginations of other researchers and educators before Tomasita. As described in chapter 1, there is an emerging field of "commodity chain analysis"[59] being developed by political economists and social scientists. Social justice activists within the field of development education or global education have also used the device very creatively—for example, excavating the social roots of chocolate in African cocoa bean production, calculating the economic and environmental costs of export-oriented banana production in Central America, and (more hopefully) proposing alternative routes in producing fair trade coffee.[60] This project thus builds on a rich tradition of popular education around globalization focusing on food.

Border-Crossing Research

Not only tomatoes and Mexican migrant workers cross borders in the Tomasita Project. The research itself has involved border crossings of several kinds: geopolitical, disciplinary, occupational, and methodological.

CROSSING GEOPOLITICAL BORDERS

The NAFTA context has compelled us to consider the shifting relationships among Mexico, the United States, and Canada, and the tomato story probes the changing meaning of these geopolitical borders. NAFTA has accelerated the building of links not only between businesses in the three countries but also between universities; Mexican, U.S., and Canadian feminist academics and popular educators in this project have crafted research across languages, cultures, and intellectual traditions.

CROSSING DISCIPLINARY BORDERS

The questions asked in this research (even such a simple one as "Where does the tomato come from?") require multidisciplinary probes. Three fields, each somewhat interdisciplinary in themselves, inform this research: political economic analysis of the food system, feminist theories (especially social ecofeminism), and cultural studies of consumption. The latter two, in particular, question the dualism, fragmentation, and positivism that have characterized not only the natural sciences but also social sciences.

The construction of disciplines in Western academia reflects such fragmentation, and we have worked across disciplines to challenge some of the boundaries between them. There are no easy recipes for interdisciplinary work, and this project has left me more humble about its possibilities. I felt its strength at the more collaborative stages of the process, particularly in editing a collective anthology[61] around issues of women, food, and globalization, with diverse contributions from fourteen women from three countries who were involved in the project. When pulling the tomato study together in this book, however, I found myself disciplinarily challenged on a regular basis and came to appreciate the value of expertise in specific fields. Despite the limitations, tracing the tomato's trail has been a rich affirmation of multidisciplinary work.

The official academic research team included economists, sociologists, and a lawyer, each bringing different methodological approaches to the women's stories. Not only did they transform the project, but some had their work transformed by it as well. After our first team meeting in Toronto in 1996, for example, we visited Mexican migrant workers who had come to Ontario on the FARMS program; unaware of this unique stream of continental labor migration, Mexican economist Antonieta Barrón decided to initiate survey research on them, proclaiming, "Enough of northern researchers coming south, I'm coming north!" Securing financial support from the Canadian embassy in Mexico, she spent two summers in Ontario, interviewing workers on fruit and vegetable farms, vineyards, and nurseries. Exemplifying interdisciplinary exchange, working with Antonieta also taught me to appreciate the quantitative research behind the economic statistics that I draw upon in my more qualitative studies, and she, on the other hand, became inspired by my use of photographs.

CROSSING OCCUPATIONAL BORDERS

The project also deliberately combined the interests and skills of both academics and activists, teachers and students, researchers and popular educators.

My closest collaborators were graduate students of the Faculty of Environmental Studies at York, employed as research assistants. In joining this adventure of "chasing the tomato," their involvement was a kind of action learning in the field. Each brought her own unique cultural experiences and class perspectives, critical analysis, and theoretical sophistication to the research questions. The student researchers also joined me in defining the parameters, working out ethical guidelines, interviewing managers and workers, weaving analytical threads, and making hard editing decisions. Some were able to design parts of the project to fit their own strengths and interests and produced theses and projects, journal articles and books, photos and videos, building on the work. As I learned with and from the student researchers, they also became my teachers. While sometimes constrained and challenged by our differential privileges and power, together we crafted new forms of teacher–student relationships.

The boundaries separating research, education, and action were regularly blurred through collaboration with the local food organization FoodShare as well as the Mexican Institute for Community Development (IMDEC). The outcomes of rich community–university interchange with FoodShare have been multiple: popular education workshops, a video, *The Global Food Puzzle,* an exhibit of storyboards by immigrant women in our annual Eco Art and Media Festival. IMDEC, for more than thirty years a key popular education training center in Mexico, has nourished the project in multiple ways. While participating in one of its Popular Communications Workshops in 1996, we adapted its strategic planning tool to plot the path of the project. In exchange, I taught photography in its training program. IMDEC staff joined us in interviewing campesinos and rural activists alike and helped translate research into popular education materials.

CROSSING METHODOLOGICAL BORDERS

Embedded in disciplines and educational approaches, in different cultural practices and geopolitical contexts are diverse kinds of knowledges and ways of knowing. Both my own voice and the voices of women in these pages reflect "situated knowledges." I take the position of feminist research that recognizes that power is always operating in these diverse contexts, and that we must continuously struggle with our own complicity with power and our choices about how we use it. Audre Lorde speaks about the "strategic use of privilege," suggesting that we not deny but rather use well whatever power we do have. Similarly, Maria Mies, with her concept of "conscious partiality," challenges the myth of impartial research. I had to come to terms with my own positions, in terms of both my social identity as a North American white middle-class professor/activist as well as my political perspectives on food, women, and globalization. I constantly wrestled with the differences in culture and in power, particularly during the Mexican fieldwork, when I composed the poem on page 85.

The construction of knowledge is always a political process, and the choice of methods for probing the knowledges of others is also political. Methods are chosen for their appropriateness both to the research themes and to the particular contexts and subjects. This project combined an eclectic array of research methods, which fall under three categories: qualitative approaches, corporate research, and visual methods.

Qualitative Approaches

In featuring the stories of women on the front line of the global food system, our research drew on "methods from the margins."[62] While collaborative in many ways, the research did not involve the women workers as agents in the process to the extent advocated by Sandra Kirby and Kate McKenna, Maria Mies, or Patricia Maguire.[63] There were real limits to the participation of Indigenous migrant women workers, for example, who did not even speak Spanish. Given the scope of the project, across sectors and borders, we applied classic qualitative methods such as participant observation research (visiting tomato fields, supermarkets, and restaurants), interviews with workers in each context, and life history interviews with a select few.

We did try to apply principles of feminist research[64] in taking a stance with and for women workers, unearthing and valuing their knowledges, and collectivizing their stories where possible. We gathered a group of women field-workers, for example, around one woman's table in rural Mexico, using photographs of them at work as catalysts for deeper, collective discussion. Similarly, a greenhouse worker invited coworkers to her home one evening for a group interview. In Canada, supermarket cashiers joined us for dinner at my house or in their lunchroom at work.

While many interviews were individual, these group experiences were by far the richest. They also offered the women workers an opportunity to share their stories with each other. In three cases, I developed longer term relationships with the women, visiting them many times during subsequent visits, whether to Mexican tomato fields or Canadian supermarkets. Where possible, I have returned photographs and draft chapters to women whose life experiences humanize this study. Returning to Mexico twice to check the manuscript, I involved greenhouse workers in editing their own pieces in the book and in choosing their own pseudonyms. The use of pseudonyms is a precautionary measure, so as not to jeopardize their jobs. In Canada, the featured cashier reviewed all drafts carefully and offered critical response to my analyses. The Mexican farmworker in Canada also reviewed, word for word, the draft of her story featured in chapter 5.

Corporate Research

The project also involved conventional research methods such as library and Internet searches. Corporate research is growing just as corporate control is becoming more entrenched.[65] Student researchers helped me access material from trade journals, CD-ROMs, and company Web sites. This was more difficult in Mexico, because corporations are not publicly traded, so we had to dig to uncover useful data. In the U.S. and Canadian contexts, however, company annual reports as well as the business pages of national newspapers offered considerable information.

Photographer/Researcher as Shadow

The early morning sun pours over the fields
in rural Jalisco in western Mexico
as I approach with my camera in hand,
my shadow meeting the shadow
of a woman tomato worker.

Northern researcher/photographer
coming South
just like the agribusinesses,
the managers and technologies,
the hybrid seeds and pesticides.

I come to take stories and images,
to find out where the food we eat comes from,
and what happens to it along the journey
from Mexican field to Canadian table.

How is my taking any different
from that of the companies
who import most of the inputs
and export most of the produce,
taking advantage of the available land,
cheap labor, and ever-present sun . . . ?

Photographic Methods: Visualizing Globalization

For the past thirty years, my camera has been an extension of my eye and arm, in research, education, and advocacy work. In the 1970s, I helped pioneer a new field of visual sociology, integrating photographs into my doctoral research in Peru on Freire's use of codes in literacy classes with Indigenous migrant women.[66] It was only natural to use photographs in this project, to "make visible" both the long, often "hidden" journey of the tomato as well as the "invisible work" and home lives of women along the tomato trail. As popular education tools, photographs help demystify the global food system.

We have used photographs in various ways: to record and document, to generate discussion with workers, to bring alive people's daily lives through photo-stories, to witness both corporate practices as well as acts of resistance, to illustrate both theories and actions, to invite the reader to make his or her own connections and interpretations.[67] Photographs can convey ideas and feelings that help us understand abstract concepts; the tangled roots photos opening each chapter offer a visual metaphor for an interlocking analysis of gender with race, class, and age, for example.

I've identified two distinct uses of photographic images in this project,[68] which roughly correspond to the globalization-from-above and globalization-from-below frame. One is the subverting of corporate images and the other is social documentary of workers' lives. Both uses assume that photography is a political act; what, where, when, and how we photograph reveal how power operates.

Subverting Corporate Images

When I tried to photograph inside a Mexican Burger King, for example, I was stopped because of "the recipe." I don't think the management believed I would slip a photo of the Whopper to McDonald's and abet the hamburger hegemony of the Big Mac, but rather they were more concerned about a potentially critical lens examining working conditions. Similarly, it took me a year to get permission to photograph inside a Loblaws supermarket, as official policy prohibited cameras, again suggesting the threat of "industrial espionage."

The control that corporations have over our visual environment was perhaps brought home most poignantly by my experience with McDonald's, when I asked permission to use a photograph of one of their restaurants on the cover of the new edition of this book. First of all, the company headquarters Web site, while offering tons of information, provides no way that anyone can contact them (e-mail, phone, fax) for two-way communications. So I had to go through the Canadian headquarters, which forwarded my request to the Chicago head office. One of the corporate communications staff asked for a copy of the proposed cover and detailed explanation of the portrayal of McDonald's. I sent the publisher's description and the cover, which juxtaposed a young Mexican tomato picker with a McDonald's on Broadway in New York, representing both the origin and the destination of the tomato in my story. When they turned town

my request, they could not offer me a cogent rationale. Most troubling, however, was the extensive proviso at the bottom of the e-mails, threatening legal action if any word of the communication were circulated. In a country that purports to honor free speech, the censoring of such an innocuous image as the outside of a restaurant, which reminds us of itself daily on billboards and in commercials and ads, appears to be either a purely defensive or a tremendously arrogant act of power. This is a contradiction that must be named and challenged.

When I realized I couldn't overcome the contradiction, I began to think about how to engage it, to work within its cracks. If I couldn't get "inside" the actual workplaces, I could at least make critical and creative use of corporate images mounted "outside" in so-called public space, or imprinted on place mats and food boxes. I borrowed from a countercultural practice called "adbusting"[69] that transforms advertisements into "subvertisements" by changing either visual elements or words, forcing the viewer to rethink both the message and its construction. When we take apart and reconstruct these representations, we can probe their ideological assumptions as well as the political economic arrangements on which they are built. The ad on page 87, which appears in chapter 4, was deconstructed and then reconstructed to make visible the workers who make the food that "means the world to us."

Social Documentary and Photo-Stories

The dominant use of photographs in this book draws on the tradition of documentary photography, exposing social conditions that are not often visible or in the public consciousness. While documentary practice has been dwarfed by expansion of corporate images in our "mediascapes" and its illusion of "objectivity" challenged, it remains a tool for social scientific exploration. It can, in fact,

remind us of the objective/subjective tension in image making, that our photographs say as much about us as they do about our subjects. I do not hide my own conscious use of photographs to promote a more critical perspective on globalization, to generate debate and action.

For years, I have produced photo-stories, integrating photographs with women's oral histories. I adapt this form here, particularly to three longer profiles: one of Marissa, the supermarket cashier (chapter 4); another of Irena, the Mexican migrant worker in Ontario (chapter 5); and a third of Tomasa, a Mexican field-worker (chapter 6). These stories have also become tools for communicating across borders. Marissa eagerly digested Tomasa's story, comparing her experiences in Canada with workers in Mexico. When I took her to visit Irena on an Ontario farm, Irena used photos to tell Marissa about her life in Mexico.

I always try to return photographs to people, as one small gesture of thanks for their participation in the research process. Redressing what is often an unequal exchange, this also affirms the histories and daily lives of these women, allowing them to see themselves in a new light. In one case, when I was not permitted to photograph inside a Mexican greenhouse, a woman worker offered to take pictures of her daily work activities (chapter 6). Putting cameras in people's hands offers another way to share their knowledge and to challenge photographic power relations.[70]

The photographs that bring these pages alive have been enlarged and mounted in exhibits to stimulate public discussion about the issues. I joined Toronto photographer Vince Pietro Paolo for a 1997 exhibit, "Who Grows Our Food," at the Art Gallery of Ontario. In June 2000, I displayed a visual synthesis of this book at a global education teach-in around the OAS meetings in Windsor, Ontario,[71] and later at a Food Forum in Toronto, the World Women's March in Ottawa, and the People's Summit in Quebec City. Such portable exhibits can travel to conferences and workshops to generate debate and inspire action. The photographs help transform the research into processes of popular education and mobilization.

Notes

1. As a graduate research assistant on the Tomasita Project, Lauren accompanied me twice to Mexico; she is now completing her PhD in environmental studies.

2. Jeremy Brecher, John Brown Childs, and Jill Cutler, *Global Visions: Beyond the New World Order* (Montreal: Black Rose, 1993), 39.

3. Maria Mies and Vandana Shiva, *Ecofeminism* (Atlantic Highlands, N.J.: Zed, 1993), 9.

4. Edward Said, *Culture and Imperialism* (New York: Vintage Books, 1993), 5–6.

5. Vandana Shiva, "The Greening of the Global Reach," in *Global Visions*, 54.

6. Shiva, "The Greening," 59.

7. Randall White, *Global Spin: Probing the Globalization Debate, Where in the World Are We Going?* (Toronto: Dundurn, 1995).

8. Philip McMichael, *Development and Social Change: A Global Perspective* (Thousand Oaks, Calif.: Pine Forge, 2000), 121.

9. The Group of Seven (G-7) includes the most dominant Western economies—the United States, Canada, Great Britain, France, Germany, and Italy—as well as Japan.

10. Xabier Gorostiaga, "Latin America in the New World Order," in *Global Visions*, 68.

11. Cuahtémoc Cárdenas, "Moving Peoples and Nations," in *Global Visions*, 274.

12. Philip McMichael, "Global Food Politics," cited in Fred Magdoff, Frederick H. Buttel, and John Bellamy Foster, "Hungry for Profit: Agriculture, Food, and Ecology," *Monthly Review* 50, no. 3 (July/August 1998): 109.

13. Magdoff, Buttel, and Foster, "Hungry for Profit," 11.

14. Gabriel Torres, *The Force of Irony: Power in the Everyday Life of Mexican Tomato Workers* (New York: Berg, 1997).

15. Anthony Giddens, *Central Problems in Social Theory* (London: Macmillan, 1979), 148–49, quoted in Torres, *The Force of Irony*, 12.

16. Brewster Kneen, *From Land to Mouth: Understanding the Food System, Second Helping* (Toronto: NC Press, 1993), 39.

17. Vandana Shiva, "Development, Ecology, and Women," in *Ecology: Key Concepts in Critical Theory*, ed. Carolyn Merchant (Atlantic Highlands, N.J.: Humanities, 1994), 274.

18. Vandana Shiva, *Monocultures of the Mind: Perspectives on Biodiversity and Biotechnology* (Atlantic Highlands, N.J.: Zed, 1993), 6.

19. Fordism, epitomized by the automobile industry, involves mass production of homogeneous products, inflexible technologies, standardized work routines, and increases in productivity coming from economies of scale, deskilling, and intensification of labor. Post-Fordism, emerging since the 1980s, focuses on customized and specialized products, smaller and more productive systems, more flexible technologies, and flexible forms of management and labor through multitasking and part-time work. George Ritzer, *The McDonaldization of Society* (Thousand Oaks, Calif.: Pine Forge, 1996), 150–52.

20. This perception of women's compliance is critically deconstructed as we move into the case studies of women workers in different sectors and in the comparative analysis across sectors.

21. Irene Dankelman and Joan Davidson, *Women and Environment in the Third World: Alliance for the Future* (London: Earthscan, 1988).

22. Egla Martinez-Salazar, "Development, Coercion, and Indigenous Peoples: The Case of Santiago Atitlan, Guatemala," unpublished major paper for the master's degree in the Faculty of Environmental Studies, York University, Toronto, Canada, August 1999, 20. Rejecting class-only, race/ethnicity-only, and gender-only analyses, Martinez-Salazar draws on other critical feminist and postcolonial scholars who have insisted on complicating our analyses, not just theoretically but in demonstrating this complexity in specific contexts. See also Jacqui M. Alexander and Chandra T. Mohanty, *Feminist Genealogies, Colonial Legacies, Democratic Futures* (New York: Routledge, 1997); Patricia Hill Collins, *Fighting Words, Black Women and the Search for Justice* (Minneapolis: University of Minnesota Press, 1998); and Sherene H. Razack, *Looking White People in the Eye: Gender, Race, and Culture in Courtrooms and Classrooms* (Toronto: University of Toronto Press, 1998).

23. I must acknowledge at least three central aspects of women's experience that have been omitted here. First, I have not examined *sexual orientation* as a part of the identity of women workers; it was not as salient a factor in determining job positions or responsibilities as other aspects of social identity. Second, the issue of *violence against women* is not exposed, even though it can be assumed to be present in both domestic and work contexts that are described here. Finally, the influence of *religion* on the lives of these women and their gendered work at home or in the food system has not been explored. In a more secular urban Canadian context, we may be blind, for example, to the centrality of Catholicism in the lives of many Mexican peasants. To address sexuality, violence, and re-

ligion would require building more intimate relationships, perhaps through longer term ethnographic studies.

24. *Mestizos* are mixed-blood Mexicans, who often identify more with their dominant Spanish roots than with their Indigenous roots. "Mestizajo . . . is in reality a very complex socio-cultural process, very often violent, through which Spanish colonizers and their descendants mixed with Indigenous peoples and African descendants brought as slaves." Martinez-Salazar, "Development, Coercion, and Indigenous Peoples," 1.

25. Beyond the unholy trinity of gender, race, and class, the variables of age and family status seem to be salient variables for women working in both Mexican fields and greenhouses as well as those working in Canadian supermarkets and fast-food restaurants.

26. I have not dealt adequately with the rural-urban dynamic in Canada or with regional differences, focusing primarily on supermarkets and fast-food restaurants that are part of my life in Toronto, the major commercial center in Canada.

27. Rosemarie Tong, *Feminist Thought: A Comprehensive Introduction* (Boulder, Colo.: Westview, 1989).

28. Dorothy Smith, *The Everyday World as Problematic: A Feminist Sociology* (Boston: Northeastern University Press, 1987).

29. See Isabella Bakker, ed., *Rethinking Restructuring: Gender and Change in Canada* (Toronto: University of Toronto Press, 1996); Leah Vosko, *Temporary Work: The Gendered Rise of a Precarious Employment Relationship* (Toronto: University of Toronto Press, 2000); and Leah Vosko (editor), *Precarious Employment: Understanding Labour Market Insecurity in Canada* (Montreal and Kingston: McGill-Queen's University Press), 2006.

30. See Ester Reiter, "Serving the McCustomer: Fast Food Is Not about Food," 81–96; and Jan Kainer, "Not Quite What They Bargained For: Female Labor in Canadian Supermarkets," 176–89, in *Women Working the NAFTA Food Chain: Women, Food, and Globalization,* ed. Deborah Barndt (Toronto: Second Story, 1999).

31. Swasti Mitter, *Common Fate, Common Bond* (London: Pluto, 1986).

32. Kathy Kopinak, *Desert Capitalism: What Are the Maquiladoras?* (Montreal: Black Rose, 1997); and Susan Tiano, "Maquila Women: A New Category of Workers?" in *Women Workers and Global Restructuring,* ed. K. Ward (Ithaca, N.Y.: ILR, 1990).

33. Ellie Perkins, "Introduction: Women, Ecology, and Economics: New Models and Theories," Special Issue on Women, Ecology, and Economics, *Ecological Economics* 20, no. 2 (February 1997): 106–9; Shlomit Segal, "Guide to the Uncounted Economy: An Alternative Look at Economics, the Natural Environment, and Unpaid Work," master's thesis, York University, 1997, distributed by the Metro Network for Social Justice; E-mail: justice @socialjustice.org.

34. Patricia Hill Collins, *Black Feminist Thought: Knowledge, Consciousness, and the Politics of Empowerment* (New York: Routledge, 2000).

35. Kirsten Appendini, "'From Where Have All the Flowers Come?' Women Workers in Mexico's Non-traditional Markets," 127–40; Antonieta Barrón, "Mexican Women on the Move: Migrant Workers in Mexico and Canada," 113–26; and Egla Martinez-Salazar, "The 'Poisoning' of Indigenous Migrant Women Workers and Children: From Deadly Colonialism to Toxic Globalization," 99–112, in *Women Working the NAFTA Food Chain;* Sara Lara, *Nuevas experiencias productivas y nuevas formas de organizacion flexible del trabajo en la agricultura mexicana* (Mexico City: Pablos, 1998).

36. Uma Narayan, "Working Together across Difference: Some Considerations on Emotions and Political Practice," *Hypatia* 3, no. 2 (summer 1988): 31–47.

37. Donna Haraway, *Simians, Cyborgs, and Women: The Reinvention of Nature* (New York: Routledge, 1991), 195.

38. Carolyn Sachs, *Gendered Fields* (Boulder, Colo.: Westview, 1996), 19.

39. Boserup's field-defining study is relevant for the Tomasita story, too, as she showed how the industrialization of agriculture promoted by market-driven development projects negatively affected women in the south by changing patterns in the sexual division of labor and displacing them from their traditional subsistence agricultural work. Ester Boserup, *Women's Role in Economic Development* (New York: St. Martin's Press, 1970).

40. Rosi Braidotti, Ewa Charkiewicz-Pluta, Sabine Hausler, and Saskia Wieringa, eds., *Women, the Environment, and Sustainable Development: Towards a Theoretical Synthesis* (London: Zed, 1994), 94.

41. While I reject an essentialist position suggesting that women have an innately closer relationship with nature, I feel that Shiva's promotion of the Hindi "feminine principle" has been misinterpreted by Westerners who don't understand it is the "source of all life" within nature and within men as well as women. "Indian cosmology refrains from viewing the feminine principle in opposition to the masculine principle but rather sees the relationship as a duality in unity. Shiva reminds us that the feminine principle, not exclusively embodied in women, represents activity and creativity in nature and in men, as well as in women." Sachs, *Gendered Fields*, 32–33.

42. Bina Agarwal, "Engendering the Environmental Debate: Lessons Learnt from the Indian Subcontinent," *CASID Distinguished Speakers Series*, Monograph No. 8 (East Lansing: Michigan State University, 1991), 8.

43. Sachs, *Gendered Fields*, 40.

44. Braidotti et al., *Women, the Environment, and Sustainable Development*, 162; Val Plumwood, "Feminism and Ecofeminism: Beyond the Dualistic Assumptions of Women, Men and Nature," *The Ecologist* 22, no. 1 (1992): 8–13.

45. I find a certain irresolvable contradiction in an essentialist argument: if it intends to challenge the historical nature/culture split, but privileges only women as potentially "closer to nature," it reproduces the split, still not reclaiming (all) humans as a part of, rather than separate from, nature.

46. Toby M. Smith, *The Myth of Green Marketing: Tending Our Goats at the Edge of the Apocalypse* (Toronto: University of Toronto Press, 1998), 78.

47. This is not to deny the importance of raising questions around spirituality and challenging the antireligious bias of Western intellectuals, which, in fact, reinforces another dualism between spirit and matter.

48. Catriona Sandilands, *The Good-Natured Feminist: Ecofeminism and the Quest for Democracy* (Minneapolis: University of Minnesota Press, 1999), 72.

49. Ellen O'Loughlin, "Questioning Sour Grapes: Ecofeminism and the United Farm Workers Grape Boycott," in *Ecofeminism: Women, Nature, and Animals*, ed. Greta Gaard (Philadelphia: Temple University Press, 1993), 149.

50. Deborah Barndt, *To Change This House: Popular Education under the Sandinistas* (Toronto: Between the Lines, 1990), 15–20.

51. Popular education legacies in North America include workers' education in the early 1900s, agricultural extension work in midcentury, the work of centers like the Highlander Center in Tennessee and the Coady Institute in Nova Scotia, and *education populaire* in Quebec during the Quiet Revolution. Rick Arnold, Deborah Barndt, and Bev Burke, *A New Weave: Popular Education in Canada and in Central America* (Toronto: CUSO and OISE, 1985), 9–27.

52. Rick Arnold and Bev Burke, *The Popular Education Handbook* (Toronto: CUSO and OISE), 1990.

53. I first articulated these creative tensions as frames for the Tomasita Project in "Tracing the Trail of Tomasita the Tomato: Popular Education around Globalization," *Alternatives Journal* (January/February 1996): 25–26.

54. Deborah Barndt, "Crafting a 'Glocal' Education: Focusing on Food, Women, and Globalization," *Atlantis: A Women's Journal* 22, no. 1 (fall/winter 1997): 43–51.

55. Deborah Barndt, "The World in a Tomato: Revisiting the Use of 'Codes' in Freire's Problem-Posing Education," *Convergence Tribute to Paulo Freire* 31, nos. 1 and 2 (1998): 62–73.

56. A seven-question guide for a decoding process appears in Barndt, "The World in a Tomato," 66.

57. Decoding shares a lot with cultural studies' emphasis on deconstruction. Stuart Hall, "Encoding, Decoding," in the *Cultural Studies Reader*, ed. Simon During (New York: Routledge, 1993), 90–103; and Stuart Hall, *Representation: Cultural Representations and Signifying Practices* (Thousand Oaks, Calif.: Sage, 1997).

58. My doctoral dissertation focused on Freire's notion of "conscientization" in the context of the lives of Indigenous migrant women participating in literacy classes in Lima, Peru. Deborah Barndt, *Education and Social Change: A Photographic Study of Peru* (Dubuque, Iowa: Kendall/Hunt, 1980), 169–86.

59. Gary Gereffi and Miguel Korzeniewicz, eds., *Commodity Chains and Global Capitalism* (Westport, Conn.: Praeger, 1994).

60. *The New Internationalist*, a magazine for development/global educators, has been an inspiration to the Tomasita Project in popularizing complex information about north-south relations. See especially "The Cocoa Chain," no. 304 (August 1998), and "The Big Banana Split," no. 317 (October 1999); Web site: http://www.newint.org. An example of tracing alternative production is *Coffee with a Cause: Moving toward Fair Trade* (Montreal: Editions des Intouchables, 1997).

61. Barndt, *Women Working the NAFTA Food Chain*.

62. Sandra Kirby and Kate McKenna, *Experience, Research, Social Change: Methods from the Margins* (Toronto: Garamond, 1989), 26.

63. Patricia Maguire, *Doing Participatory Research: A Feminist Approach* (Amherst, Mass.: Center for International Education, 1987).

64. Maria Mies suggests the seven guidelines for feminist research in "Feminist Research: Science, Violence and Responsibility," in *Ecofeminism*, 38–42.

65. "Researching the Labor behind the Label," in *Stop the Sweatshops: An Education/Action Kit*, produced by Maquila Solidarity Network; see www.web.net/~msn.

66. Barndt, *Education and Social Change*.

67. I often used photos during the writing of this book to reconnect me to the real people whose lives form the core of the study, as well as to break my feeling of isolation in the writing with memories of other more collaborative moments of the project.

68. These two uses of photographs in the Tomasita Project are elaborated in Deborah Barndt, "Zooming Out/Zooming In: Visualizing Globalization," *Visual Sociology* 12, no. 2 (1998): 5–32.

69. A Vancouver-based group has developed adbusting to a fine art: *Adbusters: Journal of the Mental Environment*, available from The Media Foundation; E-mail: adbuster@adbusters.org.

70. The more participatory practice of giving people cameras to document their own lives has been central to my work, if not to this project. Deborah Barndt, "Naming, Making, and Connecting: The Pedagogical Possibilities of Photo-Story Production," in *Participatory Approaches in Adult Education*, ed. Patricia Campbell and Barbara Burnaby (Los Angeles: Erlbaum, 2001), 31–54.

71. The portable exhibit, "Attacking the Corporate Tomato: Turning Globalization on Its Head," is available for use at conferences and can be rented for shipping costs; E-mail: dbarndt@yorku.ca.

CHAPTER 3

Arch Deluxe with a Smile:

WOMEN NEVER STOP AT McDONALD'S

We're All under the Golden Arches

I took my son, Joshua, then 11, to McDonald's when we visited Guadalajara, Mexico, in 1996; even without Spanish, he could feel at home with Ronald's plastic embrace and frozen smile. In dragging him along on my research, I was periodically reminded that he was, in fact, a key motivation for my initial interest in tracing the fast-food journey. As a single mother in a large North American city, where Disney and McDonald's are the standard diet for most children growing up in a fast-paced society, I saw this project as a way both to engage him and to challenge us around these dominant patterns and practices. I wanted to understand the seduction, too, of the food, the toys, the experience.

We begin this journey with ourselves as northern consumers, as we are drawn into this food chain at the most processed and packaged end of the tomato trail. Why start with the destination rather than the origin of the food we consume? First, given that most of us have become drastically distanced from the food production process, we are better able to enter at the point of consumption; we can more easily identify with eating than with planting tomatoes, as we do it every day. Most readers of this story are North American or European, located at the northern pole of this north-south contradiction. We consume most of the world's resources that are extracted and processed elsewhere, by other hands. Hamburgers, however, epitomize our dependency on production in the south: the beef industry has contributed to rainforest destruction in Latin America, wheat for the buns has displaced the staple corn in many Central American countries, and monocultural crops of tomatoes for agroexport have drained both water and land resources.

Globalization from Above: McDonaldization from Birth to Death

> **Forever Young** is the essence of our brand. It's what we seek to express in everything we do. Youthfully energetic, committed to well-being, a delightful experience, personally engaging, and distinctly casual—it's who we are and it guides our relationship with our customers.
>
> —McDonald's Corporation 2005 Summary Annual Report

Going to McDonald's fast-food restaurant is probably the quintessential experience of globalization, in both cultural and economic terms. And it is clearly aimed at the young—both as consumers and workers.

Welcome to Ronald's Play Place—offering you fast food and fun, in a clean, safe environment, at low cost and with friendly service.

What is the location of the McDonald's featured on these pages? It could, in fact, be one of over 120 countries since by 2006, McDonald's was serving 52 mil-

lion customers a day in 31,000 locations worldwide,[1] more outside than within the United States,[2] where it originated in 1937.[3] With the highly competitive U.S. market (Wendy's, Burger King, and Jack in the Box running a close race with McDonald's), McDonald's has in the era of globalization followed a strategy of expanding internationally. The most successful fast-food giant opens five new outlets a day; and in the 1990s, major media events were designed around the opening of McDonald's chains in Moscow (1990),[4] in Beijing (1992), Tel Aviv (1993),[5] and Managua (1998).

The outlet pictured on the opposite page is in Guadalajara, Mexico, and the young girl celebrating her Catholic confirmation (while her brother sports Mickey Mouse ears) represents a still small number of middle-class Mexicans[6] who are drawn to the golden arches, as much for the experience of "Americana" as for the Big Mac, or "McNifica" (the Spanish name for the Arch Deluxe and a play on the Spanish word for "magnificent"). Mexico's poor majority cannot afford what in North America is considered a cheap meal, and most Mexicans still prefer the classic (and tastier) Mexican fast food—for example, the predominant taco stands on most street corners.[7]

McDonald's, however, has made a few cultural adaptations to its globally expanding clientele, adding spicy omelets to its Mexican menu, for example.[8] And in the late 1990s, it targeted the growing Hispanic market and responded to the increasing popularity of Mexican cuisine in the north by becoming majority owner of Chipotle Mexican Grill. Reflecting the corporate strategy of horizontal integration, McDonald's also added two new brands to the "McFamily" in 1999: Donato's Pizza in the United States and Aroma Cafe in the United Kingdom. Besides following the broader trend of continual expansion, these acquisitions are seen as part of the "strategic effort to capture an ever-increasing percentage of the total meals-away-from-home market."[9]

The McDonald's in a wealthy Guadalajaran neighborhood represents, in fact, more a status symbol than a restaurant; its elegant mosaic designs have won architectural awards. Butterflies on beautiful handmade Mexican tiles appear to be flying north and east, reflecting perhaps not only the annual migration of monarch butterflies from Mexico to Canada and back (an ironic symbol[10] of our ecological connections) but also the increasing movement of goods and services (i.e., hamburgers and Ronald's play places) into southern countries with neoliberal trade policies such as NAFTA. McDonald's presence in Mexico increased significantly after NAFTA was implemented in 1994; by 2003, there were 268 franchises in 59 Mexican cities.[11]

McDonald's expansion in Mexico represents a major contradiction of this continental food story: that many of the ingredients for the hamburgers we eat in the north come from southern lands and labor, while the food in its processed and packaged form goes south again with fast food. Clearly it isn't just food being imported but also the technologies of cooking and serving, the design of the kitchen and dining area, the routinized work and scripted conversation, McDonald's obsession with cleanliness, its birthday parties, and the toys that accompany the combos. Not only are cultural wannabes seduced into the Americanized eating experience, but tourists also are comforted by the familiar, safe, clean, and predictable menus, settings, and paraphernalia.

McDonald's has the cultural power it has today because during the twentieth century, the market moved into the family and the family moved into the market, as fast-food analyst Ester Reiter concludes. The mass production of goods made possible by industrial and assembly line production cheapened costs, while also "creating the consumer."[12] Activities like growing and preparing food were labor-intensive, and buying prepared food was easier and cheaper. The very market for fast food, the family, also became a source of employment for a burgeoning restaurant and fast-food business;[13] they hired young people and women, in particular, both of whom had previously offered their unpaid labor to the household and would more easily accept low wages.

Both women and youth are key markets as consumers of fast food as well, and advertising often targets them. The culture of consumerism is a driving social force and value shaping our activities, indeed our very identities.[14] Recent work in cultural studies challenges the dichotomizing of production and consumption, with a claim that "in every act of consumption there is production, as in every act of production there is consumption." The emphasis is on the "production of meaning"—that is, how we actively take and make meaning from our experiences of consumption.[15] We are helped in this process by the billion-dollar advertising industry that accompanies the products we buy; we consume not only food but also the messages its producers want us to digest, even as we might negotiate our own meanings and relationships with both the food and the message.[16]

As Joe Kincheloe concludes in *The Sign of the Burger: McDonald's and the Culture of Power*, "a burger is never simply a burger, and the cultural domain is now also the primary political domain."[17] Starting at the consumption end of the tomato journey, then, invites us to consider how not only our stomachs but also our minds and hearts are touched by these processes. We can find some clues in the packages that are part of the McDonald's experience. A kid's meal bag, for example, includes on each side cartoons aimed at both male and female children.

What ideological messages about gender, race, and ecology are promoted by having a blond, white Barbie biking through the park, while Ken fishes? The park scene is for the most part environmentally friendly (though there is a car on the road, and animals are anthropomorphized), but the flip side of the bag is clearly the boys' side, with an anti-environmental message. Values of speed and competition are promoted, especially if you follow the dots and get what every

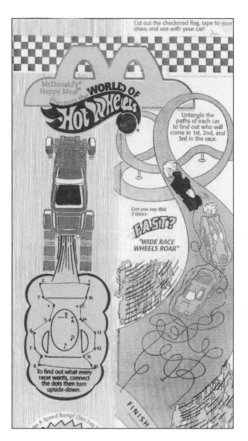

boy wants: a trophy. The exhaust fumes from the race car almost cancel out any ecological responsibility promoted on the girls' side of the bag. The ideological dominance of this side is reinforced by the fact that the free toy offered with the meal is a Hot Wheels car, a favorite of boys. If you want a Barbie, on the other hand, you have to cut out a coupon from the side of the bag and buy the doll with a one-dollar discount off the list price. What's more, we are instructed in how to transform the bag itself into a ramp for the speeding car.

The deconstruction of a kid's meal bag highlights a key aspect of McDonald's market strategy: its targeting of children—both as consumers and as drawing cards to get whole families into the restaurant. Only in the mid-1990s did the kids' favorite food chain consciously aim its marketing at adults when it announced the birth of the Arch Deluxe, a hamburger geared to "adult tastes" and including something that kids often reject—tomatoes![18]

In fact, McDonald's has increasingly found ways to insert itself—both materially and culturally—into our total life cycle, from birth to death. Love it or hate it, it is indelibly marked in our collective cultural memory. In the 1980s, McDonald's Canada offered a major donation for a prenatal unit of a hospital in an eastern province, with the condition that the company control its interior decorating.[19] Imagine a newborn opening her eyes for the first time and being greeted by Ronald the clown or the golden arches, etching in her early consciousness these icons destined to accompany her through her life.

McDonald's iconic power is important to acknowledge and can serve as a cultural code for underlying political and economic realities. In Canada, this is brought home most poignantly by the insertion of the Canadian maple leaf, excised from Canada's national flag, into the crotch of the golden arch. This subsuming of a national symbol within the most recognized symbol of global capital perhaps accurately heralds an era when the role of the nation-state seems to be eroding. It reflects, on the other hand, the rising of multinational corporate power, the triumph of global corporate capital over the state as the prime mover

of change. Indeed, McDonald's epitomizes the mobile society, supplying a fast-food pickup for constant road running. Not only the culture but also the business it promotes is on the move; it is part and parcel of the "free" trade that Ronald Reagan promised in the 1980s would reach all the way to "Tierra del Fuego," covering the Americas and moving on to conquer other continents.

In the new millennium, trade ministers north and south have been crafting other free trade deals such as the Free Trade Agreement of the Americas (FTAA) and the Security and Prosperity Partnership, in the wake of September 11, 2001. McDonald's serves as a symbol of this economic and cultural integration in the hemisphere. When the fast-food giant reopened[20] in Nicaragua in 1998, it was a national political event, with President José Alemán claiming, "With the golden arches, we are moving into the First World."[21]

A U.S.-based multinational, McDonald's represents as well the growing economic presence of U.S. private interests in Canada. The reframing of the Canadian maple leaf by the McDonald's arch incites a centuries-old debate around identity in this northern neighbor of the predominant world power. Representing both the colonizer and the colonized, Canada is said to suffer from a cultural inferiority complex although its elites benefit from the exploitation of marginalized peoples and resources by Canadian companies at home and abroad. The long-standing presence of McDonald's in Canada (since 1967, with 1,400 outlets now employing 77,000 Canadians[22]) thus inspires familiarity and pride in some but fierce nationalism in others, depending on your political perspective. When we consider the globalization-from-below perspectives of Canadian workers in McDonald's, they must be understood in part from the vantage point of a "branch plant," albeit just north of a border that is becoming increasingly meaningless. The U.S.-based multinational has already earned places of honor in this northern country, given choice contracts at the service centers on the trans-Canada highway, building eighty-one outlets in the Toronto-based Skydome stadium, and getting exclusive food-service rights at the Toronto Zoo.[23]

McDONALDIZATION: THE MOTHER OF ALL WORKPLACES?

Economically, McDonald's remains at the top, with its seemingly insatiable imperative for growth and total annual sales that surpass the gross national products (GNPs) of many countries. Part of its formula for success is its expansion through franchised or affiliated operations, 85 percent of all U.S. restaurants, which incur no capital expenditures.[24] Not only is McDonald's a powerful symbol of neoliberal trade policies, of expanding U.S. cultural hegemony, and of our present consumer-driven society, but also it has pioneered and promulgated increasingly dominant work and cultural practices. This phenomenon is reflected in the addition of *McJobs* to our vocabulary, and even to the *Oxford English Dictionary*, much to the consternation of the multinational, who charge that the term is insulting to service-sector workers.[25]

McDonald's influence on workplaces and social practices has been critically analyzed by George Ritzer in *The McDonaldization of Society*, written, from the au-

thor's perspective, "to alert readers to the dangers of McDonaldization and to motivate them to act to stem its tide."[26] Building on Max Weber's theory of rationalization (epitomized in the nineteenth-century organizational development, the bureaucracy), Ritzer sees the fast-food restaurant as the late-twentieth-century paradigm of McDonaldization, which has been extended to most social institutions and work practices in North America. Representing a deepening of rationalization, it ultimately serves to dehumanize people and cultural activity.

Ritzer names five key characteristics of this rationalizing power that permeate fast-food restaurants as well as most other contexts: efficiency, calculability, predictability, control, and the irrationality of rationality. They can be seen to represent dominant values of globalization from above. In describing their work experiences, women McDonald's workers in the Tomasita study illustrate these principles, offering us an inside perspective.

Efficiency: Fast-Food Assembly Line

McDonald's values efficiency, or finding the "optimum means to a given end";[27] this emphasis fits well with the fast pace of modern life, speeding the way "from secretion to excretion."[28] Efficiency involves streamlining the process, simplifying the product, and putting consumers to work. Many developments in the food industry have followed these mandates, creating new technologies that make food faster, easier, and more convenient.[29] Freezers, food processors, and microwaves as well as prepackaged mixes and supermarket meals have made cooking and eating in our culture extremely efficient.

The preparation of Big Macs epitomizes such efficiency. Most of the ingredients come precut and weighed, with the exception of the tomatoes that get sliced on-site. The construction of the Big Mac, in an assembly line, not only follows a very particular order (sauce, onions, and lettuce on top bun, cheese on the bottom bun, pickles and meat on the middle bun) but is calculated to take the least possible amount of time. The Arch Deluxe, the adult-oriented Big Mac with a tomato, requires firm fruit, almost like cardboard, that will survive the assembly line production. One of the wholesalers who purchases tomatoes at the Ontario Food Terminal and sells them to McDonald's restaurants in Toronto offered us a slice test when we visited his warehouse. The Mexican tomatoes were definitely tastier but were also watery and fell apart when sliced. Florida tomatoes, on the other hand, were pulpier, and easier to assemble. If offered as an extra condiment, they can sit on a plate for a few hours without disintegrating. Appearances are equally important.

McDonald's workers are trained in this extreme efficiency through routinized work practices in training modules, aided by videos and manuals. As a business student, Jennifer[30] found that working at McDonald's was "good business training," teaching her skills she could transfer to other workplaces. She described how her manager would even monitor the weather in efforts to make operations more efficient: "If it was raining, we'd expect more people through the drive through," so staff would be moved around. Perhaps the most rationalized treatment of labor relates to the "flexibility" of part-time labor, whose shifts are determined to the hour by charting customer flow. Kate explains: "Basically they're supposed to make a certain amount of money an hour; say between 12 and 1 P.M. they're supposed to make $1,300 an hour. If you make less than that, for every $50 you're minus, you're supposed to cut half an hour of labor."

Though it is illegal to ask a part-time worker to leave after one hour of her three-hour shift, younger and newer female workers especially feel pressured to go home or to ask somebody else to leave. This mentality that places immediate customer demand (or, more accurately, profits) above the needs of workers is reflected in the new just-in-time production practices originating in Japan and adapted to post-Fordist work organization.

Post-Fordism refers to the restructuring of work begun in the 1970s and 1980s that emphasizes customized products, shorter production runs, new technologies, more flexible systems, and workers with multiple skills carrying out multitasks. It contrasts with Fordist practices, which emphasize mass production of homogeneous products, inflexible technologies such as the assembly line, standardized work routines, economies of scale, and the homogenization of consumption patterns. McDonald's operations exhibit a combination of both Fordist and post-Fordist practices, yet all are geared toward efficiency.[31]

Calculability: Food and Work Reduced to a Number

Efficient workplaces depend on a quantification of all aspects of the work routine and production process. The emphasis here is on quantity (e.g., selling billions of burgers), speed (doing it in record-breaking time), and size (implied in names like "Big Mac" and "supersize fries"). In such a system, the workers, too, become quantified and dehumanized in the work process. Teresa describes the time pressure of working in the drive-through: "The order has to be taken, the money has to be taken, the food has to be (prepared and) delivered, the drinks have to be delivered to customers—all in ninety seconds."[32] Time is very literally money, but the pressure to produce fast takes its toll on workers.

Workers' performances also get quantified through the Station Observation Checklist (SOC), filled out periodically by supervisors, and measuring (in points) behavior such as one's speed in the ninety-second drive-through. Computers have facilitated the calculability as well as the control of workers' productivity, as Kate explains: "There's something called an 'hourly' that indicates how much money the store's made in an hour, how much food they've sold. You can look up how many orders that person took in an hour, so you can monitor how many customers they've served in an hour and also the amount of their order, the size of their order."

Work thus gets equated with amounts—of food, of time, and of money. A bottom-line mentality clearly reigns. Even waste is seen only in numerical and monetary terms, certainly not in ecological or social terms. More time is spent "counting the waste" to calculate the financial loss and plan better than is spent finding other uses for the waste. Kate explains that they tried composting at her store, but it was stopped because "it was costing us more money, and the farmers were not taking it." Similarly, recycling of plastics and paper in Teresa's store was discontinued because "the memo came down as money—it was money."

When money and time are totally rationalized for the sake of ever more efficient operations and ever-rising profits, the natural rhythms and needs of people, and especially the workers, are disregarded and even denied. Teresa reached her limit when her store announced it was going to be open for twenty-four hours: "I had to stay at work 'til five or six in the morning and that would ruin my sleep pattern." That led her to quit, a choice not all workers have.

Predictability: Uniformed Employees, Uniform Behavior

In workplaces driven by values of efficiency and based on calculations of time, quantities, and money, production (as well as consumption) gets reduced to a set

of very predictable routines. The setting and the products are totally predictable, as are the employees' actions and interactions. They are trained in uniform behaviors that contribute to the creation and perpetuation of what Vandana Shiva calls "monocultures of the mind."[33] The programmed activity of such jobs is created by and reinforces patterns of thinking that promote uniformity and conformity, leaving little room for diversity or creativity.

"Everything's formula," declares Jennifer. The charts, based on calculations of prior sales at the same time the previous year, dictate what and how many items are to be produced and thus stored. But Jennifer, like others, realizes the limits of such a rigid formula: "It's a lot of theory, but you don't really follow it, 'cause it's more what you feel." In a form of individual resistance, workers use their own observations and judgment at times to decide what products seem to be selling best.

Perhaps the most dehumanizing aspect of the work routine takes the form of the scripted interactions with customers. To satirize the puppetlike behavior such scripts inscribe, some female McDonald's workers mimicked the standardized lines: "How may I help you?" "Would you like fries with that?" These scripts have also been determined by the principles of efficiency and calculability (i.e., the ultimate goal of profit) described earlier. The front-line worker is trained, for example, to ask customers, "Is that supersize?" to encourage sales of greater quantities and "Will you have dessert?" to add to the orders. There is not only a false politeness in the tone and promotion in the content. The rationalization of the script reflects an effort to shorten the interaction to save time. Teresa explains that "you always say, 'Will that be a Coke?' because that's the most preferred drink. So they'll say 'Yeah.' It cuts off two seconds."[34]

Such routinized conversation does, however, take its toll on the workers. Teresa found the repetitive nature of the job wearing, to the point that "I would talk in my sleep, like 'May I help you?' or I'd pick up the phone at home and say, 'May I take your order, please?'" The mind-numbing effect of the work itself was poignantly described by another fast-food worker: "It makes a zombie out of you."[35]

Control: Hierarchies and Machines over People and Creativity

Machines now carry out many key tasks, perpetuating the McDonaldized goals of efficiency, calculability, and predictability. Ritzer suggests that "the replacement of human with nonhuman technology is very often motivated by a desire for greater control."[36] The quantified food production processes of McDonald's and the routinized interactions allow greater control of both the product and the process.

McDonald's workers must fit into a well-oiled machinelike operation, with hierarchies (from manager to assistant manager to swing manager to crew trainer to crew) and organization of their work by stations (back, front, and drive-through) as well as functions (cash, production caller, grill, maintenance, and even birthday parties). We've already seen how computerized monitoring of productivity and SOC reviews control the worker who veers from the expected behavior and speed. Jennifer describes how, as a crew trainer, she must evaluate the work of a crew member, following a checklist: "Do you wash your hands and check your appearance?" "Do you have your name tag on?" "Is your shirt tucked in?" "Are you clean shaven?" "Is your hair tied back?"

Besides the importance of personal appearance, workers are judged on their ability to perfectly reproduce proscribed work procedures. They are thus rewarded for mind-numbing repetition and discouraged from any kind of creative responses to situations. A male fast-food manager rationalized this (usually gendered) division of labor: "We do the creative work [developing the routines], so they [the women workers] don't have to think."[37]

Part of McDonaldization is the control of humans by nonhuman technologies, which includes both the work procedures described earlier as well as the ultimate control: replacement of workers by machines or even robots. This is the critical intersection of work and technology. As one food worker suggested, "It gets to be automatic; it's like you're a machine."[38] Yet, in many McDonaldized workplaces, machines are increasingly taking the place of workers, contributing to growing unemployment. This may create new kinds of work (particularly in the field of computers), perhaps more highly skilled but still lacking in meaning and creativity. The changes in supermarket cashier jobs, featured in the next chapter, also reflect this shift.

The Irrationality of Rationality: Humans Are Missing

The rationalization underlying the four principles elaborated thus far—efficiency, calculability, predictability, and control—comes with a price, however. There is an

ultimate irrationality in the rationalism, particularly when it ends up contradict-
ing the values it aims to promote. Some routinized practices may actually turn out
to be inefficient. What's more important, extreme rationality usually has an effect
of dehumanizing both the production and consumption of food. Workplaces
should be able to benefit from workers who think creatively, for example, and

workers themselves will feel much more satisfied if their various skills and potential are tapped in a job. In a broader sense, fast-food consumption patterns, whether grabbing a burger at a McDonald's restaurant or digesting microwaved precooked food in front of the television at home, have dehumanized the eating experience. These so-called rational practices have also spelled death for many social and cultural eating traditions such as the family meal, as detailed later.

There are positive aspects of McDonaldization, as Ritzer acknowledges, which many benefit from: the greater availability and affordability of goods for greater numbers of people, the convenience and dependability of many goods and services, a kind of democratization of consumption that has accompanied the homogenization, especially in the more affluent north. But in the final analysis, Ritzer offers a critique of modernity; he forcefully condemns the McDonald's model of production and consumption—based on efficiency, calculability, predictability, and control—and argues for resistance to its dehumanizing effects and efforts to create alternatives. With a tone of despair, he suggests we are already caught in an "iron cage of McDonaldization" that so permeates our daily lives and interactions that we are not even aware of it and have internalized many of the values it perpetuates.

While Ritzer's analysis focuses more on the Fordist elements of McDonald's such as "cookie-cutter products, rigid technologies, standardized work routines, deskilling, and homogenization," I agree with Joe Kincheloe that it misses the post-Fordist modes of production that are more flexible in the restructured global economy, especially in response to diverse markets and demographics.[39] Equally important to the success of McDonald's, for example, has been the "experience" the company has created for both children as consumers and youth as workers. Ritzer's analysis is also somewhat gender-blind as well as ethnocentric. Particularly in tracing the tomato and the experience of women workers in the three NAFTA countries, we need to deepen and broaden his critique to incorporate issues of equity and diversity.

Globalization from Below:
Young Workers, Young Consumers

Through the stories of the young women workers in Canadian-based outlets, I'd like to examine two aspects of McDonald's that are particularly important for a more integrative and critical social analysis of the continental (and global) food system: its seduction of youth (as both workers and consumers) and its impact on our own consumption and eating practices.

FROM McFIESTAS TO TEEN OUTINGS: THE SEDUCTION OF YOUTH

When my son, Joshua, and I visited the Guadalajara McDonald's, we recognized the predictable birthday party formula being applied to very Americanized "Mc-

Fiestas." McDonaldized parties are just one of the ways that the restaurant caters to kids and assures that large numbers of customers pass through over a short time. One worker explained that McFiestas are, in fact, limited to an hour and a half, with "no time for games." This shortened and hurried party model could potentially change cultural practices as well as intergenerational relations. Traditional birthday celebrations in Latin America involve all members of an extended family for a lengthy period of socializing and dancing through the night. McBirthdays, on the other hand, are limited to kids only, a hamburger-centered menu, an hour and a half of activity, and whatever is the latest toy.

The loot bags that have become standard birthday fare in North America in the past decade are really extensions of the ubiquitous cultural objects that seduce kids in a steady flow into McDonald's; not so interested in the food itself, they are rather drawn in by the treat of the week (comic books, magnets, stickers, etc.) as well as the toys sold at discounts. Workers acknowledge that this is a deliberate strategy. One woman recalls a training video that says "make sure you treat kids with a lot of respect, because they're our future customers."[40]

While McDonald's may offer an easy solution to the challenging task of feeding kids, parents also feel caught. One fast-food worker who's also a mother confessed, "Once you get within two blocks of it, if you have two pennies to rub together in your pocket you're going to spend it at McDonald's, because these little people drive themselves into a frenzy; my usually well-behaved children just lose their minds."[41] The same woman, recognizing how difficult it was to resist the opportunity for a free toy, also harbored a secret guilt with her own growing knowledge about the stories behind those toys: "I later found out they exploit other people [workers in Third World plants], so those toys can get here; I feel so badly now." Here, too, though, are the seeds of potential solidarity with workers elsewhere in the system which, as we can see, extends well beyond food, to the cultural industries and to the shared experiences of workers in the global economy.

The seduction of young customers has to be understood in the broader context of the economic integration in the past decade of cultural industries with businesses such as fast food. There is now a standard formula, for example, for the immediate (and constantly shifting) production of over two thousand incidental products to coincide with and promote the release of all Disney films; recall Pocahontas bubble bath, Ninja Turtle noodles, and Lion King socks, for example. A perfect marriage was consummated in 1995, when McDonald's signed a ten-year deal, an unprecedented multimillion-dollar promotional alliance with Walt Disney Co., following an earlier alliance formed with Coca-Cola.[42] Previously with each new Disney film, there was fierce competition among all fast-food companies. Until the 2000s, McDonald's was the sole promoter of Disney videos and plastic toys, and Disney got additional advertising on place mats and cups, bags, and Big Mac posters. The integration of economic and cultural hegemony was complete, and the path to a child's growing consciousness all the more direct. Perhaps the most successful recent promotion was the Teenie Beanie Babies: the strategy was to release only one or two characters per week, so that

kids would have to come back weekly to get the entire collection. Parents got in on the hysteria, creating midday traffic jams and long lines outside restaurants to get the free toys.[43]

To provide the promised "experience," McDonald's restaurants have come increasingly to resemble amusement parks, another seduction for kids and parents. One mother admits the attraction: "A restaurant with a play area! How can you compete against that as a mother?"[44] Most of the new stores include these special play places, which in some cases are as high as three stories, with slides and ropes and balls, and—baby-sitters. Young women workers, in fact, have had this task added to their jobs, as they are assigned to monitor children in the play areas as well as to organize their birthday parties.

Packaged Fun: For Child Consumers and Teen Workers Alike

McDonald's tries to package and sell "fun" not only to its youngest customers but also to its young workers. Despite the drudgery of the routinized work processes described earlier, McDonald's offers perks to its predominantly youthful workforce[45] that include weekly treats (hot dogs or fruit) as well as monthly outings of their own design (movies, ice skating, a trip to the beach). While these appear to be "free," they are often tied to performance; in training sessions, for example, prizes are offered for getting the "right answer." Amy remembers that "when the salads just came out and we answered some salad question, I got an album. It makes you pay attention at the meetings, because you want to get the answers."[46]

The outings, however, also contribute to the development of camaraderie among workers, to creating a McDonald's family feeling. In fact, for many young part-time McDonald's workers, one draw of the job is its social value, the chance to hang out with other young people; many fast-food restaurants become favorite hangouts for teenage customers as well. In this sense, the atmosphere created by perks and prizes, games, and field trips contributes to the construction of a temporary youth culture. Nonetheless, some young workers recognize that—in both economic and ideological terms—this is how McDonald's survives and maintains high profits. Norma describes the perks as a kind of compensation for low wages: "McDonald's is not known for its great pay, right? You have to really like working at your workplace in order to get what you're getting paid."[47]

McDonald's promotes itself as committed to diversity, dedicates sections of its Web site to minority populations, and flaunts itself as *Fortune* magazine's "best place to work for minorities" and one of ten "Diversity Champions" according to *Working Mother* magazine.[48] Still, only a quarter of its officers and middle-management are women and minorities, while the part-time workforce itself remains more diverse, predominantly female, and young. The corporation has also garnered environmental awards from the U.S. Environmental Protection Agency for waste management and climate protection, and conservation leadership awards from the Audubon Society and Conservation International.

Cheap labor is the key to the formula of economic success, and McDonald's has fiercely resisted unionization that would challenge that formula; also key are the use of part-time workers and the lack of benefits. Wages begin at minimum wage and increase by ten cents a year. Shifts are kept below the four-hour mark to avoid giving the legally required breaks, saving time and money. As is increasingly the case in McDonaldized workplaces everywhere, there are fewer full-time workers and a majority make up this "flexible" labor pool. Workers are not blind to this strategy: "I think they're trying to avoid having people work full-time. They don't have to give benefits. Everything has to be cost-effective. Whatever step you take, whatever decision you make, you have to make sure you're saving money." The "flexibility" of part-timers means that "they can cut their hours more than a full-time person; they can change the shifts around more if you're part-time."[49]

For newer and younger workers, the schedule varies from week to week. The unpredictability of shift work also makes it more difficult to organize a workforce that not only has little time to communicate among themselves and to build solidarity but also has little long-term investment in the work. Sara Inglis, a teenager from Orangeville, Ontario, led a valiant effort in the late 1980s to organize her outlet, but she was met by the overwhelming economic resources and union-busting strategies of the multinational in a kind of David-versus-Goliath battle that she was doomed to lose.

In 1998, both in Windsor, Ontario, as well as in Quebec, there was renewed movement among trade unionists to crack this very hard shell of fast-food organizing. Backed by the Quebec Federation of Labour (QFL), the Teamsters launched a major campaign "to pierce this stronghold of anti-unionism," as QFL president Clement Godbout called it.[50] This intensified effort came on the heels of a February 1998 attempt to organize employees at the St. Hubert McDonald's; two weeks prior to the "successful" vote, the management closed the restaurant permanently. This union-busting tactic, which the corporation has used in other countries, perhaps has helped the Teamsters' cause; 72 percent of Quebecois in the eighteen to thirty-four age group supported unionization, and 62 percent were willing to sign a petition condemning the multinational's behavior.[51] Nonetheless, the Quebec drive was also ultimately thwarted.

From the perspective of the totally rationalized workplace, then, McDonald's epitomizes the exploitation of cheap, low-skilled, temporary, and part-time employees, who are usually young as well as predominantly female. In seeking out youth as its core employees, McDonald's has entrenched a culturally sanctioned practice of seniority that rationalizes paying younger people less, seeing such work as a kind of apprenticeship for the real world of employment. The tasks themselves have become so technologized that they are easy to learn and require minimal skill. In hiring primarily women, the multinational builds on systemic and deeply entrenched sexism, not only at home but also abroad. This is one of the critical ways that McDonaldization is being reproduced in other work contexts of the restructured global economy.

Nonetheless, McDonald's remains a key employer of youth and continues to promote work at McDonald's as the perfect first job for a young person. It builds on the fact that many people have worked there as a kind of rite of passage, portraying it as a training ground for many other mainly higher status careers. The 1999 annual report features former employees of diverse ethnicities who have "made it," including a Puerto Rican media mogul, an Olympic swimmer, and a Mexican foreign currency dealer. McDonald's promoted itself as an international convener of young people when it ran a contest, Millennium Dreamers, cosponsored by UNESCO and Disney. From thousands of nominations, two thousand top youth were selected to attend an international children's summit held at the Walt Disney World Resort in Florida.[52]

McDonald's young employees seem to fall into two different kinds of categories: (1) those who are unskilled and unschooled for other occupations, who begin working there for survival's sake and may end up by default making a career of fast-food work, and (2) those who are studying for other careers and use McDonald's as a way to pay for their education or to get pocket money, a temporary stop on their journey to more skilled and prestigious work (which still may be in McDonaldized workplaces). Not surprisingly, the more permanent employees were more positive in describing their work experience: "I think it's a good place to work."[53] The students we interviewed, on the other hand, were much more critical. But three had already left the company, and they all saw their McDonald's job as a transition, providing financial support to help them through school.

Some students are forced to take two part-time jobs, to pay for college or university and, increasingly, to help support their families. This becomes tricky especially because of the constantly changing nature of the shifts; piecing together two erratic schedules that would also complement class schedules is no simple matter. Teresa finally quit when such juggling proved too difficult: "I was working an eight-hour shift in my other job, and then when I went to work at McDonald's, I wasn't putting my full force into the store. So they said, 'Forget her!' because they wanted you to make McDonald's your life."[54]

With young people increasingly faced with few employment opportunities, more and more young workers are doing just that. We heard about students who were so desperate to get and keep fast-food jobs, that they would skip classes to be able to make a shift. Others had found McDonald's not only a steady source of employment over the university years, but also a potential career path. McDonald's helped Joan, a young swing manager, through school and offered her management training. She bought stocks in the company and may seek employment either in the headquarters or in one of the fast-food giant's new outlets in the Third World, for the international experience.

For those who put several years into the company, there are even bigger perks: "Within ten years you get a diamond ring. It's not only that I think I would probably stick it out with McDonald's but I do really like their diamond rings."[55] Joan suggests that a kind of loyalty develops over time: "I do assume if you work there for a long period of time that McDonald's must have done something for you in order to stay there for that long." In fact, some managers get cars: "If you've been a head manager for two years, you'll get a Grand Prix."[56]

From Youth to Older Immigrant Women: Building on Shifting Intersections of Age, Gender, Class, and Race

Most often, the managers, however, are male; only three of the seventeen corporate officers are women. A majority of workers remain part-time workers and are female. At McDonald's (as well as Loblaws supermarkets, as detailed in chapter 4), there is a very small full-time workforce, a growing trend in the restructuring of work at a global level. Full-timers are drawn either from those who have stuck it out and worked their way up in the company or, in the Toronto context, from a new workforce of middle-aged women. *Fast Food Women*, a documentary film produced in Kentucky, features middle-aged women who sought work at fast-food restaurants mainly because their husbands have been laid off, particularly as U.S. plants have moved south to Mexico. These women have been forced out of their own kitchens into these greasier ones to become the family breadwinners.

Increasing unemployment, the growing need in families for two incomes, and a burgeoning pool of new immigrant labor have brought more older women and immigrant workers into the McDonald's workforce. Women who are entering the workforce without previous employment experience in North America are forced into low-wage, low-skilled work such as fast food. For companies like McDonald's, these women also represent a more mature and stable labor force.

They pride themselves on being an "inclusive environment" that hires a "global team of talented, diverse employees, franchisees, and suppliers."[57]

In the Toronto context, McDonald's can draw from the burgeoning immigrant workforce that is fast becoming a majority. One younger worker explains their lack of choice in this way: "I think the fact that they're immigrants from, say, India or Hungary or Germany, influences the kind of jobs they can have. You don't really have to speak English to work at McDonald's." Besides, with a limited script to learn and repeat in rote fashion, they catch on quickly. On the other hand, it was reported that those with strong accents were put in the back, reflecting a subtle racism as well as the emphasis on fast service.

With increasing unemployment, the competition for McDonald's jobs has become more fierce. One worker reported that the applications used to be short, asking only for your name and phone number. But now, candidates desperate for work are sending in résumés. The application forms, too, have changed. Job candidates must note their availability throughout a week; flexibility seems to have become an important criterion in hiring. The application form can be picked up from a display case in the restaurant, reflecting a broader recruitment strategy. McDonald's can choose from a surplus of workers and is moving away from a predominantly young and single workforce; its recruitment material offers something to people at different life stages:

> If you're still in school, we can offer the chance to learn valuable skills for your future while you earn extra spending money.
>   If you have young children and only want to work part-time, we can give you flexible hours while you earn the extra income a growing family needs.
>   If you're retired and want a job that lets you meet people and have fun while you earn a little extra cash, McDonald's can give you that, too.

McDonald's actually prides itself on its hiring of minority youth as well as on its "McMaster's program" that provides employment for seniors. Yet there are discriminatory practices, evidently, in those hirings. Carol Stack and Ellen Stein report that in the United States,[58] the competition for minimum-wage jobs is fierce, with a ratio of fourteen applicants to one hire; they conclude that fast-food restaurants have begun to prefer mature workers.[59]

Even though managers and owners stated that they wanted the labor force in their stores to reflect the racial and ethnic makeup of the neighborhoods, it was not the case; blacks were rejected at a much higher rate than Latinos and Asians. The young people in the study found it difficult to move from part-time fast-food jobs into full-time jobs elsewhere. And employers didn't seem to value the skills imparted through the jobs, noting only that they taught people "to use an alarm clock, get to work on time, and arrive clean and well-groomed."[60] On the other hand, young workers themselves believed that they learned many other skills such as "team work, how to do more than one thing at a time, planning for and anticipating the ebb and flow of work, negotiating with workers

from different ethnic groups to cooperate to deliver an order, and acquiring allies to help you out during the busiest times."[61]

No matter the age of the McDonald's workers, however, three trends remain: more than 50 percent of the workforce are female and minorities, and a majority is employed part-time. In this sense, they fit into the broader phenomenon of a flexible, casual, female, and racialized workforce, adapting to shifting consumer demands by the hour, and adjusting their weekly plans to the patchwork of part-time shifts constructed on schedules that are revised regularly by managers. The never-ending uncertainty about when you will work has become a constant dynamic in the lives of many workers. The young women students we interviewed were favored for weekend and evening shifts, and in some ways, this "flexibility" suited their lives as students, if their shifts complemented their class schedules. Yet because of their low seniority, they didn't always get the hours they wanted.

One worker who has become a manager has observed that while not many men over twenty-five apply to work at McDonald's or stick it out very long there, women do, because "they're more adaptable; they're more eager to find a job."[62] Contrary to the more common explanation by employers that they're more dependable (in other words, docile and dependent), there are other reasons why women might feel they have to "stick it out." One manager explains, "Full-timers are more women because they may have kids at home or they go to school so they can work a nine-to-five job and be home later on for their kids." Machismo is also a factor, she suggests; she's observed that immigrant men don't want to take on low-status jobs until they have exhausted all other avenues.

Gendered practices also shape the division of labor between male and female workers at McDonald's. One fast-food worker suggests that "men see themselves as higher up for doing stock or whatever rather than having to actually go out and be among the people you were serving. That's the part they didn't like. There was a lot of humiliation."[63]

Dominant gender ideologies in North America (and elsewhere) often support the role of women on the front line, seeing them as more skilled in social relations and better able to deal with customers. This purported female behavior is also congruent with McDonald's emphasis on customer service. The company once ran a campaign with the slogan "Do whatever it takes"; workers were encouraged to go out into the lobby and talk with the customers. Teresa suggests there are gendered criteria applied in assigning men to work in the back of the restaurant, while women are put in the front, because they are "more understanding; they'd smile."[64]

The ideology behind the McDonald's smile fits snugly with the company's emphasis on appearances, where workers are trained in what some refer to as a "fake friendliness," reinforced by the scripted interaction. Some workers buy into the ideology so completely that they believe it: "It's so great—you make so many friends, and everyone's so happy and cheery so you have to be. It's like a happy environment."[65] Women are also more thoroughly socialized into polite, pleasant behavior and into taking greater care of their appearances.

The emphasis on appearances, however, also feeds discriminatory practices; one worker felt that she was always put in the back, while more attractive women (and men) were assigned to the lobby. One young woman, who seems to be in the job for the long term, summarized the ideology well: "You've got to have a good attitude or you can't work there. You'd be miserable, because there's a lot of people who are unhappy and they don't like the job because you have to be happy, right? It's part of customer satisfaction."[66]

Ronald McDonald's frozen smile projecting a constantly happy image, echoing the now ubiquitous "happy face," represents this simulated environment that leaves little space for natural interactions or for a normal range of changing facial expressions reflecting shifting human moods. Ronald is similar to the hyperreal characters of McDonald's former corporate ally, Disney, which never frown, never go to the bathroom, and never die.[67]

Fast-Food Work, Fast-Food Eating: The Intimate Link between Production and Consumption

The boundaries between production and consumption blur when you probe the patterns of McDonald's women workers as consumers and not just producers of food. It becomes clear how the operation of the fast-food restaurant and the organization of work within it inevitably shape the eating practices of its workers and their families. The phenomenon moves far beyond McDonald's to reflect deeper cultural shifts. Two features stand out in these stories. One is that the constantly changing schedule associated with part-time "flexible" work wreaks havoc on any family cooking and eating rituals. The second is that working in a fast-food restaurant also affects workers' diets, in a least one way: the food is there, it's convenient, and workers can purchase it at half price. In part-time jobs with low pay and no benefits, this is touted, in fact, as the "major benefit"!

Perhaps the best way to understand this interrelation between being a fast-food worker and the culture's shifting eating practices is to examine the daily lives of several young women workers we interviewed. While there is some diversity among them, at the same time they reveal patterns, particularly as young single women.

Teresa: No Time to Eat Together

"My whole family used to work at fast-food restaurants. My mom used to work at Burger King as a manager, then I got a job at McDonald's, then my other sister got a job, and Arun got a job, the younger one. My boyfriend works at McDonald's and the guy who lives in the basement works at McDonald's. So it's like everyone, most of my friends, work at McDonald's like I do. At work, when my sister was working with me, or my boyfriend, even if I didn't bring food, they did. Or we would buy food there.

"At home, there's no time that we can all sit down and eat together. My dad works downtown as a metro police officer, so he has weird shifts, from eleven at night 'til six in the morning. He comes in and sleeps during the day, then wakes up in the afternoon. My mom works full-time, in shifts; sometimes she works during the evening and sometimes during the day. So when I'm home, I just grab something and put it in the microwave or whatever.

"But now since I've quit McDonald's, because I have to pay full price, I don't want to go in and buy it anymore. And also because I've changed my eating habits, and I want to start eating healthy and I started exercising more. So I haven't eaten McDonald's for a month, and I'm so proud of myself."

Kate: Living on Half-Priced Burgers

"When I first started at McDonald's, I had only eaten there once or twice before then. But I was struggling to get on full-time, and I didn't have time to make a big breakfast or lunch or something. And the fact that it was half price made it more desirable. I really did not have time to be making food and stuff. So I ended up eating at McDonald's.

"Then I would maybe bring something from McDonald's home, even though I'm not supposed to, because half price is only supposed to be for me. But my mom's unemployed, so I guess there's not as much food around the house.

"As for my family, for the longest time, we've been on different schedules so we don't eat together at all."

Adele: "I'm Always in a Rush"

"I don't eat very well, actually. I don't cook. I'm renting a room, and even though I have access to a kitchen, I don't like to cook. So it seems like I'm always buying food when I'm on campus, which is not good as far as nutrition, and as far as spending money, and I've spent a lot of money.

"Before going to school, I don't like to make a lunch. Like I'm always in a rush, and always running behind, so I don't usually have time to make something. I keep telling myself, OK, I have to start making meals, but I just can't get into it—I don't know why.

"As far as going to the grocery store, the one that's closest to where I live doesn't have a very large selection. I'm not the kind of person who makes a grocery list; I just don't plan ahead. I eat lots, I'm always sort of nibbling on things, but I don't really have like big meals.

"Besides most of my classes are at dinnertime, like a 3:30 to 5:30 kind of thing, so I usually end up eating on campus during the week. I would usually just grab something on my break, because I would be starving by that time."

Joan: "I Come Home Really Tired"

"I used to be a vegetarian when I was a teenager, but my mom and I would get into a fighting match every night, you know, and then when I started working at McDonald's, I started eating meat again.

"Now I live with my grandmother, who has Alzheimer's, so I cook for her. Sometimes when I come home really tired, she will eat a dinner, from Loblaws or wherever I go shopping, and they have dinners on sale. If I'm coming from work at McDonald's, I'll bring her home a McDonald's meal; she loves the McChicken at McDonald's and the apple pie."

Jennifer: "My Mom's Always Cooking"

"When I was a kid, I never ever remember going to McDonald's with my parents. And I couldn't stand hamburger meat for the longest time. At home, we sit down for every meal, from breakfast, lunch, and dinner, because my mom is always cooking.

"I'm a recovering anorexic, so I have a plan, it's psychological, related to my recovery and the organization of my eating. I know that I'm only supposed to eat at certain times of day, or I'm really turned off by stuff. So I don't eat McDonald's; I can't stand it.

"When I wake up, I make myself breakfast, no matter how late I am, even if it's like on the run. Because if I don't have breakfast, the whole day is shot. That's how my body works, and they say breakfast is the most important meal. And when I was recovering, was going through outpatient, they really stressed breakfast. And my mom keeps a lot of bran muffins and Rice Krispies squares, and bananas—on the table, waiting for us. So I grab it and run out. So I do breakfast.

"If my shift starts at one o'clock, I'll have lunch just before I go, and that means I'll get home in time for dinner. I don't eat dinner there. I always sit down with my family. Even if I get off at 10 P.M. my mom's always waiting for me, and I'll have dinner and she'll sit with me. You'd think we were living in the '50s like June Cleaver in Leave It to Beaver, *because afterward, we'd have dessert, we'd have coffee or fruit or a tart. My mom grows her own vegetables, so in the summer we have homegrown tomatoes. I don't eat tomatoes in a salad, so it's usually like tomato sauce that my mom has made and frozen from the fresh tomatoes in the backyard in the summertime."*

EMERGING PATTERNS FROM THE PROFILES

Though no sweeping generalizations can be drawn from so few cases, Jennifer's story does stand out as an exception to an emerging pattern. Her experience of eating homegrown tomatoes and tomato sauce made by her mother (who works full-time) is very rare, as is the family that still sits down together to share a meal. For the most part, the erratic schedules of young women part-time workers combined with the divergent shifts of other family members make it almost impossible to continue such a family tradition; of course, the notion and composition of today's families have also radically shifted. The "flexibility" that is predominant in global corporate labor strategies may suit the productivity and profit margins of companies like McDonald's, but it takes its toll on the very human practice of "commensality," or gathering around the table to share a meal as a social occasion.

The fast-paced life that is reinforced by such erratic work schedules also makes fast food a convenience that is hard to pass up, especially when it is close at hand and half price. Note how these workers spoke about "not having any time," being "always in a rush," just "grabbing" something, or picking up food on the way home. In two of the stories, young women had increasing responsibility for family members at home and found the cheap McDonald's meals a useful way to feed them. As social programs are increasingly cut, more and more young people, particularly women, will be taking on the care of older family members. If fast food becomes the default diet, their health will become even more precarious.

Healthy eating is threatened by several trends and is thus more and more of a challenge. There are personal preferences—for example, people who just don't like to cook or haven't ever learned; not only a younger generation but a whole population is being deskilled as restaurants replace home kitchens. There are structural constraints as well, such as the limited selection in campus food joints or neighborhood convenience stores as well as the disappearance of smaller stores in the face of competition from megasupermarkets. Developing and acting on a more health-conscious eating pattern is not an easy task. Even as a vegetarian, Joan found it hard to resist McDonald's meat; Teresa was motivated to seek more healthy practices only after she left McDonald's and as a reaction against very unhealthy eating habits. Jennifer, with unflinching support from her mother, ate more regularly and healthily. But her attention to good eating was part of a process of recovering from anorexia, a social disease (with dangerous physical manifestations) that has its roots in eating practices and cultural pressures around the notion of an "ideal" (and very thin) body for women.

What should be clear from these stories, though, is that the production practices of McDonald's—the way the company organizes its workforce to meet market-driven goals—inevitably shape the possibilities and patterns of employees' eating, in terms of both its nutritional value as well as the cultural rituals surrounding it. Fast-food eating fits into a broader social process, characterized by urbanization, mobility, and fast-paced living that have both created the demand and perpetuated the need for prepared convenience foods and very individualized (rather than social) eating practices.

THE SPECTER OF CHILD OBESITY

In recent years, however, there has been a growing public consciousness of health, linking the alarming rise of child obesity to the ubiquity of fast food in

our daily diets, as well as inactivity. According to a 2005 study, half of adults and one-third of children in Canada are overweight or obese, and predictions are grim: the life expectancy for our children has dropped due to the greater risk of heart disease.[68] Not surprisingly, McDonald's, as the epitome of fast food, has been under attack. Symptomatic of the negative association was Disney's failure to renew its very lucrative promotional agreement with McDonald's in 2005; while both companies deny it, many feel that Disney did not want to tarnish its own clean image with an association with child obesity.[69] The company has also been faced with lawsuits by obese teenagers claiming McDonald's misled consumers into thinking their products were nutritious.[70]

McDonald's has responded with some changes, offering healthier fare, such as the premium salad with grape tomatoes (at $4), advertising its food-safety record, and promising to find alternatives to the trans fats that coat the fries. Interestingly, it is women customers who seek out and pay for the more expensive salads, and women, too, are the key market for a new phenomenon: home delivery of packaged healthy food.[71] Zone Chefs in the United States and Nutrition in Motion in Canada deliver meals to stressed-out working mothers to feed their inactive kids; and at $900 a month, this McDonaldization of healthy food does not address the deeper issues of lifestyle or the question of the workers who prepare these heavily packaged options.

McDonald's Engaging the Tensions of the Tomato Story

The preceding stories of women workers reflect the four tensions of the tomato story in many ways. These tensions provide axes around which we can synthesize some of the learnings from the fast-food stop on the tomato's journey.

PRODUCTION/CONSUMPTION

By getting inside these young women's experiences as both producers and consumers, we challenge a rigid *production/consumption* dichotomy. It is clear that work practices aimed at increasing production inevitably affect the opportunities for food consumption in our culture. Women's "flexible" labor may meet McDonald's goal of maximizing efficiency and profits, but it denies the natural rhythms and needs of workers as consumers to eat well, to savor their food, and to gather around the table to socialize. Women are at the center of these shifts.

Ironically, the women workers who bring us fast food are as distanced and alienated from its production as we are. Most of the ingredients of the McDonald's menu are processed and precut and require very little skill to prepare. Tomatoes offer one of the few contacts with the actual fruit, as the workers actually slice them on the spot, even if they are the pulpier variety that have been gassed and shipped from Florida.

McDonald's also represents the dominance in the north of a consumer culture, in which the food itself is almost secondary, while the "experience" of the restaurant predominates—its seductive advertising, convenience, toys and entertainment (play places and birthday parties), and perks and outings for workers. For northern consumers, so distanced from the tomato fields, the meaning of the food is often more symbolic and cultural than material and physical.

BIODIVERSITY/CULTURAL DIVERSITY

Not only northern consumers but also wealthier consumers in the south have been seduced by the cultural experience McDonald's offers. But both production and consumption of McDonald's threaten *biodiversity/cultural diversity*. The kind of monocultural production necessary to supply the standardized fare of the McDonald's menu has had a disastrous impact on the world's biodiversity as well as on the cultural diversity of women as consumers and producers of food. In Canada as well as in Mexico, an economic and cultural homogenization threatens cultural diversity in multiple ways—through scripted interactions and practices such as globalized birthday parties as well as disintegrating home-cooked family meals.

WORK/TECHNOLOGY

The underlying rationalization of work at McDonald's has deepened over time with the introduction of new technologies. Ritzer's warning of the replacement of human by nonhuman technologies is becoming more a reality; the *work/technology* dialectic, thus, is central to understanding the shifting nature of work and its impact on women workers. The technologies of McDonald's work include not only the actual equipment, such as the machine through which the hamburger passes as it cooks itself, but also the minute tasks that have been engineered to make the human effort in this process as efficient as possible. McDonald's has led the industry and other workplaces, too, in scientific management, through which human beings become part of well-oiled machine operations.

HEALTH/ENVIRONMENT

McDonald's has been on the defensive in the past decade, particularly with concerns about both the health and environmental impacts of its menu, produce suppliers, and packaging. In fact, the company now advertises itself as promoting "balanced, active lifestyles" with more menu choice, physical activity, and nutritional information, and has created a Global Water Team, Animal Welfare Council, Sustainable Packaging Coalition, and Paper Working Group.[72] While the food giant can be seen as leading fast-food businesses in these areas, the pressure has come mainly from northern consumers; its environmental guidelines for suppliers only suggest a minimization of pesticide use, for example, so the health of workers and of the land in the supplier states and countries is still not a priority.

Once again, a global food system that keeps all of us distanced from the production practices that bring us food, fast or otherwise, contributes to this lack of consciousness and concern. And, despite a growing slow-food movement (chapter 8), the increasing speed of our lives seems to perpetuate a "grazing" approach to food—filled perfectly by the market invading the home through fast food.

The Other Globalization: Signs of Resistance, Signs of Hope

We are all immersed in the McDonald's culture, so our resistance to the extreme rationalization and dehumanization resulting from McDonaldization is always partial and contradictory. Yet since the new millennium, there has been a growing worldwide movement of consumers questioning the company's practices. Confrontations with the Golden Arches have become commonplace around the globe; one of the highlights for women attending the 1995 Beijing Women's Conference, for example, was the demonstration against the McDonald's outlet at the NGO Forum. McDonald's executives, aware of the power of the symbol to represent the United States, closed down the multinational corporation's regional office after the September 11, 2001, attack in New York City, fearing retribution from widespread anti-American sentiment.[73] Kids have also challenged the environmentally damaging use of Styrofoam containers and have been successful in getting McDonald's to change to paper containers. Ironically, though, the paper products were coated and turned out to be less biodegradable than polystyrene; in a decision that reflects the true motives of the company, McDonald's chose to respond to consumer (false) perception that the paper was better and went with that, maintaining appearances rather than protecting the environment.

One celebrated challenge to the company's exploitative practices came in the form of the McLibel trial in England. The company brought libel charges against two British environmental activists of Greenpeace, who distributed leaflets in 1986 criticizing McDonald's for promoting unhealthy food, exploiting workers, robbing the poor, damaging the environment, exploiting children through its advertising, and murdering animals.[74] The trial lasted three years (the longest running trial in British history), a David-versus-Goliath battle for which McDonald's paid over $16 million in legal fees against the penniless activists who defended themselves. The judge ordered the two to pay $136,000 in damages but sided with their statements that the company exploited children in advertising, paid low wages to workers, and was responsible for cruelty to some of the animals used in McDonald's food.[75]

The McLibel suit touched a chord with consumers as well as producers around the world. The Internet, in fact, has become one of the key tools for organizing anti-McDonald's forces globally. McSpotlight (www.mcspotlight.org) has provided a popular cyberspace for sharing information about protests all over the globe and for expressing international solidarity with local activists in less McDonaldized cultures resisting the onslaught of Big Mac into their economies and cultures. The scope of this cross-border resistance can be gleaned from the cover page of the McSpotlight home page on the World Wide Web. There are links to sites on issues like nutrition, advertising, animal welfare, employment, multinationals, and global trade. And activist efforts "beyond McDonald's" are also cited: baby milk industry, cosmetics, pharmaceuticals, oil, and tobacco. Clearly, anti-McDonald's organizing fits into a much broader globalizing movement challenging corporate rule in all spheres of life.

One organization that has often targeted McDonald's as a cultural icon is The Media Foundation in Vancouver, which produces the popular magazine *Adbusters: Journal of the Mental Environment*.[76] Promoting what it calls "culture jamming" through various subversions of corporate advertising, it forces us to question the original messages and encourages us to creatively critique the consumer culture. An example of one reconstruction of the McDonald's ideology appears on the next page.

In the past decade, there have emerged multiple forms of resistance—initiated by young and old, in North America and globally—challenging the McDonald's

Adbusters, The Media Foundation

model of fast and unhealthy food, cheap labor, and packaged fun. Chapter 8 offers examples of worldwide initiatives such as the Slow Food Movement and a new Alliance for Fair Food in the United States, stimulated by a group of Mexican tomato workers in Florida who in 2007 convinced McDonald's to pay more for the tomatoes they picked, improving wages. Here we will maintain the focus on the restaurant's target demographic, kids, and consider actions located within schools. The first example illustrates how classrooms can become sites of developing critical consciousness around food, and the second how school policies can be shifted by public (and celebrity) pressure to offer healthier food to kids.

KIDS AS FAST-FOOD DETECTIVES

A six-week "participatory research" project with more than twenty kids in my son's grade 3–4 class began with their decoding fast-food ads. We started with a few basic questions:

- What do you like about the ad?
- What does it say about food?
- Who's making the message?
- What do they get from it?

These young consumers seemed quite aware of the corporate ploy to seduce kids into their fold through ads and toys: "They try to attract you to buy food by offering a free prize and a cheap price," one explained. They also readily admitted that their interest in the restaurant itself shifted from month to month, depending on the treats and having little to do with the menu.

Another purpose in deconstructing ads was to help kids understand the constructed nature of all the media messages that bombard them daily. We wanted to encourage them to be not only critical media consumers but also creative media producers. Once they were clearer about how ads are produced ("They make the hamburger bigger than it really is to impress us," one kid concluded), they were ready to make their own ads.

First, we taught them basic skills in photography with the aid of five simple point-and-shoot cameras lent to us by the local school board. Their first assignment was to construct a new burger ad, but this time with their own particular messages, anything they wanted to say. We provided all the ingredients for a Burger King Whopper (akin to a Big Mac). Using their imagination, the kids assembled and photographed them in a wonderful variety of ways.

When the photographs were processed, the kids mounted them on a Burger King tray liner, a Leonardo da Vinci sketch, adding their own advertising slogans.[77] All of the subverted ads were put on public display in a school hallway in an exhibit entitled "Burgermania." Their constructions challenged viewers to think critically about fast food and the ads that promote it.

Though many kids still mimicked the form (and messages) of the corporate ad makers, some allowed their imaginations to flow—outside the frame, so to speak. My son, for example, perched his Whopper on a friend's head before photographing it, then mounted the photo with the slogan "Burgers aren't only good to eat, they are good for hats too."

The classroom teacher became very engaged in this project, weaving it into other lessons during the six weeks. One class session, for example, focused on nutrition issues and involved the school nurse; another class on environmentally sound eating promoted the five N's: near, natural, naked, need, and now.[78]

To further explore and expand these kids' understanding of the food system, we asked them to pick one ingredient from a Whopper and to draw a map of its journey to a fast-food sandwich. While most of the maps revealed ignorance of the real origins, the kids did recognize that the journeys were long and twisty. In an ironic twist, however, one reinforced a persistent myth of "Farmer Brown" bringing fresh produce from the country to town; this modern farmer, however, stopped along the way to fuel his appetite for fast food! The mapping process dramatically reflected how distanced from the food production process urban kids, and their families, have become.

To get them to think about the bigger picture of global food production, we shared the tale of Tomasita the Tomato. The kids, however, decided to dramatize and videotape their own variation of the story. The first scene portrayed a dialogue between two girls, asking each other where tomatoes come from. Other kids reenacted their two dramatically different answers.

The first girl recounted a long trip, the globalized version, similar to the story of the corporate tomato. The second, however, proposed a shorter journey—from her own backyard to the family dinner table. She proudly described how she and her mother prepared the ground, planted the seeds, harvested the tomatoes, and ate the fruits of their labor, thereby promoting local production.

The culmination of this project was a class field trip to the neighborhood Burger King.[79] In preparation for their participatory research at the restaurant,

Map of One Whopper Ingredient: From Production to Consumption

the kids divided into four teams, each developing the questions they would ask during the two-hour visit. The "Adbusters" photographed and analyzed the ads; the "Menu Detectives" investigated the nutritional value of the food; the "Whopper Production Line" team interviewed a worker as she put together the large burger sandwich; the "Behind the Scenes" group interviewed the store manager about where the food comes from and where the waste goes. Even as they deepened their own critical analysis, they gobbled up the free snacks and gifts they were offered before heading back to class!

The next day, we returned with the processed photos taken by the four groups. Using these, the kids summarized their research findings in photo-stories, which were then shared with other classes in the school.

A week later, to evaluate the project, we did video interviews with pairs of kids, using a TV talk-show format. In describing what they had learned from the experience, they revealed small cracks in their near-total fascination with fast food. One suggested, "I now see things in a different way when I go to McDonald's." Clearly they were entering fast-food restaurants with more critical eyes.

While there were few educational resources to support critical education around food in the 1990s, there is now a plethora of materials to teach kids about the multiple consequences of eating fast food, beyond their own health concerns. In 2006, Eric Schlosser, of *Fast Food Nation* fame, published (with Charles Wilson) *Chew on This: Everything You Don't Want to Know about Fast Food*, aimed at McDonald's prime demographic—kids. Packed with facts about how not only the ingredients but also the toys are produced,[80] the well-illustrated book reveals, for example, that a 1997 McDonald's promotion of giving away Beanie Baby toys over a ten-day period boosted sales of Happy Meals from ten million to one hundred million.[81] It also urges kids to take action, to question food in their schools, for example. Not surprisingly, McDonald's marketing executives convened a "war council" to deal with this latest popular onslaught on its representation.

VENDING MACHINES VS. SALAD BARS

The growing concern with child obesity has also shone light on the complicity of schools in providing unhealthy food and limited physical education. Following the cutbacks to public education in the 1990s, the fast-food and beverage industries enticed cash-strapped schools with contracts worth millions of dollars in exchange for installing their vending machines and selling their food in school cafeterias. Part of a broader neoliberal project of privatization and reduction of social spending, these corporate deals became a primary source of funding for computers, books, and team uniforms.[82]

Schools and universities alike have become known as "Coke" or "Pepsi" schools, but the ubiquitous presence of their vending machines has also provoked political action by students. In 2001, secondary school student Nick Dodds won a two-year battle to make transparent how much money the school received for being a Pepsi school, and how the funds were used, through a Freedom of

Information Act request.[83] In British Columbia, grades 4–12 students testified before a provincial legislative committee dealing with childhood obesity, advocating for vending machines with healthier food choices, explaining that they went for junk food because it was accessible and cheap.[84]

Pressure to change school policies and practices has come from various sources. The Ontario government has banned the sale of pop and candy from elementary schools, but has yet to do the same in secondary schools. FoodShare, North America's largest food security organization, has been part of the Partners for Student Nutrition network in Toronto and in 2002 launched a salad bar program in two Toronto elementary schools. Since then, the program has grown to include twelve Toronto schools.[85]

Efforts to change school food policies received a big boost from the dramatic action of Jamie Oliver, the popular British television celebrity chef, who in 2005 convinced the British government to ban junk food from schools. His strategy was to produce a TV series both exposing the unhealthy fare and demonstrating how nutritious and tasty food could be with "a bit of imagination and a touch more money."[86] A national junk food ban in Canadian schools is difficult because education is a provincial jurisdiction. But the forces are clearly growing toward more definitive action to transform schools into sites of health promotion.

Questioning fast food can happen within homes as well, where the market has invaded the kitchen. Such resistance, however, most often becomes the responsibility of mothers—still on the front line when it comes to purchasing, preparing, and consuming food. Women are caught in the paradox that fast food has also responded to their need for greater convenience and less time in the kitchen. Thus, any alternatives to McDonald's are not simple when it comes to women's labor.

Notes

1. *McDonald's Corporation 2006 Summary Annual Report.*

2. In 2006, 44 percent of the McDonald's outlets were located in the United States, 20 percent in Europe, 25 percent in the Asia Pacific, 5 percent in Latin America, and 4 percent in Canada.

3. Mac and Dick McDonald opened their first restaurant in Pasadena, California, in 1937, offering a "highly circumscribed menu" and operating on "principles of high speed, large volume, and low price." Ray Kroc discovered them in 1954 and became their franchising agent, finally buying them out in 1961 for $2.7 million. The profits, in fact, come from the franchises, 1.9 percent of their store sales, rather than from the initial fees for franchising. So while the McDonald brothers laid the basic foundation for the fast-food formula in the restaurant business, Kroc honed their model to its current extreme formula and expanded it—into the far reaches of the United States and later the globe. George Ritzer, *The McDonaldization of Society* (Thousand Oaks, Calif.: Pine Forge, 1996). Also Ray Kroc, *Grinding It Out: The Making of McDonald's* (New York: St. Martin's Press, 1987).

4. The Moscow McDonald's opening is the claim to fame of George Cohon, chairman of McDonald's Canada, engineered over twelve years of negotiations. When it opened in

1990, thirty thousand people lined up on a cold winter day to visit the enormous restaurant that serves seven hundred people. *Source:* Information package from McDonald's Canada.

5. There have been minor adaptations to different cultural and religious food practices. In Arab countries, for example, McDonald's complies with Islamic law for food preparation and does not display statues of Ronald McDonald since this is a prohibited "idol," while a kosher McDonald's in Jerusalem does not serve dairy products and is closed on Saturdays. *Source:* McDonald's Canada information package.

6. The 1999 annual report features a Mexican senior foreign currency dealer who had his first job at a Mexico City McDonald's. He described it as "very cool" because his customers included "many artists and musicians, such as a locally popular girls' rock and roll group." *McDonald's Corporation 1999 Annual Report*, 23.

7. During the 1990s, when I wrote the first edition of this book, my Mexican friends claimed that American fast food would never enter the Mexican culinary landscape to such an extent that it would change eating practices and preferences. But ten years later, the popular taco stands are under attack from two sources: the incursion of multiple global fast-food corporations and the rising cost of tortillas, precipitated by U.S. moves to convert corn into ethanol for fuel.

8. Joe Kincheloe argues that McDonald's "is producing a global culture—not a homogenized one." Viewed from a postmodernist perspective, "McWorld is mediated through local conditions and local perceptions." Joe Kincheloe, *The Sign of the Burger: McDonald's and the Culture of Power* (Philadelphia: Temple University Press, 2002), 167.

9. Scott S. Greenburger, *El Economista, The America's Intelligence Wire*, 1 July 2003.

10. The monarch butterfly, because of its annual migration through the three NAFTA countries, has been used as a symbol by both sides of the free trade debate. A tourist advertisement in American Airlines' magazine uses it, while I found the monarch juxtaposed with a flying U.S. dollar bill on a placard used in the annual Bread and Puppet Theater pageant in northern Vermont in August 1998, where the negative impacts of NAFTA on Mexicans were being creatively represented.

11. McDonald's presence in Mexico increased significantly after NAFTA was implemented in 1994; by 2003, there were 268 franchises in 59 Mexican cities.

12. Ester Reiter, *Making Fast Food: From the Frying Pan into the Fryer* (Kingston: McGill-Queen's University Press, 1996), 11–12.

13. Reiter, *Making Fast Food*, 45.

14. Cultural studies offer new theories of consumption, responding in part to the inadequacy of classic Marxian analyses that relegated consumption to a secondary domain, primarily economically determined by the relations of production. Challenging the rigid determinism of orthodox Marxism, critical theorists who cross disciplines have rather emphasized the superstructure or cultural aspects of production/consumption and indeed have challenged the very division of society into producers and consumers. See A. Fuat Firat and Nikhilesh Dholakia, *Consuming People: From Political Economy to Theatres of Consumption* (New York: Routledge, 1998).

15. Firat and Dholakia, *Consuming People*, 77.

16. Key cultural theorist Stuart Hall, a British scholar of Jamaican descent who experienced this kind of cultural imperialism firsthand, suggests there is a more complex process of meaning-making that we as consumers engage in. We might accept the preferred meaning of the message maker, evolve a negotiated meaning that accepts some aspects of the preferred meaning but on our own different terms, or construct an oppositional meaning

born out of a critique of the ideology underlying the corporate message. Stuart Hall, "Encoding, Decoding," in *The Cultural Studies Reader*, ed. Simon During (New York: Routledge, 1993), 90–103.

17. Kincheloe, *The Sign of the Burger*, 213.

18. The appearance of the Arch Deluxe was actually an important development for the Tomasita story and research process. The inclusion of tomatoes signaled a change in marketing strategy on the part of McDonald's, and subsequent advertisements continued to stress the "grown-up" tastes the company was adding to its menu, reflecting attempts to move beyond if not to actually shed its predominant image as a mecca only for kids. The Arch Deluxe, however, was a flop, and the CEO responsible for the debacle stepped down in May 1999 (http://www.washingtonpost.com/wp-srv/business/longterm/post200/99/toptown.htm). With six hundred calories, it was charged with contributing to heart disease and stroke (http://www.espinet.org/new/archd.html). Critics, inducting the Arch Deluxe into the 2001 Hall of Shame, concluded, "Perhaps McDonald's should have stuck with Ray Kroc's edict never to offer a sandwich with a tomato" (http://www.counterintuitivemarketing.com/hallshame.html).

19. "Big Mac in the Hospital Ward," *Globe and Mail*, 29 March 1980.

20. McDonald's had already set up shop in Nicaragua in the 1970s, invited by the dictator Anastasio Somoza, who as a former U.S. used car salesman was a major promoter of all things American. The company was expelled with the Sandinista revolution in 1979, precisely because it symbolized U.S. hegemony.

21. Personal communication with Eduardo Baez, Managua, July 1999.

22. http://www.mcdonalds.ca/en/aboutus/mcdCanada_facts.aspx.

23. Reiter, *Making Fast Food*, 59

24. Greenberg, *Annual Report*, 13.

25. In early 2007, McDonald's mobilized a coalition (including British MPs) to push to change the dictionary definition of a McJob as "an unstimulating, low-paid job with few prospects," replacing it with a definition that would acknowledge that service work is "stimulating, rewarding and offers genuine opportunities for career progression and skills that last a lifetime." Rebecca Smithers, "McDonald's Not Lovin' 'McJob' Definition," *Globe and Mail*, 25 May 2007, L4.

26. Ritzer, *McDonaldization of Society*, 203.

27. Ibid., 35.

28. Arthur Kroker, Marilouise Kroker, and David Cook, *Panic Encyclopedia: The Definitive Guide to the Postmodern Scene* (New York: St. Martin's Press, 1989), 119, quoted in Ritzer, *McDonaldization of Society*, 38.

29. In 1999, McDonald's installed a new Made for You food preparation system in all of its U.S. and Canadian restaurants that promised to "serve fresher, better-tasting food at the speed of McDonald's," as well as to "accommodate an expanded menu." *McDonald's Corporation 1999 Annual Report*, 12.

30. Group interview with the author and Karen Serwonka, 16 February 1998, York University, Toronto.

31. Post-Fordism refers to the work restructuring begun in the 1970s and 1980s that, according to Ritzer (150–52), emphasizes customized products, shorter production runs, new technologies and more flexible systems, and workers with multiskills and multitasks, in contrast to Fordist practices, which emphasized mass production of homogeneous products, inflexible technologies such as the assembly line, standardized work routines (Taylorism), economies of scale, and the homogenization of consumption patterns. I tend to agree with Ritzer that McDonald's operation exhibits a combination of both Fordist and post-Fordist practices, yet all geared toward efficiency.

32. Group interview with the author and Karen Serwonka, 16 February 1998, York University, Toronto.

33. Vandana Shiva, *Monocultures of the Mind: Perspectives on Biodiversity and Biotechnology* (Atlantic Highlands, N.J.: Zed, 1993).

34. Group interview, 16 February 1998, Toronto.

35. Interview with author and Ann Eyerman, 24 January 1997, Toronto.

36. Ritzer, *The McDonaldization of Society*.

37. A manager of a Kentucky-based fast-food chain, Druthers, quoted in *Fast Food Women*, a documentary film by Anne Lewis, Appalshop Productions, Whitesburg, Tennessee, 1994.

38. Interview with author and Ann Eyerman, 7 February 1997, Toronto.

39. Joe Kincheloe, *The Sign of the Burger*, 198–199.

40. Group interview with author, 16 February 1998, Toronto.

41. Interview with author, 24 January 1997, Toronto.

42. These corporate links are memorialized on a recent McDonald's cup that traces the development of the company around the cup, highlighting deals with both Coca-Cola and with Disney as key historical moments.

43. There were reports of parents dumping the meals after securing the free toys. Joe Kincheloe, *The Sign of the Burger*, 136.

44. Interview with author and Ann Eyerman, 24 January, 1997, Toronto.

45. By the 1990s, half of the teenagers in school were also in the labor force. For some, it is less a matter of survival than a desire/need to be able to afford the increasingly expensive forms of recreation and entertainment aimed at youth culture. Reiter, *Making Fast Food*, 17. A CBC news program on 22 May 2007 reported that high school students were working up to fifty hours a week.

46. Interview with author and Karen Serwonka, 16 February 1998, Toronto.

47. Interview with author and Ann Eyerman, 7 February 1997, Toronto.

48. http://www.mcdonalds.com/corp/values/people/diversity.html.

49. Group interview with author and Karen Serwonka, 16 February 1998, Toronto.

50. Christian Huot, "Unionizing the Impossible," *Canadian Dimension* (September–October 1998): 24.

51. Ibid., 26.

52. *McDonald's Corporation 1999 Annual Report*, 4.

53. Interview with Ann Eyerman, 24 September 1996, Toronto.

54. Group interview with author and Karen Serwonka, 16 February 1998, Toronto.

55. Interview with author and Ann Eyerman, February 1997.

56. Group interview with author and Karen Serwonka, 16 February 1998, Toronto.

57. *McDonald's Corporation 1999 Annual Report*, 6.

58. Carol Stack and Ellen Stein carried out a three-year comparative study of fast-food workers and job seekers in Oakland, California, and Harlem, New York.

59. This is similar to a phenomenon observed by Antonieta Barrón in her surveys of Mexican migrant labor; whereas women and children were previously predominant among field-workers, with more unemployment in other areas and a surplus of labor supply over demand, both men and the heartiest young women are now given priority, while older and younger workers drop off the list.

60. Carol Stack, "Job Creation, Workers' Rights and the Challenge of Welfare Reform," testimony presented to the Senate Committee on Industrial Relations on Working in California, 10.

61. Ibid., 11.

62. Interview with author and Ann Eyerman, 7 February 1997, Toronto.

63. Interview with author and Ann Eyerman, 24 February 1997, Toronto.

64. Interview with author and Karen Serwonka, 16 February 1998, Toronto.

65. Interview with Ann Eyerman, 24 September 1996.

66. Interview with Ann Eyerman, 24 September 1996.

67. Joyce Nelson, "The Culture of Agriculture," in *Road Kill/Sign Kill: From Landscape to Mediascape* (Toronto: Between the Lines, 1992), 218–29.

68. The study also showed that in regions of Ontario with twenty or more fast-food restaurants, mortality increased by 62 per 100,000 and hospitalizations for heart attacks 47 per 100,000. Andre Picard, "Live Near These and They'll Get You," *Globe and Mail*, 12 May 2005, A19.

69. "Did Childhood-Obesity Worries Kill Disney-McDonald's Pact?" http://abcnews.go.com/Business/sotry?id_1937651&page=1, accessed 8 May 2007.

70. "McDonald's Targeted in Obesity Lawsuit," *BBC News World Edition*, 22 November 2002, http://news.bbc.co.uk/2/hi/americas/2502431.stm, accessed 25 April 2007.

71. Megan Oglivie, "Special Delivery," *Toronto Star*, 9 September 2005, D1.

72. www.mcdonalds.com, accessed 08 May 2007.

73. Kincheloe, *The Sign of the Burger*, 4, 35.

74. Ester Reiter, "Serving the McCustomer: Fast Food Is Not about Food," in *Women Working the NAFTA Food Chain: Women Food and Globalization*, ed. Deborah Barndt (Toronto: Second Story, 1999), 90–91.

75. Madelaine Dronan, "Burger Chain Wins McLibel Suit," *Globe and Mail*, 20 June 1997, 1, 13.

76. Culture Jammers Campaign Headquarters, www.adbusters.org.

77. This particular tray liner mimicked the brilliant scientific and artistic drawings of Leonardo da Vinci; a new "bigger burger" was sketched beside the older smaller one within a gilded frame, exuding the aura of European classical art. The ad itself is a wonderful example of popular culture appropriating high culture.

78. Candace Sherk Savage, *Eat Up! Healthy Food for a Healthy Earth* (Toronto: Douglas & McIntyre, 1992).

79. We chose Burger King because at that time the Whopper included tomatoes, while the Big Mac of McDonald's did not. It was only in 1997 that McDonald's launched the Arch Deluxe, complete with tomatoes.

80. The Disney toys that were given away with Happy Meals, for example, were produced by seventeen-year-old Vietnamese girls who earned $4.25 per week for a seventy-hour week; in 1997, two hundred of them became ill from the toxic chemicals used in production. Joe Kincheloe, *The Sign of the Burger*, 67.

81. Scott Simmie, "Reality of Fast Food Industry Dished Out to Kids in New Book," *Toronto Star*, 10 April 2006, A17.

82. Caroline Alphonso, "Nutritious Fare Is Tough Sell in Schools," *Globe and Mail*, 20 January 2007.

83. http://aci.on.ca/~saublent/school/ipcdecision/ipcdecision.html, accessed 2 May 2007.

84. Canadian Press, "B.C. Students Demand Healthy Food Choices," *Globe and Mail*, 18 October 2006.

85. Personal communication between Amanda Montgomery and Laurie Nikkel, Student Nutrition Coordinator, Foodshare; 7 May 2007.

86. Editorial, *Globe and Mail*, 30 September 2005, A22.

CHAPTER 4

You Can Count on Us:

SCANNING CASHIERS AT LOBLAWS SUPERMARKETS

A Personal Link to My Local Supermarket

When I first met Marissa, I was amazed to learn that she had been working for twenty-five years as a part-time cashier in my neighborhood supermarket. As was the case for other women, the part-time work had initially suited her, when she was married and had small children. It had supported her since high school and through college, where she studied anthropology. But when she separated and then divorced, she was left as a single mother with a job that was too good to leave: she had high seniority, was at the top of the wage scale, and enjoyed good benefits; the flexibility she had earned allowed her to be home for her children on some weekdays. But there were costs, too: long commutes, a changing labor force that deskilled and devalued part-time cashiers, and pressures to work fast that left her numb (and hungry) at the end of an eight-hour shift.

It was no wonder that when I visited Marissa on her days off, she drew upon the anthropological studies of her student days, but this time she became her own subject. Digging into a collection accrued over decades, she unearthed for me the artifacts of her cashier career—uniforms, buttons, name tags, bags, and books. They not only told the story of her work life but were rich treasures of the history of work in the service sector, holding clues to changes in technology, in food, in management style.

I identified with Marissa, not only because I am a relentless collector of artifacts but also because as a single mother, I found myself making difficult choices about my work, struggling daily to juggle the chores of my paid work at university with the chores of my unpaid work at home. In a society that doesn't provide adequate child care, whose workplaces don't take into account the schedules of parents, where even extended family support is rare, I felt destined to feel inadequate in either my profession or my parenting, and most often in both.

When I arrived one day to find that Marissa had created a detailed outline of all her unnamed tasks as a single mother over a month, I found that her careful and reflexive research on her life, produced for my research, helped me reflect on my own life. Together we could acknowledge and revalue the unpaid and unrecognized work of parenting. The endless list of thankless tasks also made a poignant point for the need for some of the food options offered by supermarkets like Loblaws where Marissa works. She helped me understand myself better as both a worker and a consumer.

Globalization from Above: "Food Means the World to Loblaws"

> In the 1990s, the focus is on the rationalization of our business to win in a globally competitive market. We are now investing in areas where we not only can compete on a North American basis but where we can be globally competitive.
>
> —Galen Weston, chairman's letter (1994)

A billboard campaign launched by Loblaws supermarkets[1] in the mid-1990s, bearing the slogan "Food Means the World to Us," reflected the company's global vision at multiple levels. A lone figure (unisex), clothed in Arabic robes, pushes a shopping cart across a highly stylized and very barren desert.[2] The cart is empty but our imaginations can easily fill it—with Mexican tomatoes and President's Choice salsa, for example. Not only does the commercial food sector depend on moving into international markets for its survival in a globalized era, but it draws its culinary products from all corners of this shrinking planet. Supermarkets are a major destination for the corporate tomato.[3]

Like McDonald's, the story of Loblaws reveals the increasingly consumer-driven end of the tomato food chain, as well as the growing control of all food production by the retail sector. The billboard reflects three trends critical to Loblaws'

success as the largest and most profitable food retailer in Canada: the development of corporate products or "private labels" (e.g., President's Choice) to compete with brand-name labels, the marketing of ideas and images through brands, and the promotion of both to an increasingly multicultural and cosmopolitan Canadian population as well as to a growing elite of consumers in the south.[4]

In many ways, the history of Loblaws and its parent company, George Weston Ltd., covering more than a hundred years, offers insight into the evolution of the global food system, reflecting a system now controlled by large conglomerates (built on diversification, vertical and horizontal integration), by restructured workplaces (high-tech, just-in-time production, and part-time labor practices), and by marketing an image and lifestyle as much as food (through seductive store designs, product development, environmental practices, and community service). All of these features of the new global economy are illustrated in the coming pages, with a special focus on the part-time and technologized work of women cashiers.

BREAD RISING: A CENTURY OF EXPANSIONS

In contrast with some contemporary food giants,[5] George Weston Ltd. always had an interest in food, not just the *business* of making and selling it. Beginning as a baker's apprentice, Weston purchased two bread routes in 1882 and opened a model bakery in Toronto in 1897.[6] Incorporated in the 1920s, the company survived the depression by producing large volumes and selling at low cost; during and after World War II, Garfield Weston, the founder's son, began expanding by purchasing U.S. bakers and acquiring a food distribution operation.

Loblaw Grocertaria was founded in 1919 by J. Milton Cork and Theodore Pringle Loblaw, introducing the self-serve,[7] cash-and-carry concept into the Toronto grocery trade. It grew steadily through the 1920s and 1930s, pioneering self-serve practices and introducing private-label products. Around the same time (1925), National Grocers Co. Ltd. was formed from a merger of thirty-four food wholesalers in Ontario and opened the first wholesale cash-and-carry.

The 1950s was an era of expansion and major restructuring, as companies merged, stores moved to the suburbs, and many workers lost their jobs.[8] George Weston Ltd. purchased controlling interest in both Loblaw Grocertaria and National Grocers, becoming one of the first food conglomerates by integrating both retail and wholesale distribution with its food processing companies. In 1956, Weston created Loblaw Companies Ltd. as a holding company to operate all these supermarket interests, which included other retail chains and three wholesalers in eastern and western Canada, as well as the United States. In the 1960s, Weston added British Columbia fish-processing companies and an Ontario-based paper industry to its holdings, reflecting the diversification strategy of many capitalist enterprises.

The postwar period began the internationalized agroindustrial food era. Considered the fourth stage of the food economy,[9] it has been characterized by increasing corporate concentration and diversification, multinationalization of capital, the central role of mass market advertising, product differentiation and proliferation, integration of farming and agribusiness, and the emergence of food retail chains as the leading players in the food system.[10] The 1980s were characterized by ever-more aggressive corporate takeovers, in which the choice was now "eat or be eaten," and for more and more food companies the goal was to achieve such size as to be indigestible.[11] Both Loblaws and its parent company, Weston, followed this trend through the last half of the twentieth century by strategically buying up companies to diversify and consolidate holdings and, again strategically, selling off companies that were not profitable.

Annual reports of the late 1990s reflect the strategies of diversification and vertical and horizontal integration. Weston's investments in forest products, for example, reflected the strategy of *diversification*. Its involvement in both food processing and distribution represents *vertical integration* (controlling several stages in the production/consumption chain). Finally, its control of various supermarket chains (including corporate, franchised, and independent grocers) epitomizes *horizontal integration* (covering diverse target markets by owning competing companies in the grocery business).

By 1998, however, Weston reported a significant strategic realignment that involved selling off its E. B. Eddy forestry investments as well as most fish processing and consolidating the company's interests into only two divisions: Weston Food Processing and Food Distribution. Clearly the most significant growth has been through distribution, incorporated as Loblaw Companies Ltd.: the total number of Canadian stores owned (by the eighteen affiliated chains) was 9,402 in 2005.[12] Expanding its control across Canada, Loblaw bought out Quebec's biggest grocery store chain, Provigo (30 percent owned by Caisse de dépôt et placement du Québec, a provincial pension fund)[13] as well as the Atlantic division of Agora Food Merchants.

Loblaw Companies Ltd.'s merger and acquisition activity echoes other recent blockbuster mergers among top food chains in Europe and North America.[14] In fact, it fits perfectly the argument of the Business Council on National Issues (BCNI) that "companies have to be big to compete."[15] The level of corporate concentration in the Canadian food retail sector, however, has been considerably higher than in the United States: the top ten U.S. chains have less than 50 percent of the grocery market share, while in Canada, only four chains control 70 percent of the market. Loblaw Companies Ltd. is clearly the dominant power, with over 35 percent of the market, with the next three competitors holding a much smaller percentage (Sobeys—18.3 percent, Metro/A&P—15 percent, and Wal-Mart—3.4 percent). Its 2005 sales were over $27 billion.[16]

Strategically, George Weston Ltd. has structured itself to remain dominant in food retail, with three key characteristics: (1) geographic diversity, spanning regions of Canada, (2) integration of wholesaling and retailing, and (3) control of a range of store formats and ownership arrangements.[17] The latter is critical in the case of Loblaw: it can pay lower wages to workers in its franchised discount stores (No Frills, Valu-Mart), while paying higher wages to its corporate stores that serve a high-end market.

Whatever the impetus, the trend is toward ever-greater corporate concentration in the food sector. Canadian agrifood analyst Anthony Winson denounces the impacts of this excessive market power in the hands of a few firms. As retail conglomerates like Loblaw Companies Ltd. control food production, they have squeezed out small farms,[18] small processors, and small grocery stores and chains, contributing to the demise of the family farm and rural communities.[19] The excessive expenditures on marketing (packaging, store design, and advertising) waste scarce resources and are ultimately paid for by consumers through ever-increasing prices.

With the food sector as the most profitable of all Canadian retail operations, its restructuring in the 1990s was part of a broader process of corporate concentration that has deepened structural inequalities, increased the gap between the rich and poor and, paradoxically, precipitated a hunger crisis. Loblaw Companies Ltd.'s corporate strategies pretended to solve the problem that they, in fact, helped create, by offering cheaper prices in its own large discount stores (horizontal integration) and contributing its surplus to burgeoning food banks (community service). It was all part of a company plan to cover a diversity of niche markets, while maintaining an image as good corporate citizens.

A WINNING RECIPE: DESIGNER SUPERMARKETS FOR DESIGNED TOMATOES

> Operating a portfolio of banners and store formats across Canada, Loblaw seeks to grow its market share on a market-by-market basis and to satisfy its customers' everyday household needs.
>
> —Loblaw Companies Limited 2005 Annual Summary[20]

The purchase of Maple Leaf Gardens by Loblaws in 2003 epitomized the iconic status the supermarket chain has gained over the last thirty years; the massive arena in the heart of downtown Toronto that was home for sixty years to Canadian hockey teams is full of popular cultural significance, a veritable temple of the sports world. Now it will become a temple of consumerism as Loblaws applies its blueprint of gigantic, elegant, and multipurpose supercenters, transforming the Gardens into a "shopping emporium, boasting everything from pharmacies to fitness centers to furniture and financial services."[21] Key ingredients of Loblaws supermarkets' winning recipe for becoming Canada's leading food retailer included designer supermarkets, private-label development, the greening of the food industry, and community service. These strategies were cooked up in the 1970s and 1980s, after Galen Weston hired his old college roommate, Dave Nichol, and Nichol's colleague, Richard Currie (president of both George Weston Ltd. and Loblaw Companies Ltd. until 2002), to help turn around the retail business that was near insolvency. In 1984, Nichol was named to head a new unit, Loblaw International Merchants, through which he revolutionized the supermarket industry, aided by the magic touch of designer Donald Watt.

The corporate tomato, whose twenty-one-step journey we traced in chapter 1, ultimately ends up on display in a highly constructed marketlike produce section of Loblaws, ironically under the banner "Fresh from the Fields." Moving the produce from the back to the front of the store was just one of the ideas that the Watt Design Group adopted in the 1970s when it gave the supermarket not just a facelift but a total makeover.[22] Its new grocery retailing concept, "Lifestyle Retail Environment," included expanding the store space, redesigning the layout into zones, creating a mix of merchandise, and a communications strategy complete with a new logo, internal signage, and lots of yellow.

Large photographs of fresh fruit and vegetables,[23] in Loblaws' own words, "reinforced the perceptions of product freshness and quality."[24] According to Don Watt's philosophy, perception is reality.[25]

Since the 1970s, this design strategy has been elevated to cult status. Journalists have followed the openings of the latest elegant Loblaws superstores in downtown Toronto, competing for ironic hyperbole about the "fantasy" experience of shopping at Loblaws, with headlines about "spiritual supermarkets" "engineering a chamber of temptations."[26] One arts reporter analyzed the broader trend spearheaded by Loblaws: "The Canadian supermarket has been transformed in recent years from a drab warehouse into a carefully engineered persuasion machine, from a pedestrian chore into one of our society's great brainwashing experiences. Once you went to buy food; today you get sold a whole culinary ideology."[27]

When it comes to selling tomatoes, part of the strategy is to re-create the feeling of a village market, drawing on our longing for a nostalgic past when we actually knew where our food came from and felt confident about its safety. Designer Watt admits that this strategy is "to win back consumers who have been turned off by the frigid homogeneity of the big corporate supermarket, by creating a 'neighborhood' within the supermarket itself, a simulacrum[28] of the very merchants who had provided competition."[29] This illusion of the farmers' market is perhaps most poignant in the Queen's Quay superstore along the Toronto lakeshore in Toronto, not coincidentally located just two blocks south of the St. Lawrence Market, a

gathering place for local farmers, which has been forced to expand its hours and activities in response to competition from its giant new neighbor.

The simulated market design has also been applied in efforts to spruce up old stores. According to cashiers in my neighborhood store, "they tried to create that kind of feeling by putting umbrellas up and displaying things on wagons. It's brighter, more open, more products. It's the presentation." It is no coincidence that the profit is made from the carefully stacked produce under colorful umbrellas, and not in the more bland and sterile aisles of less costly bags and bottles, cans and cartons. Yet the illusion of the market is revealed through the constant spray of water that keeps vegetables "appearing" fresh as well as the air-conditioned stores that sever the produce "from the heat of labor and the heat of the (real) marketplace."[30]

The new superstores actually fall more accurately into what Watt associates call "eatertainment" and contribute to Loblaws' goal to provide "innovative shopping experiences."[31] One has a balcony surrounding its produce section, complete with café, art gallery, a stage for jazz musicians and storytellers, and space for cooking classes. In an even more upscale store, the café is built around an artificial tree on the second floor, while customers gaze out the window at the real thing. Such simulation of nature is consistent with the production and sale of "hyperreal" tomatoes whose origins are obscured and whose "appearance" is everything.

According to Donald Watt, the philosophy is: "If you can heighten the experience for the buyer, you'll keep them there and they'll buy more."[32] Another way Loblaws has kept its customers buying is by expanding its merchandise and service through corporate partnerships.[33] Standard fare now includes PhotoLab, DRUGStore, and Movenpick Marche inside the store, and close by an LCBO, PrintPost, Bell Mobility, the Dry Cleaner, and its very own PC Financial services (with CIBC).[34] Recently moving into clothing, the grocery giant now has its own fashion line, "Joe Fresh Style," a partnership with designer Joe Mimran of the Club Monaco, Caban, and Holt Renfrew labels.

SALSA PICANTE: PRIVATE LABELS AND IMAGE COLONIALISM

The other key strategy that turned Loblaws around in the 1980s was Dave Nichol's product development, variously called "private labels" or "corporate" or "retailers" brands. He first launched No Name brands in the late 1970s, generic products in bold yellow packaging with plain type, to communicate the notion that an item was produced and sold at the lowest price possible; the success of this approach resulted soon in the "no frills" supermarket, aimed at a lower-income clientele. The high-end consumers in Loblaws, however, were the target of a line of premium products under the label "President's Choice." Designed to compete with the big brands (e.g., Coke, Tide, etc.), these in-house brands promised to be better than the national brands at the same price or to be unique in the marketplace.

It is hard to separate this successful strategy from the persona of Dave Nichol himself, whose passion for food and travel, as well as his personal prej-

udices, largely shaped the development of his President's Choice[35] brand, its now-famous PC logo scribbled by his hand. Pure business motivations, however, thrust Nichol and Loblaws into full battle with the national brands (Kraft, General Foods, Nabisco, Coca-Cola) that had dominated the supermarket industry for almost a century. The strategy was to sell national brands at cost while using private labels to generate profits; Loblaws could produce its own premium brands at value pricing with higher margins.

The phenomenal success of in-house brands, nurtured first by Nichol at Loblaws, caused a veritable food retail revolution, contributing to the growing dominance of the retail sector.[36] Before supermarkets made money by selling the best shelf space to the low-cost national brands; now store brands get eye-level shelves and account for a quarter of supermarket sales in Canada.[37] George Weston Ltd. offers centralized distribution through National Grocers to its many affiliated supermarkets. Sales are also strong in the United States, and PC sauces now compete with maple syrup as a favorite carry-on export sold at the Toronto international airport.

Advertising (often featuring celebrities) was a major cost for the big national brands, what Nichol called the "brand tax" (ultimately paid by consumers), so Loblaws' strategy was to focus on less costly in-house promotion, through special campaigns and publications such as the popular *Insider's Report*.[38] Design was again an important part of the formula, proving Marshall McLuhan's notion that "the medium is the message." The Package became the overriding principle.[39]

This manipulation of perception is epitomized by the highly successful line (with over 36 percent profit margin) of "Memories of . . . (Szechuan, Kobe, etc.)" sauces, which brought Loblaws fully into the "ethnic market." Though Nichol claimed to have "discovered" the recipes during his travels, most were bought and developed in Canada. Many of the sauces are, in fact, produced in southern Ontario by E. D. Smith & Sons Ltd., a company that for more than a century grew and processed tomatoes. With free trade threatening in the late 1980s, the company downsized, subcontracted processing, and bought tomato paste from California and Chile, focusing instead on the more profitable value-added products (pasta sauces, e.g., rather than stewed tomatoes). Smith was so successful in taking on the production of Loblaws' private-label house brands that the company has since been contracted by Loblaws' competition to produce their own retailer-controlled brands.

Now, not only have Mexico and its salsa become sexy, but exotic images of almost any foreign place (if not actual recipes or production processes) have be-come important visual elements of Loblaws' distinct image, suggested by the "Food Means the World to Us" billboard. One of Nichol's favorite photographs, of a Muslim woman peering through a veil, was found in a fashion magazine and purchased for use on two different products, the Mem-ories of Marrakech couscous box and Mem-ories of Ancient Damascus pomegranate sauce, a sauce found far from ancient Dam-ascus, in Seattle, Washington. Women have long been prey to advertisers' attempts to seduce consumers to buy, but the recent ubiquitous appropriation of non-Western peoples has brought charges of "image colonialism," or media construction of the "exotic other."[40] Cultural critics suggest that "we consume less the product than its im-age, less the contents than the advertising on the bottle or box, revealing more about ourselves than any 'other' culture, more about mass delirium than fond memories."[41]

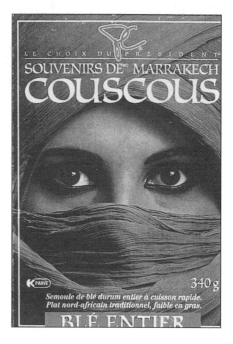

GREEN OR GREED? MARKETING THE ENVIRONMENT

> No, I am not [an environmentalist], I'm a person who brings people products they want. The reason I do that is because I want them to switch to our supermarkets.
>
> —Dave Nichol, on CBC's *The Journal*, 1989

The promotion of PC products reached a new and complex level of strategy in the late 1980s when Loblaws decided to launch its GREEN line of environmen-tally friendly products. A convergence of factors gave rise to the idea. Canadians had named the environment the number one public issue, and corporate retail-ers were being pressured by government to adhere to environmental require-ments. Nichol was discovering a burgeoning and profitable environmental mar-ket in Europe. Finally, Patrick Carson, hired by Loblaws to develop waste management procedures, proved a charismatic spokesperson for corporate re-sponsibility in the environmental crisis.[42] Into the 1990s, Loblaws created more than one thousand products, fulfilling Nichol's dream of "owning GREEN" as a winning hook for a growing consumer activist movement, offering shoppers a way to assuage their guilt and take individual action around a crisis that felt overwhelming and depressing.

The strategy paid off, at least initially. Sales of the first one hundred GREEN products went far beyond projections, but the real value was in the free advertising resulting from a carefully constructed media strategy. Surveys in the first year showed that 87 percent of Canadians were aware of the line, and *New York Times* coverage spread the word as far as China, producing an estimated publicity value of $100 million. Nichol cleverly used television as well as his *Insider's Report* to warn of "a green wave that's going to come crashing down on those retailers and manufacturers who have not 'greened' their company and their product lines."[43]

Ultimately, Loblaws' leadership (read: comparative advantage) in developing and promoting green products did have an impact on the industry, with competing companies rushing to follow suit. But there were other costs involved. A strategy that Patrick Carson had proposed, to involve environmental groups in building a green consumer movement, ran into major snags. Pollution Probe, an activist group Loblaws paid $150,000 to help develop and endorse the first eight products, almost collapsed amid internal tensions around the questionable deal. Greenpeace and Friends of the Earth, two other environmental groups who had been consulted, eventually publicly challenged the content of the disposable diapers and organic fertilizer.

This attempt at building a business–activist alliance ran head-on into a basic contradiction: environmentalists saw consumerism itself as a key source of environmental problems; buying green products did not necessarily solve them. Similar contradictions were revealed in the 1990s when the Ontario Public Interest Research Group (OPIRG) and the Sierra Club challenged George Weston Ltd. on promoting Loblaws as an environmental champion, while cutting down old-growth forests in Temagami through its affiliate E. B. Eddy. In the late 1990s, Loblaws' Environmental Affairs office was mediating such public relations conflicts, speaking to school classes about the sustainable practices of forestry companies or defending the safety of genetically modified foods.

Operationally, there have been advances. The company has an innovative waste management system, involving grinders behind the stores and underground storage tanks that hold composting tomatoes, for example, until they can be siphoned out and transported to lagoons, where they become a source of organic fertilizer.[44] Loblaws has also led the industry in monitoring fuel emissions of its trucks[45] and in instituting environmental management systems in each store, monitored by environmental coordinators who are part of the joint union–management Safety and Environment Committee. The greening program has reportedly cost about $2 million, but the company is also saving money by adopting more energy-efficient practices and by recycling wastes.[46] Part of the responsibility has been shifted to customers, who are offered a three-cent rebate if they bring their own bags or purchase from Loblaws a permanent "smart box" for carrying their groceries.

Weston's statement of environmental principles advocates the "three-legged stool" approach: balancing the economic, social, and environmental aspects of

the business. An Environmental Affairs staff member summarizes the company's position: "Our business is not saving the environment, our business is selling groceries. Doing it, minimizing our impact, and making as much of a difference as we can. But we can't put ourselves out of business to save the environment, 'cause then we won't be able to do anything."[47]

It's interesting to note that the early GREEN line products were nonfood items, responding to concerns about chemical pollutants (such as PCBs) that could contribute to the depletion of the ozone layer. More internal environmental concerns related to food and health were not predominant,[48] perhaps because they would force the company to consider ethical issues related to agricultural production in the south. Even as companies like Loblaws are now being confronted publicly about these issues, they offer a classic defense: "As far as marginalizing people, be it in Mexico or Costa Rica, the banana fields there, whatever it might be, [it's a] very complicated issue. It's very difficult for any organization to be the police, the conscience," suggests the Environmental Affairs officer. Companies would prefer that such issues remain out of sight and out of mind.

CAPITALIZING ON FEAR: THE BURGEONING ORGANIC MARKET

By 2007, however, environmental issues had returned to the top of the public's concerns, especially due to dramatic climate change that gave people a direct visceral experience of the impact of human activity on the planet. And more links were being made between environment and health, with a growing public consciousness about the health risks endemic to the global food system, in which consumers have little sense of what has gone into the production of what they eat. Mad-cow disease panics, the looming specter of avian flu, and increasing questions about the long-term health effects of pesticide-coated fruit and vegetables have all exposed the dangers of a globalized industrial and chemical agriculture that eschews borders and makes it difficult to trace the origins of contaminated food. These food scares, among other things, have fueled consumer demand for organic produce, and Loblaws was one of the first food retail giants to tap into this growing niche market. In 2001, it opened its special organic sections with great fanfare, and by 2004, it carried three hundred organic products under its new Blue Menu line, all bearing the President's Choice brand.

Loblaws has taken the demand for healthier food seriously, reflected in its publication *President's Choice Healthy Insider's Report*, which promotes the Blue Menu products while educating consumers about the nutritional value of superfoods such as tomatoes.[49] But despite a growing concern about obesity, targeting junk food diets as a culprit and predicting that 10 percent of Ontario's adults will suffer from diabetes by 2010,[50] high-sugar, high-fat products still take up as much as 30 percent of Loblaws' shelf space, are on display around every corner as well as at the checkout,[51] and get the highest returns as the most lucrative products in the supermarket.[52] When Canadian sociologist Anthony Winson proposed a tax on low-nutrition food products that could be used to promote healthy eating, Nick Jennery, president of the Canadian Council of Grocery Distributors, defended the junk-food promotions, saying, "We're in the business of giving consumers choice . . . not in the health-regulation business."[53]

Economic motives are a major driving force behind the new organic face of the company. Organic food products remain more expensive, costing up to 20 percent more than nonorganics, but consumers in high-end stores (baby boomers and young urban professionals) are willing to pay more for the peace of mind. "What was once the marginal preserves of hippies and tofu-munching zealots has become the fastest-growing and most lucrative sector of the food industry," announced the business pages of Montreal's *Gazette*, and *Canadian Grocer* magazine predicted that, based on an average annual growth of about 20 percent, the organic agrifood market could command as much as 10 percent of the Canadian retail market by 2010.[54] This reflects a worldwide trend as Agriculture Canada reported in 2003 that organics had grown from a small-scale niche market into a $23 billion global business.[55]

The entry into the organic market by large retailers like Loblaws has threatened small organic farmers and independent producers who cannot produce large quantities, move them through massive distribution networks, or offer lower prices because of the economies of scale. Loblaws deals with large-scale organic growers, such as the Quebec-based Les Producteurs Biologiques Symbiosis, which weekly sells four thousand kilograms of tomatoes alone to Loblaws stores in Ontario and Quebec.[56] The organic market becomes another site of competition with foreign markets (such as the United States, Japan, and Europe); U.S. retailers such as Texas-based Whole Foods have aggressively set up shop in Canada, for example.

LOOMING APOCALYPSE? THE WALMARTIZATION OF FOOD RETAIL

> The globalization of food industries and the expansion of su-
> permarkets present both an opportunity to reach lucrative new
> markets—and a substantial risk of increased marginalization
> and even deeper poverty.
>
> —Food and Agriculture Organization, 2004[57]

> Loblaws basically wants to compete with Wal-Mart. It's the big
> Wal-Mart scare. I think they hide behind that curtain a lot. They
> use it as an excuse.
>
> —Loblaws employee, 2007[58]

Global competition within a climate of increasing corporate concentration[59] is clearly the terrain on which Canadian food retailers like Loblaws must operate, and since the early 1990s, neoliberal trade policies have opened the doors to competing foreign retail outlets. As Angelo DiCaro of the Canadian Auto Workers Union concludes, "Without major Canadian content restrictions on these largely nonunion retailing goliaths, they are able to bring in their global supply chain networks and their low-cost megastore format anywhere they please."[60] Just as McDonald's has become the symbol for economic and cultural hegemony in the fast-food world, Wal-Mart has epitomized this new imperialism among retailers.[61] Since the mid-1990s, Loblaws has consciously shaped its strategies defensively,[62] in preparation for Wal-Mart's invasion of the Great White North, and by 2006, the apocalyptic predictions were starting to materialize. The Bentonville, Arkansas–based company, which first opened in 1962 selling dry goods in rural communities at discount prices in warehouse-style stores, entered Canada in 1994 when it bought out Woolco's department store chain. By 2006, it owned more than 50 percent of the market for general merchandise in Canada, with an estimated $13 billion a year in sales.[63]

Wal-Mart only added the grocery business to its U.S. supercenters in the mid-1990s, and now controls 35 percent of the American grocery market, ranking as the top global food retailer by 2004.[64] The giant initially appeared hesitant to bring its food sales to Canada, citing strong retail competition with private label programs and tremendous perishables; as recently as 2003, a company spokesman insisted there were no plans to open its supercenters with a stronger food presentation north of the border. That year, Wal-Mart did, however, open four Sam's Club warehouses, which carry fresh food and which many saw as a precursor to the arrival of the supercenters, signaling a coming "food-industry apocalypse."[65] By the fall of 2006, as feared, the first three supercenters opened in Ontario, with a prediction that there would be fifteen established by 2007, and thirty per year after that, controlling $6.2 billion in grocery sales by 2010.[66]

What is the Wal-Mart model that threatens Loblaws? It has developed an immense and strong supply chain, taking full advantage of neoliberal trade

policies and a cheaper global labor force; Wal-Mart ranks as China's eighth largest trading partner and is the largest importer of Chinese-made products in the world.[67] With massive economies of scale and cheap imports, the company can undercut competitors' prices. The other critical cost-cutting feature, of course, is bargain-basement wages, which are generally 30 percent lower than those at unionized supermarkets, and on average, less than the U.S. federal poverty level.[68] As a nonunionized company, Wal-Mart has also been charged with hiring illegal immigrants[69] and fostering an anti-woman culture in the United States, and with perpetrating sweatshop conditions in its overseas supplier factories.[70] It has vehemently fought efforts by the UFCW to organize workers, closing shop after a Quebec-based center successfully unionized. Finally, the supercenters represent the diversification model, providing one-stop shopping to consumers, from clothes to medicines, from hardware to food. And this model is being exported around the world; by 2006, 1.7 million employees served 138 million people[71] in 6,380 stores in 16 countries (from Argentina to Qatar), garnering sales of $312.4 billion.[72]

Wal-Mart has also led the way in high-tech innovations, including the online grocery business. Following suit, Loblaws made a short foray into that market in 2000, signing a deal with Markham, Ontario–based e-grocer eBox.com to supply grocery, pharmacy, and general merchandise items.[73] It was a short-lived experiment, however, which garnered only 3,500 customers over five years. In 2005, they scrapped the deal, blaming rising oil prices and price-conscious consumers, who "were not willing to spend more to have their groceries delivered to their front door."[74]

COMMUNITY SERVICE: BEING GOOD CORPORATE CITIZENS

> There's a good business reason for taking care of people. If they're suffering, they're not good consumers.
>
> —Dave Williams, former Weston vice president

As the private sector has grown in power and public-supported social services have shrunk in the face of neoliberal policies and globalization, corporations have been increasingly pressured to take on more community service.[75] Through the W. Garfield Weston Foundation, the Weston group supports a variety of nutrition research, education, conservation, and community projects. There is a paradox, however, in the response of big food retailers like Loblaws to a hunger crisis that they have helped create. In 1984 Weston moved its headquarters to its current elegant tower in uptown Toronto, leasing its abandoned warehouse by the lake to the Daily Bread Food Bank.

Since then, food banks have become an integral part of a very unequal food distribution system, rather than merely an emergency measure. Almost 900,000 of the poor in the greater Toronto area used food banks in 2006, representing a 79 percent increase since 1995.[76] There are two other ways that Loblaws is complicit in maintaining this "alternative" food distribution system. For one, National Grocers, the distribution warehouse for all Weston companies, donates wasted produce that is still edible to Second Harvest;[77] an estimated 70 percent of food bank donations are, in fact, the excess of food manufacturers and distributors.[78] A hidden benefit for corporations is that by giving it away, they save on the growing dumping costs.

Community service is critical to the image of the Weston companies as "good corporate citizens"; it's one way to show the community that "we're different from another grocer and we care."[79] Besides feeding the hungry with the unsal-able items, Loblaws also encourages its more privileged shoppers to buy food in the supermarket and donate it to the poor, by depositing it into a box at the door.[80] This approach, which effectively has consumers paying for the company's charitable donations, has raised criticism from social justice groups who protested in front of Loblaws stores in 1999.[81] The company claims that it is do-nating valuable space and labor by assigning employees to organize food drives. Food security organizations, such as FoodShare, suggest cash donations might be the solution, since they allow food bank organizers to purchase healthy food, rather than be stuck with items that people don't really need. Another option is community-run food discount stores, similar to Goodwill, that would provide jobs for people preparing the surplus food for sale.

MANAGEMENT TENSIONS AND LABOR CONCESSIONS

> Labor continues to be the most significant cost component out-side of product costs and remains an area of focus for the busi-ness to ensure cost competitiveness.
>
> —*George Weston Ltd. 1998 Annual Report*

Loblaws has certainly not been immune to the broader process of global eco-nomic restructuring, where new labor strategies are central. In the first years of the new millennium, the battle with Wal-Mart, dubbed the Terminator of Ben-tonville, highlighted that fact, but several interrelated forces have converged to reshape the labor force. The increasing computerization of supermarket work—production, distribution, and sales—has contributed to a total redefinition of work and to growing unemployment in some sectors (such as distribution). Just-in-time production and distribution practices have put new pressures on super-markets to respond to consumer demand by the minute, resulting in the flexibi-lization of labor. New management approaches such as "best practices" have engineered jobs so that every movement and every second are spent maximizing productivity and efficiency. Loblaws' labor strategies are driven by local and global competition and an endless search for greater profits.

The bottom-line mentality is evident in the dollar ratio, or "profit–hour ratio," used for controlling labor costs. The profit–hour ratio is determined by analyzing the "sales per person hour," projecting volume sales, and then assigning stores a precise number of labor hours. These hours are distributed among different departments in a supermarket and divided between full-time and part-time employees. There is tremendous pressure put on department managers to cut labor costs, because the more labor hours a manager can save, the higher the profit level, besides the additional incentive that managers get bonuses based on profit.[82]

Since the early 1990s, Loblaws has been negotiating labor concessions claiming they are necessary to ensure "labor competitiveness." For many, this excuse rings false, given its corporate connections. Controlling eighteen different chains, Weston in a sense owns the competition and can afford a mix of high-end unionized supermarkets and nonunionized independents and franchised stores (the benefits of horizontal integration). In the late 1990s, in fact, it bought up more independents and sold more stores to franchise retailers (often getting former managers to buy them); besides saving on labor costs, it also gets a franchising fee on sales as well as assured buyers for its corporate products such as President's Choice. When Loblaws opened No Frills and Valu-Mart in the 1980s, it got the union to agree to a lower wage structure in exchange for not closing more higher end, higher waged corporate stores.

Loblaws is the only one of the three corporations featured in this book that has a unionized labor force (134,000 employees). George Weston Ltd. has made its position clear, however, to its shareholders that the company "is willing to accept the short-term costs of labor disruption in order to achieve competitive labor costs for the long term which help to ensure sustainable sales and earnings growth."[83] Loblaws' executives argue that labor cost is what most limits the company; 13 to 14 percent of its total operating costs is for labor, compared to 9 to 10 percent for other unionized stores and 7 to 8 percent in nonunion stores.[84]

Management used the argument of a deepening threat of competition from the discount stores during negotiations with the United Food and Commercial Workers (UFCW) in the early and mid-1990s. In 1990, Local 1000A of the United Food and Commercial Workers[85] and Loblaws bargained an hours-based wage increase scale to replace the existing seniority-based wage increase scale. This meant that pay raises would be based on the number of hours worked rather than years of company service. While this was the first major supermarket contract to implement the new scales, they are now standard fare in supermarkets across the country.[86]

The negotiations of 1996 are seen as a major turning point in labor relations, and set the stage for all subsequent concessions. The UFCW, representing 90 percent of unionized retail food workers, felt it was negotiating with Loblaws in what it saw as a life-or-death struggle for jobs. While the company has succeeded in getting wage concessions in the face of market competition, the union has felt trapped between the choice of wage rollbacks or losing the jobs altogether. Through the concession bargaining in the 1996 negotiations, the UFCW agreed to a two-tiered wage structure, buyouts, and an elimination of full-time jobs with a subsequent increase in part-time positions.[87] While avoiding a total wage rollback, the union negotiated wage freezes for current employees, but lower ceilings for new hires, both full-time and part-time; this has essentially created an unequal pay structure, where new full-time cashiers can only reach a top level of $16/hour (instead of $18 for current employees), and new part-timers will be capped at $12.50 (instead of $15). While the union felt there was no alternative, the two-tiered wage structure has created divisions among workers and threatened efforts at collective action.

A critical development in labor relations took place behind closed doors in late 2003, and once again, the specter of the "evil empire" of Wal-Mart was framed by management as the catalyst for a preemptive move. The company announced its strategy to change all of its Ontario locations to a Real Canadian SuperStore (RCSS) format, combining grocery sales with department store goods (mimicking Wal-Mart supercenters); workers in the SuperStores, however, would have their wages capped at $10 per hour, with Christmas bonuses, sick days, and Sunday premiums all eliminated. Because this was midcontract, Loblaws negotiated the rollbacks in secret with union staff and local reps "so that it could be leaner for the upcoming Wal-Mart battle."[88] While for some critics the midcontract concessions represented a "sweetheart deal" and a "real-time demise of the union,"[89] union brass defended the decision and the seemingly undemocratic process with a sixteen-page special report to union members, ensuring that workers in existing conventional Loblaws supermarkets would not experience wage cuts and that workers who voluntarily moved to the RCSS stores would get a generous transfer allowance. The pact also guaranteed there would be no concessions on wages and benefits for the next collective agreement (2006).[90]

Three years later, however, that proved to be a broken promise. The collective agreement negotiated in 2006 for workers at Loblaws, Zehrs, Real Canadian SuperStores, and Fortino's in Ontario allows the supermarket chain to convert up to one-third of the stores into the new SuperStore format, under which the pay rates are lower. Employees can be offered a buyout or a "buy-over" in cases where they decide to stay on at the converted store at the new lower wage. The same pay structure is to be applied as well to another new format, The Great Canadian Food Store, which promises to offer more choice and better service than a traditional food store.[91]

Under the pressures of the Wal-Mart invasion and labor strife (a strike was closely averted during negotiations), Loblaw's management showed signs of buckling under. In 2006, CEO John Lederer attempted to streamline administrative costs by moving two thousand people to new headquarters in Brampton, Ontario, on President's Choice Circle; he also closed thirty-six warehouses and cut fourteen hundred jobs. New information technology was introduced to upgrade the supply chain.[92] Along with accelerated openings of Real Canadian SuperStores, these restructuring efforts created supply chain chaos and appeared to be too much, too fast for investors. Six months later, in the midst of labor negotiations, Lederer resigned in the face of weak financial results and stock losses.[93] He was replaced by a youthful triumvirate headed by Galen Weston Jr., son of Galen Weston, former Loblaw chair and still chairman of George Weston Ltd.

Not coincidentally, two of the new senior management team had previously worked internationally for Wal-Mart, reflecting yet another realm of global

competition, this time for top management.[94] The younger scion of the Weston dynasty announced his new strategy to Loblaws' store employees in early 2007 as "Simplify, Innovate, and Grow," aiming to streamline administration by cutting 800–1,000 jobs in head and regional offices, while promising not to reduce store staff.[95] This was all part of a "Make Loblaw the Best Again" campaign that Weston subsequently outlined to sector analysts, which simultaneously proposed refocusing on food and pushing its Joe Fresh clothing line while aiming to lower prices (given that Loblaws' prices were 20 percent higher than Wal-Mart's in some categories).[96] One Loblaws worker offered this perspective:

> I hear customers and employees saying, "Look, you guys were good food grocers, that was your specialty, stick to it, and forget about the rest of it." Then we get the feeling that it's greediness. They're looking at Wal-Mart sales thinking, "We can capitalize on those, selling general merchandize, you know."[97]

Kainer suggests that Loblaws is applying both "functional flexibility" (multitasking) and "numerical flexibility" (use of part-time workers) to maximize efficiency and profits.[98] Multitasking intensifies the work of employees by asking them to take on other jobs. Cashiers, for example, are asked to stock shelves when things slow down at the checkout lanes.

A major corporate strategy has been the trend toward part-time work, offering the ultimate in labor flexibility and savings. Part-timers work shorter shifts, so require fewer breaks (one on a five- or six-hour shift, instead of two plus a half-hour unpaid lunch break on an eight-hour shift). As just-in-time workers, they can be called on to fill the constantly changing shifts determined by the ebbs and flows of supermarket traffic.

   Part-timers are discouraged from moving to full-time status because they can no longer get credit for their part-time service if promoted, having to start from square one with wages and vacation entitlement. It is not uncommon for part-timers to be asked to work what is the equivalent of full-time (thirty-seven hours instead of twenty-four), though this contravenes the collective agreement.

   Wages are kept down even longer by the part-time wage progression for employees hired after the 1996 collective agreement. Previously, workers got raises automatically every six months; now part-timers must work for 500 hours before getting a raise (hired at a starting salary of $6.85) and must work more than 8,750 hours to reach the top wage of $12.50.[99] New hires are only guaranteed one four-hour shift a month. As one cashier explains, "If you're at the bottom of the seniority list, you're lucky to get four hours a week. So, it's going to be years before you get that first increment, it's going to be years before they start paying benefits[100] to you."[101] There is added pressure on new hires, too, putting them "on call" to work on long weekends and holidays when stores are short-staffed.

   When the 1996 collective agreement came into effect, management issued a new "Declaration of Availability" form, emphasizing that "scheduled shifts are determined solely on the basis of business requirements, and are consistently subject to change, based on shifts in business trends."[102] Scheduling is a sore point between Loblaws management and the union. The company would like to have greater control over the scheduling process (essentially computerizing labor shifts in harmony with just-in-time inventory monitoring), while the union has insisted on maintaining part-time scheduling practices that consider employees' weekly submissions of availability and follow seniority in assigning shifts. Seniority addresses age discrimination but does not address gender. Gender issues are, however, embedded in the construction of the cashier job, the focus of this case study.

Globalization from Below: Loblaws Cashiers on the Line

> At the front end, that's where it all happens. That's where we sell the stuff.
>
> —Loblaws store manager

The changes in supermarkets over the past fifty years come into clearer focus at the checkout line, and there, too, future trends can be forecast.[103] With technology a leading weapon in global market competition, cutting-edge companies are introducing shopping carts and boxes that allow customers to pass through cashierless lanes while their goods are scanned by the entire box instead of item by item. In corporate language, this area is called the "point of sale" (POS); it has also historically been the front line for customer relations.

   It is no coincidence that women have predominated in cashier jobs where speed and accuracy as well as human relations are required. As in other food

system jobs examined in this book, gender ideologies that claim women are in-herently more agile and congenial have historically shaped the division of labor. It is also no coincidence that these primarily female jobs are the ones that are lit-erally on the line, being cut back, constantly changing to adapt to new technolo-gies, and increasingly eliminated. Cashiers' perspectives on globalization, then, offer a particular window on the deeper motives and gendered consequences of the corporate strategies revealed earlier.

A history of women in the food retail industry provides a broader context for understanding the present struggle.[104] A somewhat rigid sexual division of labor has defined grocery store jobs since their growing presence in the early part of the twentieth century. Men were usually hired in what was considered production work (meat cutting, baking, stocking), while women were hired for service jobs that were associated with their gendered skills of homemak-ing and interpersonal relations. From the start, women were hired at lower rates than men, as it was assumed that they were still primarily committed to their domestic duties and were willing to work part-time for "spending money." This classic sexual division of labor in the Western industrial era de-valued the many skills (food related and otherwise) of unpaid domestic work, and, despite challenges from the women's movement, continued to shape job classifications throughout the twentieth century.

In the postwar period of the 1960s and 1970s, supermarkets flourished, while women entered the workforce in increasing numbers as their income was needed for ever-increasing levels of consumption. Men have continued to fill the major-ity of managerial positions and production jobs, which are presumed to require more skill and strength, and are directly tied to profit creation. Women have taken on new service jobs in diversified supermarkets, which have added bakeries (especially cake decorating), delis, pharmacies, garden centers, floral shops, and banking services. They have always predominated in the front-end work described earlier, as cashiers. As the service sector has burgeoned in the last two decades, women's presence in service jobs has also mushroomed. Retail work is the top job category for women today, while cashier work is the fourth most common job among Canadian women.[105]

Historically, the early craft-based unions were also built on a sexual division of labor within emerging industries, assuring a family wage for industrial workers with the assumption that women would reproduce the producers (i.e., their husbands and sons), supporting them at home without pay. Canadian retail unions have inherited some of this legacy, in giving priority to full-time production-oriented jobs, primarily held by men.[106]

Managerial positions in Loblaws are held primarily by men; as one immigrant woman worker concluded, "Always boss is man." In terms of the hierarchy in my local supermarket, the store manager is a man and all department managers are male, except the head checker or customer service manager, who oversees the cashiers and does the payroll. Beyond the local store, the hierarchy at the head office is also defined by gender. According to one part-time cashier, "There is a major glass ceiling. Women will rise to certain positions and then stop. All those executive positions are male-dominated, while entry-level jobs and a lot of middle management are women."[107] The 2006 company annual report revealed one woman out of nine top executives and nine women out of thirty-three company officers, a slight rise from previous years. It is interesting to note, in times of consumer backlash, however, that women are on the "front line" as managers in the public relations office.

In 1988, a Pay Equity Act was passed in Canada, requiring employers to equalize wages in comparable job categories. However, it was never ratified before the conservative government gained power in 1994. Nonetheless, that period is now seen as a rare moment of gender awareness. One cashier recalls, "In the 1980s, there was a push toward equal pay for equal work, that's what they were physically trying to show people, to make it noticeable that Loblaws was part of this. But now we don't have women butchers, and there are no more male cashiers. And in the bakery, the guys are doing the baking, while the women are doing the decorating."[108]

Breaking the stereotype of the typical cashier was a challenge not only for the public but also for potential employees. Even as pay rates become more equal, it is still women who tend to apply for jobs on cash, while males apply for clerk jobs, stocking shelves and lifting goods.[109] In the 1996 contract, full-time wages were divided between only two categories: "Clerk" (deli, grocery, produce, front end or cashier, wrapper, and bakery service) and "Meat Cutters and Baker/ Decorators," who are paid slightly more. This roughly corresponds to the service-versus-production distinction shaped over the century.

It's among part-time workers that gender divisions become most pronounced. All cashier positions are now part-time, female, and an increasingly precarious job category. Ironically, however, unionized part-time Loblaws' cashiers have more job security than some women working full-time in the company's head office, who are not unionized, are hired on contract, and thus don't have job security. Many of them have come up through the ranks, so they have kept their part-time jobs in the stores, while also working full-time at the head office. Putting in the requisite number of hours per month preserves their seniority in the cashier lines, so they have a fallback should they ever lose their full-time office job.[110] This is another stark indicator of the value of unionized-versus-nonunionized jobs.

What are the gendered dimensions of cashiers' jobs? It depends on who you talk to, how you see the job, and how you understand gender roles. Physically, fine-motor coordination is needed for quick scanning, weighing, and bagging in the checkout lane, as well as the care of more delicate items. Socially, customer relations require pleasant interactions with the shoppers. The two key criteria seem to be a combination of these skills, what I'm calling "fast and friendly." Women are seen as more agile in handling food, more trustworthy in tendering cash, and more skilled in interpersonal relations, in dealing with customers—whether sharing information, making personal connections, or mediating conflicts. All of these skills are acquired through their socialization as girls who, in contrast to boys, often grow up more connected to food shopping and preparation, and more focused on relationships.

There is also an assumption that women seek part-time work, reinforced in this proclamation of a female manager: "It's a great part-time job for someone. You can pick your hours, depending on your availability and your seniority, even working weekends; if your spouse was home, that would be perfect. You could be home during the week. Your kids come home, you work a couple of evenings and weekends and there you go."[111] This assumes a lot: that women take the major responsibility for child rearing and housework, that they have another source of support through a spouse's income (or even that they have a spouse), and that they really have much choice of hours worked. These notions are challenged in some of the forthcoming stories.

ON THE FRONT LINE: CASHIER AND TOMATOES

Most people assume that new technologies have made the cashier's job easier. But according to one seasoned Loblaws cashier, "Now we've got more things to do."[112] Their work has both expanded and intensified in recent years, as multitasking predominates and job specialization declines. One cashier offers this explanation: "Years ago, there was somebody specific to do certain things, but now because sales have gone down, they are cutting back on staff, so basically whatever two people were doing before maybe one person is doing now."[113] While scanners may cut down on punching-in time for bar-coded products, cashiers have the added task of weighing the tomatoes (previously done in the produce department) as well as punching in the product look-up (PLU) codes for fresh produce. Scales were moved to the front end to spare customers waiting in two lines and because women cashiers were assumed to know the produce.[114]

They also do more bagging now, with fewer bag-your-own lanes and no hired bagging help. When business is slow, they are expected to help restock shelves, put back returned items, organize the magazine or candy displays, clean the cash registers, and take out the garbage. They may be assigned to the drug aisle or the customer service desk, where they sell film, razor blades, and lottery tickets, prepare unsold newspapers for return credit, or rent out carpet cleaners. Those at the customer service desk must also deal with customer complaints. Their frontline work at the point of sale means as well that they deal most directly with money (though less directly since the InterAc bank machine came in); while this represents a heavy responsibility, cashiers have the extra pressure of

being watched by undercover security guards to make sure they don't steal.

Another change that cashiers note, especially those with lower seniority, is that they feel they have less control over their schedules: "They have all these odd shifts, like 3 to 7 P.M. (which takes your whole day), which don't really suit our needs, it's the business, the business, the business." This is the scheduling nightmare mentioned earlier, a combination of the company adopting just-in-time production practices[115] with more flexible part-time workers and the union insisting on seniority as well as workers' input on their availability.[116]

The greatest differences are between the part-timers with seniority, often older women, mothers who have been working at Loblaws for years, and those at the bottom of the seniority list, usually young women and often students. There is a sense that the demographics are shifting, however, as more older women are now being hired or students stay on after finishing their studies. One young cashier suggests that "the change is a product of economic conditions. Full-time isn't what it used to be and you take what you can get."[117] There is a danger, though, of intergenerational tensions, not only because of wage differentials but because the younger hires may adapt more easily to technological change than older employees. It works both ways: while senior staff can resent the "young tykes," more youthful staff may resent the veterans who are sometimes seen as "doing time." The issue of seniority, while critical as a worker's right, is complex and can be divisive.[118]

The 1996 contract offered attractive buyouts to both the few full-time cashiers left as well as well-established part-timers. In my local Loblaws at least one full-timer, an older widow, took the package and then accepted a part-time position at a much lower wage, just to get out of the house and occupy herself socially. It's the new hires who are left with the least desirable hours—Thursday, Friday, and Saturday nights. Many are students who do homework during the week; as one cashier explains, "They're sixteen years old, right, and they want to go out [on the weekends]." They're probably the most unhappy about the scheduling, but they must accept it in order to accumulate hours; what's more, they can now be pressured to work on holidays or risk losing their job.

FAST AND FRIENDLY

Perhaps the greatest contradiction a cashier faces in her job is the pressure to deal politely with customers while also scanning and bagging items accurately and efficiently. The manager of technical training for Loblaws considers cashiers' goals as "representing the company correctly in front of the customer and having a satisfied customer, but also providing the correct service and ensuring that the correct sales are coming into the company for the product that has been purchased."[119] Exploring each of

these central roles separately may deepen our understanding of the cashier's experience as well as the tension of trying to be both fast and friendly.

Marissa recalls when cashiers were asked to wear a button proclaiming, "I promise to check you out fast!" When management realized the phrase could be misinterpreted, however, the buttons were recalled. But *fast* has nonetheless been an operative word at the checkout lane, especially since scanners replaced the manual cash register. The scanning technology first developed by the Ohio-based National Cash Register company required a new system of organizing merchandise, the now ubiquitous ten-digit bar code adopted as the industry standard in 1972 by an Ad Hoc Committee on Universal Product Codes (UPCs), made up of U.S.-based manufacturers and retailers. There were two options for the scanners: the handheld variety was easier for the cashier who put it right on the label, while the bottom scanner (which had to be read at an angle) allowed a cashier to have both hands free, increasing her productivity and speed. The latest version at Loblaws has two "magic windows," as one manager calls them, a second one perpendicular to the bottom scanner. It's been estimated that cashiers can check out groceries 30 to 50 percent faster with scanners than with the old cash registers.[120]

From the management perspective, scanners provided a computerized pricing system, allowing managers to institute changes by computer from a central location. But this also meant considerable job loss for stockers who had previously removed and replaced price stickers with each new price change. While management saved in reduced labor both at checkout and with stockers, both unions and customers initially resisted the introduction of scanners. Unions fought the job loss, while consumers didn't trust the new technology that eliminated price labels on items and feared companies would use it to manipulate prices. In recent years, however, customers have warmed up to it, particularly as they are able to monitor their accumulating bill on the screen as cashiers scan in each item.

The point of sale is not only the strategic location of the cashier but also has become the technological center of myriad store activities: the same computerized device combines functions for checkout, retail inventory, customer tracking, general ledger, accounts receivable, accounts payable, time and attendance, and labor scheduling.[121] Computerized ordering is another key use of the scanning technology in what is sometimes called an *automated management system*. "The advantage is basically for the company itself," a cashier told us, "because once you scan something the inventory record minuses it, so they can order more."[122] As part of a recent business initiative, Efficient Consumer Response, this approach assures a continued flow of products to meet consumer demand, through a paperless computerized system between retail checkout and manufacturers.[123] Computerization has also made available to the company information about its customers, which can help it determine the key markets it wants to reach. A union officer explained, "With check cashing or coupon cards, they know what family, what kind of groceries each family is purchasing, how many kids in the household, what are the items that are most advantageous to the customer."[124]

Technology social critic Heather Menzies makes the link between the introduction of bar codes, scanners, ordering, and staffing in supermarkets: "Value-added software analyzes the data pouring in through the scanner and out through the cashier's keyboard, allowing stores to trim inventories through a just-in-time system of stock reordering," adding that it also allows them to rely on less qualified part-time staff as well as to trim staff through just-in-time scheduling.[125]

Scanning has dramatically affected the cashier's job. Productivity is more carefully monitored, food knowledge has been computerized, and new health problems have arisen. Taken together, these changes have increasingly deskilled and intensified the cashier's job. One cashier showed us a computer printout that tallied her week's work, to the hundredth of a second, according to the average number of scans per hour, and how much time she spent per hour scanning, tendering money, or in "idle time" (between customers); it also indicated her average time per item (4.64 seconds) and per transaction (1.45 minutes) as well as how much money she had tendered per hour ($1,808). Her performance is thus reduced to quantitative measures—time and money. More recently, cashiers can

Trans	725	Scanned	70.7%
$/Trans	43.80	Coded	28.6%
Items/Trans	18.9	Paging	0.0%
Alt Dif	103.58	Pr/Dept	0.7%
Alt Units	-64	Item Corr	0.3%
No Sales	16	Item Void	0.1%
Tender Corr.	0	Cpn Scan	0.9%
Express Trans.	246	Add'l MC Val.	0.00

Average time for one customer (in minutes)

	HHH:MM:SS	%MT	%AT	SEC/ITEM	MIN/TRAN	$$/HR	ITEMS/Hr
Manned Time	17:33:54			4.64	1.45	1808	775
Active Time	14:47:53	84.2		3.91	1.22	2146	920
Item Time	10:14:21		69.2	2.71	0.85	3101	1330
Subt Time	4:15:19		28.8		0.35		
Tender Time	0:18:13		2.1		0.03		
Idle Time	2:46:01	15.8					

Weekly productivity report of Loblaws' cashier

Average time to scan an item (in seconds)

Average cash tendered (per hour)

no longer make corrections, and are asked to fill out a form each time they get an unscannable item. While helping management computerize all inventory, this additional task also takes time and thus lowers a cashier's productivity.

THE ALL-SEEING EYE

Menzies suggests that technologies such as scanners "seal people into a completely computer-defined sense of their work, which they are then almost forced to internalize."[126] Echoing Michel Foucault's notion of the superpanopticon (the prison structure that allows wardens to see inmates at all times but not be seen), computerized job monitoring represents an "all-seeing eye" focused on every minute detail of a cashier's job. Such constant watching leads to internalized regulation, as was evident in one cashier's story. Marissa described her efforts to beat her own record of items scanned per hour, far surpassing the store quota of 500 by reaching 681. While this diligence can be seen as an admirable desire to challenge herself and to make the monotony of the job more interesting, it certainly also serves the company's goal of training productive workers.

Cashiers review their productivity reports weekly with their customer service manager. The company is mainly concerned if someone has a lot of "voids" on record, indicating a lack of accuracy, or a very low items-per-hour count. The printouts also reveal the traffic flow at different times of day or days of the week, and the activity by lane, guiding scheduling decisions and job assignments.

The intensification of the job through computerized monitoring is evident, ironically, in descriptions of how cashiers deal with the slowdown often brought on by the use of debit cards, an electronic process that is supposed to simplify and speed up payment. As debit card technology improves, some stores have better systems that shorten the time, setting an unfair competitive standard for those with slower systems:

> Interac delays the tender time; it's a lot slower because it takes time to print up the whole transaction on the slip. But while it's doing that, you

can start the next order. I can usually scan about ten items before the debit is closed and it has a memory in the machine so you just ring it all up. Some people get really annoyed because you really haven't finished with the last customer and you're dealing with two at a time.[127]

Loblaws has followed, like other industries, the trend to develop "best practices," which usually translates to greater productivity. For example, it's undertaking engineering studies on the minimum time and movement required to move and to scan each different item:

> There is already a set engineered standard out there for putting up a crate of canned tomatoes. The company's just trying to get the employees so they aren't wasting—what they perceive as wasting—time. And in doing that, they cut down some time that will in turn increase productivity. For cashiers, it probably means there will probably be a small percentage of increase for them to take a few extra cans. So, the company has less labor costs.[128]

BODY LIMITS

Company best practices encourage not only speed and accuracy but safe work, as workplace injuries are ultimately expensive. But speeding up work, while increasing productivity, also increases the possibility of injury. Cashiers' bodies are regulated and shaped by the quick scanning motions, and some are resisting. First, they must stand for hours: "Your legs get very, very tired, particularly your calves. And my feet get sore. You're standing all the time and you just want to go

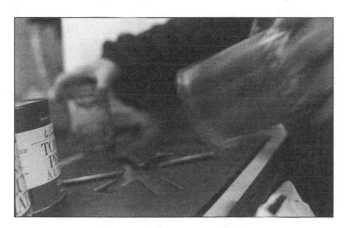

home and soak in a bath." Grabbing and repeatedly scanning produce other ailments: "I'm not a very strong person; I try to grab it [a pack of cans] myself and I've messed up my shoulder."[129]

The express lane is known to cashiers as the "penalty box," because it is narrower and leaves little room for movement; one cashier bruised her hip while working in it. More common are complaints about wrist pain, repetitive strain, and carpal tunnel syndrome. It's over time that cashiers feel the impact: "One morning I'll go to reach for my coffee pot at home and it's just like your wrist is going to give, like you're just ready to drop it."[130] Cashiers are increasingly wearing wrist bands and hand bands.

Both management and union have recognized these occupational health problems and have been working to address them, through training (about proper grabbing and lifting) and through structural changes. A major concern raised by cashiers is health and safety: "repetitive strain, lower back from standing, wrist and shoulders from scanning with the new scanner and the increased speed of the product they are now putting through compared to twenty years ago." One union response has been to make sure they get breaks after three hours.[131]

Following a pay equity exercise in the early 1990s, the job of cashier was assessed as one of the most difficult jobs in the supermarket, in terms of responsibility, effort, and working conditions. The study spurred a joint union–management health and safety committee effort to redesign (with the help of an ergonomist) the check stand for cashiers, to eliminate some of the side strains and lower-back strains. Though very expensive, the new stands have been implemented in new stores.

COMPUTERIZED FOOD KNOWLEDGE

Also impacting cashiers' work has been computer software that gives them detailed information about produce such as tomatoes. Since fresh produce such as tomatoes cannot be scanned, they are stickered with a PLU code rather than a bar code. The PLU code identifies the variety of tomato; it's an internationally standardized number shared by all producers of that variety. Instead of scanning, then, cashiers must punch in this code, but if they want to know more about the tomato, if the sticker has fallen off, or if they think the sticker might be wrong, they can check through their computer monitor, where photos of a variety of tomatoes and their codes appear, along with a list of characteristics of the produce. While this teaches cashiers about foods they might not know, it is one element of deskilling, a computerization of food knowledge that lessens that responsibility of the cashier.

From the perspective of the Loblaws training staff, however, a minimum knowledge about food is critical to the company's earnings. A company trainer emphasized the importance of a cashier being able to distinguish between varieties of tomatoes:

> If they use the wrong code in ringing in a tomato, they could be causing great losses to the company or they could be overcharging a customer. A cashier will always tend to take the safer route, not wanting to offend the customer and therefore will tend to use the most frequently used code. So the more exotic tomato that we have brought in to address a certain audience, may indeed be rung in as another type of tomato. Now, the customer is happy because the customer has most likely purchased it at a lesser price, but from a company perspective and the cost we have had to pay to import that more exotic tomato, it could be a great business loss.[132]

The hypothetical example of the tomato was actually calculated on the wall of the training center, warning of million-dollar consequences if such a mistake were to be massively reproduced.

During sixteen hours of orientation, cashiers must memorize as many as sixty codes; it is hoped that they will not have to check the monitors but will remember the PLU numbers, saving precious checkout time. Food knowledge has, in some sense, been substituted by this memory work as the most demanding mental activity for cashiers, who internalize these numerical identifiers. This was brought home poignantly when I visited a farm with Marissa, who quickly identified the produce in the fields by their PLU numbers!

Cashiers are, in fact, continually monitored for their accuracy. Senior cashiers are asked to give periodic "produce tests" to newer cashiers, for example, to check their memory of PLUs. It was reported that management hires "professional shoppers" to go through checkout lanes posing as customers, in order to check a cashier's accuracy and service. The computer systems that monitor performance also single out those who don't measure up, and they are sent to counseling sessions to help them improve.[133]

CUSTOMER SERVICE WITH A SMILE

If the front line is critical to supermarket business, "where you sell the stuff," as the manager said earlier, then it is also where human relations are key, where the first and last impression is left with the consumer. "You are the most important person dealing with the customer in checking them out," said one cashier.[134]

The emphasis on customer service has had its ebbs and tides over the years. Older cashiers recall a major push in the late 1980s when the company offered them a series of seminars on customer relations,[135] called "You can count on me." "Count on us for more" is the updated slogan for cashiers, a perfect double entendre for their responsibilities, both fiscal and social.

Cashier training emphasizes the importance of customer contact: "We have an image. . . . Cashiers represent . . . the last person the customer sees before they leave. That cashier can greatly influence a customer's perception."[136] Cashiers thus fit into the design strategy described earlier, their smiling faces essential to the company's overall presentation.

With the speeded-up work of scanning and quotas to be met, being friendly is sometimes just an added pressure: "You're always in motion, and you have to smile all the time, talk to customers, be very friendly, do price checks. I'm not going to lie—it's hard to do. You try to be the nicest person you can be while you're there because you don't want to lose the customer."[137] This cashier concludes, "It's hard to be nice twenty-four hours a week."[138]

Cashier–customer relations take both positive and negative forms. Some cashiers who have been there a long time have built up relationships with the customers, and the social contact is important to both: "A lot of customers come in every day, they might come two or three times a day because it's their walk for them and it's social contact. I'm almost like a bartender, we know their family problems. We ask 'How is your granddaughter?' It's a nice sort of continuity . . . it sort of makes it feel like a family." In some ways, these very personal exchanges offer one of the few spaces in the job where the monotony and pressure are broken by more spontaneous human contact: "People wait in my lane so they can see me. Even if I'm busy I'll talk to them."

These relationships can also involve exchanges of food knowledge: "I'll ask a customer, 'What do you do with this? I've never seen this before.' Or with products in the store, you might say, 'I've tried that and it's really good. You may want to try it this way.'"[139] There is a fine line, however, between sharing knowledge and selling products, which cashiers are more and more encouraged to incorporate into their repertoire. Promotion is subtly inserted into suggested scripts: "I'm not into saying, like we are supposed to say, 'Did you find everything you were looking for?'" One cashier says she refuses to repeat that phrase, claiming it's "too Wal-Mart"!

Since the inception of the corporate brands in the 1980s, cashiers have been encouraged to sample new foods, so that they can then promote them with customers. At one point, some managers insisted that each cashier select an item to promote, each in her own way: "It was sell, sell, sell, sell. Pick a product and launch that product, say, those cookies. Make an announcement, things like that."[140]

This may be more than what cashiers bargained for in taking on the job: "They'll give us regular buttons to wear, like 'Ask our pharmacist about this drug store.' When the new movies come in, especially the Disney ones, they'll give you little buttons, and people ask, 'When is that going to be released?' So we're sort of advertising. I hate wearing those buttons. I figure I'm there to be a cashier; I'm not there to be pushing products."[141]

In early 2000, cashiers were invited to compete for prizes in a "Win a Million Points" contest that pushed for greater accuracy (minimal voids), less waste (five bags or less), and monitored customer service. "Mystery shoppers" passed through checkouts to judge a cashier's performance on the following behaviors: (1) make eye contact with the customer; (2) greet the customer; (3) ask, "Will that be on your President's Financial Choice debit card?"; and (4) finish with "Thank you for shopping at Loblaws." Prizes included charms and T-shirts, while a winning front-end team could get watches.[142]

Cashiers must also deal with complaints and manage conflict. As the most exposed staff, they're on the front line of fire: "Cashiers are the last person anybody sees when they come into the store, so in a way, you have this little diplomatic role. Because if they're going to get mad, they'll get mad at you and it's your job to resolve it. Crazy people, too, pass through and I just try to get them out before something nasty happens."[143]

The pressure to be polite can collide with the pressure to be productive, creating a kind of double bind for cashiers. There is some resentment, too, that the compensation does not reflect their central role: "Managers tell us, 'You're the front end, you're so important.' Sometimes we're the only contact the customer has. You've got all this pressure on you and yet what do you get for it? Then the managers get a bonus in the New Year."[144] Cashiers' work has certainly intensified, both physically and socially, as reflected in the "You can count on us for *more*" on their jackets. It is little wonder that some cashiers actually prefer the short shifts often mandated by management, their bodies and minds resisting eight hours of such pressure, perhaps wishing for *less*, not more.

You Can Count on Me: The Single Mom Express

Women cashiers face constant demands not only from their customers and their employers but also from their families. Like many women working today, they piece together part-time jobs and juggle paid work with unpaid domestic work. Digging deeper into the daily life of Marissa, a single mother who's worked for over twenty-five years as a Loblaws cashier, we can get a fuller picture of women behind the checkout counter and the intertwining of their work life with their home life.[145]

"When I started working here, I was sixteen and in high school. When you are low on the seniority list, you are lucky to get any hours. They might only call you in once every two weeks for a four-hour shift. And Friday and Saturday nights you had to work. That suited me fine because my parents wouldn't allow me to work during the week, because of homework.

"Then I went to university for a while, and I fit it around my courses. After that I took a full-time job, but I still kept up with Loblaws because the benefits were better part-time than at my full-time job. It's always been a good company for taking care of its employees.

"After I got married, we moved up to Markham, and I quit my full-time job. But I stayed at Loblaws and started a family. And it was great just to get out of the house. I'd work two evenings a week, from four to ten (I'd drop the girls at the sitter's at three; my husband would pick them up at seven). I didn't feel guilt or anything.

"Now it's a bit harder because (since the divorce) I'm on my own, so I have to take into account travel time. I would like to be able to work at a Loblaws that is closer to my home, but if I transfer stores I lose my seniority! Now I work two days a week, depending on the custody arrangement, because he gets the kids three weekends out of four. When they're with their dad on the weekend, I'm working. The day care costs are unreal ($4 per child per hour, plus $5 more for dinner), because I have to add in the travel time. It ends up being almost $60 a day.

"I work three weekends out of four, which Loblaws loves because they've got a senior girl for their busiest period, and it works out for me because I'm not paying for day care. It works out for all of us."

Marissa's trajectory across the decades reflects a common dilemma for women her age: since she has reached the top level, her pay and benefits are better than she might get at another job. Yet while she has much more choice about her hours than newer cashiers, she is bound by two major constraints: she must commute two to three hours to and from work (she can't transfer without losing her seniority),[146] and there is no public or company child care program that would make her scheduling less patchwork and less expensive. In other words, both the company and the state benefit from her "flexible labor," while she spends her weekends without her kids, driving into Toronto for the busiest and longest shifts. The hidden costs of child care and family disintegration are not calculated by either employers like Loblaws or the federal government, which has failed to implement a long-promised national child care program.

What does a typical work day look like for Marissa?

"I drop the kids off at the sitter's, which is just around the corner from me, at quarter to eight. My kids are sleepers so it's tough, especially when there's something like Brownies going on the night before. It's hard in winter, too, when you've got to put in an extra fifteen minutes just to get snowsuits on. And it's extra child care for me because I won't get home until 7:00.

"I like to make the lunches in the morning.

"I have my juice and coffee, and then I usually make a sandwich and put a banana in my lunch bag. I'll eat that on the way to work, down the highway. Some women put their makeup on; I'm eating.

"I always like to get to work early, have a coffee, relax a bit, unwind, talk to the people.

"I'll work all day and then right at 6:00—boom—I'll punch out because I don't know what the traffic is going to be like and I feel really pressured.

"I give myself an hour and a half to get to work, but I only give myself an hour to get back. 'Cause I figure, 6:30, that's a long haul for my kids, you know. And there's a big difference between 6:30 and 7 if it's bath night.

"I get there and—boom—I'm attacked by the kids as soon as I get in. 'And this happened in school and blah, blah, blah.' Usually the notes come out of the bag as well as the Tupperware containers.

"For a long time I was coming home from work and tending to them. And I was just so wiped by nine o'clock. So, now I come home and say, 'Look, you guys, you've had your lunch and you've had your supper. Mommy hasn't had her supper,' and I sit down and eat. Sometimes I'm so tired, I don't know what I want to eat, so I may just have toast or sometimes nothing at all.

"I think dinner time is very important time for, you know, learning about everybody's day and everything. I was brought up with that—the family sits and eats dinner.

"I'm not a TV person; I like to read after they go to bed. I might sit there with the newspaper, or I start doing stuff like paying the bills. I got a letter from my lawyer, and there was a bill that is unpaid, and emotionally I'm a wreck because I am going through this divorce.

"Sometimes when there are thunderstorms, I find a body in bed beside me."

Over the months that Marissa and I talked about her work and home life, I became increasingly conscious of the incredible daily juggling act of working and parenting. During one visit to her house, I was surprised to find she had made up a monthly calendar, detailing her tasks as a single mother.

"I did this just for you, because you started sparking my interest thinking how much organizing I have to do. When I started writing this, it really depressed me.

"This is my October calendar, and these are some of my concerns: I'm still looking for a painter to paint my house, I had the flu from September to October 6. The other day I realized that Connie's Girl Guide pants needed to be shortened, so I had to go down to the cleaners. I take medication every day and I realized I was out of medication and I need blood work for it; it takes three days to get back from the lab. Then I realize my library books were very overdue, right? The kids have a PD [professional development] day and you came over, and later we went to the bank at the mall because I had two bills that were due."

The calendar reflects not only the multiple skills and tasks of domestic work, which are rarely counted, but also how she organizes her work around her children, their schedules and needs.

"This feeling of the kids being shuffled all the time—I don't like that. I hate that feeling of not seeing them. My objective is to keep them home as much as possible, to work around their schedule."

"I'm a single parent, so I'm taking them to school, doing the piano lessons, the Brownies, that kind of thing. They may have a PD day so I don't go into work that day."

Like many other part-time workers, Marissa also tries to supplement her income with extra home-based work.

"I sell things out of a Regal book, paper and gift items; I've done it for years, since I was sixteen, for extra income ($80 to $100 per month). I used to sell Avon, too, but that was a big rip-off."

Occasionally, she doesn't get much sympathy from supervisors at work about the conflicts that can arise when parental and worker duties collide:

"A few years ago, neither of my two supervisors had children, so they were not sympathetic to what I was going through. One day I went to the bakery to see if anybody had a radio because at ten they were going to announce about the possible teachers' strike. And they said, 'You're not supposed to be listening to this on the job.' I said, 'I have to make day care plans for my kids, next week.' You have to plan this ahead of time."

Marissa is always carrying this double day pressure with her, and, even at the checkout lane, she finds herself thinking about things that must be done when she gets home. Responding to the slogan "Count on Us for More!" she is caught among the demands of her kids, her customers, and her employers.

"I take care of everybody else, but nobody's taking care of me."

Marissa is pretty much alone in piecing together her responsibilities as mother, salaried worker, and casual worker. And she represents a growing number of single mothers whose domestic duties are not shared with a partner at home. The many skills that she brings to child care go unrecognized, both financially and socially.

She is among the many women who have entered the workforce in the past two decades, whose wages and working conditions still assume a working husband[147] and whose domestic responsibilities still seem to assume a stay-at-home mother. While the women's movement has challenged the gendered nature of housework, pay inequities, and lack of public child care, working women still averaged 28.7 hours domestic labor per week in 1998, 12 hours a week more than men[148]—that is, if they had spouses at home. As the options for women like Marissa become increasingly limited to part-time work, she joins a growing number of women who combine part-time jobs, patching together paid formal and informal labor with unpaid domestic labor—work that is not always counted, even as she continues to be counted on—both at the supermarket and at home.

The other constituency that Loblaws draws into its part-time low-wage cashier corps is young women, often students. The needs of the company for flexible workers, similar to McDonald's workers, makes this generally powerless and passive labor force a captive source of cashiers. Their responsibilities are not to children, but rather to their studies, or to their social life. One such young worker, Carol, offers a perspective that is somewhat different from Marissa's.

Carol, Student Cashier: Young and Flexible

"I started here when I was nineteen (they don't usually hire under sixteen, but I know a few who have lied and started at fourteen or fifteen). It was kind of fun, because it was just supposed to be a way for me to finance my education—a very temporary thing—and like, six years later, I'm still here. The longer you're there, the more you can claim responsibility.

"If you talk to people who have used the store to finance their education, they say, 'You have to be really careful about this because you can get into a rut, get too comfortable with it, and one day, you wake up, you're thirty-five, and you're still working at the store.'[149]

"I took different courses so I know about the methane environment and poverty conditions about the workers. But I'm like an exception to the rule.

"When negotiations started last summer, they held a meeting to find out what we wanted. And I brought up the environmental conditions: the way the store used to be set up, there were four desks directly in front of the doors during the winter. During the month of December, that door is basically open, so, it's like absolutely numb. We have little microfurnaces at our desks, and we're wearing jackets and at one point they had given us gloves with the fingers cut off. So I went to this meeting, and I said, 'OK, what are you going to do about this? Can you fix the doors, or can we get some kind of compensation for having a poor environmental area?' And they said they would look into it; in the contract there was no mention of environmental concerns, but the problem was addressed later through renovations.

"Part-timers tend to be a lot more sedate than full-timers. That way the company can have a very passive workforce—they can get away with a lot more. I happen to think the 1996 contract was really bad and should never have been signed. But people just took it. At the ratification meeting, 78 percent attending were full-timers, while part-timers are the majority."

Carol reflects the precarious status of young workers, many who move from temporary to permanent part-time status, with less and less hope for full-time employment. Her critical analysis and activism also remind us of the skills and energy that part-time workers could contribute to the labor movement or other social movements. Yet the very erratic nature of part-time shift work, such as cashiering, stands as an obstacle to developing a collective consciousness and a more organized workforce.

Tensions along the Front (and Bottom) Line

How do the key tensions of this study play out in the Loblaws case?

PRODUCTION-CONSUMPTION

At the level of corporate strategy, Loblaws has maintained its competitive edge by moving into product development (subcontracting processors of corporate brands) as well as organics, leading the retail sector in its increasing control over food production. The strategy, however, has been aimed at consumers through seductive packaging and what Naomi Klein calls "branding." Advertising giant J. Walter Thompson reflects this shift from production to consumption: "A product is something that is made in a factory; a brand is something that is bought by a customer." Klein suggests that "what is of true value [is] the idea, the lifestyle, the attitude. Brand builders are the new primary producers in our so-called knowledge economy."[150] Loblaws is certainly the food sector's shining star among the "brand bullies," more focused on consumers than on producers, yet controlling production.

Both products and workers in supermarkets, however, have also been branded—with code numbers. Cashiers' relationship to tomatoes, for example, has been framed by a computerized and standardized coding system, a PLU code for fresh tomatoes and a bar code (UPC) for canned tomatoes or bottled sauces. Even employees have numbers, bar codes on the back of their name tags that they swipe to check in and out of shifts. They internalize the PLU codes even more than the characteristics of the food, and the food's value becomes defined both by its price and the time it takes to scan. The codes or numbers, of course, primarily serve the company's needs to control inventory, organize just-in-time production, and maximize efficiency and profits.

While the cashiers' relationship with tomatoes has become technologized at the checkout, cashiers have mixed experiences with food as consumers. Young Italian cashiers like Carol, for example, spoke about family gardens in their urban backyards, where their parents grow fresh tomatoes for sauce and salads: "The tomatoes at the store are perfected, actually. They are very, very round and very, very red and that sort of thing. And the stuff I get at home is odd shaped, oval as opposed to round, and they're red in spots. They're still ripened; they're just not perfected." She realizes that the perfect tomatoes she sells are hyperreal and ultimately not as tasty.

While Carol can fall back on her own mother's home cooking, cashiers who are also mothers find that their erratic schedules and cooking responsibilities sometimes collide. Marissa has come to rely on the growing market of prepared foods that Loblaws has entered: "It's great to just pick up a frozen lasagna or chicken and at home make some rice and a vegetable. I feel like I'm still giving them a meal."

Cashiers are a captive market for Loblaws' products, and they are further tempted to buy from their employer because it is convenient. And while they don't get the 50 percent discount that McDonald's workers do, they do know the specials, and so are often the first to buy reduced products.

In their production and consumption activities, then, women cashiers reveal a combination of major trends in food retail work and eating practices, which have grown one out of the other. First, the growing number of women in the labor force has changed the shopping patterns of families; more men are shopping, for example, and more women and men are shopping in the evenings and on weekends instead of weekdays. This, in turn, has changed the intensity of activity in supermarkets during those times, requiring more part-time workers. These workers are often women, such as cashiers (often those with less seniority), who thus cannot go home to cook and eat with their families. They, in turn, become dependent on the convenience of already prepared foods in their own supermarkets. They are thus both workers and targeted consumers.

BIODIVERSITY/CULTURAL DIVERSITY

In a broader sense, megasupermarkets such as Loblaws keep the globalized food system going by filling their aisles with the fruits of monocultural production of large agribusinesses in faraway countries. Yet the retailers (as buyers) and we (as consumers) are kept so distanced from the actual production of the food sold on our supermarket shelves that we are never compelled to investigate the impact such production practices are having worldwide on biodiversity. These issues are explored in the case of a Mexican agribusiness in chapter 6.

At the consumption end of the tomato chain, then, Loblaws' role has been not only to sell tomatoes but also to sell us an illusion of diversity. In terms of tomatoes, for example, cashiers intimated that there is a greater variety being sold. Indeed, tomatoes arrive daily on flights from several countries, but it is likely that each variety is grown in large monocultural fields, eliminating a greater biodiversity of tomatoes that have been abandoned for these standard more marketable types.

Loblaws has become a master in selling diversity, not only through the seeming variety of fresh produce but more dramatically through its processed and packaged foods, such as the Elección del Presidente salsa. Packaging diversity has become a stock in trade in multicultural Canada, and a thinly disguised strategy to stave off critiques of a cultural dominance that is still very evident in the company's boardrooms.

More insidious is the erosion of "cultural diversity," as Vandana Shiva describes it, by "monocultures of the mind" promoted in homogenizing production practices. She denounces "the technological and legal trends toward monoculture and uniformity,"[151] reflected in the redefinition of cashiers' jobs by highly computerized behavior and scripted interaction. It hardly matters what the different backgrounds or interests of the cashiers are; they must meet the goals of productivity, which have been reduced to items scanned, money tendered, and speed of activity. While there is some effort to highlight diverse cultural practices in store activities, such as Caribbean week, Chinese New Year, or Hanukkah, they remain marketing strategies to capture customers, not a way of embracing the different backgrounds and personalities of the women workers on the front line.

WORK/TECHNOLOGY

As argued earlier, supermarket cashiers are a prime example of the female part-time labor phenomenon. They must meet the constantly shifting demands of shoppers and employers, as well as seniority/scheduling requirements, while adjusting their own daily activities to somewhat erratic shifts that are reconfigured each week. Only women with seniority have some control over their time.

As work is being redefined both within and outside of the supermarket, it is technological restructuring, claims Heather Menzies, that is "turning full-time jobs into lousy part-time, shift, and temporary jobs." Of all the case studies in this book, Loblaws cashier work is perhaps the most affected by technological changes. It comes close to fitting the McJobs that Menzies describes, in which "tasks are so completely determined and controlled by the computer system that job performance can be measured and monitored by the system itself." Technology-driven labor practices are even more salient with the incursion of Wal-Mart on the Canadian grocery scene. As we've seen, cashiers' knowledge about food has been substituted by computer programs they can click into for the required information. Time motion studies have determined the minimum time required for scanning and punching in different items, taking into account certain body movements. Menzies denounces this new cybernetics of labor that raises fundamental questions of human identity and social justice.[152]

The internalization of this regulation, at the same time physical and mental, transforms the cashier's work into routinized, repetitive, accelerated, and highly pressured work. In the context of such monitoring, it is not surprising that Marissa would try to disrupt the routine by playing a game to beat her own record in items scanned per hour.

She appropriates the number as a kind of badge, a public record of her accomplishments. It's a contradictory reward, however. While it gives her one way to combat the monotony of the job, it can also work against her and other cashiers, if her increased productivity raises the norm and sets a new standard to be followed by all cashiers. With years of experience, this seasoned cashier can still maintain personal contact with customers, even as she scans in competition with herself.

"I can talk while I scan. I don't have to pay attention to the prices, whereas before we had to. We had to say that's twenty-nine cents, and we had to look at the keyboard and press twenty-nine cents. When you've scanned for a long time, you know where the bar code is on the jar. Your hand even knows. So if you see it coming down the belt, you'll just pick it up and start automatically turning it. And it'll probably catch the bar code. So you just look and talk, look and talk. That's where you get your chance to communicate."

Marissa's body, like a cyborg, has merged with the computerized system of identifying and pricing, recording and ordering inventory, monitoring time and speed, goods and earnings. She acknowledges, "Your hand even knows." And while her hand carries on the work, automatically and at record speed, she carries on a conversation. The contact with customers, in this context, becomes one of the small "free spaces" where she may still be creative, human, original.

In terms of work, the health effects of jobs speeded up by computer technology are starting to be publicly recognized. Clearly, the "environment" for the cashier begins with the computerization of her work that regulates and marks her body. The UFCW, along with Loblaws' management, has sought technical solutions to leg and back strain, as well as the carpal tunnel syndrome caused by repetitive movement of the cashier's wrist in scanning. But more ergonomic checkout lanes and scanners are high-tech responses reflecting a management mentality; they only lessen the impact of the technology but do not address the question of speed in its use, for example, or other deeper structural issues such as work totally driven by efficiency and profit. It's no wonder cashiers end up preferring the shorter shifts.

Health and environment issues dominate concerns not only of supermarket workers but also of many consumers, who are increasingly questioning the safety of the food they buy. Ironically, while Loblaws is touted as an industry leader in promoting environmentally sound operational practices, in developing an organics line and in educating consumers about the health benefits of this line, the company, like other food giants, has not really challenged the underlying global food system. Unsustainable agricultural practices contribute to environmental degradation (especially in the south) and produce food of questionable nutritional value; even large-scale organic production, while chemical-free, may reproduce harmful effects of industrial agriculture, such as unfair labor practices. It has only been in the past few years, with a growing food security movement, that questions of food safety, health, and environment have come to the forefront.

The Other Globalization: Resistance Is Fertile

In early 2000, a burgeoning and vociferous movement of Canadian activists brought to the public debate some of the key issues raised in this book. During International Resistance Is Fertile Week, for example, Vandana Shiva spoke to sellout crowds at the University of Toronto on her way to an international Biodevastation Conference in Boston. She called for a five-year moratorium on genetic engineering and public financing of scientific research. Relevant to supermarkets, she suggested that basic foodstuffs should be taken out of the marketplace, food and agriculture should be taken out of the World Trade Organization, and life forms and biodiversity should be out of the Intellectual Property Rights Legislation.[153]

The same week, the Mexican Senate tabled a health bill that would require genetically modified foodstuffs to be labeled,[154] and in 2004, the Mexican congress passed a law allowing limited release of genetically modified (GM) crops.[155] The Canadian government has been more timid on the issue of genetic engineering, and in the fall of 2001, the Parliament defeated a bill requiring mandatory labeling of GM foods.[156] They sided with the United States and against Europe at an early 2000 international conference in Montreal discussing the rules, limitations, and trade of GM food; while Europe and the Third World prioritized the right to health, the North Americans argued for freedom of enterprise. The head of the Canadian delegation was quite clear: "the health of the population is not on the agenda of this meeting."[157]

"With such government cheerleading," writes Leah Rumack, "supermarkets don't think they have to speak to consumer anxiety."[158] Government agencies have acted primarily within the interests of large retailers and pharmaceutical companies that have helped fund research. The government of Canada is at least waking up to citizen concern, and in 2001, it issued to all doorsteps a twelve-page booklet on "Food Safety and You," to assure the reader that new foods are strictly evaluated by scientific experts, comparing transgenic manipulation to using yeast to grow bread.[159] The purposes of the flyer seem to be to calm fears and to corroborate the claim of Jeannie Cruickshank, of the Canadian Council of Grocery Distributors, that "there is no safety issue with these products."[160]

Many Canadian consumers are not convinced, however, and national environmental and social justice organizations joined forces to launch a national campaign against genetically modified food. The Sierra Club, Council of Canadians, and Greenpeace have independently and collectively raised public consciousness about the issue, adopting a consumer-driven strategy. As the country's largest retailer, Loblaws has become a favorite target. Greenpeace met with company representatives in the early 2000s and secured an agreement that Loblaws would provide a special section in the supermarket clearly marked for non-GM foods.

Nonetheless, Greenpeace decided to step up the protest, linking the giant retailer to the actions of giant food processors, such as Kellogg's, whose popular cornflakes is a perfect entree for exploring impacts of GM corn, touching children and parents alike. Families were out in full force in the spring of 2000 for demonstrations at various Loblaws stores. In the next two pages, I juxtapose photos of this protest with excerpts from the flyers of the protesting organizations, revealing the positions, goals, and strategies of these active resisters.

CONSUMERS CLAIM THEIR POWER

For the past few years, a few huge companies have been quietly replacing ingredients in your food with GMOs. More than 60 percent of processed foods contain GMOs. GMOs are created by taking a gene strand from one life form and inserting it into another, making a completely different life form. It could be a gene from an animal or a bacteria being inserted into a plant.

Among the few chosen for creative genetic manipulation, a tomato has been inserted with a fish gene to allow it to survive in colder weather. Risks include the development of antibiotic resistance, allergic reactions, the development of superweeds and superpests resistant to agricultural chemicals, increased pesticide and herbicide use, harm to beneficial insects, and loss of biological diversity, to name a few.

There's already evidence that GMOs are harming the environment. It could take decades for all of the effects to be known. In the meantime, we're all being used as guinea pigs, taking part in a genetic experiment without our knowledge or consent.

Not nearly enough testing has been done. These same biotech companies have mostly controlled what little testing there is. And the results are not available to the public.

In Europe and Asia, major manufacturers like Kellogg's and Nestle have responded to consumer demand and removed GMOs. Canadians deserve the same protection! Send the manufacturers of the food we eat a message.

The anti-GMO organizers also raised deeper issues that are ecological, social, political, and economic in nature:

Why we should worry about genetic engineering:

1. *Health risks*
2. *Biological pollution*
3. *Corporate interests*
4. *Farming crisis*
5. *Government regulatory failures*

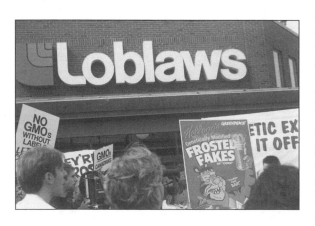

In targeting supermarkets instead of farmers, activists are confirming the power of the retail sector in bringing food to our tables. As farmers predicted their own demise, National Farmers Union representative Darrin Qualman identified a deeper concern for the increasing concentration of the control of seeds in the hands of a few companies.[161] Clearly, activism has to become as transnational as the ruling corporations (chapter 8).

UNION ACTION FOR CASHIERS

One of the key movements to expose the exploitation by transnational companies of cheap Third World labor is the Stop the Sweatshop movement.[162] In contrast to the consumer-based strategy of environmentalists demanding that Loblaws address the issue of food safety, these activists focus on production—denouncing the wages, working conditions, and environmental impacts of production practices that have been relocated in Third World countries. Mexican agricultural workers have not yet become part of the consciousness of the food security movement in Canada. Nor has there been much public concern for the working conditions of the cashiers and other Canadians working in our supermarkets.

Canadian retail workers' concerns have been left primarily to the labor movement. Loblaws cashiers, the key subjects of this chapter, are represented by the UFCW. As the second largest private-sector union in Canada (with 215,000 Canadian members, 1.4 million including U.S. members), it represents the largest number (42,000) of retail grocery workers in Ontario.[163]

In her gendered analysis of the supermarket industry, Kainer charges that retail unions have not challenged the employer around gender wage differentials of full-time workers. "Women continue to be paid at wage rates which devalue the worth of their work. Once again, the industry is building upon the historic sex division of labor to restructure work in the supermarket."[164] Kainer suggests that a lack of feminist consciousness in the union leadership is rooted in the male-dominated butcher craft traditions. There have been advances, with the UFCW establishing a National Women's Committee in 1990; but while the majority of the members are women, few are local and national executives. In 2005, however, CAW Local 414 representing 10,000 supermarket workers in Ontario, elected a female president for the first time in its history.

The tough bargaining of the mid-1990s again raised questions of gender blindness, as full-time jobs in the male-predominant job classifications were preserved,[165] while part-time and female-predominant jobs such as cashiers lost full-time positions and had their wages lowered. This left older cashiers like Marissa either accepting buyout packages or a wage freeze and new hires with lower starting and top salaries. The two-tiered wage concession, unfortunately, contributes to divisions among workers. UFCW officers maintain that they fought for the part-timers' cause by protecting scheduling by seniority, while Loblaws wanted to be able to schedule them according to shift, time, and skill. Admittedly, this served the most senior cashiers, while the most junior became more susceptible to holiday and weekend call-ins.

Union negotiators have felt caught not only in the larger corporate battles for control of the sector, especially given Wal-Mart's relentless expansion, but also in the unrelenting pace of technological change: "We can't just stick our heads in the sand and say we're going to fight technological change. The industry is changing, and if we just say no to the change, probably we will end up with store closures and losses of more jobs than we otherwise face."[166] In terms of cashiers, the UFCW president fears that their jobs are literally on the line, as the company considers options such as scanners on grocery carts, shifting their work to the customer. Yet 2003 and 2006 contracts did not reflect a strong gender analysis or a defense of part-time workers. Reflecting more a social unionist perspective, he tries to put this labor struggle into the broader context of the impact that work restructuring is having on our society:

> The real answer to the political issue of whether society is ready for that kind of job losses—that's a political agenda as well as a labor agenda. It is a much larger picture—it's going to take much more than one employer and one union to resolve. It's really going to take a meeting of the minds of government, business, and labor, because ultimately you're going to find revolt, reaction, loss of jobs, high unemployment—it's going to put a price to pay on society. We'll end up with a lot more crime in the street, and a lot of drug issues, and a lot more youth that are disenfranchised and feel like there's no security and no future. Those are bigger issues. They're hard to deal with because the employer wants to deal with today, tomorrow, and maybe a five-year outlook.

The UFCW president recognizes that the general climate is not favorable to unions. Still, he maintains, "There is a lot of protection in a unionized environment. It's not a perfect world. I wish we could wave the magic wand and when you join the union everything becomes perfect. It's an opportunity for workers to try to group themselves and have a voice to try to deal with workplace issues." As for participation of the rank and file, he admits that it is limited: "The problem is, you still only reach a small percentage of your membership. Because the reality is, aside from contract time, people have busy lives today, you know, they are struggling to make ends meet and attending their local membership meeting isn't the highest priority."

Having seen the impact of erratic scheduling of shifts based on the infinite "flexibility" of a cashier such as Marissa, it is easier to understand how the restructuring of work, and thus of home life, makes it even more difficult to build a coherent union movement, one that responds to the needs of men and women, full-time and part-time, in an era when work itself is being totally redefined[167] by corporate interests.

Notes

1. The epigraph is from *George Weston Ltd. Annual Report 1994*, 2.

2. For a more elaborated deconstruction of this image, see Deborah Barndt, "Zooming In/Zooming Out: Visualizing Globalization," *Visual Sociology* 12, no. 2 (1997): 10–12.

3. I am indebted to Stephanie Conway, who, as graduate research assistant with the Tomasita Project, did much of the research and interviews that form the basis for this chapter. Not only her careful work but her sharp analytical skills have influenced the ideas developed here.

4. President's Choice products, for example, are being sold in Colombia.

5. Philip Morris, which until 1986 was the world's premier tobacco company, by the mid-1990s had become the world's second largest food conglomerate, gobbling up food giants Kraft and Suchard through corporate takeovers, part of a merger wave encouraged by President Reagan. Richard Barnet and John Cavanagh, *Global Dreams: Imperial Corporations and the New World Order* (New York: Simon & Schuster, 1994), 211.

6. Information on the history of George Weston Ltd. and Loblaws is drawn from three key sources: "The History of Loblaws," a two-page summary provided by Loblaws' main office; the company Web site; and Anne Kingston, *The Edible Man: Dave Nichol, President's Choice, and the Making of Popular Taste* (Toronto: Macfarlane Walter & Ross, 1994).

7. It is interesting, in an era when labor is increasingly being replaced by technology, and supermarket cashiers may be replaced by automated checkouts where consumers will scan their own boxes, to consider that the origins of Loblaw Grocerterias were also based on cutting back on labor and transferring the work of shopping to the customer.

8. Personal communications with Jan Kainer, May 2000.

9. Louis Malassis suggested four stages, the first three being the preagricultural food economy, the agricultural and domestic food economy, and the commercialized and diversified agricultural food economy. Louis Malassis and Martin Padilla, *Economie agro-alimentaire*, vol. 3 (Paris: Cujas, 1986), 10.

10. Anthony Winson, *The Intimate Commodity: Food and the Development of the Agro-Industrial Complex in Canada* (Toronto: Garamond, 1993), 111.

11. Barnet and Cavanagh, *Global Dreams*, 228.

12. The data offered here are drawn from the 2005 annual report of George Weston Ltd.

13. Paul Waldie, "Loblaw Gobbles Up Biggest Quebec Grocer," *Globe and Mail*, 31 October 1998, 1, 11A.

14. With the $20.3 billion takeover of Best Foods in late 2001, the Anglo-Dutch Unilever Group became the world's largest food manufacturing firm, with combined sales of $52 billion (web.northscape.com/content/gfherald/2000/06/26/agweek/626merger.htm).

15. An April 2000 manifesto issued by the Business Council on National Issues (BCNI), a body that represents 150 of Canada's largest corporations, sparked much public debate about the "big is better" argument: "Jean Monty of BCE Inc. told the group [BCNI] yesterday that the toughest message to get across in Canada is that companies have to be big to compete. Michael Phelps of Westcoast Energy Inc. said that all things being equal, big is better. Okay, it's not easy being big in Canada, where many people equate being big with being American." Madelaine Drohan, "Big Business Feels Misunderstood in Canada," *Globe and Mail*, 6 April 2000, 7B.

16. *Loblaw Companies Ltd. 2005 Annual Report*.

17. Winson, *The Intimate Commodity*, 180.

18. Loblaws supermarkets will buy fresh local produce in season, but from larger producers, not small farms.

19. Winson, *The Intimate Commodity*, 157.

20. *Loblaw Companies Ltd. 2005 Annual Report*.

21. Marina Strauss, "Maple Leaf Gardens to Become a Loblaws," *Globe and Mail*, 22 October 2003, A9.

22. Weston, Currie, and Nichol visited successful North American supermarket chains to gather ideas, and they were most influenced by California retailers, borrowing the idea of the *Insider's Report* from Trader Joe's and spray systems and produce stacking from Gelson's Markets in Los Angeles. Kingston, *The Edible Man*, 29–30.

23. Produce staff daily inspect and discard "blemished" produce into a composter. Interview with part-time cashier, May 2000.

24. "Loblaws Grocery Stores: Shifting the Retail Paradigm," in "The Watt Design Group" section of the Loblaws Web site.

25. Kingston, *The Edible Man*, 127.

26. Bronwyn Drainie, "Prepackaged Prophecy and Spiritual Supermarkets," *Globe and Mail*, 30 May 1996; Doug Saunders, "Engineering a Chamber of Temptations," *Globe and Mail*, 16 November 1998; Don Gillmor, "Groceryland: Is It a Store? A Theme Park? A Biosphere?" *Report on Business Magazine*, October 1998; Susan Cole, "Queasy at Loblaws," *Now Magazine*, 2–8 December 1999.

27. Saunders, "Engineering a Chamber of Temptations," 20C.

28. The notion of the "simulacra," first coined by Jean Beaudrillard, is very appropriate here; from tomatoes to supermarkets, our illusory perceptions of fresh food and intimate experiences have replaced the real thing. Jean Beaudrillard, "The Evil Demon of Images and the Precession of Simulacra," in *Postmodernism: A Reader*, ed. Thomas Docherty (New York: Columbia University Press, 1993), 194.

29. Don Watt, paraphrased by Saunders, "Engineering a Chamber of Temptations," 20C.

30. "Maintained in a constant bath of refrigerated air, these fruits are incapable of producing scents, harboring bugs, growing molds, and becoming decayed." Susan Willis, *A Primer for Daily Life* (New York: Routledge, 1991), 50.

31. *Loblaw Companies Ltd. 1999 Annual Report*, 8.

32. Don Watt, quoted in Saunders, "Engineering a Chamber of Temptations," 20C.

33. Thanks to Stephanie Conway for pointing this out.

34. CIBC was already in the family, in some ways, as the principal banker for both Loblaw Companies Ltd. and its corporate parent, George Weston Ltd., and with Galen Weston, the chair of both companies, sitting on the bank's board of directors. John Partridge, "Loblaw, CIBC to Open In-Store Bank Branches," *Globe and Mail*, 10 December 1997, 1B.

35. Ironically, the "president" in "President's Choice" refers to Richard Currie, president of both Loblaw Companies. Ltd. and George Weston Ltd. from 1996 to 2002. Most people, however, associate it with Dave Nichol, who was in fact replaced by Currie in 1984 as Loblaws' president and demoted to president of Loblaws International Merchandising, through which he developed the PC line. Behind the label, in fact, is an intriguing story of sibling rivalry and power struggles. See Kingston, *The Edible Man*.

36. Dave Nichol himself has continued to carry his passion for product development elsewhere. While still with Loblaw International Merchants, he helped develop "Sam's Choice in America" for Wal-Mart; he left Loblaws (under much innuendo) in 1994 to join Gerry Pencer of Cott Corp. to manage private-label food development as part of a major campaign to take on national brands in North America and Europe. By 1996, he had left Cott and his money-losing division and launched his own company, Dave Nichol & Associates. Kimberley Noble, "Pitchman Nichol Lands on His Feet after Leaving Cott," *Globe and Mail*, 9 September 1997, 1B.

37. Gillmor, "Groceryland," 124.

38. As a strategy, the *Insider's Report* (an idea and name Nichol bought from Trader Joe's in California) created a new form of advertising, actually educating consumers about food while urging them to try new products at introductory low prices (which would eventually rise). Kingston, *The Edible Man*, 72.

39. Kingston, *The Edible Man*, 145.

40. There are myriad analyses of this phenomenon within the field of cultural studies, drawing on classic advertising theorists such as Raymond Williams, who suggests there's a kind of magic in advertising that promotes social and personal values more than the products themselves. See Raymond Williams, "Advertising: The Magic System," in his *Problems in Materialism and Culture: Selected Essays* (London: Verso, 1980). Another key theorist, Edward Said, labels the Western gaze and stereotypical views of the East as "orientalism." See his *Orientalism* (New York: Random House, 1994).

41. Clara Sacchetti and Todd Dufresne, "President's Choice through the Looking Glass," *Fuse Magazine* (May/June 1994): 30.

42. Patrick Carson became the guiding light for the environmental thrust of Weston companies from the late 1980s until the mid-1990s, when environmental concerns faded from the corporate agenda. While he at times seemed too radical for the boardroom, pushing an analysis that considered not only the symptoms but the (political and economic) sources of the environmental crisis, he did leave a blueprint for the business world, a legacy that companies could use out of mercenary, altruistic, and/or ecological interests. See Patrick Carson and Julia Moulden, *Green Is Gold: Business Talking to Business about the Environmental Revolution* (Toronto: HarperBusiness, 1991).

43. Quoted in Kingston, *The Edible Man*, 203.

44. Organic Resource Management is the company contracted by Loblaws for instituting this in-store system. Interview by author and Stephanie Conway with Vive Wark, 31 January 1997, Toronto.

45. Johanna Powell, "National Grocers Brings 'Greening' Motto to Life," *Financial Post*, 23 November 1996.

46. Powell, "National Grocers Brings 'Greening' Motto to Life."

47. Interview by author and Stephanie Conway with Marcela Diaz-Granados, 8 May 1997, Toronto.

48. The Loblaws/Pollution Probe collaboration in the late 1980s also involved a coproduction with McClelland & Stewart and Doubleday of the first Canadian *Green Consumer Guide*. Activist journalist Warner Troyer worked with Pollution Probe on the project, but

while he wanted to raise health-related issues such as pesticides and food safety, they wanted to focus on more mainstream concerns such as acid rain, waste management, and transportation. Kingston, *The Edible Man*, 207.

49. *President's Choice Healthy Insider's Report*, 6; see also www.healthyeatingisinstore.ca.

50. Joseph Hall, "Diabetes Soars in Ontario," *Toronto Star*, 2 March 2007, A1.

51. In my local Loblaws, two of the ten checkout lanes have been converted into displays of junk food and candy specials.

52. Peter Rakobowchuk, http://news.yahoo.com/s/cpress/20060221/ca_pr_on_he/food_obesity_tax.

53. Ibid.

54. Deirdre McMurdy, "Organic Foods Are Hot as Health Awareness Grows," *Gazette*, 26 August 2004, B8. See also Michael Valpy, "Has Big Business Turned Organics into Yuppie Chow?" *Globe and Mail*, 30 May 2007, A9.

55. Craig Wong, "Stores Rush to Meet Soaring Demand for Organic and Natural Foods," *Canadian Press Wire*, 2 October 2005.

56. Allison Lampert, "Organic Food Sales Growing," *Gazette*, 8 June 2006, B3.

57. Excerpt from "State of Food Insecurity" document of the FAO, quoted in ETC group, "Oligopoly, Inc. 2005: Concentration in Corporate Power," *Communiqué* 91 (November/December 2005): 8.

58. Interview with Loblaws' employee, Toronto, 23 February 2007.

59. By 2005, the world's top ten seed companies controlled one-half of the global seed trade, the top ten biotech businesses controlled three-quarters of biotech sales, and the top ten pesticide producers controlled almost 85 percent of the market. Some companies, like Monsanto, were in the top five in all three categories. ETC Group, "Oligopoly, Inc.," 2.

60. Angelo DiCaro, "Buy Canadian: Made in Canada Matters," *CAW Local 414 Banter*, December 2006, 5. DiCaro also notes that the number of U.S.-based retailers operating in Canada has risen from 21 in 1991 to 135 in 2003.

61. As a symbol of the struggle between two visions of the world, Fishman suggests that "Wal-Mart is either one of the boldest, most democratic creations in human history, a validation of free markets, harnessing its enormous power on behalf of the needs of ordinary people, or it is an insatiable, insidious beast, exploiting the people it pretends to defend." Charles Fishman, *The Wal-Mart Effect* (New York: Penguin Press, 2006).

62. Loblaws is not alone in reorienting its strategies to fight off the Wal-Mart threat. Over 80 percent of U.S. retailers named the behemoth as their greatest competitive threat. Jenny McTaggart, Debra Chanil, and Stephen Dowdell, "Survival of the Fittest," *Progressive Grocer*, 14 April 2006, 48.

63. Dana Flavelle, "Ontario Grocers Ready for Battle," *Toronto Star*, 13 August 2006.

64. In 2004, Wal-Mart controlled 8 percent of the global market share of grocery retail, more than twice its closest competitor, Carrefour of France. In a highly concentrated industry, the top ten food retailers controlled 24 percent of global sales of $3.5 trillion. ETC Group, "Oligopoly, Inc.," 7.

65. Zena Olijnyk, "Battle of the Giants," *Canadian Business*, 23 November 2003, 29.

66. "Wal-Mart's Canadian Supercenter, Estimating Trade Area Damage," CIBC World Markets Report, 3 August 2006.

67. UFCW 1000A Special Report, 11. Human rights observers have charged Wal-Mart with lowering labor standards in China.

68. Anthony Bianco et al, "Is Wal-Mart Too Powerful?" *BusinessWeek*, 6 October 2003, http://www.businessweek.com/magazine/content/03_40/b3852001_mz001.htm.

69. Wal-Mart avoided criminal charges for hiring undocumented workers by paying a $11 million settlement. ETC group, "Oligopoly, Inc.," 9.

70. Five hundred thousand workers in Bangladesh, China, Swaziland, Indonesia, and Nicaragua filed a class action suit against Wal-Mart in September 2005, "Oligopoly, Inc.," 9.

71. "Oligopoly, Inc.," 9.

72. *Supermarket News* 54, no. 22 (May 29, 2006): 22.

73. "Sobeys and Loblaw Hop on the E-Grocer Channel," *Canadian Grocer* 116, no. 9 (November 2002): 19.

74. Hollie Shaw, "Loblaw to Unplug E-grocer: Rising Oil Prices Cited," *Financial Post*, 14 September 2005, FP3.

75. The epigraph is excerpted from a speech that Dave Williams, then vice president of Weston, presented to the Food 2002 conference in May 1998, which brought together representatives of government, industry, and community agencies to plot a common strategy for eradicating hunger in Ontario by 2002.

76. "Who's Hungry: 2006 Profile of Hunger in the GTA," www.dailybread.ca, accessed 7 March 2007.

77. Interview with Gary Lloyd, 20 February 1997.

78. Kingston, *The Edible Man*, 63. There is pressure in Canada to institutionalize this "alternative" food distribution system as has happened in the United States, where food manufacturers get lucrative tax write-offs for their donation of surplus or damaged goods. Winson, *The Intimate Commodity*, 183.

79. Interview with author and Stephanie Conway with Ken Mulhall, 8 May 1997, Toronto.

80. Food bank organizers have repeatedly requested cash donations in lieu of many of the food donations they receive that are not necessarily what people need.

81. It may not be a coincidence that a few months later, in early 2000, the company ended the lease with the Daily Break Food Bank.

82. Jan Kainer, "Flexibility and Low Pay: Restructuring in Ontario's Food Retail Sector," unpublished paper, York University, December 1996, 13.

83. *George Weston Ltd. 1998 Annual Report*, 23.

84. Interview by Stephanie Conway with Kevin Corporan, executive vice president, United Food and Commercial Workers International Union, Local 1000A, Toronto, 25 April 1997.

85. While the UFCW serves employees of Loblaws, the Canadian Auto Workers (CAW) merged with Retail Wholesale in 1999 and currently represents about five thousand workers in Newfoundland and Ontario under the banners of No Frills, Valu-Mart, and Your Independent Grocer. Angelo DiCaro, personal communication, 26 February 2005.

86. Angelo DiCaro, personal communication, January 2007.

87. A precedent had already been set for concession bargaining by the UFCW in its negotiations with Miracle Food Mart in 1993–1994. After a three-month strike, the longest in the history of retail in Canada, which ironically was to resist concessions and maintain industry standards, the union finally settled for lowering of wage levels, a buyout program, and the introduction of new part-time wage categories, deepening the schism between full-time and part-time workers. Jan Kainer, "Gender, Corporate Restructuring, and Concession Bargaining in Ontario's Food Retail Sector," *Relations Industrielle/Industrial Relations* 53, no. 1 (1998): 195.

88. Adria Vasil. "Aisles of Trouble," http://www.nowtoronto.com/2003-0731/news_feature_p_html.

89. Hugh Finnamore, "A Sweetheart Deal," http://www.ufcw.net/articles/HJ_Finnamore/2003-07-25_a_sweetheart_deal.html.

90. UFCW 1000A Special Report, 3, 8.

91. Dana Flavelle, "Union Okays Loblaw Revamp," *Toronto Star*, 17 October 2006, C1.

92. Jerry Tutunjian, "Loblaw Opts for Short-Term Pain for Long-Term Gain," *Canadian Grocer* 120, no. 3 (April 2006): 7.

93. Marina Strauss, "Troubled Loblaw to Lose Another Key Executive," *Globe and Mail Report on Business*, 29 September 2006, B5.

94. Gordon Pitts, "The Loblaw Evolution: A Revolution in Style," *Globe and Mail*, 6 January 2007.

95. "Loblaw Announces Changes That Will Lead to a Leaner and More Responsible Structure," Loblaw Companies Ltd. Bulletin issued to employees, 22 January 2007.

96. Dana Flavelle, "Loblaw Stakes Future on Apparel," *Toronto Star*, 22 February 2007, C1–11.

97. Interview with Loblaws worker, Toronto, 23 February 2007.

98. Kainer, "Gender, Corporate Restructuring, and Concession Bargaining," 193.

99. Most of the details outlined in these two paragraphs are drawn from the "Proposed Settlement between UFCW Local 1000A and Loblaws Supermarkets Ltd. Including Supercentres," 1996.

100. Most new hires are students who live at home, so they are often covered by their parents' benefits. But specific benefits kick in at different times; for example, after three hundred hours, a part-time worker gets vision care.

101. The epigraph is from an interview by author and Stephanie Conway with Marissa Ronen (pseudonym), Toronto, May 1997.

102. Cashier Notice Re: Declaration of Availability, 1996.

103. The epigraph is taken from an interview by author and Stephanie Conway with Andrew Stock, store manager, Loblaws, Dundas West and Bloor, Toronto, 14 March 1997.

104. Much of the data in this section is drawn from Kainer, "Flexibility and Low Pay: Restructuring in Ontario's Food Retail Sector," unpublished paper, York University, December 1996.

105. Pat Armstrong and Hugh Armstrong, *The Double Ghetto*, 3d ed. (Toronto: McClelland & Stewart, 1993), 55.

106. The United Food and Commercial Workers (UFCW) itself was formed in 1979 out of a merger between the Amalgamated Meat Cutters and Butchermen (known in Canada as the Canadian Food and Allied Workers) and the Retail Clerks International Union; butchers were in fact often placed in a separate bargaining unit from retail clerks, creating divisions that are still felt today. Kainer, "Flexibility and Low Pay," 6.

107. Interview by author and Stephanie Conway with Camila Mejia (pseudonym), Toronto, 4 May 1997.

108. Interview with Marissa Ronen, Toronto, May 1997.

109. Interview by Stephanie Conway with Kevin Corporan, 25 April 1997.

110. This survival strategy, employed by what may be seen as the most privileged women employees, was revealed by two head office workers we interviewed as well as two in managerial positions.

111. Interview with Sandra Lot, manager for systems training, 5 June 1997.

112. Interview with Marissa Ronen, Toronto, May 1997.

113. Interview by Stephanie Conway with Rosa Viccelli (pseudonym), 20 April 1997.

114. "The assumption by management as well as checkers is that the mostly female checkers will know the different fruits and vegetables because of their experience as con-

sumers." John Walsh, *Supermarkets Transformed: Understanding Organizational and Technological Innovations"* (New Brunswick, N.J.: Rutgers University Press, 1993), 142.

115. Increasingly sophisticated software links cashiers' schedules to the ebbs and flows of day-to-day, week-to-week sales. Cashiers' availability forms are inputted in the program that allocates work hours based on projected sales volume (based on the previous year's data). This has greatly facilitated the scheduling process, which was previously done manually by front-end managers. Personal communication with Angelo DiCaro, Canadian Auto Workers, January 2007.

116. The company tried to gain more control over scheduling in the 1996 negotiations, but the union maintained the seniority system. Loblaws probably hoped to facilitate the scheduling process by computerizing it as many other food services have done. Starbucks uses a software program called Star Labor that allows it to tailor-make shifts to maximize coffee-selling efficiency. As one worker describes it, "They give you an arbitrary skill number from one to nine and they plug in when you're available, how long you've been there, when customers come in and when we need more staff, and the computer spits out your schedule based on that." Quoted in Naomi Klein, *No Logo: Taking Aim at the Brand Bullies* (Toronto: Knopf, 2000), 243.

117. Interview by author and Stephanie Conway with Carol Melucci, Toronto, May 1997.

118. Personal communication with Jorge Garcia-Ogales, UFCW staff, April 2000.

119. Interview with Sandra Lot, 5 June 1997.

120. John Walsh, *Supermarkets Transformed*, 94–95.

121. Nisant Thusoo and Senthil Kumar, "Leveraging Store Technologies for the Customer Experience," *Chain Store Age*, ABI/INFORM Global, January 2006, 34A.

122. Interview with Marissa Ronen and Karla Bocello, Toronto, May 1997.

123. "ECR—Where It's Coming From," *Canadian Grocer* (July/August 1996): 53.

124. Interview by Stephanie Conway with Kevin Corporan, Toronto, 25 April 1997.

125. Heather Menzies, *Whose Brave New World? The Information Highway and the New Economy* (Toronto: Between the Lines, 1996), 70.

126. Menzies, *Whose Brave New World?* 117.

127. Interview with Marissa Ronen, Toronto, May 1997.

128. Interview by Stephanie Conway with Wayne Montgomery, 13 May 1997, Toronto.

129. Interview by author and Stephanie Conway with Karla Bocello, 13 May 1997, Toronto.

130. Interview with Karla Bocello, 13 May 1997.

131. Sometimes cashiers may, however, work five and a half hours without a break, when the customer service manager schedules the first break after the first hour of an eight-hour work day and the last one hour before the end of the work day.

132. Interview with Sandra Lot and Kim Scharnowski, 5 June 1997.

133. Angelo DiCaro, Canadian Auto Workers, personal communication, January 2007.

134. Interview by Stephanie Conway with Rosa Viccelli, 20 April 1997.

135. The "You Can Count on Me" program was canned, apparently, when the man in charge of it was found swindling money. An ironic end, as two cashiers joked: "You can count on him, eh?!"

136. Interview with Sandra Lot, 5 June 1997.

137. Interview by Stephanie Conway with Laura Donello, Toronto, 18 February 1997.

138. See Arlie Hochschild's classic work, *The Managed Heart* (Berkeley: University of California Press, 1983). She notes how the pressure to be "courteous and pleasant" in service jobs such as cashiers can be very emotionally wearing over time.

139. Interview with Carol Melucci, 4 May 1997.

140. Interview by Stephanie Conway with Rosa Viccelli, Toronto, 20 April 1997.

141. Interview with Marissa Ronen, Toronto, May 1997.

142. Loblaws' handout for employees, early 2000.

143. Interview with Carol Melucci, 4 May 1997.

144. Interview with Marissa Ronen, Toronto, May 1997.

145. At the time of the second edition, Marissa had secured a permanent job as an inventory analyst and was soon to celebrate thirty-five years of service. She also remarried (a Loblaws coworker) and her children were young adults, no longer living at home.

146. This restriction on seniority does serve workers to a certain degree, as Marissa might bump another worker with less seniority if she transferred. Personal communications with Jorge Ogales-Garcia, April 2000.

147. "The ideology of family affects women in paid employment. The assumption that women workers are wives with husbands to support them has been used to justify paying women less than men." Meg Luxton, Harriet Rosenberg, and Sedef Arat-Koc, *Through the Kitchen Window: The Politics of Home and Family* (Toronto: Garamond, 1990), 16.

148. Statistics Canada (www.statcanada.ca/english/pgdb/People/Families/famil 36c.htm).

149. There is an increasing probability that students who have worked on McJobs to finance their education will end up stuck in those jobs after graduation, not because of their own inertia but because the options for young people have been narrowing at an alarming pace. A young Starbucks employee bemoans this reality: "This isn't how we want to spend the rest of our lives, but for right now the dream job isn't waiting for us anymore. . . . I was hoping that Starbucks would be a stepping stone to bigger and better things, but unfortunately it's a stepping stone to a big sinkhole." Quoted in Klein, *No Logo*, 236.

150. Klein, *No Logo*, 195–96.

151. Vandana Shiva, *Biopiracy: The Plunder of Nature and Knowledge* (Toronto: Between the Lines, 1997), 121.

152. Menzies, *Whose Brave New World?* 29–32.

153. Vandana Shiva speaking at the Life Sciences Building, University of Toronto, 24 March 2000.

154. Reuters wire service, 31 March 2000.

155. Opponents to the Mexican legislation dubbed it the "Monsanto Law" suggesting it benefits only multinationals. "Mexico Approves New GM Law," *Bridges*, The World Conservation Union, www.ictsd.org/biores/04-12-20/story3.htm, accessed 8 May 2007.

156. Joanne Paulson, "Biotech Firms Dodge Bullet: MPs Vote Down Bill Requiring Mandatory Labelling of GM Foods," *Saskatoon Star Phoenix*, 18 October 2001, D1.

157. John Erity, quoted in Marco Mostellino, "The Sour Taste of Transgenic Foods: The War Is Waged between North America and the EU Member States," *Tandem/Corriere Canadese*, 6 February 2000, 3.

158. Leah Rumack, "Stalking the Supermarket," *NOW Magazine*, 23–29 September 1999, 19.

159. Government of Canada, "Food Safety and You," distributed door to door, April 2000, 9; also see www.canada.gc.ca.

160. Jeannie Cruickshank, Canadian Council of Grocery Distributors, quoted in Rumack, "Stalking the Supermarket," 19.

161. Rumack, "Stalking the Supermarket," 33.

162. See Klein, *No Logo*, 347–63. Also Maquila Support Network, 606 Shaw Street, Toronto; E-mail: perg@web.net.

163. The other union representing a smaller number of food retail workers is Retail Wholesale Canada (RWC); until 1999, it was part of the Canadian Service Division of the United Steel Workers of America; it is now part of the Canadian Auto Workers Union. The joining of smaller unions to the larger affiliates is part of a trend within labor, parallel to the corporate trend of increasing concentration. It is argued that the only way labor can hold its ground in the face of corporate giants is by joining forces.

164. Kainer, "Flexibility and Low Pay," 35.

165. In the case of meat cutters, however, this meant being transferred from an increasingly technologized job to another category.

166. Interview with Kevin Corporan, 25 April 1997.

167. Some would argue that work as we know it is being redefined out of existence. See Jeremy Rifkin, *The End of Work: The Decline of the Global Labor Force and the Dawn of the Post-Market Era* (New York: Putnam, 1995).

CHAPTER 5

On the Move for Food:

TRUCKERS AND TRANSNATIONAL MIGRANTS

Bumping into Border Crossers

I met the two people featured in this chapter in very serendipitous ways. I first saw Humberto Carillo while visiting the packing plant of Empaque Santa Rosa in Sirena, Jalisco, Mexico, in 1997. He was hanging out at a food stand outside the plant, with other truckers, waiting for the tomato shipments to drive north.[1] It was thus a total surprise when I ran into him again two years later, in early 1999, in Nogales, Arizona, entering one of the warehouse destinations of Jalisco tomatoes, forty hours north of Sirena and in another country.

Irena Gonzalez also came into my life by a circuitous route. When Antonieta Barrón, a Mexican collaborator on this project, came to Canada to study Mexican farmworkers in Ontario, she introduced me to a trio of women picking tomatoes on a farm two hours outside of Toronto. Irena was clearly the mother figure of the group and she soon took us, the researchers, under her wing as well. Every year since 1996, we have visited her at her adopted Canadian farms. Often I have taken along other Mexican friends, or students, or supermarket cashiers; always we share stories as well as *mole, pozole,* and tortillas, in an exchange that is both culinary as well as cultural. In 1997, after Irena had completed our harvest season and returned to Mexico, Antonieta and I made the journey to visit her in her hometown of Miacatlán, Morelos. Since then, she, too, has visited my home in Toronto, most recently to spend a week exchanging agricultural knowledge with urban farmers who are creating food alternatives in Canada.

When I make the two-hour trip out to the farm where Irena works, I sometimes get stuck in highway traffic. I find myself particularly frustrated by the increasing number of larger trailer trucks hauling goods across borders, especially since NAFTA has made the crossing easier. Then I think of Humberto, forced to leave his family behind for twenty-three-day stints driving the tomatoes to their destination, and Irena, forced to leave her family behind for four months while she picks our summer tomatoes. I think of both of them as border crossers, on the move for their own survival and the survival of their families. Perhaps I am a border crosser, too, especially as I make this twisty journey chasing tomatoes, truckers, and women workers up and down the tomato trail.

In this chapter, we take a pause along the highway. The journey from the commercialization and consumption of food in Canada (chapters 3 and 4) back to its production in Mexico (chapter 6) requires a considerable leap—both in distance and in conceptualization. While this book is highlighting only three sectors involved in the tomato's transformation, we see in chapter 1 that there are many other stops along the trail.

Free trade supposedly opens the borders to encourage an easier movement of goods from one country to another. In the post-NAFTA era, there is also an increasing movement of certain workers across those borders. With the enormous increase in the traffic of goods, for example, there are greater numbers of workers needed to lift, pack, drive, inspect, repack, lift, pack, and drive again. While the Tomasita Project focuses on women workers in the food chain, the picture would not be complete without the (mostly male) truckers who move the tomatoes north. The stories of Humberto, a Mexican trucker, who crosses the border into the United States, and Jim, who brings tomatoes into Canada, will help fill this gap.

Not surprisingly, Mexican farmworkers who have been left landless by neoliberal policies are migrating in ever greater numbers to support their families; they are perhaps the most flexible labor force of the free trade era. And the U.S. $20 billion in remittances[2] these migrant workers send home are a critical source of foreign exchange, second only to oil. With deepening economic integration, leaders of the three NAFTA countries have been pushing for an expansion of this model to other sectors, such as financial services, energy, and transportation. In 2007, thirty CEOs from Mexico, the United States, and Canada proposed measures to smooth border crossings between the three countries. The business leaders' report was submitted to the 2005 Security and Prosperity Partnership (SPP) proposal aimed at greater trilateral cooperation in security, economic, and regulatory standards. Ironically, just as construction began on a 1,125 kilometer-long wall at the U.S.–Mexico border, President George W. Bush in his 2007 State of the Union address called for legislation to create "a legal and orderly path for guest workers." In May 2007, compromise legislation was proposed to grant legal status to twelve million illegal immigrants[3] and to bring four hundred thousand to six hundred thousand foreign workers into the United States annually through a temporary worker program.[4]

The largest numbers of migrant workers go to the United States.[5] In Canada, with private contractors increasingly seeking temporary foreign workers, the number was 145,871 in 2005.[6] A smaller number of farmworkers come to Canada through a government-sponsored program, the Seasonal Agricultural Workers Program (SAWP), that flies them to our fruit and vegetable farms for the growing season, and flies them back home when all the tomatoes have been harvested. Few Canadian consumers realize that not only their imported winter tomatoes but also the locally grown summer tomatoes may have been picked by Mexican women's hands. The story of Irena makes visible this little-known piece of the food puzzle.

The Canadian artist Ron Benner[7] has traced the journey of food from Mexico from its pre-Hispanic roots along a trail leading north. He reminds us that trade is not a new phenomenon, but the trails themselves have certainly changed, especially in the past fifty years. While trains transported goods in the nineteenth and early twentieth centuries, the postwar development of superhighways, largely subsidized by governments, has made large trucks the key mode of transport, especially for fresh produce such as tomatoes.

These large truck trailers are key culprits in the ecological devastation wrought by a continental food system, digesting hundreds of liters of fossil fuel and spewing exhaust into rural and urban areas alike as they barrel across borders. In peak season in early 1999, truck traffic at the Nogales, Arizona, border crossing exceeded twenty-five thousand shipments. An average of 100 trucks of tomatoes cross that border daily; in 1998, 40,486 trucks carried 513,978,826 kilograms of tomatoes to northern consumers.[8]

Trucking has long been a job associated with men. Whether loading small pickups with loose tomatoes for domestic production or steering twenty-five-ton trailers with well-packaged tomatoes exported to the foreign market, men draw on physical strength, an entrenched sexual division of labor, and a dose of machismo to operate in the trucking world.

Tales of Tomato Truckers: Humberto and Jim

Humberto,[9] a trucker with many years of experience, reflects this rarely questioned attitude: "There aren't any women truckers. Mexican women aren't interested. I did see one woman driver once, however, in San Cristobal." Humberto was socialized into this male job:

"My father was a truck driver, and when I was a kid, he taught [me] how to drive and I liked it. My brother also drives trucks. Since I didn't go to school, I decided to do it, too.

"I've been driving for UTTSA Trucking. It's a big company, with one hundred trucks and one hundred drivers, that transports only tomatoes. UTTSA has

a reputation for being one of the fastest companies, so producers contract it more than others.

"I work all year round, following the harvests: from October to January, I bring tomatoes from Jalisco; from January to May, I bring them from Sinaloa; and from May to October, from Baja California. Every year I see more tomatoes going north for export.

"When I arrive in Sirena (where Santa Rosa produces tomatoes), they assign me to a truck at the packing plant. I make about three trips every two weeks from Jalisco to Nogales. It takes about two days, then there are two days to sell the tomatoes. If you can make the journey in one day, then you have three days for selling.

"If I leave on a Monday about 5 P.M., when the tomatoes are all packed, I might arrive in Nogales on Wednesday. The journey is about thirty-six to forty hours, depending on whether I'm alone or not. If alone, I drive for twelve hours, then stop to sleep for five hours, drive again for twelve hours, and sleep for five. Now that it's the peak season, we work in pairs, so we never have to stop. If I have an assistant, then I can sleep for eight hours.

"When we get to the border, the truck gets weighed, and they give us permission to cross the border [for about twenty miles] and insurance to cover twenty-four hours. At the customs, there is the Department of Agriculture and the Department of Narcotics—they're police. They inspect the truck to be sure we're not carrying any drugs or pests, and they do a quality check of the tomatoes to be sure they're not rotten or covered with pesticides. Mexican producers send the best-quality tomatoes to the United States, so we usually don't have any problems.

"The regulations in the U.S. are a lot stricter than in Mexico. We have to make sure that the refrigeration works and have to check the equipment, water, oil, batteries, et cetera. The temperature has to be around 45 or 50 degrees Fahrenheit. But when it's hotter, the refrigeration has to work harder.

"This truck holds thirteen hundred liters of gasoline, which costs about three thousand pesos (about U.S. $300) to fill. The refrigeration unit uses two hundred liters costing about six hundred pesos (about U.S. $60).

"When I get to the warehouse in the United States, it takes about an hour to unpack the truck. There are about fifteen skids weighing about fifteen thousand kilos."

Having delivered the goods, Humberto then turns around and returns to Mexico, retracing the forty-hour trip back to Jalisco. If he's completed a three-week stint, he might be able to stop off for a three-day visit with his family.

"I'm married and have a six-month-old daughter; she and my wife live in Guadalajara, near her mama and papa, so they can help. I only see my family every twenty days, for about three days, then I'm off again for twenty more days, then three days at home, and so on."

A story similar to Humberto's, but from the northern end of the tomato chain, came to me by e-mail in early 2007, in response to a CBC radio interview I did about the supply chain of tomatoes, focusing on the Florida-based Mexican migrant workers who supply McDonald's (chapter 8). A Canadian trucker, Jim Bradbury, revealed some of the underbelly of the trucker's life: "I go to Immokalee [Florida] and I am expected to wait, sometimes all day. The trucking industry standard is that the first two hours of my time is covered by the pickup or delivery fee. Then, after waiting, I am expected to get the tomatoes delivered on time."[10]

At his Canadian destination for these tomatoes, the Loblaws warehouses in Ontario, Jim experiences a related frustration:

"A typical delivery starts at 1 A.M. or 3 A.M. The 1 A.M. appointment finishes at 7 A.M. and the 3 A.M. finishes up at 2 P.M. Then I have to go on to the next warehouse. To top it all off, Loblaws refuses to stamp my bills coming and going so there is no proof of my time at the warehouse."

All of these [unpaid] delays exact a personal toll: "Keep in mind that I left on Sunday and it is now Thursday night and then all day Friday. I want to get home to my family, because it starts all over again on Sunday."

"Food really is a nasty business," Jim concludes. "I'm so glad there is a shortage of drivers. I can threaten to quit when I have to do the food runs."

He does, however, find camaraderie in the human relations along the tomato trail. "I have to say, I really enjoy talking and spending time with the Mexicans. They are a good people and hard working."

Irena: One Widow, Two Countries, Three Jobs

"I was harvesting squash in the fields near my village one day, when my patrón came and said, 'Irena, you should go to Canada. There's now a program there for women.' And I said, 'How can I go to Canada, if I haven't even been to Mexico City [two hours away]?'

"When I went to the city to apply for the job, they asked for my husband's death certificate and my children's birth certificates.

"I didn't hear from them, but five months later I went with another woman to Mexico City; we left at 2 A.M. to be the first in the line when the office opened at 5 A.M. They had just received a request for two women, so we went quickly to get our medical exam and our passports.

"I was crying when I told my family I was going. My father said, 'If you're afraid, don't go, you won't starve here eating beans.' But I wanted to help my kids get ahead, so, tears and all, I said, 'I'm going.'"

The first time she came to Canada in 1989, Irena joined five thousand other Mexicans who, in her words, "are rented by the Mexican government to the Ontario government." Building on a program for temporary agricultural workers set up for Caribbean off-shore workers in 1966 and expanded to include Mexicans in 1974, the Seasonal Agricultural Workers Program (SAWP) is considered the crème de la crème of migrant worker schemes in North America.

The SAWP program originated in a period of low unemployment in Canada, when many Canadians did not want to do this kind of work. Today, coordinated by the Foreign Agricultural Resource Management Services (FARMS), it is a significant sector of the labor force, accounting for over 52 percent of agricultural workers.[11] In 2006, around 20,000 Mexican farmworkers came to Canada, with over 8,000 in Ontario.[12] From the beginning, the two governments agreed to annual controlled migrations of healthy farmworkers, who would have limited labor rights: minimum-wage salaries, medical insurance, and a Canadian pension, but no unemployment insurance, no unionization, and no overtime pay. The contract usually stipulates eight-hour workdays at six days a week. This doesn't mean there is no overtime work; in fact, farmworkers often seek it and agree to longer hours. In Irena's current situation, the regular workday is eleven hours, six and a half days a week. Since her primary reason for being in Canada is to make money, she wants to use every waking hour for that purpose.

It should be noted that there are some differences between the treatment of workers in different provinces, and private contractors are now bringing workers into Canada with even fewer rights.[13] Only since 1989 have women been included in the SAWP, brought to pick and pack fruit and vegetables during the four months of the harvest season or for longer production periods in the increasing number of greenhouse operations, where Canadian hydroponic tomato production has become internationally competitive. As Ofelia Becerril argues, their economic success is built on the specialized flexible labor force of Mexicans in the SAWP,[14] not only cheap but "captive."[15]

While their numbers increased from 37 in 1989 to 359 in 2005,[16] women still only account for less than 4 percent of the total seasonal work force. There continue to be strong gender ideologies entrenched in Canadian agrarian patriarchal culture where women are seen as "unable to carry out heavy work but suited to those tasks requiring the gentle touch, patience, and greater care."[17] Leigh Binford suggests that this narrows the field to certain jobs, along with the Mexican government's requirement that the women be single mothers, widows, or divorcées.[18]

"Most of us who are working in this program are widows," Irena explained. "They're afraid that a single woman might stay in Canada, or that a married woman might leave her husband.

"I've been a widow for eighteen years now. My husband died from drinking too much. With so much violence and alcoholism in the rural areas, there are some women who become widows after one year of marriage."

The only reason that women like Irena can consider leaving home for four months is that they have an extended family to support them. Irena lives with her elderly father and mother, who are left with the child care and domestic work. Her mother feels the load, too: "When Irena goes to Canada, I miss her, because she leaves the youngsters with me."

The practice of family members migrating for work and sending money home is common for most rural Mexican families. The United States has been the major destination, and Irena remembers her father going north just as she now must leave her children. "My father went twice to work in Texas. The second time he stayed for two and a half years," she said.

With the deepening poverty of the countryside, most Mexican families cannot survive without combining the incomes of several family members. Irena's older sons have also left in recent years.

"One of my sons goes to work in Quebec through the same program. He gets paid $7.50 an hour and works for fourteen or fifteen hours a day, seven days a week.

"My other son went this year to Kentucky to pick tobacco. Now there are contracts there, but they have to pay their own flight. I begged them not to go illegally, because it is dangerous; besides, you have to pay a coyote (the person who helps smuggle illegal migrants), and you can go into debt."

Irena's work, however, is totally dependent on the Canadian farmer who requests her labor.

"The economic situation in Mexico made me think about going to Canada," Irena said. "If God wills, I'll be there again. As long as the patrón keeps inviting me, I have work in Canada. If for any reason he doesn't ask for me, I can't get into Canada. I obey the person who pays me."

This patrón relationship is central to the SAWP program; migrant workers dare not displease their farmer/boss, or he may not request their return the following summer.[19] Once in Canada, the farmworkers are totally dependent on the farmer not only for transportation but also for permission to leave the premises, and they thus live almost like indentured workers. Ellen Wall suggests that this paternalistic relationship where migrant workers are housed on their employers' property, may depend on them for translation, filling out forms, and communications home, also makes it difficult for workers across farms to develop any solidarity around their common situation, let alone form some kind of workers' organization.[20] This paternalism often incorporates classist, racist, and sexist behaviors.

Employers' individual behaviors only mirror structural inequities in these government programs that reinforce racialized and gendered labor dynamics, shaped also by the asymmetry between the participating nations.[21] For example, while the SAWP program began with Caribbean workers, their numbers have decreased relative to the Mexicans, as racism shapes governmental policies as well as decisions made by employers about who will be hired and who will be asked back. One woman worker claimed her Anglo boss "always treated us as worthless Mexicans," while favoring Korean immigrants who were more productive because they were used to sitting close to the ground and their work required that.[22] Racism is also evident in the towns that workers visit for their weekly shopping or to attend mass on Sundays; they feel ignored and excluded.[23]

Irena has worked on several farms over the years, primarily with other Mexican workers, and claims that she has been treated fairly by the farmers who have employed her. When we visited her in 2000, the farmer and his family joined us for a picnic, and had made an effort to learn a little Spanish. But one incident revealed the limits of his generosity. One of the three Mexican women working on the farm asked me to translate a delicate conversation with him, in which she revealed she had been sexually assaulted by a male Mexican farmworker the previous night; she wanted her employer's assurance that this man would not be invited back the following year. However, Irena phoned me from Mexico a few months later to report that the employer had instead decided to hire only male workers! Fortunately, she was given another assignment, this time with a berry business where she shared a small trailer with two other women.[24]

In general, migrant workers like Irena in the SAWP program put up with the problematic labor relations, long hours of grueling work, social isolation, and often substandard housing conditions because they know it is temporary and lucrative.[25] While they are covered by the Occupational Health and Safety Act, they have not been able to unionize.

After eleven years of seasonal work in Canada, Irena still only makes slightly more than minimum wage. But because the program is based on the inequities between the two countries, the economic rewards of the program make it worthwhile for Mexican workers.

"In Mexico, we're paid by the day, thirty pesos ($6 to $7 a day). But we have to fill fifteen or twenty pails. The time it takes depends on how fast you move your hands. But in Canada, we're paid by the hour, $7 an hour, and you can work as many hours as you want. If we work eight hours, which is what the contract says, we get $56, which is seven times as much as we get in Mexico."[26]

While the SAWP program clearly exploits the asymmetry between Mexico and Canada in terms of wages, it provides a quick way for Mexican workers to amass an income, earning in one hour at minimum wage almost as much as they would in one day for similar work back home. Because these temporary migrant workers migrate alone, they are "freed" from family responsibilities for those few months, have minimal costs, and can work long hours. Irena recalls working once on a shorter contract for nineteen hours a day, starting at 5 A.M. and finishing at 12. While appalling to me, it was a gold mine for her, as she made $1,000 over two weeks.

In general, the working conditions in Canada are considered to be better by migrant workers like Irena:

"Agricultural work is harder in Mexico," said Irena. "Everything is done by hand. There, for example, we have to carry two boxes on our heads, full of tomatoes. In Canada, I can leave the tomatoes I've picked along the edge of the field and a truck will pick them up. In Mexico, if it's raining, we don't have anything to protect ourselves. But in Canada, they give us everything—a raincoat, a hoe, we don't have to buy anything. In Mexico, there's no protection from the fumes when they spray pesticides on the fields. In Canada, if you work for a good patrón, there is."

I was curious about what difference the four months in Canada made on Irena's survival back in Mexico. How does she spend the money she has earned? What does she do during the eight months she is at home? During a visit to her home in late 1997, I got some answers. In her living room were some of the immediate benefits of her Canadian earnings, new appliances that she had brought back: a TV, stereo, sewing machine, and fan. Her earnings mainly go to provide housing and security for her kids.

"With what I've earned in Canada, I've been able to pay for the legal title for a piece of land that my father gave me. I've divided it up for my kids and am helping both my sons purchase their own plots. My oldest daughter lives in California and works in a restaurant with her husband but may come back; my youngest daughter is studying to be a teacher. My hope is that all of my five children (between the ages of eighteen and thirty-two) as well as my grandchildren will eventually have a place here to live.

"I am trying to construct a more secure house. I have added rooms on to my house and have finally installed a bathroom. Everything here is very expensive.

I have to buy shoes and books for my daughter, who's just finished high school. I have ten cows. We're getting by. At least we have enough to eat."

Far from living in luxury on her Canadian earnings, Irena must keep working in Mexico at two jobs to support her family, and ironically, for most of the week, she must leave her children again.

"When I return home to Miacatlán, I work on weekdays in Cuernavaca (one hour away) as a live-in domestic worker, taking care of two invalids. Then I make and sell tacos in my village on Saturday and Sunday."

Irena feels, however, that her children understand and appreciate the sacrifices she makes for them, that they have better lives, and their relationships are more mature and loving. The concept of the "good mother" is being redefined by these female transnational migrants, according to Kerry Preibisch, who analyzes their experiences with SAWP as a "gender transformative odyssey."[27] While male farmworkers fulfill their traditional gender role of breadwinner by coming to Canada as seasonal workers, women are often stigmatized for abandoning their traditional caregiver roles.[28] Their time in Canada is seen as both liberating (unsupervised, free of traditional gender and sexual roles) and subjugating (bound to seventy-hour workweeks and their employers' rules). Women like Irena, in fact, reframe their role as both sacrificing mother *and* breadwinner.

"I have to leave so they can continue surviving. I know that I'm the only one my children depend on. Being far away from my children, because I am making sacrifices for them, I feel closer to them. My children also understand this. Especially now that they have their own families and have followed the same kinds of paths to feed their families, now they understand.

"I know many kids that have everything they need but they don't respect their parents. I never had problems with my kids, they were educated in poverty, but they were educated with respect. I do this to see them advance. I can't become a teacher or a nurse, but I give my all so that they may be able to get better work. Now my daughter may become a teacher. I feel myself realized through her."

I was struck by the fact that Irena's survival depends on patching together work in different parts of the food system, whether as a migrant farmworker in Canada or cooking for a middle-class Mexican family in Cuernavaca, or selling tacos on the streets of her home village. She epitomizes women's centrality to the planting, picking, packing, preparing, and selling of food. And, ironically, as a marginal Mexican woman worker, all of her food-related jobs take her away from her own land and family.

A BUDDING MIGRANT WORKER RIGHTS MOVEMENT

In 2003, Min Sook Lee premiered a National Film Board production, *El Contrato*, offering a critical inside look at the working conditions of Mexican farmworkers in a large greenhouse production in Leamington, Ontario, near the Windsor-Detroit border.[29] One of the workers came masked in a bandana; he had quit his job and was now doing public advocacy on behalf of workers in the SAWP program. Clearly, organizing seasonal workers is dangerous territory, and the film itself became a cause celèbre when the greenhouse owners sued both Lee and the NFB.[30]

A re-edited version of the film featured during an Art for Social Change festival in Toronto the following year drew many of the key actors in a growing multisectoral movement for migrant farmworkers' rights. I shared a panel with other activists, including Teresa Alemán, a Mexican woman on a tour organized by the United Food and Commercial Workers (UFCW), denouncing the treatment of workers in a new low-skilled worker program, which has even less government oversight than the SAWP; she had quit after being subjected to inhuman conditions in a business that had her working all night to fill a quota of ten bags of worms for fish bait.

UFCW has led the charge to try to organize these farmworkers, despite tremendous obstacles such as the temporary nature of the work, language barriers, and employer pressures. Their tactics have been two-pronged: 1) to serve the workers through setting up Migrant Resource Centres in four towns in Ontario and one in Quebec, offering English and French classes, health and safety training, and assistance in securing health services and in filling out tax forms,[31] and 2) to challenge the current regulations through the courts. In late 2001, the Supreme Court of Canada ruled that "agricultural workers have a constitutional right to unionize without fear of reprisals."[32] In 2003 SAWP workers were granted the right to form associations, but not the right to form unions and engage in collective bargaining.[33] The UFCW then challenged this Labour Relations Board decision as a denial of basic Charter rights and also sought to eliminate the requirement that SAWP workers pay employment insurance that they never will be able to claim as temporary workers.[34]

In an attempt to stall the legal process, the government argued against the UFCW's right to represent the workers' interests in the courts, suggesting the workers should represent themselves; the UFCW challenged this and won the suit in 2005. It only highlighted the fact that migrant farmworkers are at the mercy of their employers, who are threatened by the efforts to organize because collective bargaining might very well drive smaller family farms out of business. The UFCW has taken this into account, proposing differential wage scales based on the size of the farms.[35] In September 2006, Mexican migrant workers on three farms in Quebec and one in Manitoba petitioned to organize unions under the UFCW; these cases are under review, but could ultimately have an impact on the whole SAWP program.[36] A most significant decision by the Supreme Court of Canada on June 8, 2007, however, ruled that the right to collective bargaining is guaranteed to all workers in Canada under the Charter of Rights and Freedoms; confirming that this includes migrant workers, the Manitoba Labour Board certified a union of migrant workers at Mayfair Farms in Portage La Prairie in early July 2007.[37]

The Mexican consulate assigns staff to monitor working conditions; they are caught in a double bind as they must both mediate worker-employer disputes as well as recruit and retain more employers, in the face of increasing international competition for workers.[38] Consulate officials appear threatened by the groups attempting to service and organize a population they see as theirs to oversee. In 2005, they set up a consulate office in Leamington, now competing with the UFCW workers' center as well as the work of groups like Justicia 4 Migrant Workers. Justicia has taken a different approach, building a common front of Caribbean and Mexican workers, a campaign that is "based on workers' experiences" and "ultimately driven by workers themselves," and draws on the work of antiracism movements, integrating an analysis of class, race, location, and gender.[39] Other Canadian advocacy organizations such as ENLACE, Frontier College,[40] the North-South Institute, and the Latin American Worker Network, have also taken up the mantle of migrant rights;[41] KAIROS, a coalition of national churches, sponsored a conference with advocates from various social justice sectors in 2006.

Transnational coalitions of unions and human rights and community groups have also taken up the issue, using the political space created by instruments such as the North American Agreement on Labor Cooperation (NAALC).[42] In 2005, a transnational gathering of scholars and activists issued the Cuernavaca Declaration, challenging the underlying premise of migrant worker programs, claiming that they "distort the concept of development, basing it on the export of workers and capture of remittances."[43]

Clearly, migrant workers themselves risk the most in the organizing efforts to improve or challenge programs such as SAWP. Some worker-led strikes have led to deportations.[44] Workers who staged a one-day wildcat strike in Leamington in 2001 articulated their common problems: lack of translation for medical appointments, unsatisfactory bank service in sending remittances home, poor housing, excessive costs for meals, and abuse by employers; indeed, for this action, twenty-one workers were immediately repatriated to Mexico.[45] Another strike in 2003 protested a new computerized system of piecework payment replacing hourly wages; thirty of the sixty workers participating were deported.[46] They recognize that the precarious situation of campesinos in Mexico means they can be easily replaced by a revolving transnational flexible labor force.

But their actions have birthed a growing advocacy movement in Canada. And they take strength from other movements of farmworkers and the new civil rights movement of undocumented Latino workers in the United States.[47] In Canada, they are speaking out for their rights: the SAWP office registered as many as thirty complaints a day in 2005; a group of thirty-two Mexican workers in British Columbia stopped working and demanded to be sent home.[48] They refuse to be victims, either of the neoliberal policies destroying livelihoods in their homeland or of the guest-worker schemes of their governments. Teresa Alemán feels a part of a broader process, leaving her legacy in Canada: "I feel a lot of pride going back to Mexico, having begun this. It takes a lot to say that you are not going to give in. Something inside you reels and you say: 'You have to go on.'" Her hope is that her children and others will be inspired, will remember "the noise we made for our people, for the Mexicans, so that we do not allow ourselves to be stepped on. We are equal, we are human, and we can succeed."[49]

Notes

1. We were told by some truckers that, if the prices were low in the United States, the shipments might be delayed two or three days, which would also leave the truckers waiting.

2. Alan Freeman, "Meanwhile, Back at the Ranch . . . ," *Globe and Mail*, 10 April 2006, A13.

3. Donna Smith, "U.S. Immigration Bill Attacked from Left and Right," Reuters Alert-Net, http://www.alertnet.org/thenews/newsdesk?N19252884.htm, accessed 22 May 2007.

4. Democrat Representative Xavier Becerra charged this program would "create a permanent underclass of imported workers to fill American jobs." Robert Pear and Jim Rutenberg, "U.S. Senators in Bipartisan Deal on Immigration Bill," *International Herald Tribune/Americas*, http://www.iht.com/articles/2007/05/18/america/18immig.php, accessed 22 May 2007.

5. Ibid. Under the official H-2 program, there were only 121,000 guest workers in 2005; this number doesn't come close to accounting for the more than 11 million undocumented Mexicans in the United States.

6. Katherine Harding and Dawn Walton, "Canada's Hottest New Import? Employees," *Globe and Mail*, 24 February 2007, A14.

7. Ron Benner, *All That Has Value* (London: University of Western Ontario Gallery, 1995).

8. Total Trucks, 123, a document created by Teresa M. Clerc and provided by U.S. Customs officials in Nogales, February 1999; United States Department of Agriculture, "Fruit and Vegetable Imports, Nogales, Arizona, Fiscal Year 1998."

9. This testimony is from an interview with Humberto Carillo (pseudonym) by author and Sheelagh Davis, Joanna Shaw, and John Vainstein, 16 February 1999, Nogales, Arizona.

10. E-mail communication with Jim Bradbury, 13 April 2007.

11. A. Weston and L. Scarpa de Masellis, "Hemispheric Integration and Trade Relations—Implications for Canada's Seasonal Agricultural Workers Program," Research report (Ottawa: The North-South Institute, 2003).

12. Personal communication with Jose Martinez de la Rosa, Mexican Consulate, Toronto, 17 May 2007.

13. In June 2003, for example, the Quebec government issued a document stating that unskilled farm labor would not be subject to minimum wage. A. Weston and L. Scarpa de Masellis, "Hemispheric Integration and Trade Relations," 8.

14. Ofelia Becerril, "Transnational Work and Labour Politics of Gender: A Study of Male and Female Mexican Migrant Farm Workers in Canada," unpublished paper, 2004, 6.

15. Tanya Basok, *Tortillas and Tomatoes: Transmigrant Mexican Harvesters in Canada* (Montreal: McGill-Queen's University Press, 2002).

16. Kerry Preibisch, Global South Seminar, York University, Toronto, April 2005.

17. Kerry Preibisch, "Gender Transformative Odysseys: Tracing the Experiences of Transnational Migrant Women in Rural Canada," *Canadian Women Studies* 24, no. 4 (summer/fall 2005): 91–97.

18. Leigh Binford, personal communication, November 2006.

19. According to Roberto Nieto of the Centre d'Appui pour les Travailleurs et Travailleuses Agricoles Migrants du Quebec: "A boss can send a worker back to Mexico for whatever reason—no judge, no appeal. The boss says the word, and the worker pays the ticket." IWC Research Group, "Dirty Work," *Alternatives Journal* 32, no. 3 (2006): 15.

20. Ellen Wall, "Personal Labor Relations and Ethnicity in Ontario Agriculture," in *Deconstructing a Nation: Immigration, Multiculturalism and Racism in 90s Canada,* ed. Vic Satzewich (Halifax: Fernwood, 1992), 261–75.

21. Kerry Preibisch (referencing D. Sasiulis and A. Bakan, "Negotiating Citizenship: Migrant Women in Canada and the Global System [New York: Palgrave Macmillan, 2003]) suggests that "High-income nation-states not only enjoy the hegemonic authority to selectively bestow mobility rights, but also to make discriminations based on gender, age and national origin." Kerry Preibisch, "Gender Transformative Odysseys," 92.

22. Teresa Alemán as told to Kerry Preibisch, "One Woman's Grain of Sand: The Struggle for the Dignified Treatment of Canada's Foreign Agricultural Workers," *Canadian Women Studies* 24, no. 4 (summer/fall 2005): 98–101.

23. Kerry Preibisch, Global South Seminar, York University, March 2005.

24. This employer offered to drive Irena two hours into Toronto for the launch of the first edition of *Tangled Routes* and actually bought the first copy!

25. Tanya Basok, "Forms of Control within the Split Labor Market: A Case of Mexican Seasonal Farm Workers in Ontario," paper presented to the Rural Sociology Conference, Toronto, Ontario, August 1997.

26. The wages Irena describes here refer to levels in 2000. In 2007, Mexican tomato workers earned about 100 pesos or approximately CAN $11 per day, while the Ontario minimum wage, as of 1 February 2007, was $8.00 per hour, so the daily wage would be $64–$96 for 8 to 12 hours. Mexican data from Antonieta Barrón, personal communications,

12 April 2007; Canadian data from www.labour.gov.on.ca/info/minimumwage, accessed 17 May 2007.

27. Preibisch, "Gender Transformative Odysseys," 95.

28. Women also suffer most from the separation, and are most prone to mental health problems; there is evidence, too, that the separation does impact their children. Kerry Preibisch, "Social Relations Practices between Seasonal Agricultural Workers, Their Employers, and the Residents of Rural Ontario," Research paper prepared for the North-South Institute, Ottawa, 2003.

29. Leamington is considered Canada's tomato capital and the largest greenhouse vegetable production area in North America. Large corporate greenhouse operations employ almost 40 percent of SAWP workers in Ontario, 99 percent of them from Mexico. Becerril, "Transnational Work and Labour Politics of Gender," 4.

30. The greenhouse owners wanted footage that portrayed them in an unfavorable light to be removed. Lee refused to edit her film; the NFB, however, conceded to the owners' demands.

31. Mark Michalak, unpublished MES paper, York University, 2006.

32. Kirk Makin, "Workers' Right to Unionize Backed by Top Court," *Globe and Mail*, 21 December 2001, A1.

33. Leigh Binford, personal communication, November 2006.

34. Apparently, by the spring of 2007, the UFCW had withdrawn its challenge around the EI payments, because workers were successfully applying for parental leave benefits. Personal communication with Leigh Binford, 22 May 2007.

35. Ibid.

36. One fear is that, while wages and benefits might increase, employment opportunities could actually decrease, with farmers replacing workers with increased mechanization or moving toward private contracting. The North-South Institute, Report on Migrant Workers, Ottawa, 2006.

37. "Commentary by Wayne Hanley, National President, UFCW Canada, regarding the unionization of migrant farm workers at Mayfair Farms in Portage La Prairie," http://www.ufcw.ca/Default.aspx?SectionID=226d6838-e873-4d74-bf68-a1a5615a6cae& LanguageId=1, accessed 9 August 2007.

38. The North-South Institute, Report on Migrant Workers, Ottawa, 2006.

39. Justicia's statement of commitments, noted in an announcement of meeting on 7 September 2005, see www.justicia4migrants.org.

40. Frontier College, an adult education organization with more than a one hundred year history, has for many years placed students on farms where they have worked alongside migrant workers, while teaching literacy in the evenings; they have also linked to the U.S.-based organization Student Action for Farmworkers (http://cds.aas.duke.edu/saf).

41. See Petra Kukacka, "Articulating the Migrant: An Interrogation of the Movement for Agricultural Migrant Workers' Rights in Ontario," unpublished major paper for the Masters in Environmental Studies, York University, 2005, for a postmodern probing of the mind-set and motives of migrant worker rights' advocates, of which she is one.

42. Michalak, unpublished MES paper, 12–14.

43. University Consortium on the Global South, "Migrants Are Not Just Anonymous Producers of Dollars," e-mail from the Centre for Research on Latin America and the Caribbean, York University, 2005.

44. SAWP workers have also been deported for illness, refusing to undertake unsafe work, and complaining about housing conditions.

45. Becerril, "Transnational Work and Labour Politics of Gender," 17.

46. Ibid., 18.

47. Hundreds of thousands of immigrants and activists converged on the U.S. Congress in the spring of 2006 to demand immigration reform and some form of amnesty of undocumented migrants, a majority of them Latinos. This movement has given Hispanics a newfound power and is being heralded as a new civil rights movement. Alan Freeman, "Meanwhile, Back at the Ranch . . . ," A13. Canada, with an estimated 200,000 undocumented workers, has been deporting them by the thousands, while some argue they are desperately needed in the workforce, and should be given temporary work permits if they have skilled jobs in the underground economy. Editorial, *Globe and Mail*, 28 March 2006, A18.

48. Jonathon Woodward, "B.C. Farms Face Crackdown Over Migrants," *Globe and Mail*, 6 October 2005, A8.

49. Alemán, "One Woman's Grain of Sand," 100.

CHAPTER 6

Picking and Packing for the North:

AGRICULTURAL WORKERS AT EMPAQUE SANTA ROSA

In search of tomato workers, I found Tomasa.

As Lauren and I worked our way through the rows of tomato plants, we found ourselves awkwardly making conversation with women who were bent over, mouths covered with handkerchiefs, hands rapidly filling pails of fruit, to make their forty-pail daily quota. One woman, however, chatted easily and cracked jokes with us and other workers. From the start, Tomasa, a sixty-eight-year-old forewoman at the time, made us feel welcome; she even invited us to visit her in her nearby village on a day off.

Months later, after a premature freeze cut short the harvest, I found Tomasa and Pablo, her husband and coworker, out of work and in their home in Talpapa. Once again, she offered a warm welcome, and I ended up staying for dinner, then coming back another day to meet with her and her coworkers. During a subsequent visit, Tomasa and Pablo took us to their cornfield outside the village, to show us their intercropping of corn, squash, and beans—the traditional practice now challenged by monocultural production. Tomasa represents through her life the many different forms of work that Mexican peasant women engage in: growing corn for her family's consumption, working as a temporary salaried worker in a large agribusiness during the harvest season, sending her kids away to the United States to work and send money home, undertaking informal work in the off-season making straw mats, and finally, securing a permanent job in a year-round U.S.-owned and operated greenhouse production, Sunshine Produce.

Globalization from Above: Empaque Santa Rosa in Context

"I've heard that the tomatoes go *al otro lado* [to the other side]," declares Reyna Gomez, a sixteen-year-old Indigenous worker who came with her husband from the south to pick tomatoes for Empaque Santa Rosa in the central western Mexican state of Jalisco. Whether she says *al otro lado* (to the other side), *al norte* (north), *afuera* (outside), or *allá* (there), Reyna is most likely referring to the United States, the giant to the north that not only swallows up the majority of tomatoes produced in Mexico and directs Mexican agroexport production from primarily U.S.-based multinationals but also has drawn migrant workers, many of them Indigenous people, across the border as cheap labor in American fields, for over a century.

Whether they're working in fields on the Mexican side of the border or on the U.S. side, they are picking corporate tomatoes primarily shaped by and destined for northern markets. Many of Reyna's friends and family members have also migrated to the United States seeking better wages and working conditions. Digging

into the history of any Indigenous campesino community reveals a similar pattern: a majority migrate north for many months out of the year, either to the richer productive regions of northern Mexico or into the United States and, in Irena's case, even as far as Canada. Their families now count on the remittances sent home for their very survival. It seems that everything and everybody goes *al otro lado.*

How did it come to this? Or, as Angus Wright poignantly asks in his investigation of the pesticide-related death of Indigenous migrant farmworker Ramón Gonzales, "Why is it that people like Ramón can no longer make a living from their own land and must work instead where they own nothing and control nothing and where their only apparent future is to move on to work in yet some other alien and unfriendly land?"[1]

In trying to understand the stories of women workers in the Mexican agribusiness, I found myself with similar questions, especially after Reyna Gomez almost lost her baby to pesticide poisoning as she breast-fed the child while working in the Jalisco tomato fields. Her precarious presence in this chem-

ically cultivated plantation compelled me to investigate the history of agriculture in Mexico, a deep and complex history: land, chemicals, migration, racism, and sexism are all woven into the tangled roots of this tale.

Two events on 1 January 1994 encapsulated (not coincidentally) in one day the contradictions at the root of the struggle of globalization from above and globalization from below. While multinational business and financial elites as well as signatory governments hailed the implementation of the North American Free Trade Agreement, poor Indigenous campesinos from Mexico's southern state of Chiapas challenged NAFTA as the latest in a long series of neoliberal actions that exploited them as cheap labor while marginalizing them as citizens and producers on the land.

The uprising of the Zapatistas (EZLN) had its roots in Indigenous rebellions during centuries of colonial rule and in the revolutionary struggles led by Emiliano Zapata in the early 1900s for "Land and Liberty." It is part of an ongoing dialectic, especially acute in recent decades, between a vision of the land and of agriculture that honors ecological integrity and local survival, and a vision that privileges the needs of export markets and northern consumers. This chapter shows how historically tomatl and the corporate tomato, introduced in chapter 1, are intertwined and in struggle with each other in the Mexican context. We find the tomato in both subsistence agriculture, based on traditional Indigenous practices, as well as in agroexport agriculture, based on a Western model that has commodified and globalized production. The two stories remain linked today through the campesinos, with a focus here on women agricultural workers, who provide the cheap labor for the export-oriented agribusinesses and whose low wages are based on the assumption that they will continue to grow food for their own consumption.

To place Empaque Santa Rosa in context, particularly for readers in the north, I provide a short review of Mexican history, marked by key periods and events that have shaped these two different but interrelated agricultural practices: (1) European colonization (1500–1800); (2) independence (early 1800s); (3) the Mexican Revolution (1910–1917); (4) agroexports and the Green Revolution (1920–1960); (5) debt crisis and structural adjustment (1980s); and (6) neoliberalism and NAFTA (1980s–1990s).

EUROPEAN COLONIZATION (1500s–1800s)

While the arrival of Europeans in the Americas had the most dramatic effect on land ownership patterns and agricultural practices, current ecological crises and social inequalities have roots that are even deeper than Spanish colonization. Social hierarchies of pre-Columbian peoples in Mexico,[2] such as the Mixtecs in Oaxaca, were often embedded in diverse and sometimes contradictory agricultural practices. The lama y bordo, or mud and dam system, used by the Mixtecs, for example, allowed commoners to farm on steep slopes, but the terrace system also deforested the hillsides as the rich soils were washed to the fertile valleys controlled by the nobility. Other pre-Columbian legacies were healthier: the *chinampa* system of the Aztec culture was a very ecologically sound and self-sustaining system of raised beds in canals that used the silt as fertilizer. Such "traditional practices,"[3] perhaps best reflected in the *triculture* system (the interplanting of beans, squash, and corn), maintained soil fertility and provided well-balanced diets for centuries.

The Europeans brought new crops (e.g., wheat), new pests, and new forms of cultivation. Agricultural land was further destroyed when the Spaniards replaced the digging stick with the plow (bringing rocky subsoil to the surface and burying rich topsoil) and introduced domesticated grazing animals. The conflict between European and Indigenous agricultural practices can be seen in ecological terms as competing views of nature: one built on the domination of nature, the other on intimate knowledge of the complexity of nature; in political economic terms: the enslavement of people and their labor to extract their resources for the wealth of the colonizers; and in social terms: a racism that denied the complex knowledge systems of Indigenous peoples and disdained their traditional practices. Spanish colonizers, for example, laid the ground for ongoing migration north by forcing Indigenous people (mainly men) to migrate to work in the mines and haciendas; women's role in subsistence agriculture was critical then, as they were left behind to tend the land and children.

INDEPENDENCE FROM SPAIN, GROWING
DEPENDENCE ON THE UNITED STATES (1800s)

With independence (1810–1813), wealthy mestizos or creoles (Spanish descendants) took control of many Indigenous communities, merely replacing colonial rulers with national elites. The consolidation of their power is reflected in the painting on page 209 illustrating the institutionalized power of the economic elites, the church, and the military (once again tangled roots). In the last half of the nineteenth century, private foreign investment was encouraged, paving the way for an ever-deepening dependence on the U.S. economy. The 1857 constitution in postindependence Mexico represented a victory for the liberals (over the conservatives) that, influenced by European and U.S. liberal ideology, privatized property of the church and Indigenous peoples and established a strong role for the state in developing a market that was already being shaped by international forces. Land expropriations left over 90 percent of the population landless by the early 1900s and were one of the forces that ignited the Mexican Revolution.

During the presidency of Porfirio Díaz (1880–1910), the development of a railroad system facilitated the beginnings of a growing agroexport sector, particularly in lowland regions. This brought Indigenous people and campesinos down from the highlands to work on the large estates. For Indigenous women, migration to the lowlands stimulated artisan production and commercial activity; mestiza peasant women, on the other hand, shunned market activity and sometimes joined their husbands as hired field hands, but at lower wages. In the

ranchero regions, however, when men began to migrate to the United States, their wives remained home with in-laws, often restricted to supplementary activities like raising pigs and chickens.[4]

MEXICAN REVOLUTION AND EJIDOS (1910s–1940s)

The Mexican Revolution of 1910–1917 brought some hope for Indigenous peoples and campesinos, as the revolutionary hero Zapata declared, "the land belongs to those who work it." The 1917 Constitution created *ejidos*, a community-based landholding system that returned land to some campesinos who for the most part worked it individually, but with various forms of cooperative support. For Indigenous communities in southern Mexico, this often meant gaining access to badly eroded land, while wealthier creole landowners still controlled the best agricultural land or secured ejido lands (and lower taxes) by devious yet legal means.[5]

While the ejido system represented a return of land to poor Indigenous and mestizo campesinos, it was insufficient for all and actually forced many men to migrate north for work. On a national level, the rich and powerful agriculturalists in the northern states (more identified with the United States) represented an elitist and racist dynasty, which not only drew migrant farm labor from the poorer southern states but considered traditional farming practices as obstacles to progress. On the other hand, Indigenous peoples, whose system was more communal, were resistant to the individualizing tendencies of modernizing agriculture.

When the populist Lázaro Cardenas became president of Mexico in the 1930s, he proposed a radical agrarianism that revalorized Indigenous organization within ejidos. There was a major redistribution of land to peasants while Cardenas was in power, but such reforms lost U.S. support when he expropriated and nationalized oil companies. Even though he offered more access to land for campesinos, Cardenas nonetheless promoted a Western modernizing project of agriculture, not one that necessarily honored traditional practices.

One aspect of agricultural history that is not revealed in studies that separate the public and private, or producing for the market and for domestic consumption, is the ongoing role of women in subsistence activities: growing plants around the house, caring for animals in the patio, cultivating basic crops in the *milpa* (or cornfield). The preparation of food, too, has been hidden from all accounts as a key subsistence activity. With the development of the *molino de nixtamal* (mill for grinding corn flour), the use of domestic gas, and more accessible water, women's work in preparing tortillas, for example, was drastically cut, and they became more available to join their husbands in the ejidos or for paid agricultural work in the expanding agroindustry. In addition, as more and more men went to northern Mexico or the United States as migrant farmworkers for months or even years, campesino women took on greater agricultural responsibility at home.[6]

AGROEXPORTS AND THE GREEN REVOLUTION (1940s–1970s)

Agricultural exports have been central to the process of national development in Mexico, because they have encouraged foreign investment and spurred industrial growth. In fact, critics point to the fact that Mexican policies since the 1940s have increasingly favored urban industry and industrialized agriculture to the detriment of a campesino population and nation that used to be self-sufficient in basic foodstuffs and is now dependent on food imports.

In chapter 1, we saw how the Green Revolution, coming into force in the 1950s and 1960s, contributed to the process of integration of Mexican agriculture into the global market. First, Mexican agroindustries became increasingly dependent on purchasing from foreign (mainly U.S.) sources most of the inputs of the technological package: hybridized seeds, agrochemicals (fertilizers and pesticides), as well as devices for applying them, and water pumps for irrigation systems, particularly critical for tomato production. Central to this corporatized model of modern agriculture was monocultural production; the Mexican state favored large cash crop producers with credits while campesinos increasingly lost subsidies to support individual production. Nonetheless, even small producers were drawn into buying the latest chemical miracle, each time hoping that this one would restore balance and stop the continual "creation of pests and diseases" that Vandana Shiva calls the "only miracle of the Green Revolution."[7]

The structure of Mexican agriculture since the 1940s has been called "bimodal," depending on a functional integration of both commercial (large-scale

Diego Rivera Mural

agribusiness producing monocultural export crops on the best lands) and non-commercial (small private farmers growing basic foods on less fertile lands). Campesinos have been central to this model, as (until recently) they produced cheap basic foodstuffs for local populations while also providing cheap seasonal labor for agroexport industries. The abysmally low wages of salaried workers in agribusiness are, in fact, built on the assumption that as campesinos, they would still grow their own food for subsistence and thus not depend solely on their salary for survival. In other words, the development of the corporate tomato has depended on its coexistence with tomatl, representing subsistence practices.

"Trimodal" might more accurately describe the categories of farmers today: (1) capitalist producers, (2) medium- and small-scale farmers who may sell to the market but only with family labor, and (3) subsistence farmers, many of whom are migrant farmworkers now moving from harvest to harvest with little time (or land) to maintain their own subsistence crops.[8] While this study speaks mainly to the situation of the third group, who are migrant farmworkers employed by the first group, large agribusinesses, all Mexican campesinos have been affected by this export-oriented and chemical-dependent model of agriculture, which drives the journey of the corporate tomato. Their plight is poignantly revealed in the testimony of Benito Suarez, an independent producer growing tomatoes in Tlayacápan, Morelos.

Benito Suarez: One Campesino's Testimony

"What people grow is an economic issue. They will always grow corn and beans to eat, but the other crops depend on costs. It's whether or not we can get a good price for our produce. The capitalist system has never offered the campesino the security of guaranteed prices; it's left to the buyers and their whims. This is what has finished off campesinos.

"It's an economic question and not a question of conscience whether or not we can rotate crops so that the land won't become impoverished. Those who own the warehouses at the Central Market control everything. They come to the rural areas to buy tomatoes, they set the price, they buy them, and then resell them at double the price.

"There's no control in the sale and use of pesticides. They sell them at astronomical prices for the campesino. These products are so toxic that special equipment is needed to apply them. But here in Mexico, we don't use anything to protect ourselves.

"U.S. companies sell us pesticides that they can't sell there because they're too toxic. But they won't buy the products that are produced using those pesticides, because they are aware of the possible impact of these contaminated products on their health, and won't let them across the border. Instead they get sold to the domestic market here in Mexico.

"These toxic chemicals have a negative effect on nature. Many species have been destroyed by them. There are species of birds, for example, that no longer exist, because they ate the seeds from corn that were thrown out in the field. Over the years, many species have been affected: rabbits, crows. We are all part of a food chain; if one is affected, it affects others.

"There is a link between the earth and the [hu]man, between the plant and [hu]man that goes further than simply the idea of cultivating a plant, no? One feels the growth of the plant, it's a relation that grows, it's like a child. It's like talking in silence, getting to know what the plant needs. You feel it very deeply.

"We are a people with roots, and we understand the earth, we live and grow with her, we're part of her, and so we feel a very personal relationship. You can see a campesino working from dawn until dusk, working his land alone. Feeling it, touching it, massaging it, giving it a massage so that it will bear good fruit. That's what's important in the campo, the love that you have for the earth, that's what maintains the roots. And the desire that the earth won't disappear."

Many Mexican campesinos, like Benito, have lost not only their more ecologically sustainable practices but also their sacred relationship with the land. Their families have disintegrated and their communities have been shattered as they have been forced to move *al otro lado* to survive. While migration is certainly not new, the reasons for moving and the numbers migrating have multiplied in recent decades, especially since the Bracero Program facilitated migration to the United States in the 1940s.[9] In the early 1980s, there were about seven million farmworkers in Mexico, with four and a half million of these being *jornaleros*, or temporary seasonal workers; an estimated one million of these are migrants, moving from one harvest to another. Most remain seriously underemployed, with the average farm laborer working sixty to ninety days a year, for an average annual cash income of U.S. $175.[10]

Since the Green Revolution, however, a major cause of migration has been fertilizer debt. Steven Edinger reports that over 90 percent of the households in a Mixtec community in the southern state of Oaxaca had family members migrating, most shifting from one location to another, and gone from two months to two years at a time. These more recent migrants are trying to pay off fertilizer debts and to feed a new dependency on outside manufactured goods. Their earnings go for clothes, building materials, fertilizer, fiestas, but little for purchasing land.[11] All of this has contributed to a growing schism between the campesino and the campo (the land). Now forced to move to work for agribusiness, landless campesinos are *sin campo*, literally "without the land" that has always defined them. Some contend that the campo itself, once central to Mexico and its people, is disappearing as well, both physically and culturally.

Hubert Carton de Grammont suggests that the economic integration proposed by neoliberalism and NAFTA has created an agrarian structure with not just two but rather three poles in its division of the land: the large modern competitive agribusinesses, poor campesino farmers with little technology and less able to produce for subsistence, and land that has become useless or infertile, wasted by the unsustainable practices promoted by international competition.[12] In all cases, the relationship between the human and the earth has been estranged.

DEBT CRISIS AND STRUCTURAL ADJUSTMENT (1980s)

With the world oil crisis in the late 1970s, the bottom dropped out of the Mexican economy (which had been borrowing heavily to build the oil industry as its cornerstone); its foreign debt skyrocketed to U.S. $100 billion by 1987. Until that time, Mexico had been seen as a model for Third World development; to survive the debt crisis, it became a model for deregulation and trade liberalization. This process was guided by multilateral financial institutions (the World Bank, the IMF, and the Inter-American Development Bank) that increasingly replaced the state as key architects of development from the 1980s on, through their structural adjustment programs (SAPs).

As a prophetic sign of debt crises to come, Mexico had to be rescued by the very bodies to whom it was indebted, but at a price that was much more than economic. The reforms dictated by these international lending agencies reversed what had been the key components[13] of a more nationalist Mexican economic policy: strong state participation in the economy; control of prices, interest rates, and exchange rates; protection of domestic industries with trade and investment barriers; and basic social security for the population through subsidies and services. In a pattern repeated throughout the developing world, structural adjustments that were the conditions of the IMF and World Bank loans pushed Mexico to transfer the role of directing the economy from the state to private interests, to reduce credit supports to small producers and food subsidies, to open up commerce to foreign interests—in other words, to let the free market reign.[14]

Not surprisingly, these reforms paved the way for a greater role for multinational companies and private capital investors and for a lesser role for the government in a deregulated Mexican economy. This could not have happened, however, without the support of a Mexican technocratic elite and its political henchmen of the ruling PRI (Partido Revolucionario Institucional),[15] whose personal and class interests were also served by the commercial opening. Miguel de la Madrid, Carlos Salinas, and Ernesto Zedillo, the three presidents from 1982 to 2000, gave up populist notions (if not the rhetoric) of national development and promoted Mexico's integration into the global market as the path to economic and social progress.[16]

NEOLIBERALISM AND NAFTA (1980s–1990s)

The political struggles leading up to NAFTA reflect, on the one hand, the victory of the neoliberals over the nationalists and the dominance of the multinational industrial sector over the *campesinado*, or peasantry. Neoliberalism,[17] as "a set of economic beliefs that subordinates all social and development considerations to the demands of private capital and the world market,"[18] also has roots that go much deeper than the recent decades of global economic restructuring. Since independence, most Mexican presidents (with the exception of Lázaro Cardenas) maintained development and agrarian policies that favored large commercial export-oriented industries, leaving the worst land for campesinos and their subsistence.

In the post–World War II era, there was a contradictory dynamic, however. While the U.S.-dominated efforts to promote economic growth according to a Western-style development model were felt strongly in Mexico, there was a countervailing nationalist orientation, also rooted in the Mexican Revolution. Oil had been nationalized through PEMEX, and reforms under both presidents Luis

Diego Rivera Mural

Echeverría (1970–1976) and José López Portillo (1976–1982) promoted national pride (along with *tercermundismo*, or Third Worldism) and self-sufficiency, even as the Mexican economy became increasingly entrenched in world markets. Echeverría revived the agrarian populism of Cardenas, collectivizing ejidos and encouraging campesino organizing; he also built on the World Bank's critique that the benefits of development were not trickling down to the poorest and set up PIDER (a rural development agency), CONASUPO (for food storage and distribution), and BANURAL (providing credit to campesinos). López Portillo, though moderate, nationalized the private banking system, limited oil exports to the United States, and established the Mexican Food System (SAM), achieving food self-sufficiency by 1982.

With the forces of neoliberalism dominating after the debt crisis, however, De la Madrid dismantled the SAM, while Salinas pushed through the Agrarian Law of January 1992, a constitutional amendment to Article 27 (which had established ejidos), terminating Mexico's agrarian reform program and laying the ground for privatizing the ejidos. The specific forms that neoliberalism took in the Mexican countryside, then, included the end of land distribution, the selling of ejido land to private interests, the liberalization of agricultural commodity prices, the end of most food and agricultural production subsidies, and the abandonment of the state's role in marketing and distribution.[19]

The dual structure of agricultural production deepened, however, as the agroexport industry became central to the redefined Mexican economic plan. This fits a pattern of asymmetrical north-south relations in which multinationals in northern countries supply the inputs, extract the surpluses, and provide the markets, while southern countries supply the favorable climate, easy access to land, and cheap labor for production controlled by foreign interests. At the same time, agricultural surpluses from the north are dumped on Third World countries as cheap food or food aid (e.g., often as a reward for supporting U.S. foreign policy), forcing countries such as Mexico, formerly self-sufficient in food, to dismantle their national food programs, which can't compete with the cheaper imports. The campesinos who are the salaried workforce in the growing agroexport economy no longer have access to land for their own subsistence, have been deprived of their small producer credits and food subsidies, and must piece together their survival often with a patchwork of part-time and seasonal waged work, informal sector jobs, and subsistence activities such as farming their own plots or making their own food.[20]

Agroexports are a source of foreign exchange to pay off national debts. Even for medium-scale producers, the risks have increased with the growth of the agroexport sector; contract farming is central to the multinational agribusiness strategy. Thus, foreign companies often control the entire production process, require farmers to buy inputs (seeds, fertilizers, pesticides, machinery, even boxes) from outside Mexico, provide foreign technical assistants who manage the technology, and dictate the prices, marketing, and distribution mechanisms—without taking any of the risks of actually producing the food.

The North American Free Trade Agreement has added just one more pillar to the neoliberal structure that holds the Mexican economy together today. It has merely made permanent the export-oriented model imposed on Mexico by earlier structural adjustment programs of international agencies,[21] a model built on and dependent on low wages for Mexican campesinos and other existing social inequalities. Once self-sufficient in food, Mexico now imports more than one-third of its food needs. This makes little sense except to the financial (foreign and national) interests that benefit from this strategy of development.

In Mexico, the fruit and vegetable sector, however, has benefited from NAFTA, while the "traditional" production of basic grains has steadily dropped. Mexico is the largest producer and per capita consumer of fresh tomatoes in North America, exporting 46 percent of the yield in 2003. Field growers, along with new investors in agriculture, have been moving into greenhouse production, and Mexico now surpasses both the U.S. and Canada in greenhouse production.[22] Mexican producers have the comparative advantage over their two northern partners, with the neoliberal reforms of the 1980s and NAFTA itself making land more accessible, a year-around growing climate, and, particularly, the cheap labor of Mexican campesinos. With the U.S. market opened up to its nontraditional agroexports,[23] Mexico is in fact paying for the increasing food imports.

The most poignant example of this contradiction is corn, so central to the survival and cultural identity of Mexicans over centuries. With over half of the corn now imported, the threat of contamination of the original maize varieties by imported genetically engineered (GE) crops, and rising international corn prices spurred by demand for grain-based ethanol fuel, corn epitomizes the economic integration of the Americas, and its most frightening consequences.[24]

GROWING RESISTANCE, DEEPENING REPRESSION (2000S)

Since the publication of the first edition of *Tangled Routes* in 2002, Mexico has been on the verge on exploding and imploding. Economically, small producers and subsistence farmers have been increasingly swallowed up by expanding export-oriented agribusiness and decimated by the reduction and elimination of state supports. In January 2003, 100,000 campesinos marched on Mexico City under the banner "El campo no aguanta más" or "The countryside can't take it anymore!" (chapter 8). Representing a broad coalition of rural producer organizations, they made six demands "to save and revalue the Mexican countryside," including a moratorium on the agricultural side agreement of NAFTA, measures to revitalize rural development, food policy, and recognition of the rights and cultures of Indigenous peoples.[25] They were supported by international alliances such as Vía Campesina and the People's Food Sovereignty Network, suggesting that food should not be part of the World Trade Organization agreements.[26]

Politically, the 2006 presidential election of PAN candidate Felipe Calderón was considered fraudulent by many, who proclaimed the PRD candidate, Manuel Lopez Obrador, head of a largely symbolic parallel government; at the same time, there were vociferous calls for the resignations of four corrupt state governors. Mexican police brutally repressed groups protesting corporate development in Indigenous land in mid-2006. A few months later, violent attacks on a coalition of teachers and Indigenous groups in Oaxaca resulted in deaths and deepening repression. The paramilitary attacked Indigenous communities in Chiapas state and continually threatened Zapatista autonomous communities. The very existence and strength of the emerging coalitions are a threat to the political, economic, and military control of the Mexican state as well as national and multinational corporate interests.[27]

EMPAQUE SANTA ROSA: PRIMED FOR EXPORT

> As we move towards the twenty-first century and international free trade, Empaque Santa Rosa enthusiastically embraces the opportunity to compete literally in a global market—not only in the produce industry, but in a wide range of diversified quality products and services.
>
> —President, Empaque Santa Rosa

This quote[28] from the glossy promotional package of Empaque Santa Rosa[29] invites shareholders to join in the promising benefits of the commercial opening provided by NAFTA. Founded in the 1970s, it is one of the three largest tomato producers in Mexico, one of the five largest in North America. The four Leon brothers, sons of the founder, run the family company, while two sisters apparently "don't get involved in the business."[30] Although Santa Rosa started on a small scale, by 1996 it was a very large corporation with $300 million in sales. It employed twelve thousand employees, of which about 90 percent were field-workers, to plant and harvest more than six thousand hectares of field tomatoes and eighty hectares of greenhouse production.

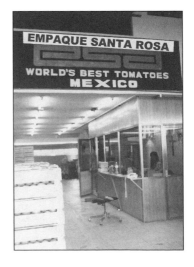

Clearly Santa Rosa was poised to take advantage of the trade liberalization of the 1980s and the new opportunities provided by NAFTA. While the agroexport industry was established in the nineteenth century, neoliberalism and NAFTA have placed additional pressure on what were once primarily domestic companies to become global. And with the fruit and vegetable market in general and tomatoes in particular one of the few Mexican winners in this free-trade game, Empaque Santa Rosa has recently been on a fast track for expanding and technologizing production, packing, and sales.

Empaque Santa Rosa is one of the few large companies that control fruit and vegetable production in Mexico, part of economic networks located in finance capitals and closely linked to North American financial and agroindustrial capital.[31] The success of this elite group depends on its access not only to land but also to markets. Its concentration and control of land are clear: the largest companies (those cultivating more than one thousand hectares) comprise only 0.2 percent of the agribusinesses yet cover 4 percent of the land, while 59 percent are cultivating only 5 percent of the land. In terms of markets, large domestic companies have become "global" by joining financial groups and by setting up their own distribution centers not only in the largest markets (in Mexico City, Guadalajara, and Monterrey) but in the United States, and in some cases even in Canada and Europe. Empaque Santa Rosa, for example, has its own trade center in the southern United States, where it manages exports and imports not only of fresh produce but also of canned food, and dealing not only with the United States and Canada but also with countries such as Ecuador and Korea.

With the commercial opening of the 1980s and early 1990s, the Leon brothers diversified their investments, just as Loblaws did in Canada during this same period. At one point, the brothers had shares in MexLube, the lubrication division of PEMEX Oil and Gas; owned 30 percent of Banco Cremi, and had shares in two other banks (BANCRECER and BANPAIS). The brothers were also shareholders in Factor PROFIN, ABACAO, and controlled 10 percent of Del Monte Fresh Produce. In Tijuana, Baja California (at the border), they owned the largest industrial park, where several foreign businesses had set up shop. There were also the more clearly personal interests, reflected in the ownership of the Guadalajara-based Chivas soccer team, one of the most popular soccer teams in Mexico, and a high-end restaurant in Mexico City. And, significantly, new investments outside of Mexico included an investment company in southern California (TCS Enterprises, involved in milk processing and academic text publishing) and a joint venture with the Canadian Bank of Nova Scotia. By the mid-1990s, the Leon brothers owned 160 properties, twenty-four of them outside of Mexico, with a total value of $75 million. They were thus part of the growing group of millionaire businessmen who control 53 percent of the national wealth, often secured by questionable practices.[32]

The NAFTA Impetus

Santa Rosa was commended by U.S. officials for its leadership in preparing the ground for the implementation of NAFTA in central Mexico. Established domestic producers were definitely at an advantage when the export market opened up. As the company's international operations head expressed, "NAFTA is common sense. The guy with the best product, that has the best price, that has the best efficiency, will win. NAFTA leveled the playing field and said the best players play. Your government can't protect you. The best players are those who have the best natural resources, the most efficient people."[33]

Following the models provided by foreign companies and technicians, the success of Santa Rosa has also been based on a more rationalized use of both technology and labor, echoes of the McDonaldization described in chapter 3. Increased investment in machinery and agrochemicals (including a more rationalized use of water, e.g., through drip irrigation in greenhouses) has resulted in a decrease in wages and a savings in water costs. All in the name of "efficiency," workers' productivity, too, has increased, both due to technological advances (e.g., biogenetically engineered seeds that produce more homogeneous ripening and thus make picking easier) as well as the speeding up of work. A European engineer hired by Santa Rosa to organize its greenhouse production, while noticing some improvement in workers' speed and accuracy, complained that the Mexican workers would "never be as productive as European workers."[34]

In the early years of NAFTA, there was a kind of "feeding frenzy" of foreign companies stimulated by the lowering of tariff barriers and new opportunities for investment in Mexico. But the peso crisis in late 1994 changed all that. With the devaluation, many pulled out, and imports dropped. Santa Rosa faced a severe economic crisis after the tremendous growth of the company into importing and investment; it began liquidating the companies that didn't apply to agriculture. The company was restructured for greater export-oriented production, and now supplies northern markets with 85 percent of its produce. It could be 100 percent, except that, according to one manager, Santa Rosa "has an obligation to the people of Mexico to be able to eat." The United States accounts for more than 90 percent of the exports, with only about 5 percent going to Canada.[35] There is interest in opening up the Canadian market in British Columbia, particularly because of its access to the even larger and more lucrative Asian market.

Girasol: Following the Sun

Large agribusinesses that take advantage of the diverse growing seasons within Mexico have been called *girasols*, or sunflowers, because they follow the sun. In the 1980s, Empaque Santa Rosa expanded its production capacity in three states—Baja California, Sinaloa, and Jalisco—maintaining tomato production all year round. While 70 percent of the total production takes place in Sinaloa, the richest tomato-producing state, there is a strong interest in expanding the facility in Baja California, because it is closer to the U.S. border and thus offers advantages of proximity, saving on transportation and time. This case study focused on the operations of its smaller plant (employing just over two thousand) in Jalisco, between 1994 and 2000. While the company leased rather than owned most of the productive land, its greatest resource was the ample supply of local campesinos (20 percent) and migrant farmworkers (80 percent); in total, Santa Rosa employed 12,000 temporary workers and 850 full-time workers.

Equally as expendable as the temporary workforce has been the land on which the tomatoes are produced. In the late 1980s, several agribusinesses rented plots in Autlán, in the southeastern end of Jalisco, operating with a "mining mentality"

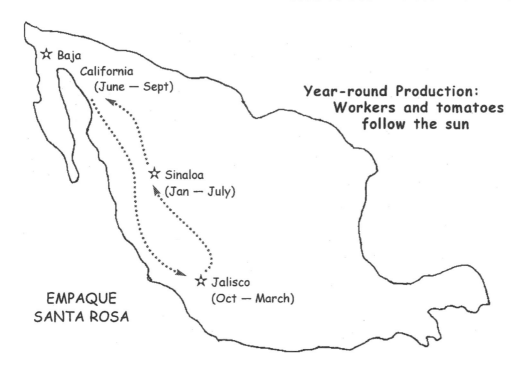

aimed at getting quick profits. After several years of monocultural production with intensive agrochemical use, they left the region, when an insect plague struck that could not be controlled, forcing them to abandon the infected and depleted land, which led to falling profits.[36] The white mosquito that destroyed the crops had deserted the mountainside for the fields, due to deforestation caused by clear-cutting for constructing crates to pack tomatoes for export.[37] Local residents, in fact, have nicknamed these companies "grasshoppers," a metaphoric critique of how companies "hop" on to the next fertile field, leaving behind a degraded environment and a community that has come to depend on the economic activity.[38] Ironically, a few years after the first edition of *Tangled Routes* was published, Santa Rosa and other tomato companies hopped on once again, deserting Sirena and returning to Autlán, which they had left more than a decade earlier. The culprit this time was a small white mosquito, aided by the greed and lack of foresight of some agribusinesses. The Plant Pest Control Board, an independent body of producers concerned about the increasing white mosquito population, decreed a hiatus in cultivation between January and April 2003, hoping the colder weather would limit the reproduction of the insects. Despite the ban, however, three companies, not wanting to miss the best season for the U.S. market of their crops, went into full production, provoking a massive mosquito infestation. The secretary of agriculture declared an emergency, fined the guilty companies, and prohibited further planting. A persistent lack of understanding of ecosystems continued to pervade Mexican agribusiness, revealing as well a short memory of recent similar crises. By 2004, the only production remaining in Sirena was greenhouse production, which allowed more control of the environment and signaled the future of tomato production.[39]

Vertical Integration

production

sales

distribution

The photos on the previous page illustrate the vertical integration strategy of Santa Rosa: engage in production, sales, and distribution of tomatoes, both domestically and internationally. It maintains offices, for example, north of the U.S. border, in both Arizona and California, to manage the distribution of its tomatoes north through brokers to several hundred clients in the United States and Canada.

By the late 1990s, Santa Rosa cultivated 2,550 hectares of tomatoes, with an annual production of 165,000 tons.[40] It operated twelve wholesale *bodegas,* or stalls, in the food terminals of Guadalajara and Mexico City, controlling much of the intermediary activity that goes on in the big centralized markets; in the Guadalajara central market, the company was the most powerful of the seven controlling families, with seven bodegas.[41] It monitored both production and distribution through sophisticated information technologies. In Guadalajara, it owned a building with Del Monte Fresh Produce that had fifteen refrigerated rooms, with a capacity to store up to seventy-five trailers' worth of fresh produce. Because they are highly perishable, tomatoes are usually not stored for longer than a day; but they may be held until they are picked up, when there is overproduction or while waiting for prices to rise. They are then often gassed (with ethylene) before being shipped so they will ripen by arrival.

High-Tech Production

The latest technological development and investment have been in greenhouse production, which takes advantage of the accessible land, prevalent sun, and cheap labor and further controls plant growth through drip irrigation and some organic fertilizers. Santa Rosa holds the majority of shares in a greenhouse operation where sixty hectares of tomatoes are grown eight months out of the year, yielding four times the amount possible in open field production.[42] The technologies are imported (primarily from the United States, Israel, and Europe), from the most sophisticated to the simplest: "We are the consumer—of seedling packs, fertilizers, machinery, computers that sort the tomatoes by size and color, boxes (eight to twelve million), plastic that covers the seedlings, gasoline, oil to move all the trucks we have to move, topsoil, sticks (twenty million sticks), even the string that holds up every plant."[43]

In what's becoming a pattern for Mexican agribusinesses, reflecting a kind of maquilization of the whole country, most inputs are imported and all outputs are exported. In 1997, the greenhouse operation exported 100 percent of its produce to the U.S. and Canada for a value of U.S. $14 million. By 2007, the Mexican countryside was increasingly dotted with endless rows of greenhouses, particularly in central Mexico where the year-round temperate climate and higher altitudes result in higher yields. Greenhouse production focuses primarily on cherry tomatoes, responding to the demands of the U.S. consumer market for luxury varieties. The growing season has been further expanded with new technologies of drip irrigation, hydroponics, and transgenic varieties.[44]

From Tomatoes to Banking: The Underbelly of Globalization

For many years, Santa Rosa distributed much of its tomato crop through Del Monte Fresh Produce, headquartered in Irapuato, Guanajuato. With the deregulation and privatization initiated during the Salinas years, which encouraged domestic companies to expand, Santa Rosa joined with other Jalisco investors who were associated with the Western Business Group (GEO) to buy Banco Cremi[45] for U.S. $248 million. In 1993, the bank was sold to the agroindustrialist and financier Carlos Cabal Peniche and others, after which time Santa Rosa became a minor shareholder but was still associated with the Cremi-Union Financial Group.

The company joined a group of investors, the Mexican Agricultural Owners Group (GEAM), to buy Del Monte Fresh Produce (the third biggest merchant of tropical fruit in the world) from the English firm Polly Peck International in 1992. This purchase was also masterminded by Cabal Peniche and incorporated the three largest tomato producers in Mexico, as well as other top food and beverage producers (including Pepsi), transport companies, and financial groups.

Cabal Peniche was a friend of former presidents Carlos Salinas and Ernesto Zedillo. He had bought the formerly state-owned Banco BCH as well in 1991 and had assets of over $2 billion by 1994. Peniche already had a history of accumulating food companies and financial institutions, and he tried to convince 152 investors that they could turn Del Monte Mexico around to their benefit. He actually borrowed U.S. $700 million for the purchase and offered credits from his Banca Union to other partners in the deal (which included many prominent politicians and businessmen) who thus didn't even have to invest any cash directly.[46]

This incident became one of the largest financial scandals in the history of Latin America. Cabal Peniche had made himself a personal loan between his own two banks, Banco Cremi and Banca Union, misdirecting almost $900 million. Banca Union collapsed when Cabal Peniche was accused of improper loans. This was only one of several criminal investigations targeting Cabal Peniche, who had also been accused of running drugs through his banana export business. He fled prosecution, apparently to Colombia, and left his business partners to clean up the mess.[47]

When the scandal broke, Empaque Santa Rosa was eager to wash its hands of this association, to sell the company's shares, and unload its debt load. NAFINSA, the government agency created to rescue businesses and public companies, absorbed the loss of Cabal Peniche, and a Colombian company bought Del Monte Fresh. A business connection remains between the two companies, in that Del Monte still distributes Santa Rosa tomatoes, but the intimate relationship has been strained.

Stories of such deals are actually quite common in the newly liberalized Mexico, where the number of billionaires has sharply increased since NAFTA. Shifting ownership from one multinational to another (along with jockeying among shareholders, mergers, and buyouts) is also a regular feature in the new global economy. Corruption is seen as a major impediment to development in Mexico, yet it is so pervasive that it is almost normalized. Indeed, the Leon brothers faced other charges in the late 1990s, from allegedly illegally buying executive jets to failing to pay field-workers who protested by setting fire to tomato poles.[48] In the context of expanding trade under NAFTA, Mexican companies such as Santa Rosa find this bad public image a major obstacle in building trust among new investors.

Globalization from Below: Picking and Packing for Survival

The story of tomato production in Mexico is told quite differently by the women who work at Santa Rosa as pickers and packers, in the fields, packing houses, and greenhouses. From the perspective of the owners and managers, these workers are crucial in a labor-intensive agroindustry, seen primarily as factors in production, ready to be called into action when the seeds are to be planted or the tomatoes are ready to be harvested and packed for export. Moving from a globalization-from-above to a globalization-from- below perspective, their stories make visible work that is often hidden from the rest of the world, and reveal some of the complexities and differences among women workers themselves.

GENDERED FIELDS

The "feminization of labor" has been central to the development of agroexport economies such as Mexico's.[49] Lara's comprehensive study of the history of the tomato industry reveals that women entered the production process as packers after a U.S. embargo in 1932 forced producers to improve their practices to compete with American producers.[50] Even then women were considered more "flexible" and "gentle" with the fragile fruit. Kirsten Appendini sees this phenomenon as integral to the more recent growth of fruit and vegetable export agriculture, suggesting that "firms use gender ideologies to erode stable employment and worker rights where women are concerned."[51] Antonieta Barrón points out that in the transnationalization of Mexican agriculture, it is in primary markets, characterized by large capitalist producers such as Santa Rosa, that there is a more rigid sexual division of labor, and women's participation has increased in recent years. Since the mid-1990s, these "temporary-permanent" migrant workers have been predominantly female, two-thirds of them under twenty-four, and a majority between fifteen and nineteen years old.

FAMILY WAGE ECONOMIES

The family as a unit, in fact, is (and has always been) central to agricultural production. While small farms are run on family labor, campesino families also depend on remittances from members who migrate, and migrating families often offer several family members as salaried workers to agribusiness. While there is particularly an international outcry about child labor in economies such as Mexico, managers themselves, such as Santa Rosa's production head, rationalize it as the only way out for poor families: "The reality is that the Mexican minimum-wage salary is so low, that we are compelled by the campesinos themselves to give work to the whole family. If we had a better social assistance program in Mexico, if these children could be in school, protected, and cared for, it might be different."[52]

The survival of families depends on combining the income of several family members, especially since NAFTA and the ensuing peso crisis. Kathy Kopinak suggests that this family wage economy characterizes Mexico's majority, in contrast with the family consumer economy predominant in the north, modeled on European industrial development, in which it was assumed that the male's individual wage would support his family, if subsidized by a woman's unpaid work in the home.[53] This is simply not enough for Mexican campesinos who have not only lost access to land for subsistence but have lost the safety net of national food subsidies. While in 1981, just under two minimum-wage salaries were needed to cover the basic survival needs of a family of five, by 1993, it was estimated that more than five family members' salaries were needed to pay for basic needs.[54]

The desperation of campesino families has pushed them to move not only from one harvest to another but also from the countryside to cities and from formal-sector work to informal economic activities.[55] They become the epitome of the "flexible" and "permanent temporary" labor considered most desirable by global capital and its proponents in industry and agribusiness, ready to move from day to day, place to place, whenever and wherever any kind of work is available. Women workers at Empaque Santa Rosa reflect this constant movement for survival in their work and home lives.

SEXUAL DIVISION OF LABOR AT SANTA ROSA

In its division of labor, Santa Rosa reproduces traditional notions about what is appropriate men's and women's work, noted in the chart on the following page.[56]

In his classic study of tomato workers, Gabriel Torres suggests that the criteria for this division of labor are economic, political, and cultural. It is argued that men are better at the heavier jobs requiring physical strength, as well as the managerial jobs that require experience, access to technical information, and the "initiative and ability to exert authority."[57]

Gendered Tasks in Tomato Work

	Male Tasks	Female Tasks
Preliminary tasks	Clean and plow land with tractors Maintain equipment Manage production	Plant and care for seedlings in greenhouses
Planting	Deliver seedlings Guard fields	Make 10- to 15-centimeter holes with stick or fingers Plant seedlings
Cultivation	Hoe fields Spread fertilizer Mound furrows Irrigate Bore holes for stakes	Prune plants Tie plants to stakes
Fumigation	Mix agrochemicals Spray pesticides, herbicides, and fungicides	
Harvesting	Farm manager Foreman Pick tomatoes Move boxes from fields to plant	 Forewoman Pick tomatoes Record production
Packing	Box makers Carriers (by hand or electric lifts) Assemblers Sealers Ticket boxes Move boxes to storage and/or to trucks Operate gassing rooms Clean the plant	Wash tomatoes Select by size, color Pack tomatoes Put stickers on fruit
Management	Company executives Plant supervisor Field production manager Fumigation manager	Secretaries Receptionists

Women are the majority in jobs such as planting, pruning, sorting, and pack-ing, and they often make up the majority of the pickers. Managers claim that women are more skilled at the intricate tasks (the famous "nimble fingers" mantra) and are more efficient, productive, and responsible than men. It's also clear that they're often preferred because they are paid lower wages and are seen to be more compliant. An executive at Santa Rosa reflects these entrenched gen-der ideologies, as he tries to explain why 80 to 90 percent of the labor force in his packing plants is female: "Women 'see' better than men; they can better distin-guish the colors, and they treat the product more gently. In selection, care, and handling, women are more delicate. They can put up with more than men in all aspects: the routine, the monotony. Men are more restless, and won't put up with it."[58] These "explanations" don't recognize the social construction of these gen-dered tasks. They also deny the women their own agency, or any recognition that they "put up with" exploitative conditions out of necessity, sacrifice, and a com-mitment to feed their families.

Sara Lara, in her historical study of the feminization of labor processes in the fruit and vegetable industry, notes that women have always predominated in the packing and processing of tomatoes in Mexico, carrying out 90 percent of the tasks. She explains this as due not to any inherently biological propensities women have toward these tasks, but rather to their socialization as girls in tasks related to food:

> Women are found in those tasks that require quick movement and dex-terity, and especially delicate treatment and the perfection of move-ments that correspond to highly developed fine motor skills, learned by women through centuries of education transmitted from one generation to another, i.e., a series of abilities that are social and culturally acquired by women that makes them preferred in the work of this sector and not low-skilled.[59]

Lara's analysis actually questions the way that "skill" gets defined, and shows how women's work, often highly skilled, has been devalued and labeled "low-skilled" by male management. While employers suggest that women aren't offered the more highly skilled jobs, because of their lack of technical compe-tence in operating machinery, Lara argues that such discrimination is sexist. At the same time, they are considered much more skilled than men in greenhouse and packing tasks that require patience and delicate treatment. After generations of developing such specialized skills, Lara contends, their capacities are neither recognized nor remunerated but rather considered natural.[60]

According to Lara, the restructuring and technologization of tomato produc-tion during the 1990s did not change this sexual division of labor, but, in fact, ex-ploited it even further. By employing greater numbers of women, companies contract skilled but devalued labor that is not only qualitatively but quantita-tively flexible.[61] With the major shift to greenhouse production after the turn of the millennium, women continued to be assigned the tasks of pruning, sorting, and packing. But Antonieta Barrón found a decrease of women in salaried work in the agroexport industry. She speculates that because greenhouses offered permanent (9–10 months) rather than seasonal work (3–4 months), the men took these year-round jobs, providing a more secure income for their families and returning some women back to full-time domestic work in the home. This is especially true in northern Mexico, where families are now settling down, and where there are more work options for skilled workers in maquila industries or across the border in the United States.[62]

MORE THAN JUST GENDER: AN INTERLOCKING ANALYSIS

Any analysis of Mexican women workers in tomato agribusiness must take into account, in fact, not only gender dynamics but historical and structural inequalities based on class, race and ethnicity, age and marital status, as well as uneven development between cities and the countryside, between the northern and southern regions of Mexico, and between the three NAFTA countries. The stories that follow reflect an interlocking analysis (chapter 2) that recognizes how groups are historically constructed, contextually developed, and placed within hierarchical relations. Thus, while the gendered nature of women's work is highlighted within the case studies, we show how class, Indigenous identity, age, and family status shape particular constructions of gender. There are clear patriarchal and racist tendencies, for example, in the persistent patterns of Indigenous workers relegated to the slogging field work, young mestizo women sorting and packing tomatoes in the plants, and more highly skilled mestizo men in management positions.[63]

Once again we uncover tangled roots. Job categories and divisions of tasks within tomato production have evolved over the decades (indeed centuries) to reflect and reinforce institutionalized classism, sexism, racism, and ageism. Santa Rosa has followed hiring practices, consciously or not, that isolate and pit workers against each other. I am suggesting six different categories for women's work within three different work contexts, which are highlighted here; each one is represented by a woman whose profile reveals both the commonalities and the differences among women tomato workers.

Three Workplaces/Six Women Workers		
1. *Packing plant*	Packer: Josefina	Sorter: Yolanda
2. *Greenhouse*	Packer: Yvonne	Planter: Soledad
3. *Fieldwork*	Local: Tomasa	Migrant: Reyna

A MOVING MAQUILA: THE "COMPANY GIRLS" WHO SORT AND PACK

The packing plant is one of the places where entrenched gender ideologies clearly reign. Women are considered both more responsible and more delicate in their handling of the tomatoes; and because the appearance of the product is so critical

to tomato exporters, there is at least some recognition of this work as a skill, even if it is considered innate rather than part of female socialization, as Lara argues.[64]

Women who sort and pack tomatoes for Santa Rosa are drawn from two sources: local girls living in the town and mostly young women hired permanently by the company and moved from site to site, harvest to harvest. The latter are the most privileged and are clearly "company girls," a kind of "moving maquila." They provide the flexible labor and the skills needed by Santa Rosa at the important stage of sorting and packing tomatoes for export.

We had an opportunity to visit with a group of these women in their temporary home in Sirena, when they arrived home, exhausted, at 8:30 P.M., after a twelve-hour workday. Juana, thirty-seven, the oldest of the group, prepared dinner on a hot plate in their small room, while the others collapsed on the two beds they shared. It was a tender scene: an older woman stroked the hair of a teenaged worker, reflecting this new form of family, a woman-centered home, constructed by the demands of the company.

They were all from Sinaloa, where the largest production site of Santa Rosa is located, and where they were trained in the precise and delicate work of selecting and packing. It is easier for the company to move these skilled workers on to other sites as the harvest shifts from one part of the country to another than to train new workers at each site.

◖◖◖◖◖

Juana, Packer

"I completed grade 5 in Sinaloa, and began working when I was fourteen, accompanying my mother who was working in a packing plant there. I'm thirty-seven years old now. I've been following the harvests for twenty-three years. I like this work; I'm still here.

"*We are brought from Sinaloa with all expenses paid; the company covers the costs of transport, food, and once here, we get a house with a stove, beds, mattresses. Our house is close to the plant, and we share it with sixteen other workers. In the end, we're all a family, those of us who are here.*

"*I usually get up at five to bathe, prepare food, and leave some dinner ready, so that when we come back at 1 P.M., all we have to do is warm it up.*

"*We go from here to the Santa Rosa plant in Sinaloa, and from there we go to San Quintin, Baja California, and then back to Sinaloa—every year we make the round. The houses in Baja California and Sinaloa are much better: there's a Social Security clinic right in the plant, a chapel, washing machines, and fifty-four spacious rooms, two women to a room. They even have teachers for kindergarten and primary school for the kids.*"

Yolanda, Sorter

"*I'm twenty-one and have been working for Santa Rosa for six years. My father was a manager at the packing plant in Sinaloa, and I began working there during school vacations. I liked packing work better than school. The atmosphere is different; it's more fun, and you can make money.*

"*I came here from Sinaloa and share an apartment with my mother, sister, and brother-in-law. He works in the Santa Rosa office and gets special living expenses. I earn almost one thousand pesos ($200) a week. I'm saving money for a house I'm building back in Sinaloa.*"

While certainly better off than the field-workers, these two mobile workers bear different levels of responsibility for their families. Juana sends money home to help support her eight siblings, while Yolanda saves all her earnings for the construction of her own house in Sinaloa. Many young women her age see this as temporary work, a good way to make some money, travel, and perhaps find a husband, so that they could then get on to the real business of settling down and raising their own families. Older women like Juana, who do not marry and leave the job, have become virtually wedded to the company, with no time or space for creating their own lives. They move from harvest to harvest, like swallows, returning annually to their home base.

None of the sorters or packers appears to be Indigenous (though this is not always easy to determine), and so they also represent mestizo privilege. They are the women who are in closest contact with the company management; the most privileged, in fact, seem to be women with connections to men who have administrative jobs with Santa Rosa, like Yolanda's brother.

Ironically, while they make three or four times as much as field-workers, and enjoy better working and living conditions, sorters and packers are often required to work much longer hours. In the peak harvest season, they may work twelve hours or more a day, six or seven days a week; they thus accumulate a lot of pesos, but they also accumulate exhaustion. One woman recalled working once until 3:30 A.M., and there were reports that the packers were fed amphetamines to keep them awake.

In any case, some flexibility seems evident here, as one worker reported staying home to sleep for a day after a particularly long stretch. The company seems to tolerate this erratic work attendance as part of an implicit agreement: workers must be flexible enough to move for the company and work long hours, while the company is flexible in not firing them for missing work but allowing them to recover energies for another long workday.[65] Companies lose nothing with such a practice: they don't have to pay absent workers because it is a piecework system and there is always a reserve of women waiting for work, from day to day.

There is, however, a hierarchy of skills and of treatment between the two main jobs of sorting and packing, with the packers being the more favored in several senses. "The sorters have to sign in, but we packers don't. The sorters have to stand all the time. Packers can sit on wooden boxes." The sorters start at 9, the packers at 10 A.M. Perhaps the biggest and most crucial difference is the wage level and form of payment. Sorters are paid by the hour, while packers are paid by the box. At 33 cents a box, a packer might average two hundred to five hundred boxes a day, or 66 to 150 pesos, or $13 to $30 a day; a sorter, earning 5 pesos an hour, would average 35 to 60 pesos, or $7 to $12 a day. Both of these far surpass the field-worker's wage of 28 pesos ($5) a day for back-breaking work under a hot sun. With speed and extra hours, packers can do very well, though the results can vary: "The most I've earned is 1,170; the lowest is 400. When you get below 300, the company gives us 100 pesos for food."

Male workers in the packing plant are still the most privileged, however. On Saturdays, when workers go to the office to get their weekly pay, the queues themselves reveal the ultimate divisions. In the words of one of the packers, "When we go to get our money, there are three lines: one for sorters, one for packers, and one for the men." For comparison, one woman mentioned that most *cargadores*, or carriers (those who move boxes), make up to twelve hundred pesos a week, while packers average between six hundred and nine hundred.

Benefits, too, are limited. As contracted workers, they don't get paid vacations (only full-time employees, mainly men, do). Like most Santa Rosa workers we spoke with, they report that there is no union (even though a sign outside the plant mentions the CTM as the official union). When they are sick, they get passes to the social security clinic, and with a doctor's signature, they can get paid for half a day's work, but packers get this pay at the sorters' wage level.

There is no formal training offered; women reported learning by watching or having someone, perhaps a friend or relative, show them how to do the work. Nor was there any orientation in the use of the equipment or the chemicals, even though the women reported some health and safety problems associated with the work: "People get sick from the wax that's put on the tomato; it makes the skin on their hands peel. It's cool in the plant, then you go outside in the heat. When I wash my hands, the water and soap is cold and gives me rheumatism." The hand washing is done to protect not the workers, but the tomatoes, as are other precautions: "First they told us to cut our nails so we wouldn't mistreat the tomatoes; now we wear gloves for that, though we have to buy our own. We wear aprons not to stain our clothes."

In the end, while they are treated better than field-workers, it is the product that reigns in management's eyes. The appearance of the tomato is in some ways more important than the health of the workers.

FACTORIES IN THE FIELDS: HIGH-TECH GREENHOUSE PRODUCTION

The future of tomato production in Mexico seems to be in greenhouses, which allow year-round production and almost total control of key factors such as climate, technology, and labor. The proliferating blocks of white plastic greenhouses increasingly dot the countryside, yet another sign of the industrialization of an agri-

culture shaped primarily by export demands and designed by foreign business architects and technicians.

Empaque Santa Rosa was the major shareholder in a model greenhouse experiment begun in 1991, an hour outside of Guadalajara. Greenhouse production is expensive, at least the initial investment in infrastructure, which was $30,000. The company rented 120 hectares of prime agricultural land,[66] and set up sixty-two different units of white plastic (made in Israel). It brought in engineers from France and Israel to set up and manage this high-tech production facility.

The company only leases the land and brings all the inputs from the United States. Pierre, the French production manager, describes the raw materials used: the seeds are biogenetically modified "long shelf-life" seeds from Israel; the drip irrigation system and the engineer brought to administer it are from Israel as well.[67] Some of the equipment, such as the computerized irrigation system and a computerized sorting facility, is from Holland. Most of the fertilizers are from the United States, as are the cardboard boxes for packing the tomatoes and the strings for tying them up. Only the tables and carts are made in Mexico by local contractors.

Greenhouse production can be seen as the epitome of the "maquila" model, which since NAFTA has now moved from the northern border to be applied to businesses throughout Mexico. Maquila industries are characterized by four dimensions: feminizing the labor force, highly segmenting skill categories (majority unskilled), lowering real wages, and introducing a nonunion orientation.[68] The key Mexican inputs are the land, the sun (the company saves on electricity and heating), and the workers. And like most maquilas, 100 percent of the produce is for export (10 percent going to Canada but most to the United States).

Only in recent years has it become culturally acceptable for young women to enter the paid labor force at all, and then only out of necessity. Yvonne remembers, "At first, my parents wouldn't let me work. I kept asking and my papa kept saying no. He thinks women belong at home. First he let me accompany him to the *milpa* (family plot), then, finally, he let me take this job."

Most young people have taken these jobs because nothing else is available and because their income is needed for the family wage. But there is an extremely high turnover: "If you don't like it, you can leave. Because there are lots of people who want to work. We do it for obligation, to put food on the table."

Greenhouse work offers a new form of employment that combines planting and packing, and in terms of wages and status, falls somewhere between the field-workers and the packers at the larger plants. There are a total of 650 employees from fourteen different towns in the area, brought daily on eleven buses. Less than 40 percent of the workers are men, who do the so-called heavier jobs: soil preparation, fumigation, maintenance of equipment, carting boxes to the refrigerated storage rooms (where tomatoes might be gassed) or directly to the trucks. Some men share with women the tasks of planting and picking. For women, there are basically two different kinds of roles: working in the green-houses planting and picking tomatoes, or working in the packing house in a more sophisticated process that combines selecting and packing. The next two profiles feature one woman worker in each area: Soledad works in the green-house and Yvonne in the packing house.

⌐⌐⌐⌐⌐

Soledad, Greenhouse Planter

While Soledad is a very feisty and social fifteen-year-old, her name means "loneliness" or "soli-tude." When she was three years old, her parents moved to Los Angeles, and she hasn't seen them since. They have had five more kids there, and they send money home, about $500 every two weeks, to support Soledad, her sister and brother, and grandparents, with whom she lives. This is not an uncommon family configuration, as relatives share child rearing on both sides of the border, and those who remain in Mexico are tied both emotionally and financially to their families in the north.

Still, Soledad and her siblings contribute to the fam-ily wage, and she has been working at the greenhouse since she was thirteen, following her uncle who is a foreman there. Her work involves caring for the seedlings, pruning the plants, and tying them up on strings, while moving along on tall rolling carts. In picking season, she averages thirteen rows a day, responding to pressure to surpass the quota of eight rows to get a bonus; the carts are somewhat risky, however, and her sister was seriously injured by falling off one.

Soledad makes 180 pesos (U.S. $26) a week, 30 pesos (U.S. $4 to $5) a day for six days, or 4 pesos (under $1) an hour—only slightly more than the field-workers. There are bonuses for going beyond the quota, but no double pay for overtime. Social Security gets 12.81 pesos, 7.94 is taken out for taxes, and a food subsidy of 20 pesos is pro-

vided. There are rumors that many workers are not officially registered with the Mexican Institute for Social Security (IMSS) but considered part-time workers, so the company doesn't have to pay social security, vacation, or the two-week bonus at the end of the year.

There are complex stories, too, behind the food subsidy. First, the normal workday begins at 8 A.M. and ends at 5 P.M. or so (though it goes until 8 or 9 P.M. in peak season); there's a half-hour break at 10 A.M. for "lunch," an hour-long break at 1:30 P.M. for dinner, the major noontime meal, and another break in the midafternoon. Most workers buy food from the cafeteria within the plant, which has a variety of typical dishes. If they don't bring food (or have it delivered by family mem-bers), they may end up spending three to four pesos for lunch and six for dinner, totaling almost sixty pesos a week, far beyond the twenty pesos provided. Buying food at work has been further encouraged in the past year as the midday break was shortened to a half hour, making it impossi-ble for some who previously went home for this major family meal.[69]

Yvonne, Greenhouse Packer

Yvonne undertakes the other major task assigned to young women, working in the enormous pack-ing house. In her three years at the greenhouse, she has passed through various jobs and has wit-nessed the move into high-tech packing. The computerized system that weighs the tomatoes and also measures their color (from green to red), on the one hand, makes Yvonne's job easier. But the phys-ical site itself reflects the dynamic of worker control: there is a small glassed-in and elevated control booth, with a computer, that oversees the two long conveyor belt packing lines; on each side of a line are twenty to thirty women, in white coats, working at lightning speed to fill cardboard boxes lined with black plastic casing shaped to receive each individual tomato. Women grab five tomatoes at a time from the cups, turning around and dropping them simultaneously into the appropriate boxes.

The pressure that the computerized process on the lines creates within and among the work-ers is palpable. The French manager's strategy has worked on people like Yvonne, who has suc-cumbed to the competitive dynamic:

"I was depressed at first because they would tell me, 'You're below the quota.'" I would be ashamed, because this means you're not worth anything. So I was very tense, con-cerned about getting faster, so they'd have a better impression of me.

"There's a competition between the lines. There are some who work at an incredible speed, and I said to myself, 'I'm never going to beat them.' Once I was washing pots, where most do 500 to 750 a day, and I was next to a woman who did more than 1,000. After a few weeks, I had reached her level, and now I'm used to going fast, so she doesn't beat me like she used to."

Ironically, these workers are paid by the hour and not by the piece; they only have to ful-fill a certain quota, and there is a bonus if they go much beyond it. But Yvonne has internal-ized this competitive race so much that she dreams about it: "Once I dreamed that some coworkers were cleaning the tomatoes faster than me. I kept thinking, 'How am I going to catch up to them? How nice it would be to beat them.' In the dream, I won."

Both Soledad and Yvonne reflect the impact of work reorganization that has been imposed by foreign management and clashes with cultural practices. The change in eating practices that keeps workers in the greenhouse all day, and purchasing food from the plant, is a classic dynamic in ur-banizing and industrializing societies but has a profound impact on family relations. Yvonne's ef-forts to keep up with the new technology and to prove herself a productive worker also reveal the internalization of new work values, not unlike the pressure that Marissa experienced as a Loblaws cashier. "Good workers" are being shaped in Mexico by the combination of controlling technology and foreign management.

Once again the male workers are paid more: "If we make 100, men make 175. Some rationalize: The men are faster in this work because they're stronger and can pick up many more boxes. We can only pick up one at a time, so it would take us much longer." Enrique closes and stacks the boxes, wraps ninety-six together, and moves them by electric cart into storage or onto big trailers. He earns 230 to 280 (U.S. $37–40) pesos, 100 more than the women.

ⓡⓖⓑⓞⓡ

INTO THE FIELDS

The women workers who are closest to the land, the plants, and the tomatoes themselves are also the lowest paid and least skilled in the hierarchy outlined here. They are the most exposed to the hot sun and the rain, as well as the pesticides sprayed incessantly in the fields. Two stories here reveal two major sources of tomato field-workers: local campesinos and Indigenous migrants from the south.

ⓡⓖⓑⓞⓡ

Tomasa, Local Field-worker

Pablo and Tomasa live in a house that was built by them and their neighbors over ten years ago, part of an earthquake relief project; the state government offered the land, and Canadian agencies offered the building materials. The small brick house is surrounded by flowers and fruit trees, and the kitchen is in the center of the outdoor patio in the back, where Tomasa makes tortillas and prepares her family's meals.

As an older woman (sixty-eight years old), Tomasa is perhaps not a typical field-worker. But her story reflects many important characteristics of migrant labor in Mexico. First, her personal history growing up as a campesino girl in the countryside reveals the deeply rooted sexism that produces and reproduces the gendered division of labor in the agricultural sector. Second, as older workers, she and her husband, Pablo, have witnessed the tremendous changes in agriculture of the past seventy years and can thus compare current with past practices. Like many other peasant families, they combine subsistence farming with salaried work for agribusiness. And finally, her story reveals the family wage economy that is the major strategy of survival for poor Mexicans.

"*Both Pablo and I were born in Tapalpa. I don't remember the year of my birth. We weren't a large family, only five—two brothers and three sisters.*

"*We raised ourselves, that is, my father died when I was two, and so my mother was left alone to raise us; she had to work to feed us.*

"*As a child, I played around the house, but when I was eight or nine, my mother put me to work—sweeping, fetching water from a faraway stream. When I became older, I helped grind and mix the corn meal to make tortillas.*

"*My mother wasn't able to help us study, and I never went to school. I remember that somebody sent books to the ranch, and my brothers taught themselves to read. Surely I didn't have it in me, I wasn't capable of learning, so I didn't teach myself. I'm like a donkey. I know a lot, but I miss not knowing how to read. You need it for so many things (when you're buying something, and you can't recognize the price, it's so embarrassing). If you don't study, you get stuck in work that is not your choice. But there is no other struggle. As long as God gives us life, we have to work.*

"*Pablo used to come by our rancho. We got married when I was seventeen and he was twenty. We had sixteen kids; nine are still alive, seven died of bronchitis (from the cold). The oldest is forty-eight, then forty-seven, then every other year, I had one—that was easier. The youngest is twenty-one. You can understand why I'm so exhausted, after having so many kids!*

"*My kids helped me with the housework and they still help. God has blessed us. None of my children drink or smoke; they just go to work and then go home. They come to visit often and bring us things to eat. We survive by sharing, as long as we live and God gives us life.*

"*Two of my sons have gone to work in the U.S. and send money back. My other sons work in the lumber business, cutting pine trees nearby. The women don't work in the field; they stay at home with their family. I'm the only one who runs around like a fried chile, picking tomatoes! My youngest daughter stays at home, and has food ready for us when we return from the fields.*

"*Women's lives have changed a lot. Before women practically killed themselves working, but they don't have to work so much now. There are store-bought tortillas, washing machines, et cetera. When I was growing up, we worked harder: grinding the corn meal, fetching water from the streams; but now there are tortillas in the tortillería and water in the house—you just turn on the washing machine and that's it. I used only cloth diapers when I raised my kids; now everyone buys paper diapers, but they're expensive.*

"*Now many women are also leaving the house to work. We are more equal now, men and women. Neither has to work too hard. Men work less now, with the help of fertilizer. Before they had to plow the rows to use it. Now the tractor plants, the tractor fertilizes. Now men don't even have to work!*

"*But housework never ends, and is never paid for. When it comes to housework, men are useless. Maybe some men know how to cook but not here. I'll speak for mine—he doesn't do anything; he just comes in, sits down, and says, 'Give me my dinner; I'm hungry and I want to eat.'*"

The unpaid domestic work that keeps Mexican campesino families alive is not accounted for in any of the official calculations. Tomasa, in fact, works a triple day: as a salaried worker for agribusiness, as a subsistence farmer on their family milpa, and as the cook and caretaker of her family. Her survival, nonetheless, is totally dependent on the family wage and her partnership with her husband, Pablo, both as foreman and forewoman in the tomato fields and as subsistence farmers in their own plot. Pablo reveals both the subsistence side of their survival strategies, as well as the mixed farming practices influenced by industrial agriculture.

"I still have my milpa," he said, "but now I use the fertilizers like the boss told me. They cost a lot but I struggled to get them, I bought some pills (I'm not sure what they're called), and I put them on. But the fertilizer we're using now only lasts for one growing season. The stronger ones cost more, and they kill the squash and beans. The milpa becomes sad.

"Tomasa helps me. The corn grows very beautiful, and just when it's beginning to emerge from the husk, you put some more fertilizer and it becomes even better. That is, it grows faster. And instead of being sad, it now becomes prettier.

"Before . . . we did have to work more, doing everything by hand, preparing the ground. Now I work in the milpa for short bits of time. I come from working in the tomato fields, and I go to work in the milpa, cultivating my little corn. I've already sold some of it. The land here is very fertile; it produces even without fertilizer, and if you add just a handful, it will grow better."

Though Pablo seems caught in this vicious agrochemical treadmill, buying fertilizers every year, trying new ones that he can't even name, he still feels a stronger connection with his milpa than with the tomato fields.

"Just like the tomatoes on the plantation are fertilized and grow to be beautiful, my milpa, too, is fertilized. I like working both there and here and think it's good to be doing both jobs. But I feel more related to that which is mine, to the milpa here. The land there at Santa Rosa is not mine, but because this is mine, I take advantage of it to grow things to provide for the family."

By 1999, Tomasa and Pablo had left Santa Rosa for permanent jobs at Sunshine Produce, the largest greenhouse operation in North America, with headquarters in Texas and four production sites around Jalisco employing several thousand workers. Their days are longer: they rise at 4 A.M. to be picked up by a company bus at 5 A.M., arriving at work by 7 A.M.; with a one-hour lunch break, they finish work by 5 P.M., are back home by 7 and in bed by 9 P.M. But they see it as a luxury to work only five days a week, their wages are 670 pesos a week (about $60 CAN), and they get a two-week vacation, something seasonal migrant farmworkers could not even dream of.

When I visited them in late 2006, Tomasa was almost eighty and about to retire. But her granddaughter, Ana Maria, was following the family trajectory of tomato picking. She works in a different greenhouse, closer to home but owned by the same company, and her job combines the tasks of Juana, Yolanda, and Yvonne of the stories above: "Before we only sorted, and sent the tomatoes to a packer, but now we must sort, eliminate the green tomatoes, weigh them, and pack them. It hurts my back, standing all the time." In her early twenties, Ana Maria is more conscious of the health risks of tomato production than workers seemed to be a decade earlier. "They show us how to take care of ourselves and insist we wear gloves and closed-toe shoes." Nonetheless, she has witnessed the impact of the drip irrigation system which includes agrochemicals: "Some women are allergic and get rashes from the tomatoes."[70]

From generation to generation, Tomasa's family remains dependent on capitalist agribusiness; whether owned by Mexicans or foreigners, both businesses are taking advantage of their cheap labor. And the companies benefit not only from their low wages, but from the family wage economy that incorporates family remittances, subsistence farming, and Tomasa and her daughter's domestic

labor. While they may appear a triple burden for Tomasa, not even these options are open to most In-
digenous migrant women, the most exploited in the hierarchy of workers.

If gender discrimination is entrenched in the tasks offered women workers and in their double or triple days, racism is manifested against the Indigenous migrant workers who are brought in packed trucks by contractors, without certainty of getting work and with even worse living and working conditions than local campesinos. Often housed in deplorable huts, without water, electricity, stores, or transport, they come as families to work in the fields and move from harvest to harvest. The women bear the brunt of this lack of infrastructure—cooking and washing, taking care of kids (even while working in the field), and dealing with their own exhaustion and the poor health engendered by the conditions of extreme poverty. Because their own regions offer even less opportunity, they are forced to endure these jobs and the racist treatment built into them.[71]

Reyna, Indigenous Migrant Farmworker

"We're from Guerrero state in southern Mexico. Contractors came to our town to find people to work here. After we finish our contract, they take us back in trucks.[72]

"The economic crisis has affected us in many ways. Many people took their kids out of school, because they couldn't afford to pay for their education. Three of us were going to secondary school, but my parents couldn't handle it, and my papa said, 'Well, we'd better leave now; everything costs more now and we don't have the money.'

"In Guerrero, we grew our own vegetables at home. But not here.

"Some women carry their children on their backs while they're working, because they don't have anyone who can take care of them.

"We live with my parents; we're eleven brothers and sisters. Eight of us work, and we share the pay. My husband says that the younger ones should work, too. I'd like them at least to study a bit, even to finish primary school, but they don't want to.

"We only have one room. How can they bring more people when there aren't enough rooms? We don't even have a kitchen, just a place to sleep. We share the housework: Mama washes the dishes, I wash the clothes, and the others help clean the house.

"We earn twenty-eight pesos a day. It's never enough to save anything. Sometimes the children need shoes and it's not enough. They give us some clothes, because twenty-eight pesos is nothing. There's no union and no vacations.

"One day my husband came home with a stomachache and a headache, vomiting white foam. The doctor said that he had been intoxicated with the fertilizer and that he should cover his mouth with a handkerchief."

Promised Land: Up in Flames

Sirena is a small provincial town of thirty thousand inhabitants, a center of a mixture of rural and urban activities. When I first visited the Santa Rosa plantation in the mid-1990s, perhaps the most visible evidence of discrimination and inequalities between the Indigenous and mestizo tomato workers was in the housing provided by the company. A few blocks from the Spanish colonial town square stood in stark contrast the migrant labor camps, or *albergues*, provided by Santa Rosa as housing for Indigenous workers like Reyna. Rows of tarpaper shacks, with only doors and no windows, were connected by clotheslines. A single faucet offered water to the six hundred living in the camp, and a makeshift communal shower was set up nearby. It was made from discarded plastic woven

bags that held fertilizers; doors were constructed from cardboard tomato boxes, and old pesticide cans have become recipients for water.

Two Mixtec guards from Guerrero hired to keep watch over the camp offered a clear denunciation of the situation: "They promised us new houses, with rooms, bathrooms, electricity, but look what we got."

Living in the camps and working in the fields constituted daily risks of their lives. Between 1996 and 1998, there were two major fires that spread rapidly through rows of huts, almost leveling the camp. By the time we returned in July 1999, there was no trace of the albergue at all; the company had been shamed into providing better housing in the town, and the land became a field once more.

The Youngest Victims

By the late 1990s, human rights activists and local residents concerned about the Indigenous migrant workers had begun exposing the inhuman conditions of the camps. Nothing caught the attention of the public (particularly international)[73]

more than the phenomenon of small children working alongside their parents in the fields. There was no child care or schooling available for them; besides, it would have required expenses (books, uniforms, etc.) that their families couldn't afford. They could never imagine participating, as the town's children did,

in first communion or in religious festivals (such as that of the Virgin of Guadalupe, ironically honoring a dark-skinned Indigenous Virgin Mary).

No provisions for children were available in the camps or in the town's schools. And kids interviewed, such as eleven-year-old Carmen de Jesus Maldonado, also claimed to prefer working. "I've been working here for one year, picking tomatoes," she said. "I work all week and get paid twenty-eight pesos a day. The money that I earn, I hide it. My papa told me to work. I prefer working in the field to going to school. We're six brothers and sisters, and my parents. We all work, to be able to buy food."

While children are paid the daily rate, it is often the case that their parents, especially mothers, will rush to fill their own quota, so they can help their children complete theirs. This dynamic makes the fieldwork much more intense and more like piecework.[74] Mothers must also carry their babies on their backs as they work in the fields. In breast-feeding her child, Reyna passed the pesticides from the plants on her hands, which then got into his mouth, and almost poisoned him. Indigenous women and children are clearly in the most precarious position of all who bring us the corporate tomato. Their plight has been the focus of human rights organizing featured at the end of this chapter.

In the six stories presented here, the multiple strategies for survival become clearer. Women are key protagonists for their families, in their triple functions: as salaried workers (with varying status and wage levels), as subsistence farmers (when they have access to land), and as domestic laborers (with a wide range of living conditions, from the horrific albergues of Indigenous migrants to the better-equipped but transient homes of the mobile packers). But no one woman's story can be understood in isolation from her family's story, or separately from her ethnicity, age, marital status, and experience. Globalizing agribusinesses such as Santa Rosa have built their workforces on these historically entrenched inequalities and differences, which keep them separate, even as their fates are intertwined.

Tensions among the Tangled Roots and Routes

What do these workers' stories contribute to our broader understanding of the issues and tensions being explored here? Let's return to the four axes of analysis: production/consumption, work/technology, health/environment, and biodiversity/cultural diversity. While the McDonald's case focused more on the axis of production/consumption and the Loblaws case illuminated the work/technology relationship, the Santa Rosa case, grounded in the production end of the tomato food chain, offers most critical reflection on the health/environment and biodiversity/cultural diversity axes. Still, each axis serves as a thread for a deepening and more holistic analysis of the tomato story.

PRODUCTION/CONSUMPTION

A key contradiction in the production/consumption story is how salaried workers in Mexican agribusiness who produce our food have lost other sources of food for personal consumption. There is the much bigger question, of course, of how Mexico itself has lost its self-sufficiency in food; it must now import corn and export its best tomatoes, while its people eat the second-rate ones—that is, if they can afford them. For migrant worker families, there has also been the loss of access to land and time to farm it for subsistence production. Tomasa and Pablo still combine subsistence production and salaried work, but even this option is increasingly unavailable to poor Indigenous workers.

In addition, major shifts have occurred in cultural eating practices, in terms of what, when, and how food is consumed. Tomasa, for example, now buys tortillas to take for lunch in the fields, instead of making them from scratch. The greenhouse workers have had to adapt to a European work schedule that has eliminated the major ritual of the noontime family meal. The food subsidy of twenty pesos per week cannot possibly cover the costs of the meals sold within the plant. A worker may end up spending three to four pesos for lunch and six for dinner, totaling almost sixty pesos a week. Thus, he or she is spending more for food and missing the social experience of commensality, the time when Mexican families gather at the table to eat, visit, and rest. This is a poignant example of how foreign management can impose work routines that ultimately impact key cultural practices.

For those who do try to maintain traditional practices, days become very complicated, especially for women who usually carry the load. Yvonne is one of the lucky ones who still receives hot meals delivered daily from her mother, who organizes her day around the different shifts and food needs of her children:

"At 7 A.M., Yvonne goes to work and one son goes to school; at 8 A.M., my younger daughter goes to school. At nine, I'm preparing all the meals, so that at ten I take lunch to my son at the high school. I then give breakfast to my other son before he goes to work at the bakery at eleven. Then I prepare the dinner so it can be taken to Yvonne and those in school before the 1 P.M. meal break. At 2 P.M., I send dinner to the son at the bakery, and at 3 P.M., those of us at home have our meal. All day working in the kitchen! I take a break at four, then start washing clothes. This is my daily routine."

Clearly, the competing schedules and dynamics of shift work wreak havoc on family practices of eating. They leave some women, like Yvonne's mother, more bound than ever to the kitchen. And for those who must migrate long distances for work, families are scattered; not only the family meal but the family itself is disintegrating.

WORK/TECHNOLOGY

Tomato production remains extremely labor intensive, much more so than other crops, in fact. And though there are mechanical harvesters in the United States, the primary tasks of harvesting remain manual work for cheap Mexican labor.

Greenhouses, however, are changing that, ushering in a more highly technologized tomato production. Drip irrigation, which includes agrochemicals in the water system, has eliminated some jobs while cutting down on spraying. It is in the packing, however, that high technology has most drastically restructured the work for women on the line. Along with the new computerized sorting equipment has come European management with their own notions of productivity and efficiency. Pierre, the French engineer, seems to be the one who instituted the scientific management approach, doing a time/motion survey when he first arrived. He offers his own position on Mexican workers and their productivity: "Man [sic] by nature doesn't want to work. About half of those hired leave because they're not accustomed to so much work. . . . The trick is to motivate them. . . . The goal is to get them to a certain level, but they'll never be as productive as European workers."[75]

HEALTH/ENVIRONMENT

In countless conversations, we found that there was massive denial about the health impact of pesticide use on both the workers and the land itself. Some workers were reluctant to talk about any problems, and those who did revealed a kind of hopelessness in being able to address them. The men who apply pesticides are perhaps most at risk. But women workers, such as Luz Maria, are often in the line of fire as fumigators move constantly through the fields:

"Whenever the fumigator passes, leaving us behind following it, we breathe in the fumes. I often get a sore throat, headache, and become nauseous. We have to keep working and after the machine passes by, we feel better. But if you leave the row to get away from the fumes and to wait awhile, then they're always shouting at you to get back to work, and if you don't, you might be dismissed and not paid for that day. For complaining, you can lose a whole day and perhaps even your job, so it's really hard to do anything about it.

"They don't give us instructions on how to protect ourselves; they just say it won't harm us, that it isn't damaging. But it is. We cover our faces with handkerchiefs to protect ourselves from the chemicals as well as from the sun, which burns our skin.

"It's very risky and dangerous working with pesticides. A year ago, I was in a field they were spraying, and I had an asthma attack from the chemicals. I couldn't breathe, so they took me quickly to the Social Security clinic and gave me oxygen. But what can you do? I need the work.

"There have been many intoxications, because we're not protected. You see it more and more, and the bosses and supervisors don't do anything, even though the workers ask for help." The workers find small ways to protect themselves from the sun and pesticides, often covering their faces with handkerchiefs and wearing long sleeves.

If workers find it difficult to name, denounce, and treat the impact of agrochemicals on human health, their impact on the land is even harder to challenge. Yet time after time, workers expressed their concern about the ecological effects of the current system. A greenhouse worker was despairing about the longer term effect of this kind of production: "I think when they stop growing tomatoes here, not even a piece of grass will be born from this land, because the chemicals affect the soil. It's simple: if you plant different crops, you fertilize the soil, but if you use chemicals, the soil decomposes. The land gets tired from so many chemicals and won't produce anything."

These comments seemed prophetic, because by the time of our second visit, a year later, the land had already tired. The tomato plants were now growing directly out of bags of soil which had been brought in, making the leased land merely a site of production.

BIODIVERSITY/CULTURAL DIVERSITY

While many tomato workers reveal an understanding of more sustainable practices, they are caught as salaried workers in the monocultural cash-crop agribusiness. Pablo and Tomasa represent older campesinos who, while working for agroexport companies, continue subsistence farming. Their very dependence on this combination has kept alive more traditional agricultural practices and, therefore, a sense of alternatives. Pablo carries with him ancient knowledge about how to work the land, knowledge that he grew up with.

"When I was young," he said, "we planted the seeds by hand, making a hole in the dirt with only our hands, while my grandparents and my papa plowed the field of the milpa with oxen, and we watered the plants by hand. We didn't use fertilizer then. We just used the wastes of the animals, we put it on every plant. And it would grow very well, it was the best fertilizer; it would last two or three years.

"Before, beans, corn, and squash could all grow together. We cultivated all three in the same field, rotating them from one land to another. The corn used to grow big and beautiful ears, without fertilizers."

The milpa supplies the family with enough cornmeal for tortillas year-round and with some surplus to sell. For Tomasa, and indeed for all Mexicans, the tortilla remains the basic diet and the symbol of daily culture, even though it is under threat from new kinds of imported flour and industrialized tortillerías.[76]

"I get up at 5 A.M. and start cooking coffee with cinnamon. I go to the mill to get tortilla flour made from the corn we've grown. Many people here in the rancho keep on making their own tortillas, even though you can now buy them already made; they cost two pesos the kilo."

Both Pablo and Tomasa use words to describe the corn that perceive it as a living entity: Tomasa talking about it "beginning to be born" after the first rains, Pablo speaking of the ear "wanting to come out," emerging from the husk, like a birth.

Indigenous workers, too, still recall a more intimate connection with the earth, the plants, and the growing process. Those who have had to leave behind their lands and subsistence production understand the upheaval of their lives as totally related to the shift to chemical-intensive agriculture. Jesús, one of the Mixtec guards at the Quemado camp for migrant workers, reflected on the historical forces that caused them to migrate in the first place:

"From the time of our grandfathers, we had our own seeds, we didn't use chemical fertilizers, and the plants yielded a lot. But now we have to buy the seeds, and even though the yield is great, the land is getting destroyed. Before, no, it was pure soil, blessed by the gods.

"If I don't have enough money to buy fertilizers, how can I cultivate the land that is now accustomed to fertilizers? You have to make an effort to buy them, and if you don't, then you have to leave, to go look elsewhere for work.

"There is no work there. And I don't have any land. We are almost like slaves of our government. We'll never be equal to the rich. There are organizations, people blocking the highway in protest, demanding what they need. The government is killing those who speak up."

In a very real sense, the struggle to maintain the biodiversity of the land is integrally related to the struggle for cultural diversity and autonomy. This has been clear in the Zapatista struggle, too, for a sovereignty that is political, economic, cultural, and ecological. The EZLN has been able to draw support from NGOs throughout Mexico and around the world, as their cause has symbolized the survival of Indigenous people and practices against the forces of corporate globalization.[77] In 2006, Subcomandante Marcos and Zapatista leaders organized "The Other Campaign," through a nationwide tour to promote dialogue within and among grassroots groups to envision a more inclusive participatory democracy built from the bottom up, outside of a party-based electoral system (chapter 8).[78] These new forms of coalitions are reflected in the fight for better working and living conditions of the Indigenous migrant families working for Santa Rosa.

The Other Globalization: Stories of Resistance

All the actors who've spoken in these pages are caught, in one way or another, in a global food system that puts profits above the health and dignity of workers and the earth. While many conclude, "What can you do? You have to work," they also find multiple ways of resisting this seemingly immutable system, from small and individual actions to the organization of hemispheric coalitions confronting head-on the political and economic forces that maintain it for their own interests.

At an *individual* level, for example, workers find ways to chat with each other in a packing plant where talking is prohibited and to joke as a way to survive the monotony of their jobs. Packers who were forced to put in twelve- to fifteen-hour days during the harvest season sometimes stayed home the following day to recover energies; the high turnover at the greenhouse was due not only to frequent layoffs but to workers leaving because they didn't like their jobs (a form of resistance that only works if other options are available).

Collectively, it is a challenge to take action. First, the transiency of migrant workers makes them very difficult to organize. There are further obstacles of language between mestizos and different Indigenous groups. Most of the Santa Rosa workers we spoke with, whether in the field or packing plant in Sirena or the greenhouse, claimed that there was no union to defend them, and so they saw little possibility of organized resistance to fight for their rights. But on the outside of the greenhouse, there is a sign indicating the workers are "officially" part of the Confederación de Trabajadores Mexicanos, or CTM; the fact that they don't know this reveals its complicity with Santa Rosa owners, as Socorro's uncle explains: "It [the CTM] favors the boss; they only come to check the quotas and the books, to make sure they're complying with the law. But if something happened, they would probably support the boss." Even without the union, however, there were reports of "strikes" by workers, spontaneously organized to put forward certain demands.[79]

STATE AND CIVIL SOCIETY COALITIONS FOR MIGRANT WORKERS' RIGHTS

In our efforts to link our research with efforts to organize for the workers, we were thus limited to local NGOs that were concerned about human rights violations being perpetuated by the agribusinesses. Early in the project, we made a link with the Grupo de Salud Popular Nuestra Vida (Popular Health Group "Our Life") and later with Amigos de la Naturaleza (Friends of the Earth). These groups were made up of (many poor) citizens of Sirena committed to social justice and concerned about the health of the population as well as the land, and they included progressive doctors with previous experience with Indigenous peoples.

They focused primarily on the Indigenous workers brought by the companies to work and live in the makeshift camps on the fringe of Sirena. Most of the migrant workers came from the poorer southern states of Guerrero, Oaxaca, Chiapas, and Veracruz, forced to leave because there was no work nor land for them in their home states. The group's first efforts involved doing workshops on nutrition with women in the albergues, getting to know them and helping them figure out how best to feed their families with such limited resources.

Since 1994, there have been various denunciations by the Sirena Human Rights group, charging all companies, but particularly Empaque Santa Rosa, with violating the human rights of Mixtec workers from Guerrero. Visits in 1994 and 1995 by officials from the Social Security and Labor and Social Welfare ministries resulted in the pressuring of Santa Rosa management to improve the health standards of the camps. The company was also charged with registering workers officially in IMSS but not with providing Social Security benefits to all of them.

In late 1996, a few pieces of investigative journalism in the local newspapers exposed the horrific conditions of the migrant worker camps, and some state agencies scrambled to respond publicly to the charges. On 3 January1997, concerned Sirena citizens (led by the NGOs) presented to the authorities a petition signed by more than two hundred residents demanding that key state government bodies address the lack of adequate housing, health care, and education for the Indigenous families. Citing both the United Nations' Universal Declaration of Human Rights and the Mexican Constitution, they denounced the situation of the three thousand Indigenous workers living on the outskirts of Sirena. They described families sleeping outside while they had to build their own inadequate barracks, lack of potable water and of latrines (forcing defecation in the open air), and cooking in the huts with no escape for the smoke, creating health problems and causing fires. They also noted that local merchants took advantage of these migrants and that the children weren't allowed to go to school, so they accompanied their parents to the fields, being exposed to the elements and pesticide spray.

Directing their petition to the municipal and state authorities, including the Human Rights Commission, the Education and Health ministries, and the DIF (Desarrollo Integral de la Familia, concerned with family welfare), they proposed concrete short- and medium-term actions: (1) housing of appropriate materials, (2) adequate sewage and garbage disposal, (3) potable water, (4) child care services, (5) teachers for school-age children, (6) recreational space, (7) pesticide spraying after work hours, (8) inspections of cheating merchants, (9) health education, and (10) control of the use of agrochemicals, research on their impact on the land, and a search for alternatives.

Finally, in mid-1998, the Jalisco Human Rights Commission (CEDH) pressured government offices to respond to the January 1997 petition from the Sirena citizens, and slowly their reports trickled in. The federally sponsored Program for Agricultural Day Laborers also responded to these demands. The Health Ministry set up mobile medical units, and the Transport Ministry agreed to talk with truck owners bringing migrants from the south to conform to standards. The Ministry of Labor was conspicuously silent. The agency to offer the most concrete response was the DIF, which sent a social worker to Sirena to set up child care centers in the albergues and to organize classes for school-age children.

The accumulated pressure began to pay off in some small ways, as was clear in the earlier admission by Santa Rosa's field manager that they had closed down the camps and had moved migrant families to houses in town; he also suggested they were moving toward organic production in response to the uproar about pesticides. While Santa Rosa seems to have been less open to making changes, one of its competitors in the area has been the most responsive in trying to improve both working and living conditions. They have more adequate housing, have provided health care, and have strongly supported the DIF-sponsored programs.

The doctor hired by DIF to establish child care centers and schools for migrant children has become a key community organizer and negotiator with the companies in efforts to improve other aspects of their lives. By mid-1999, 90 percent of the children of migrant families were in the day care centers or schools, run by Indigenous women themselves, paid by the companies at the rate of field-workers.

The DIF-appointed doctor also got the companies to support workshops she offered on pesticides, primarily to educate those who apply the pesticides about the health risks of their jobs and how to protect themselves. One major issue is the contamination by the toxic chemicals: workers learned how to dispose of the wastes and the water used to wash the tomatoes, how to avoid the use by workers of pesticide cans as cooking or washing containers, and how to prohibit the burning of tires (one of the few sources of heat), which emits extremely noxious fumes.

Leonardo Lamas, an activist doctor who spearheaded much of the local organizing around the environment, health, and migrant workers' rights, was named Sirena's first director of ecology in 2001. With a team of six, he initiated four municipal projects: the first two, Clean Sayula and Green Sayula, addressed issues of waste management (recycling, diversion) and reforestation (planting three thousand trees in the region). The third project promoted environmental education in the schools and barrios, aimed at creating "a culture of environmentalism."

The fourth project addressed directly the actions of the local tomato companies, passing regulations that required them to offer better housing and health services to migrant farmworkers and to adopt more ecologically sound production practices. Medical researchers, contracted to undertake scientific studies, had confirmed the rise in respiratory diseases—asthma and emphysema—directly correlated with the use of agrochemicals. The new regulations prohibited the spraying of pesticides within a one kilometer radius of the town. While companies at first protested that this was their most productive land, the ecology directorate encouraged them to use it for organic production, which one company eventually did. Organic pest management treatments are now being sold, especially to local greenhouses.

Lamas described the conflicting interests at stake: "The companies only see the economic while we see the human dimensions of production. The organic initiative is just one small step: at least people will eat more healthily and workers won't be intoxicated by pesticides. But we have to ensure the other conditions necessary for these workers to live a life with dignity."[80]

Unfortunately, the 2004 municipal elections ushered in a more conservative leadership and the ecology program was eliminated. By 2007, however, an environmentalist mayor gained power, and promised to reinstate the program. A major new initiative is the construction of a regional environmental education center, which will have dormitories, a library, and an auditorium for educational events as well as demonstrations of environmental practices, encouraging local alternatives to agribusiness.

While committed to fighting continually for the rights and health of the workers and the land, the Sirena activists realize they are up against a bottom-line corporate mentality and will need support from groups on the other side of the border as well. As one key organizer suggested, "What most concerns the companies is that their tomatoes be bought when they get to the other side of the border. And once it gets to the other side, it doesn't matter to anyone how they were produced, if human rights were violated in their production."

Thus, efforts to improve the lives of Mexican farmworkers must also involve alliances with human rights and environmental and social justice groups in the United States and Canada. Whenever we asked the Sirena groups about what we could do in Canada to support them, they cautioned against boycotts of Mexican tomatoes, because thousands of poor Mexicans now depend on work in the tomato fields. But as an initial strategy, they proposed, "Get consumers to demand organic produce; at least that could help improve the health of Mexican workers."[81]

Becoming aware of the conditions under which the tomatoes we import from Mexico are grown will likely make us rethink our patterns as consumers. But any actions we take—whether individual or collective—should be determined in collaboration with groups in Mexico that are working for environmental and social justice. They know the context better and can judge the impact of different responses. There are many ways that we can become involved in the issues raised in this chapter, through trade unions and NGOs that are linking workers, women, and environmentalists in the NAFTA context or more broadly in the hemisphere, for example.

Notes

1. Angus Wright, *The Death of Ramón González: The Modern Agricultural Dilemma* (Austin: University of Texas Press, 1990), 9.

2. This very brief review does not pretend to do justice to the incredible diversity and richness of both pre-Columbian cultures as well as the various Indigenous groups that have survived colonization.

3. As Harriet Friedmann reminds us, we must use the word "traditions" carefully, as every traditional practice is constructed within a particular historical and social context, out of other traditional practices; what's more, they are never static processes but constantly evolving, merging, and/or dying out. I particularly want to guard against reinforcing a tendency to equate "Indigenous" with "traditional." See *Women Working the NAFTA Food Chain: Women, Food, and Globalization*, ed. Deborah Barndt (Toronto: Second Story, 1999), 36–60.

4. Patricia Arias, "Three Microhistories of Women's Work in Rural Mexico," in *Women of the Mexican Countryside, 1850–1990*, ed. Heather Fowler-Salamini and Mary Kay Vaughan (Tucson: University of Arizona Press, 1994), 159–74.

5. For example, though large landowners were permitted to keep 150 hectares (always selecting the best land) and could also subdivide and sell land not required to be distributed to campesinos, this became a scam as they "sold" these properties to family members or *prestanombers* (name lenders). Judith Adler Hellman, *Mexican Lives* (New York: The New Press, 1995), 118.

6. Maria da Gloria Marroni de Velázquez, "Changes in Rural Society and Domestic Labor in Atlixco, Puebla, 1940–1990," *Women of the Mexican Countryside, 1850–1990*, 210–24.

7. Vandana Shiva, *Monocultures of the Mind: Perspectives on Biodiversity and Biotechnology* (Atlantic Highlands, N.J.: Zed, 1993), 56–57.

8. Tom Barry, *Zapata's Revenge: Free Trade and the Farm Crisis in Mexico* (Boston: South End Press, 1995), 27–28.

9. Established in the 1940s, the Bracero Program brought Mexican farmworkers voluntarily to work on U.S. farms. The industrialization of agriculture in Mexico also increased internal migration: the burgeoning cotton industry in Sonora state in the 1950s drew the first large wave of migrant labor from southern states; the second wave of migration in the 1970s and 1980s was stimulated by the growing fruit and vegetable industry. Personal communication with Antonieta Barrón, Miami, March 2000.

10. John Warnock, *The Other Mexico: The North American Triangle Completed* (Montreal: Black Rose, 1995), 205.

11. Steven T. Edinger, *The Road from Mixtepec: A Southern Mexican Town and the United States Economy* (Fresno, Calif.: Asociación Cívica, 1985, 1996), 225.

12. Hubert Carton de Grammont, "Algunas Tendencias de la Reestructuración Productiva del Sector Hortícola Mexicano," paper presented to the Nineteenth Congress of the Latin American Studies Association, Guadalajara, Mexico, April 1997, 1–2.

13. David Barkin, Irene Ortiz, and Fred Rosen, "Globalization and Resistance: The Remaking of Mexico," in *Contesting Mexico: NACLA Report on the Americas* 30, no. 4 (January/ February 1997): 20.

14. Maria Antonieta Barrón, "Mexican Women on the Move: Migrant Workers in Mexico and Canada," in *Women Working the NAFTA Food Chain*, 114.

15. The role of the PRI and the struggles within the party are central to understanding the political dynamic that supported nationalist interests, on the one hand, and a development model based on Western notions of modernization and neoliberalism, on the other. It remains to be seen what difference it will make, now that the seventy-one-year party rule was broken by the election of Vicente Fox of the National Action Party (PAN) in July 2000.

16. Barry, *Zapata's Revenge*, 47.

17. The term *neoliberalism* has been heavily adopted in Latin America since the early 1980s as a code name for global restructuring that favored less statist intervention in the economy and reaffirmed classic liberal positions on individual rights, civil liberties, and private property. Barkin, Ortiz, and Rosen, "Globalization and Resistance," 20.

18. Barry, *Zapata's Revenge*, 54.

19. Barry, *Zapata's Revenge*, 56.

20. Poor campesinos employ a variety of strategies for survival, including sharecropping, tenant farming, subcontracting, agricultural collectives, and government development projects, such as Solidarity. Warnock, *The Other Mexico*, 205.

21. Ecumenical Coalition for Economic Justice, "Free Trade Won't Help Mexico's Poor," in *Trading Freedom: How Free Trade Affects Our Lives, Work, and Environment*, ed. John Cavanagh, John Gershman, Karen Baker, and Gretchen Helmke (Toronto: Between the Lines with the Institute for Food and Development Policy and the Institute for Policy Studies, 1992), 57.

22. Mexican Greenhouse Tomato Industry, "Greenhouse Tomatoes Change the Dynamics of the North American Fresh Tomato Industry," ERR-2 Economic Research Service/USDA, www.ers.usda.gov/publications/err2/err2d.pdf.

23. Since the 1970s, there has been a boom in the production of fashionable high-value agricultural export-oriented products in the south, known as nontraditional agroexports (NTAEs), whose production is highly labor intensive. The growth of NTAEs in Latin America has been stimulated by changes in international trade policies and technologies, shifts in dietary preferences, increased consumer income in industrial countries, and greater penetration of transnational food companies in the south. Once again, it's the investors and foreign distributors who reap the major benefits, because of the high per-unit value, while workers and the land suffer. Most NTAEs require heavy application of pesticides, endangering the health of farmworkers and even consumers threatened by the long-term impact of pesticide residue. Lori Ann Thrupp, *Bittersweet Harvests for Global Supermarkets: Challenges in Latin America's Agricultural Export Boom* (Baltimore, Md.: World Resources Institute, 1995), 3.

24. The rising corn prices have precipitated the worst tortilla crisis in modern Mexican history, threatening thousands with hunger. Manual Roig-Franzi, "A Culinary and Cultural Staple in Crisis," *Washington Post*, http://www.washingtonpost.com/wp-dyn/content/article/2007/01/26/AR2007012601896_pf.html, accessed 2 June 2007.

25. Armando Bartra, "Milpas Airadas: Hacía la Autosuficiencia Alimentaria y la Soberanía Laboral," in *México en Transición: Globalismo Neoliberal, Estado y Sociedad Civil*, Gerardo Otero, ed. (Universidad de Zacatecas y Simon Fraser University, 2006), 41–42.

26. Peter M. Rosset, *Food Is Different: Why We Must Get the WTO out of Agriculture* (Halifax, NS: Fernwood Publishing, 2006), 125–40.

27. For a comprehensive assessment of the challenge the EZLN poses to the Mexican state, see Gerardo Otero, "Contesting Neoliberal Globalism from Below: The EZLN, Indian Rights and Citizenship," in *México en Transición*.

28. President, Empaque Santa Rosa, quoted in promotional booklet, 3.

29. I am using a pseudonym for the name of the Mexican agribusiness featured here, as well as for its owners, because companies in Mexico are not publicly traded, nor is information about them easily accessible. I prefer to protect both the workers and the managers I interviewed from any repercussions that could result from my investigation and interpretation.

30. The historical data on the company are drawn primarily from an interview with the head of International Operations, Guadalajara, July and December 1997.

31. Carton de Grammont, "Algunas Tendencias," 3.

32. Carlos Fernández-Vega, "Hasta un avion chocolate recibieron como pago," http://www.jornada.unam.mx/1999/08/02/expediente.html. In recent years, it has been difficult to find information about this company, as private enterprises in Mexico do not have to declare themselves publicly.

33. Interview with international operations manager, Guadalajara, July and December 1996.

34. Interview with greenhouse manager, Jalisco, 24 July 1996.

35. Santa Rosa's head of international operations suggested that, given that the Canadian population is only 10 percent of the U.S. population, 5 percent is not such a low figure.

36. Humberto Gonzalez Chavez provides a very nuanced study of the companies involved in Autlán in *El Empresario Agrícola: En el jugoso negocio de las frutas y hortalizas de México* (The Hague: CIP-DATA Koninklijke Bioblioteek, 1994), 12. His study confirms the "deterioration that this kind of monocultural production causes in the ecosystems where it develops."

37. Personal communications with Antonieta Barrón, Miami, March 2000.

38. Lauren Baker, "A Different Tomato," in *Women Working the NAFTA Food Chain*, 252.

39. This explanation of the flight of tomato companies was offered by Leonardo Lamas, interview with author, 10 December 2006, Sayula, Mexico.

40. Much of the information about the recent expansion and business dealings of Santa Rosa has been drawn from a study of the eight largest fruit and vegetable producers by Flavia Echanove, "Los Empresarios hortícolas y sus procesos de integración y diversificación," Centro de Investigación y de Estudios Avanzados del Instituto Politécnico Nacional, Mexico City, 1997.

41. The Guadalajara food terminal, one of the three largest in Mexico, is composed of more than one thousand stalls and handles daily fifteen hundred tons of produce. Santa Rosa's status in this market is an important part of its control of the agribusiness. "Controla un grupo el mercado de abastos," *El Occidental*, 22 July 1996, 1 and 12.

42. Interview by Roberto Ernesto Antillón Mena with manager of international trade, Empaque Santa Rosa, Guadalajara, Mexico, July 1996.

43. Interview with international operations manager, Guadalajara, July 1996.

44. Jorge Enrique Rocha Quintero, "Globalización y Desarrollo Local en el Sur de Jalisco," in *Sustentabilidad Rural y Desarrollo Local en el Sur de Jalisco*, eds. Jaime Morales Hernández y Jorge Enrique Rocha Quintero (Tlaquepaque, Mexico: ITESO, 2006), 201.

45. Banco Cremi was one of the eighteen banks privatized during the six-year presidency of Carlos Salinas de Gortari, laying the ground for a neoliberal economic policy that came into full force with NAFTA.

46. *Periodico el Financiero*, 1994: 52, quoted in Echanove, "Los Empresarios horticolas," 22.

47. Warnock, *The Other Mexico*, 242–43.

48. In 1997, the company sought credit of $100 million from Banco Cremi (where all brothers were shareholders) to cover debts for two questionable financial crises. One was to pay the day laborers in their tomato fields in Baja California after the workers had protested the lack of pay by setting fire to one million tomato poles. (They apparently decided not to pay the workers in other locations because their numbers were smaller, and so didn't represent such a risk of revolt.) The other was to pay $775,000 to legally register their Learjet, a so-called chocolate airplane, because it had been brought into the country illegally by undocumented migrant workers, thus the name. Carlos Fernández-Vega, "Hasta un avion chocolate recibieron como pago," http://www.jornada.unam.mx/1999/08/02/expediente.html.

49. Swasti Mitter, *Common Fate, Common Bond: Women in the Global Economy* (London: Pluto, 1986); Cristina Gabriel and Laura Macdonald, "NAFTA and Economic Restructuring: Some Gender and Race Implications," in *Rethinking Restructuring: Gender and Change in Canada*, ed. Isabel Bakker (Toronto: University of Toronto Press, 1996), 167.

50. Sara Lara, *Nuevas experiencias productivas y nuevas formas de organización flexible del trabajo en la agricultura mexicana* (Mexico City: Pablos, 1998), 160–61.

51. Kirsten Appendini, *Re-Visiting Women Wage-Workers in Mexico's Agro-Industry: Changes in Rural Labor Markets* (Copenhagen: Centre for Development Research Working Paper, July 1995), 7.

52. Interview with vice president of production, Empaque Santa Rosa, Guadalajara, December 1996.

53. Kathy Kopinak, *Desert Capitalism: What Are the Maquiladoras?* (Montreal: Black Rose, 1997), 94.

54. Kopinak, *Desert Capitalism*, 195. According to the UN Human Development Poverty Index in 2006, over 20 percent of the Mexican population was living on less than $2 per day.

55. Hubert Carton de Grammont, "Algunas reflexiones en torno al mercado de trabajo en el campo latinoamericano," *Revista Mexicana de Sociología* (year unknown): 49–58.

56. The information used to compile the chart was drawn from the rich research of Sara Lara and Gabriel Torres as well as my own observations. Sara Lara, "Feminización de los procesos de trabajo del sector fruti-hortícola en el estado de Sinaloa," *Cuicuilco* 21 (April–June 1988): 29–36; Lara, *Nuevas experiencias*, 198–207; and Gabriel Torres, *The Force of Irony: Power in the Everday Life of Mexican Tomato Workers* (New York: Berg, 1997), 64–72, 89–95.

57. Torres, *The Force of Irony*, 91.

58. Interview with vice president of production, Empaque Santa Rosa, Guadalajara, Jalisco, 6 December 1996.

59. Lara, "Feminización de los procesos de trabajo," 35.

60. Lara, *Nuevas experiencias*, 208.

61. Lara, *Nuevas experiencias*, 210.

62. Interview with the author, 24 December 2006, Mexico City, Mexico.

63. Rocha Quintero, "Globalización y Desarrollo Local," 202.

64. Lara, "Feminización de los procesos de trabajo," 29–36.

65. Personal communication with Antonieta Barrón, Miami, March 2000.

66. Because of the intensity of production in greenhouses, the Santa Rosa greenhouse operation of 120 hectares yields the equivalent of 5,000 to 6,000 hectares in field production. Interview by Sheelagh Davis with Gabriel Torres, November 1999.

67. Interview with Pierre Riel (pseudonym), San Isidro Mazatepec, December 1996.

68. Defined by J. Carrillo, *La nueva era de la industria automoriz en Mexico* (Tijuana: El Colegio de la Frontera Norte), 67–114, cited in Kopinak, *Desert Capitalism*, 13.

69. Since the 1950s, workers in urban centers such as Mexico City have abandoned their longer noontime meal at home, particularly because it became impractical with growing commuter traffic. Jeffrey Pilcher, *¡Que vivan los tamales! Food and the making of Mexican identity* (Albuquerque: University of New Mexico Press, 1998), 126.

70. Interview with Tomasa and Pablo, 10 December 2006, Gomez Farías, Mexico.

71. Lara, *Nuevas experiencias*, 210–15.

72. The schism between the Indigenous and mestizo worlds in Mexico was brought home poignantly as we tried to interview Indigenous women workers. A mestiza resident of Sirena who is an activist with the groups advocating for the rights of the Indigenous workers carried out the interviews. She was clearly a sympathetic and local person, less strange than a gringa researcher. The experience helped her and her group in developing relationships with the migrant farmworkers. But the barriers remained deep and strong: first, most of them did not speak Spanish and she did not speak their Indigenous language. At one point, she asked, "¿No me entiendes?" acknowledging that "You don't understand me, do you?"

The words of Indigenous workers used here should be read, then, for the silences as much as for what they actually say. These are key voices in this story; our inability to hear and understand them is deeply rooted and an ongoing challenge we must continually confront.

73. Linda Diebel, *Toronto Star*, 16 March 1997, 5F.

74. Personal communication with Antonieta Barrón, Miami, March 2000.

75. Pierre quantifies his comparative judgment by explaining that Mexican workers pack four tons an hour, averaging about 90 kilos an hour per person, which is still far from the European standard of productivity at 150 kilos an hour. Personal interviews, San Isidro Mazatepec, 24 July 1996.

76. Mexico's shift from being a corn-producing country to being dependent on corn imports was facilitated by Carlos Salinas's brother, Raul, when he headed up CONASUPO and began increasing the imports of cheap animal feed corn from the United States. One peasant complained, "They take our white corn and send us yellow corn, but we're not animals." Personal interview, San Isidro Mazatepec, July 1996. See also Kirsten Appendini, *De la Milpa a los Tortibonos: La restructuración de la política alimentaria en México* (Mexico City: El Colegio de México y Instituto de Investigaciónes de las Naciones Unidas para el Desarrollo Social, 1992).

77. While the Ejercito Zapatista de Liberación Nacional (EZLN) was formed around classist demands (work, land, housing, food, health, etc.), dialogues with Indigenous communities shifted their emphasis to the defense of Indigenous culture and rights. Gerardo Otero, "Forjando Democrácia: Economía Global, Política Local," in *México en Transición*, 301.

78. There was a charged debate among the left about the strategy of the Other Campaign, with its emphasis on working outside the electoral system; some felt it was partially responsible for the election of conservative PAN candidate Felipe Calderón in the 2006 presidential elections, because it diverted votes that might have ensured the victory of Manuel Lopez Obrador, the progressive candidate of the Partido Democrático Revolucionario.

79. There is a somewhat hidden history of organized actions by tomato workers that were violently repressed by local police and by direct government intervention defending

companies' interests, especially during the 1970s and 1980s, when the defense minister was García Barragán, a key political and economic player in Jalisco agriculture. Torres, *The Force of Irony*, 24.

80. Interview with Leonardo Lamas, 10 December 2006, Sayula, Mexico.

81. Leonardo Lamas, quoted here, has been a key advocate on behalf of Indigenous migrant workers. Two Sirena NGOs, Grupo de Salud Nueva Vida and Amigos de la Naturaleza, are now receiving royalties from the first book produced by the Tomasita Project, *Women Working the NAFTA Food Chain*. Reportedly, these funds have supported a series of educational workshops on sustainable development, agroecology, and pesticide use.

CHAPTER 7

Crossing Sectors and Borders:

WEAVING A HOLISTIC ANALYSIS

Retracing the Trail

We started this book with the question, "Where does our food come from?" and we looked for answers first in the tangled roots and routes of Tomasita the tomato in chapter 1. In tracing the trail of the traditionally produced tomatl as well as the corporate tomato, we were reminded that both are cultural and historical constructions and that they represent competing visions of the earth and of development.

We deepened our understanding of the current global food system that brings the tomato from the Mexican field to the Canadian table, by stopping along its trail at three key sectors that produce, commercialize, and sell the corporate tomato—agribusinesses, supermarkets, and fast-food restaurants (chapters 3, 4, and 6). A globalization-from-above perspective was revealed through the corporate stories, while women workers in the three companies offered a globalization-from-below perspective; they challenged particularly the impact of the current system on marginalized peoples (with a focus on women workers) and on the land (with a focus on tomatoes). Finally, social and environmental justice activists not only supported these challenges through acts of resistance in each sector but offered an alternative, "the other globalization," promoting a vision of a more just and sustainable development.

As a code for globalization, the tomato allowed us to explore four dialectical tensions implicit in the food system: production/consumption, biodiversity/cultural diversity, work/technology, and health/environment. Each case raised questions about how these relationships have evolved and how they have been shaped by corporate interests—often by economic motives at the expense of social and ecological costs.

Just as the tomato crosses borders, so, too, we must cross borders to weave a comparative analysis between the three sectors studied, one that might enlighten us about both the similarities as well as the differences among them. It is a tricky undertaking to try to compare the vastly different contexts of Mexico, the United States, and Canada, and yet in a post-NAFTA era, a process of continental integration is afoot, and some common strategies are being applied. Not only have corporations been eschewing borders through their profit-driven mergers and exporting of technologies and work practices, but civil society groups have also been making new links with organizations that challenge that very profit-driven system.

This chapter revisits each of the four tensions that we first explored chapter by chapter, picking up the threads that help us weave together a more holistic understanding of this bigger continental food system, the struggles for its definition and survival, and, particularly, the experiences of women workers within it. In engaging each tension, we will elaborate the key concepts introduced in chapter 2: distancing, fragmentation and uniformity, flexible labor, and holistic and ecological health.

Production/Consumption: No One Knows Where the Tomato Goes

Chances are that, in reading this book, you have learned something new about the long journey north of the tomato and that some hole in your understanding of the continental food system has been filled in. Most of us would likely draw maps not much more complex than those created by the elementary schoolchildren tracing the ingredients of a hamburger in chapter 3. The fact is, the food production/consumption chain has become so long, complex, and tangled that no one knows exactly where the tomato goes.

The Canadian food analyst Brewster Kneen introduced the concept of *distancing* in his classic critique of the food system, *From Land to Mouth*. Kneen was referring to not only the physical distance from, say, the Santa Rosa tomato fields in Jalisco to the McDonald's restaurant table in Toronto. He suggested that all the technological tools and processes that "treat" the tomato before it enters our

mouths also serve to distance us from the fruit. Raw food production is separated from consumers in multiple ways:

- by breeding and engineering long shelf life into a commodity;
- by processing and product differentiation;
- by increasing food's durability through preservation techniques;
- by packaging that allows greater handling, storage, and shipping.[1]

According to Kneen, each of these steps that separate us from food and that transform the fruit into a commodity also adds cost to the final product and, by extension, adds profit to those who control its production. Moreover, he maintains that, as the price goes up, the nutritive value goes down:

> A freshly picked tomato from the home garden is not the same thing as the one designed and "developed"—or genetically engineered—for mechanical harvesting and days and thousands of miles of transportation. Anything picked fresh, and virtually still alive when eaten, is going to be of different nutritive value than something that has been dead, or dying for days, refrigerated, and/or gassed into or out of a coma before it gets to you.[2]

The stories from each sector in the production/consumption chain of the tomato reveal another way that food has become distanced. Not only are we as consumers disconnected from the processes of production, but the workers along the tomato trail are also in the dark: "I often wonder," a Mexican field-worker mused, "who eats these tomatoes, where do they take them? When we're picking tomatoes, we often ask, 'And this one, where is it going?'"

The distancing, in this case, is maintained by strict divisions of labor (based on gender, race, class, age) through multiple stages of production as well as by the alienation of the workers from the fruit of their labor. When I showed photographs of women in the packing plant to Tomasa, a field supervisor, she was not even aware of the packers who worked within a hundred meters of the fields. She could, however, see the big trucks waiting outside the plant: "They come from far away, and they go far away—we don't know where. The tomatoes don't stay here."

Her comment reveals the other aspect of distancing, the disconnection Mexican workers feel from the food they plant, pick, and pack. They know that it is destined for northern markets, and that only second-rate produce will feed the majority of poor Mexicans. The tomatoes are thus symbols of what they can't have and the privilege of people far away who can afford them. In a way, the workers at the production end are more aware of those inequities than we are at the consumption end, perhaps preferring not to know that we are eating what one Mexican activist called the "fruits of injustice." A more socially critical packer expressed her own understanding—indeed, resentment—of this process: "This tomato, that lands on the table of Canadians, comes to you thanks to the efforts of the Mexicans, who are paid little to bring it to you. It upsets me that we do our best, give our all so that they are taken away; it feels strange. It's the owners who benefit; we workers don't really reap the benefits. We're like the blacks, working from sunrise to sunset, for low wages. Very few benefit, only the owners who export the tomatoes."

She thus alludes to the economic system constructed to produce both tomatoes and profit. Both tomatoes and labor are commodified in the continental tomato chain, as labor competitiveness is a key factor in the global race to be ever bigger and more profitable. In some cases, the tomatoes, as delicate perishable commodities, receive even better treatment than the workers, who are considered easily replaceable. Recall how Santa Rosa field-workers were not given gloves to protect themselves from the pesticides on the plants, while packers were asked to cut their nails or wear gloves (which they had to buy), so that they wouldn't damage the tomatoes. Similarly, Loblaws cashiers in training were warned that if they didn't get the right name for the tomato at the checkout, and would thus punch in the wrong code, they would cause the company to lose millions of dollars.

Distancing has increased with the "bigger is better" phenomenon reflected in the flurry of mergers and creation of new conglomerates over the past two decades. In the 2000s, the global integration of related industries—such as seed and agrochemical companies, pharmaceuticals, nanotechnology, and food retail—has become even more insidious, resulting in what the Erosion, Technology and Concentration (ETC) Group calls an "oligopoly," with fewer and fewer companies controlling all aspects of food. All three of the companies examined here have been involved in significant merger activity. The swallowing up of one company by another, which may actually be profitable for the executives of all parties, nonetheless distances the decision makers even further from production. This means that they can claim ignorance and innocence if something goes wrong, on down the line, with many aspects of production so far out of their sight and reach that they couldn't possibly know about it.

With a decentralization of production, contracting out has become standard practice for most large multinationals. For agribusinesses, especially, it is a way of avoiding responsibility for the vagaries of agricultural production, such as unpredictable weather, pests, shifting prices, and so on. Santa Rosa may organize production in Mexico, but as with many smaller farmers who are subcontracted, the production technologies and work structures are largely determined from the outside, by the food companies who buy the tomatoes.

Both Loblaws supermarkets and McDonald's restaurants contract out production. Loblaws epitomizes the trend of retailers controlling production (of both fresh and processed food), but its famous corporate brands are all produced by small subcontractors. McDonald's has been forced by consumer activists to be more careful about who it contracts in far-off places, as it denies, for example, contributing to the destruction of rainforests by cattle grazing in the countries from which it imports beef.[3] Fast-food consumers have become more aware of who grows the tomatoes bought by the company through the actions of Mexican tomato workers such as the Coalition of Immokalee Workers in Florida, who in 2007 succeeded in getting McDonald's to pay more attention to the labor practices of their suppliers (chapter 8).

Distancing also keeps us in the dark about the health impact of production practices. There are, of course, trade laws that set certain standards, those limiting the amount of pesticide residue permitted on tomatoes crossing the Mexico–U.S. border, for example. Mexican producers are pressured to keep up to U.S. standards. But as we saw at both borders, inspections tend to focus on narcotics and human smuggling, and food gets cursory treatment.

The shirking of responsibility by corporations and even by governments was evident in the booklet that the Canadian Food Inspection Agency distributed to all Canadians in early 2000. By asking consumers to "Fight BAC!" (BAC for *bacteria*) by carefully washing all fresh produce, the government not only shifts the responsibility from the producers and regulators to consumers, it also raises new suspicions about food safety and belies its inability to control a system that has so expanded that no one knows exactly what's happening at any other point in the process. In a system where economic costs reign, social and environmental values do not figure in the balance sheet; environmentalists, on the other hand, advocate a more inclusive "full-cost accounting."

Consider some of the ways that the three companies in question are constructed on a narrow bottom-line mentality and how such a logic ignores social and ecological impacts. While the large plantations of Santa Rosa are still labor-intensive and have not adopted mechanical harvesters, for example, it is because the labor costs are still so low as to make it profitable. The greenhouse operations reflect the more dominant form of agroexport production in the post-NAFTA era: all of the inputs (machinery, seeds, boxes, etc.) are imported, while all of the outputs (tomatoes) are exported. The very sophisticated drip irrigation systems have, in fact, left the land wasted, requiring new soil to be brought in. The women who risk their lives on moving carts picking tomatoes are not even allowed to take them home. They are workers in a global system, which benefits from the Mexican sun, easy access to land, and their relatively cheap labor—the epitome of distancing.

Loblaws' corporate brand products have been the key to their economic success in competition with national brands over the past decade. Neither shoppers nor cashiers have much sense of the production process behind the enticing labels; the no-name products are especially difficult to trace. Ironically, however, the company has moved into the ethnic market, by producing an array of global products bearing foreign names and images to meet the demands of a multicultural population as well as to appeal to our desire for the "exotic." Here there is an illusion of distance, when in fact the products are developed and produced close to home, while the images that sell them tap our fantasies about the faraway. At the same time, the corporate tomato that has journeyed over four days through the twenty-one steps we trace in chapter 1 is advertised as "Fresh from the Fields."

The food preparation process at McDonald's is the most globalized and highly controlled, based on the rational values of efficiency, quantifiability, and predictability explored in chapter 3. Everything is standardized, from the kitchen equipment to the precut french fries; menus and work practices alike are exported to 120 countries along with the franchise and the seductive golden arches. Such uniform food production is the epitome of distancing, though at least in the Big Xtra, there is slice of a raw yet firm tomato to remind us that this food was once alive and growing. The tasks of the workers are also carefully engineered, even scripted, and have less to do with preparing food than with offering, as the McDonald's CEO promises, "the world's best quick-service restaurant experience."[4]

The stories of workers in both McDonald's and Loblaws reveal that they perhaps feel even more distanced from production than the Mexican agricultural workers. Their jobs have been as rationalized, standardized, and quantified as the food they prepare and sell. In this context, they think of themselves as consumers more than as producers, and, as Susan Willis suggests, "if gratification is associated with consumption rather than working, doing, and making, we have only to bear in mind that this is a society where work is either unattainable or alienating. The contradictions we identify at the level of consumption are in fact the contradictions of production."[5]

Finally, in the stories of women workers, we saw how the reorganization of work in these companies has influenced their family eating practices, revealing a clear link between production and consumption in their daily lives. Most dramatically, the Indigenous migrant workers brought by trucks from the poorer states in Mexico to work for Santa Rosa have been distanced from their own land, history, and traditional subsistence agricultural practices.

This is the most tragic part of the story. In some cases, the land that they previously cultivated has become wasted by intensive agrochemical use, or they have incurred tremendous fertilizer debts from being sucked into chemically dependent agriculture. In any case, without the land or time to grow their own food, they are forced into the market economy and must work (growing our food) to buy food that previously they grew. The extremely low wages of salaried workers at Santa Rosa are based on the assumption that they will continue subsistence agriculture, but they don't make enough to buy healthy food. Moreover, as migrant workers, they are estranged from their land and the kinds of crops they would grow at home.

The growing dependence on part-time labor in the retail and service industries in Canada also affects the eating patterns of workers within them. Although Marissa has the benefit of seniority as a Loblaws cashier, her schedule sometimes requires that she leave home before her kids have breakfast or that she return home after they've had dinner. For those cashiers with less seniority, working short shifts at odd hours, eating patterns become totally erratic. These workers, often young students, are similar to McDonald's employees, in their tendencies to eat on the run, just as their job is to feed people on the run. Loblaws cashiers are also prime targets for the ready-made food that is increasingly filling supermarket shelves just as McDonald's workers are key consumers of the same half-priced fare that they whip into Happy Meal bags at the counter.

Both the production and consumption of food have been drastically reshaped in the past fifty years, as can be seen at every stage of the tomato chain and through the lives of food system workers. Indeed, every one of us is affected by these changes; our health and social relations have been transformed. The distancing is not just a result of an industrialized food system in isolation, but part of a broader and deeper process with tangled roots in the scientific, industrial, chemical, and genetic moments revealed in chapter 1. Urbanization and advertising, cars, and televisions are also part of this bigger picture. As key U.S. food analysts conclude in "Hungry for Profit,"[6] those who control production, processing, distribution, and commercialization of food benefit from this system, while the majority of consumers, workers, and the environment suffer, perpetuating the great paradox of hunger coexisting with extreme wealth.

Toby M. Smith reminds us that the expansionist's growth-oriented ethic, on which industrial capitalism in general and the global food system in particular is built, is historically constructed and is thus not inevitable. "Alternative values and ways of living work like water frozen in the fissures of a rock. What once seemed so solid, sure, and absolute, is beginning to destabilize, revealing cracks that, in fact, have always been there."[7]

Alternatives persist, however, not only in traditional practices, but in the emergence of locally based production practices, which aim to narrow the distance between production and consumption. The child in chapter 3 who described growing tomatoes with her mother in their Toronto backyard gave us a glimpse of one kind of alternative, available to a privileged few who own land and have the time to cultivate it. More collective and institutionalized alternatives, such as community gardens or national advocacy organizations, are explored in the next chapter. They all reflect a response to the alienation fed by distancing, and a deep desire in humans to reconnect with the processes and the products from which we have become so estranged.

Bio-/Cultural Diversity: Monocultures of the Mind

The distancing elaborated above, which commodifies both tomatoes and work-ers, is based on a *fragmentation* within the food system and a *uniformity* that al-

Mask by Louise Casselman

lows greater control by corporate decision makers. The two tomatoes—tomatl and the corporate tomato—actually represent two competing visions of nature, as Vandana Shiva has suggested (chapter 1): one that sees nature as self-generative and self-organizing, and includes human beings as an integral part of nature, and one that conceives of nature as a resource to be controlled, managed, and exploited by human efforts, with the help of technology.

The architects and managers of global food production and consumption have standardized everything in the tomato chain: from the seeds hybridized and engineered for greater control, to the machinery, chemicals, and work practices in Mexico, from the skids and stickers that make border crossing quicker, to the supermarket designs and ready-made food, precut ingredients, and identical fast-food kitchens—all aimed at greater efficiency, higher yield, and greater profits. Efficiency in itself is not a negative value, but it has often taken precedence over the health of workers and the environment. The biodiversity of the planet and the cultural diversity of its inhabitants are both threatened if the corporate tomato continues to crowd the trails.

THREATS TO BIODIVERSITY

It may seem that biodiversity is more threatened by the production end of the chain, and cultural diversity by the consumption end, but they are intimately related, like tangled roots. It appears obvious, for example, that Mexican ecosystems are more directly disrupted by monocultural production of tomatoes than are the U.S. or Canadian ecosystems of those northerners who consume the exported tomatoes (even though the urban contexts where most northern consumers live are often built on ecosystem destruction). Monocultural production, when viewed holistically, has many side effects as well. The hybrid varieties of seeds engineered to grow uniformly and ripen at the same time require "high inputs"—artificial fertilizer, pesticides, and water—at substantial economic as well as ecological costs.

The history surrounding Mexican agribusinesses such as Santa Rosa has earned them the notorious nickname "grasshopper" because they move from one location to another every several years, engaging in chemically intensive agriculture, until the soil itself is so depleted they must move on looking for new ground to contaminate. The plaintive phrase I heard often from Mexican peasants was "la tierra ya no se da," which means "the land doesn't give anymore," or is infertile. The close connection between forestry and agriculture was shown in the case of Autlán, where export-driven agribusinesses deforested hillsides to make wooden crates for shipping, causing the whitefly that lived on the trees to invade nearby tomato crops and send companies fleeing the area. The ecological lesson was not learned, it seems, because more than a decade later, in 2005, those same companies had to flee Sayula, having ignored warnings of another whitefly infestation that they could have avoided by letting the land lie fallow for a few months. As ecosystems disintegrate, delicate balances are lost. And there is

increasing evidence that monocultural production not only doesn't make ecological sense but is also not economically justifiable.[8]

The links to consumption are direct, once they are made visible, as we have
seen through the stories told here. McDonald's critics worldwide have reminded
us that the massive monocultural production required to fill the forty million
stomachs served daily by the fast-food giant draws primarily from Third World
resources: wheat, beef, tomatoes. Many of the value-added processed goods that
get choice shelf space in Loblaws supermarkets also originate in soil that previously was used for subsistence by marginalized peoples. As consumers, we are
thus (consciously or not) complicit in the daily destruction of habitats of not only
nonhuman species but human cultures as well.

Cultural critics such as Arturo Escobar suggest that we consider biodiversity
not only in biophysical terms but as a discourse that is being contested by a large
network of actors with diverging biocultural and political perspectives:

> By reinterpreting the "threats to biodiversity" (putting emphasis in-
> stead on habitat destruction by megadevelopment projects, the mono-
> cultures of mind and agriculture promoted by capital and reductionist
> science, and the consumption habits of the North fostered by economist
> models), biodemocracy advocates shifting the attention from South to
> North as the source of the diversity crisis.[9]

Escobar points out that this is a "radical redefinition of production and productivity away from the logic of uniformity and toward the logic of diversity."
Shiva also deeply questions development based on a reductionist Western science
that underlies industrial agriculture's attempt to control nature. Social ecofeminist
perspectives argue that this form of agriculture, shaped by patriarchal and colonial
practices that enslaved people to extract the wealth, is still exploiting women workers as it drains the Third World of its greatest treasure, a rich biodiversity. The story
of Tomasa in chapter 6 most poignantly illustrated this struggle between two views
of biodiversity and conflicting agricultural practices, as she shifted daily from being a salaried worker in a massive export-oriented agribusiness in the morning to
working the family's own more sustainable cornfield in the afternoon. But the
women working at the commercial and retail end of the chain are also the most exploited workers in the north now dominated by a service sector dependent on
cheap part-time female labor.

THREATS TO CULTURAL DIVERSITY

Both Escobar and Shiva make the link between biodiversity and cultural diversity,
bringing campesinos and workers, economic actors and political activists alike into
the struggle for diversity versus uniformity. In her classic *Monocultures of the Mind*,
Shiva argues that agricultural practices are not just patterns of land use but ways
of thinking. The same monocultural production at the core of industrial agriculture

and the global food system is threatening the diverse ways of thinking and forms of knowledge that have kept biodiversity thriving for millennia. She considers dominant Western knowledge systems as both parochial and colonizing, with a globalizing gaze that makes local knowledges disappear through eliminating the practices that use them and/or negating their very existence.[10] In arguing that the ideas behind Western systems of production represent a particular cultural system with a particular relationship to power, Shiva suggests that because its relationship with the project of economic development has been invisible, "it has become an effective legitimizer for the homogenization of the world and the erosion of its ecological and cultural richness."[11]

Aboriginal activists, such as Winona LaDuke, contend that it's more than ecological and cultural erosion we have been witnessing under this Western economic system but, in fact, "a great holocaust. There have been more species lost in the past 150 years than since the Ice Age. During the same time, Indigenous peoples (over 2,000 nations) have been disappearing from the face of the earth. . . . There is a direct relationship between the loss of cultural diversity and the loss of biodiversity." While sending an ominous warning, LaDuke also sees hope offered by this link: "Wherever Indigenous peoples still remain, there is also a corresponding enclave of biodiversity."[12] In fact, in the new millennium, Indigenous groups and peasant-led organizations such as Vía Campesina have been gathering strength in their efforts to defend their rights to lands, resources, and cultural identities (chapter 8).

We see examples of the threat to cultural diversity in the daily experiences of workers in the three companies. While the Mexican women working for Santa Rosa draw upon their socialization in food growing and preparation at home as they join the rows or lines of industrialized agribusiness production, they are also being deskilled by monotonous routinized jobs, exuding uniformity. Indigenous and campesino women who can no longer cultivate their own plots are reduced to picking tomatoes for export and are thus slowly losing the knowledge of generations that maintained sustainable agricultural practices. Women packing greenhouse tomatoes in assembly-line production are numbed by the repetitive motions of partially automated packing plants.

Such mindless activity echoes the scanning that dominates the days of Loblaws supermarket cashiers and semiautomated food preparation by McDonald's workers. As one fast-food executive proclaimed, "We do the creative work, so they [the workers] don't have to think!" The kind of creative work this manager refers to is the development of systems and procedures that are the most efficient and profitable. Yet they often curb the potential for creative input or any diversity on the part of workers.

In the retail and service jobs we've examined, whether at the checkout lane or fast-food service counter, women are trained not only in routinized tasks but in scripted interactions with customers. Young McDonald's workers mimicked the lines they are taught such as "Will that be a Coke?" that might shave two seconds off an interaction and thus increase their productivity. Loblaws cashiers are prompted, too, to say things like "Did you find everything you were looking for?"

to encourage customers to keep buying. Both are examples of uniformity applied to work practices, which deny the workers' unique identities and creative capacities. Customer relations, in fact, is one of the few aspects of both cashier and fast-food work where there might be room for creativity, and yet profit-driven, scientifically managed work procedures and company-determined scripts limit the possibilities. Even the pressure to constantly smile denies the natural rhythms of workers' moods and diverse relationships.

In all sectors of the food chain, deeply entrenched gender ideologies construct certain women's tasks as "natural," thus devaluing the skills they require as well as the domestic practices through which women have acquired them. The dexterity required for packing delicate tomatoes, as well as the relational skills needed for the frontline work at checkout lanes and fast-food counters, were developed through gendered childhood and family roles.

Cultural diversity is also challenged by the reorganization of work in the food system and the entry of the market into the family, both homogenizing diets and reshaping family eating practices. In one generation, "we have gone from a traditional food producing society to a food grazing society—one where we eat wherever we happen to be"[13]—in the car, as Marissa does on her way to work at Loblaws, or in the kitchen of McDonald's, where Kate gets a discount on the burgers she makes.

In such speeded-up environments, food has lost its meaning as sustenance or family time, and eating out is more about the "experience" associated with the restaurant, again promoting homogeneous culture rather than diversity. The market has taken over family practices not only of eating but also of entertainment (Ronald's playhouse and McBirthdays) that are more the attraction than the food itself. Similarly, Loblaws offers shoppers an experience that not only simulates a farmers' market but also offers cooking classes, cafés with artificial trees, and jazz concerts.

Commensality, the social act of gathering around the table to share a meal, is becoming a lost art. This is true not only in the fast-food-crazed north but also in Mexico, due to work schedules imposed by foreign managers that keep workers in the greenhouse cafeteria, for example, rather than going home for the typical midday family meal. In the north as well, in retail and service-sector work, the redefinition of work for just-in-time production has left many workers eating as they move through their day, on the road or in front of their TVs. This redefined work, which promotes uniformity and limits diversity, is further explored next, in relationship to new technologies that in themselves threaten both biodiversity and cultural diversity.

Work/Technology: Who's Flexible and for Whom?

One of the major reasons that family meals are becoming a thing of the past is that corporate strategies in the new global economy are built on the infinite *flexibility* of the labor force. In the food system, this usually means flexible women workers,[14] as they predominate both in the fields and packing plants in the south as well as in food retail and service in both the north and the south. In fact, entrenched gender ideologies have contributed to the construction and definition of flexible labor

that is so central to new practices such as just-in-time production.

Since the 1970s, many feminist scholars have pointed to the dependence of mobile corporate capital on a female labor force, most dramatically in the export processing zones of Asia and the maquiladoras region of Mexico.[15] Building on an already established sexual division of labor and institutionalized sexism and racism in the countries where transnationals set up shop, the employment of primarily young women in low-skilled and low-wage jobs has also deepened the "feminization of poverty."[16]

While some young women entering the labor force experience it as a liberation from patriarchal family structures and an access to salaries they've never had, most are contributing to the family wage in poor communities where all family members must combine incomes to survive.[17]

With the trade liberalization of the 1990s, exemplified by agreements such as NAFTA, free-trade zones and geographically defined maquilas lose their uniqueness. In fact, maquilization, which referred originally to the northern border region in Mexico that allowed U.S. industries to operate freely, now refers to a more generalized work process characterized by (1) the feminization of the labor force, (2) extreme segmentation of skill categories, (3) the lowering of real wages, and (4) a nonunion orientation.[18] With the dropping of trade barriers, not only all of Mexico but even northern countries such as Canada have virtually become giant maquilas.

Maquilization, initiated in the south and now appearing in the north, and McDonaldization, initiated in the north and spreading into the south, are interrelated processes in the new global economy. Common to both phenomena is their dependence on flexible, part-time female labor. From a globalization-from-above perspective, this means cheaper and sometimes more compliant labor; in the corporate world, flexibility is ultimately about maximizing profits and minimizing obstacles (such as trade tariffs, government regulations, underused labor, and trade union organization). From a globalization-from-below perspective, this often means the disintegration of the family—all in the name of providing for the family's survival. Let's consider the cases of the three sectors studied here.

The Indigenous migrant workers brought by truck from the poorer states to the Santa Rosa plantation for the harvest represent the most "flexible" members of the workforce. They are so flexible, in fact, that they take their kids out of school, leave their own plots of land behind, and move entire families to horrendous migrant labor camps surrounding the tomato fields. There, women not only bear the burden of backbreaking work under the hot sun, but many carry their babies on their backs and double their picking pace to fill the quotas of their working children. They are literally in foreign territory, as most don't speak Spanish, the dominant language, and can't ask for the support to which they're entitled. They must use their minimal wages to purchase food often sold by the company and find it difficult to maintain their own culinary practices, let alone eat healthily. If they get ill from pesticide exposure, they have difficulty securing medical assistance. Their domestic duties are also more arduous, since their living quarters usually lack basic necessities such as water and electricity.

As we saw within the hierarchy of women working for Santa Rosa, class and race conspire with gender to create different conditions. The mestizo packers brought by the company as a mobile maquila fare much better than the Indigenous field-workers. They make as much as eight times the wages of field-workers, partly because they are flexible (without family responsibilities) and can work ten- to twelve-hour days during peak season. Their schedules and assembly-line tasks are determined by company needs and rhythms, and they comply. In turn, the company does not punish them when they take a day off to recover energies, because they are being paid by the hour and can be temporarily replaced. Their ultimate flexibility is in their willingness to leave their families behind and move from one production site to another, the skilled female labor of the tomato business. Some see this as a temporary sacrifice, allowing them to amass savings to buy land, get married, and settle down, but older women have become wedded to the company and have lost all opportunity to create a family, due to their flexibility to meet corporate needs. For many, this is the only way they can contribute to the family wage, and so it is, once again, a sacrifice of family for family.

This paradox was most dramatically illustrated by the story of Irena, the transnational migrant worker,[19] in chapter 5. She leaves her family behind in Mexico for four months every year to pick locally produced tomatoes in Canada. While her wage is considerably higher than that of Mexican internal migrants, she must still work during the eight months she is at home, however, leaving her family once again to take care of a couple of invalids as a live-in domestic in a nearby city.

What does flexibility look like at the consumption end of the tomato chain? The epitome of part-time workers, McDonald's employees, especially young women, are sought for their willingness to meet erratic and short shifts, allowing the company to avoid paying benefits. Scheduling is determined by the labor/hour ratio, and workers complain of being asked to leave when restaurant traffic is slow. As we saw in the profiles of five young McDonald's workers, their flexibility at work also translates into eating practices that are, at best, equally flexible and, at worst, isolating and unhealthy.

Loblaws' labor strategies in the past decade have also mirrored this trend toward increasingly part-time and ever more flexible labor. Cashiers, primarily female, have effectively lost full-time status, as concession bargaining has increased the part-time contingent, buying out higher paid full-timers and part-timers alike and rolling back wages to lower starting salaries and longer waiting periods before receiving benefits or raises. When Loblaws opened the Great Canadian Superstores in the early 2000s, the company negotiated even greater wage concessions, allegedly to position the company to compete with Wal-Mart, which has moved aggressively into food retail in Canada.

For part-time cashiers, seniority reigns in scheduling. This means that the younger students who've put in less time with the company may only get four hours a week of work and can be called to work on the weekends when they'd like to be out socializing. It is assumed that, like young McDonald's employees, they will be flexible as part and parcel of their apprenticeship in the business world; low wages and erratic hours go with the territory of youth employment, seen as a sacrifice they make in working their way up the ladder.

While such flexibility may often suit student needs, it most definitely suits corporate interests, as food companies like McDonald's and Loblaws determine labor needs in concert with customer flow and inventory control. The just-in-time production of post-Fordist practices not only extends the scientific management that serves the profit motives of the corporations but is made possible by both flexible labor and new technologies. In the Loblaws case particularly, the same scanning technology that has allowed global monitoring of inventory has speeded up cashiers' work and increasingly monitored their productivity. Ironically, the very technology that makes them more efficient for the company's bottom line could eventually replace them. This is why unions like the United Food and Commercial Workers claim concession bargaining is a defensive strategy to save jobs, even as those jobs get reduced in time and wage levels. They fear not only that companies like Loblaws will move their operations to their nonunionized, lower waged affiliated discount stores but that jobs like cashiers will be eliminated by new technologies that require minimal work at the front end. Supermarkets have been experimenting with "smart boxes," for example, which allow customers to pass their groceries through the checkout without human assistance.

The Mexican feminist economist Sara Lara brings a north-south analysis into the discussion of flexibility, building on older notions of "center" and "periphery"[20] that are reconfigured in the new global economy. She considers the strategies of Mexican domestic companies, while being increasingly globalized, as still being managed by a "primitive flexibility" that depends on labor-intensive processes of production, sorting, and packing. In the agroexport economy, there is a growth of such unstable and temporary employment, relegated primarily to the most "flexible" workers in the rural labor market—women, children, and Indigenous peoples. Lara contends that agribusinesses exploit these groups that already play socially marginal roles based on their gender, race, or age: "women as housewives, Indigenous peoples as poor peasants, children as sons and daughters, young people as students, all as the ad hoc subjects of flexible processes."[21] We could certainly see this pattern in the flexible labor of Indigenous families working for Santa Rosa. Multiple oppressions are intertwined among workers with the lowest wages and worst working and living conditions.

Lara contends that in contrast to the "primitive flexibility" practiced in the south, multinationals headquartered for the most part in the more industrialized north manage higher skilled labor according to a "negotiated flexibility." Here again we see how global food production has built on regional and national inequities. The majority of transnationals in the north control production through ownership, subcontracting, and advanced technology—which includes biogenetic engineering, sophisticated food processing, production of most of the inputs and machinery of production, and design of the commercialization and distribution systems. They employ a nucleus of skilled workers, who are offered relatively stable employment and are managed through "negotiated flexibility."

Lara misses the fact, I think, that even though part-time women workers in the north, such as Loblaws cashiers, may bring more technical skills to their jobs, they still represent a precarious workforce, one that is built on similar discriminatory practices as the marginalized workers in the south. In some ways, the technologization of their work, while making company labor practices and inventory more flexible, has also bound them within rigid definitions of work, highly engineered, speeded up, and even scripted. This may be the ideal that the French manager in the Mexican greenhouse was referring to when he said that Mexican workers would never be as productive as European (or North American) workers.

The real question, then, is "Flexible for whom?" Even the most privileged women workers in northern supermarkets, those with high seniority such as Marissa, must gear their schedules to the demands of a double, or even triple, day, juggling responsibilities as parents and as casual workers supplementing their part-time incomes. Recall that, with twenty-five years of experience, Marissa "chose" to work three eight-hour days. She did that partly because she had to commute two hours to get to work, because if she transferred to a closer store, she would lose her seniority. She also "chose" to work weekends because her former husband could offer "free" child care.

The flexible and part-time labor of women in food retail and restaurant service is thus based on an assumption that they still take major responsibility for child care, without significant support from either spouses or from publicly funded day care. As Lourdes Beneria argues, "the private sphere of the household is still at the root of continuing asymmetries between men and women."[22] In the case of Ontario workers, increasing cutbacks in social services have increased women's workload not only in child care but also in health care and elder care, a growing burden as the population ages. It is on the basis of these multiple responsibilities that women accept flexible part-time labor, not, as some suggest, because it suits their desires to be at home with their children.

In fact, as we've seen in the earlier discussions of production and consumption that threaten not only biodiversity but also cultural diversity, family eating traditions have been drastically transformed by the flexible labor of women entering the workforce. Partly, the market has entered the household to compensate for their absence, offering ready-made food in supermarkets and cheap fast-food restaurant alternatives. Women are thus both the producers as well as the target consumers of this corporatized fast food. For women like Marissa, eating has been reduced to downing a banana on the road, as her flexibility takes her on the long commute to work; the car has, in fact, increasingly replaced the kitchen dining table for many people in our fast-food society.

The ability to move geographically to distant work sites as well as to move daily through shifting time schedules both constitute flexible labor, what might be called spatial and temporal migration. While Indigenous workers such as Reyna leave home for most of the year to seek survival in rotating harvests, more privileged Mexican workers like Irena fly across borders to pick our tomatoes for four months out of the year. Marissa commutes from the suburbs to an even more privileged job at a downtown Toronto supermarket, her working and living conditions far more humane than either Reyna's or Irena's. Still, the flexibility of all of them—women workers along the tomato trail—ultimately suits corporate interests, while wreaking havoc on families. They are part and parcel of lean production, which maximizes efficiency and profits, while leaving marginalized and primarily female workers bound to the shifting winds of just-in-time production. In the end, they are just-in-time workers with no time of their own. Ironically, as workers in the food system, they spend less and less time growing or preparing healthy food for themselves and their families. And there are other scars as well—on their bodies as well as on the earth itself.

Health/Environment: Sustaining Bodies and the Earth's Body

What are the long-term costs of such flexible labor practices and of the current globalized system of production and consumption? Following the tomato story has compelled us to consider the impact of its production on both the earth that generates food as well as on our bodies that, as workers, produce it, and as consumers, ingest it.

This probing has caused me to question how we in the west conceive of both the environment and our bodies within it. Susan Griffin also questions this "Western habit of mind (in which) the earth is no longer enchanted with its own significance. A forest exists for lumber. Trees for oxygen. A field for grazing. Rocks for minerals. Water for irrigation. Inch by inch the earth is weighed and measured for its uses and in the process the dimensions of the universe are narrowed."[23]

As I suggest in chapter 1 and substantiate in chapter 6, the current global food system is built on a notion of the environment as a resource to be exploited for human use, and ultimately, profit. Deeply rooted in the Western scientific

separation of nature and culture, this perspective has encountered limits, particularly as food systems have further globalized and food corporations have expanded into massive conglomerates. The distancing examined earlier in this chapter has allowed multinational executives to make decisions that disrupt and even destroy Third World ecosystems and, in turn, threaten the health of peoples who depend on them for survival. The environmental crisis, epitomized in food

safety scares and the erratic weather caused by global warming, has at least alerted economic and political leaders to the limits to growth and the need to curb rampant exploitation of nature with more sustainable practices. But the roots of the crisis are much deeper, as Escobar and Shiva argued in warning about loss of both biodiversity and cultural diversity. And while politicians of the twenty-first century are finally waking up to the seriousness of climate change, they are still not addressing the systemic causes of the crisis or considering a revamping of the economic system that perpetuates not only environmental but also social injustice.

We come face-to-face with our alienated understanding of the earth when we begin to see connections between human destruction of the environment and the destruction of human bodies and cultures. In Western culture, there is a deep denial that humans are an integral part of nature, a contention that Griffin challenges: "We are inseparable from nature, dependent on the biosphere, vulnerable to the processes of natural law. We cannot destroy the air we breathe without destroying ourselves. We are reliant on one another for our survival." She sees intimate links in the way we have been taught to see the natural world and our sense of our own bodies: "The life of the body is also reduced by this truncated idea of use. Like the physical acts which bring sustenance, the needs of the body have become mechanical, too; they are no longer numinous sources of knowledge."[24]

Just as this book highlights the stories of women workers in the food system, we can explore the enormous question of ecological costs, then, by starting with these women, their work, and their bodies. Adapting a social ecofeminist perspective, we don't assume that women are by "nature" closer to the earth, but that their domination has paralleled and, indeed, reinforced the domination of nature by Western industrial agricultural practices. As the most marginalized (read: flexible) workers in the tomato chain, they are, in some ways, closer to the processes and products of the food system, like canaries in the mine.

In a food system that commodifies both tomatoes and women workers, the health of the land and the workers is secondary. We saw in Santa Rosa that fieldworkers were not trained around health and safety issues and had to provide their own handkerchiefs to cover their mouths or gloves to protect their hands from pesticides. By not offering orientation or protective gear, Santa Rosa management kept workers in the dark about the dangers. Some women denied that the chemicals affected them, while others began to make the links between asthma attacks and rashes and the excessive use of agrochemicals. All felt powerless to question or act on the dangers. Fortunately, local environmentalists organized around these issues in the early 2000s, offering instruction on the use of pesticides for the male workers who apply them in the fields and providing day care for the children so they wouldn't have to accompany their mothers to work and be exposed to the chemicals.

In the mid-1990s, when I visited the makeshift camps set up for Indigenous migrants, I was most disturbed to see pesticide containers being used to carry water and communal showers constructed in the open air made out of discarded pesticide bags. But beyond the obvious risk of exposure to toxins sprayed in the field or their residue left on recycled containers, the very working and living conditions for migrants constituted tremendous health risks. The cardboard houses, without floors or windows, were extremely flammable; in fact, several serious fires took whole rows of them down in the late 1990s. There was only one water tap and no potable water; sewage was nonexistent, and people defecated in the fields. All of these conditions breed cholera and other contagious diseases. It was only with pressure from the state human rights commission and other political allies that in the early 2000s, the worst offenders among the agribusinesses were forced to provide better housing for the Indigenous migrant workers.

As Egla Martinez-Salazar points out, the inhuman living conditions are perpetrated by mestizo owners whose racist attitudes make them actually believe that the Indigenous workers do not take care of themselves because of their culture and carelessness. The field production manager shifted the blame to these workers when their huts went up in flames: "Luckily we haven't had any human losses, but it's better to prevent this. It's just that these people aren't very careful."[25] In fact, the classism and racism built into the division of labor in present-day agribusinesses probably affect more deeply the ill health of these workers than do toxic chemicals.

In linking "deadly colonialism to toxic globalization," Martinez-Salazar reminds us that Indigenous women and men have resisted over centuries forced migration, institutionalized assimilation, and racist ideologies that have naturalized their poverty.[26] The fact that most of them do not speak Spanish meant that they were not informed of their rights by the company, nor could they read instructions on pesticide cans, for example. They were reportedly denied medical health passes, because one mestizo clerical employee claimed they would not be able to understand anything the doctor said.

While some women described symptoms of respiratory diseases and skin rashes, it is harder to know the longer term effects of low-level exposure on their health. As there is little regulation of pesticide use in Mexico nor study of its impacts, many workers just swallow the toxicity along with other indignities that are part of the exploitative system, because they feel they have little choice. For Indigenous migrants, for example, returning to their homes in the poorer states is not necessarily a better option. Since the land reform act was drastically changed in the early 1990s, the formerly communally worked land has been privatized and can be expropriated. What's more, decades of chemical use and poor agricultural practices have left lands badly eroded and barren. Again, the direct link between the environment and health is not only physical but also determined by economic interests, political decisions, and cultural beliefs in chemically intensive scientific agriculture.

Just as our definition of the environment must expand to include humans and socially constructed political and economic systems, so, too, our definition of health must be expanded to include the social and spiritual as well as the physical conditions created by humans and systems built by humans. Within both traditional health practices in the south as well as health promotion movements in the north, there is a growing understanding of the socioeconomic determinants of health and a vision of *holistic health* challenging a purely physical definition of health that focuses on a medicalized body.

While it may seem more obvious in the extreme conditions of eroded and expropriated lands of sick and poor campesinos in Mexico, the working environment of retail and service workers in the north must also be viewed in a more holistic fashion. Here technologies such as scanners and deep fryers constitute the work environment, each offering its own risks. We learned about the carpal tunnel syndrome suffered by cashiers who rush to break their quotas of scanning five hundred items an hour, as well as back and leg pains resulting from standing, reaching, and grabbing.

The response to these health problems by food retailers and retail unions alike has been to create ever more sophisticated technical solutions. But these problems have been produced not only by the technologies of work but also by the organization of work driven by speed and productivity, efficiency and profit. McDonald's workers experience some of the same symptoms from the pressure to work fast, to carry out routinized tasks, and to never stop. The famous slogan "Clean, don't lean" encourages workers who find a spare moment to pick up a broom and sweep the floor or wipe off a countertop, rather than sit down and take a breath. Time is indeed money, and bodies are seemingly endless sources of money-making activity.

We must remind ourselves, however, that the environment also includes the mind-numbing computer-monitored activity of the tasks of both fast-food workers and supermarket cashiers who are considered, like tomatoes, commodities in a global world of labor competition. The mental impact of such jobs cannot be separated from their physical impact. The loss of dignity that comes with low wages, highly automated jobs, scripted interactions, and invisible (electronic) supervision has long-term effects on women's self-esteem and physical and mental health. There is a deep exhaustion, not only of the body but also of the soul.

The deeper schism created by the current food system, between humans and earth, is reproduced in the thinking that creates the technologies and work systems of all three sectors studied. Understandably, Mexican campesinos have a clearer sense of that relationship, as many still maintain an intimate connection with the earth through more sustainable subsistence agricultural practices. Tomasa still talks about the corn "beginning to be born," a living entity. The cultural diversity and traditional knowledges threatened by the current food system remain sources of inspiration and alternatives.

Braided Threads: The Axes Spin Together around the Planet

This attempt to weave together key threads of comparison across sectors and borders and to elaborate central concepts underlying the case studies has revealed, once again, the importance of interdisciplinary and interlocking analyses that acknowledge the complexity of the tangled roots and routes of today's food system. Clearly the four axes around which the tomato story has been spun are intimately interrelated; the distancing that characterizes the relationship between production and consumption is based on narrow definitions of health and environment, which are reinforced by the reorganization of work with new technologies and which threaten both biodiversity and cultural diversity. Ultimately, competing visions of development and the environment are in conflict through the life cycle of the tomato (tomatl vs. the corporate tomato) and through the lives of women workers along the tomato trail. While massive and powerful, the economic system that moves the corporate tomato and shapes many daily practices is not inevitable, universal, immutable, and unchallenged. It is being contested at every step of the journey.

Charlene Spretnak synthesizes the obstacles—at the same time political and philosophical—that we face in promoting alternatives to a profit-driven system:

> The human is considered essentially an economic being, homo economicus. Consequently, the arrangement of economic matters is believed to be the wellspring of contentment or discontent in all other areas of life. Economic expansion, through industrialization and computerization, is the Holy Grail of materialism, the unquestioned source from whence follows abundance, well-being, and the evolution of society. That evolution is understood to be decidedly directional: The human condition progresses toward increasingly optimal states as the past is continuously improved upon.
>
> Modern socialization structures our understanding of the world via objectivism, rationalism, the mechanistic worldview, reductionism, and scientism. The design and organization of work in modern societies is based on standardization, bureaucratization, and centralization. Modern interactions with nature are anthropocentric and are guided by instrumental reasoning. Above all, modern culture defines itself as a tri-

umphant force progressing in opposition to nature. As such, it harbors contempt for non-modern cultures, which are seen to be "held back" by unproductive perceptions such as the "sacred whole" and reciprocal duties toward the rest of the Earth community.[27]

A food system totally defined and controlled by market forces, of course, benefits certain people such as investors, owners, managers, and wealthy consumers—at least in the short term. But any longer term vision recognizes that the costs are not just economic—they are ultimately ecological, social, cultural, and spiritual. As the fate of humans is intimately tied to the fate of the earth, no one is immune from the impacts of an unjust and unsustainable system.

If we begin to take seriously the knowledges of peoples who are most affected by this globalizing process, and draw upon our own intuitive understandings and collective memories of a more intimate connection between our bodies and the natural world, we may reroute the tomato's journey as well as our own futures. Nurturing a more holistic conception of health—as well-being that is at the same time physical and spiritual, individual and collective, human and nonhuman—is a starting point. But it also requires action, collective and coalitional efforts that move beyond concern for our own bodies, to a commitment to the sustenance of the collective body, of the earth's body. Tales of resistance and stories of hope in the final chapter can serve to kindle such reflections and actions.

Notes

1. Brewster Kneen, *From Land to Mouth: Understanding the Food System, Second Helping* (Toronto: NC Press, 1993), 39.

2. Kneen, *From Land to Mouth*, 47.

3. In its pamphlet "The Planet We Share," McDonald's states that it "does not now purchase, nor has it ever purchased beef grown on rain forest (or recently deforested rainforest) land." Source: McDonald's information packet.

4. Jack M. Greenberg, CEO, *McDonald's Corporation 1999 Annual Report*, 15 March 2000, 1.

5. Susan Willis, *A Primer for Daily Life* (New York: Routledge, 1991), 59.

6. Fred Magdoff, Frederick H. Buttel, and John Bellamy Foster, "Hungry for Profit: Agriculture, Food and Ecology," *Monthly Review* 50, no. 3 (July/August 1998): 11.

7. Toby M. Smith, *The Myth of Green Marketing: Tending Our Goats at the Edge of the Apocalypse* (Toronto: University of Toronto Press, 1998), 25.

8. "A growing body of evidence suggests that large operations are actually far less productive and efficient than areas of equivalent size and quality worked by similar producers. And big operations generate far more waste and pollution per unit area." John Tuxill, "The Biodiversity That People Make," *World Watch* (May/June 2000): 35.

9. Arturo Escobar, "Whose Knowledge, Whose Nature? Biodiversity, Conservation, and the Political Ecology of Social Movements," *Journal of Political Ecology* 5 (1998): 59.

10. Vandana Shiva, *Monocultures of the Mind: Perspectives on Biodiversity and Biotechnology* (Atlantic Highlands, N.J.: Zed, 1993), 9.

11. Shiva, *Monocultures of the Mind*, 60.

12. Winona LaDuke, *All Our Relations: Native Struggles for Land and Life* (Cambridge: South End Press; Minneapolis: Honor the Earth, 1999), 1.

13. Susan Strasser, *Never Done* (New York: Pantheon, 1982), 297, quoted in Ester Reiter and Richard Slye, *Making Fast Food: From the Frying Pan to the Fryer* (Montreal: McGill-Queen's University Press, 1991), 15.

14. Many of the ideas in this chapter I have previously developed in two other articles: "Whose 'Choice'? 'Flexible' Women Workers in the Tomato Food Chain," in *Women Working the NAFTA Food Chain: Women, Food, and Globalization*, ed. Deborah Barndt (Toronto: Second Story, 1999), 62–80; and "On the Move for Food: Three Women behind the Tomato's Journey," Earthwork: Women and Environments, *Women's Issues Quarterly* 29, nos. 1 and 2 (spring/summer 2001), ed. Diane Hope and Vandana Shiva.

15. Swasti Mitter, *Common Fate, Common Bond* (London: Pluto, 1986); Susan Tiano, "Maquila Women: A New Category of Workers?" in *Women Workers and Global Restructuring*, ed. Kathryn Ward (Ithaca, N.Y.: ILR, 1990); Diane Elson and Ruth Roach Pearson, "The Subordination of Women and the Internationalization of Factory Production," in *The Women, Gender, and Development Reader*, ed. Nalini Visvanathan, Lynn Duggan, Laurie Nisonoff, and Nan Wiegersma (Halifax: Fernwood, 1997), 191–203.

16. Gita Sen and Caren Grown, *Development, Crises, and Alternative Visions: Third World Women's Perspectives* (New York: Monthly Review Press, 1987), 25.

17. Deborah Barndt, "Women in the Food Chain: Bound, Freed, and/or Connected?" in *For Hunger-Proof Cities*, ed. Mustafa Koc, Jennifer Welsh, and Rod MacRae (Toronto: University of Toronto Press, 1999), 162–66.

18. Developed by J. Carillo, these four dimensions of maquilization are elaborated by Kathy Kopinak, *Desert Capitalism: What Are the Maquiladoras?* (Montreal: Black Rose, 1997), 13.

19. A much larger number of women, primarily from the Philippines and the Caribbean, also leave their families behind to support them. These domestic workers care for children of Canadian upper- and middle-class families through the government-sponsored Live-In Caregiver Program.

20. The terms *center* and *periphery* have been used since the 1960s in development theories to explain the concentration of power in the so-called industrialized developed nations, or the center, which depend on the resources of the peripheral developing nations.

21. Sara Lara, "La flexibilidad del mercado de trabajo rural," *Revista Mexicana de Sociologia* 54, no. 1 (January–February 1994): 41 (translated from the original Spanish by the author).

22. Lourdes Beneria, "Capitalism and Socialism: Some Feminist Questions," in *The Women, Gender, and Development Reader*, 330.

23. Susan Griffin, *The Eros of Everyday Life: Essays on Ecology, Gender, and Society* (New York: Doubleday, 1995), 57.

24. Griffin, *The Eros of Everyday Life*, 121.

25. Interview by author and Sheelagh Davis with field production manager, Sayula, July 1999.

26. Egla Martinez-Salazar, "The 'Poisoning' of Indigenous Migrant Workers and Children: From Deadly Colonialism to Toxic Globalization," in *Women Working the NAFTA Food Chain*, 102–3.

27. Charlene Spretnak, *The Resurgence of the Real: Body, Nature, and Place in a Hypermodern World* (New York: Routledge, 1999), 40–41.

CHAPTER 8

Signs of Hope:
TAKING ACTION FOR JUSTICE AND SUSTAINABILITY

Any attempt to examine the dynamics of globalization, even if focusing on one sector such as food, can feel overwhelming. An even greater danger is that the process of peeling away the layers, or following the seemingly endless journey of a tomato, can also prove despairing. My own digging into the tangled routes of the corporate tomato has made me wonder at times how we got here and also how we could ever possibly challenge or transform any of the structures or ideas that hold the system in place.

Yet the very digging has unearthed not only the roots of current concentrations of wealth and power but also stories of individuals and groups who have creatively struggled for alternative visions of a society, one that is both more sustainable and more equitable. The framing of the three sectors in the food chain, around the dynamics between globalization from above and globalization from below, is one attempt to acknowledge that wherever there is hegemonic control, there is not only consent but also resistance and transformation. The stories of the women workers, on the one hand, represent a view from below and within, but growing collaborative efforts by civil society groups reveal "the other globalization." Some of the very processes that have facilitated global economic integration have opened up possibilities for cross-border linkages among people and groups who are resisting and revisioning something beyond the seemingly monolithic global food system.

What has kept me going through the process of this project have been the signs of hope, the resistance and resilience of women workers, and the initiatives of individuals, groups, and coalitions to create more healthy and just communities.

I frame their activities broadly, illustrating four levels of resistance: individual responses, local/global education, organized collective actions, and transnational coalitional initiatives. They represent a reframing of resistance as multipronged and pro-active.

INDIVIDUAL CRITICAL THOUGHTS AND ACTIONS

> Traditional understandings of resistance as social rather than individual, political rather than personal, and inclusive of large numbers of people in conscious alliance working toward a common goal often inaccurately define women's activities as outside the political realm, assume that women accept their subordinate position, and situate women as ultimate victims.
>
> —Carolyn Sachs[1]

Despite tremendous pressures—both in the workplace and at home—women workers constantly find ways to resist the impacts of globalization in general and the corporate food system in particular. These can take the form of activities that counter corporate control of one's daily life as well as new ways of thinking—critical thought is itself a form of resistance. A Mexican immigrant to Canada reflected this level of resistance in describing her shift in consumption patterns: "As much as I can, I'm going to avoid buying vegetables. And even if I have a little balcony in an apartment, I'm going to grow my own vegetables. We have to start by taking the matter into our own hands."[2]

It is important to recognize and honor the small everyday ways that women resist and contribute to the creating of alternatives. We explore examples from both Mexico and Canada.

LOCAL/GLOBAL EDUCATION

This level of activity involves people learning in a social process based on popular education (chapter 2). Recall that popular education is a process of developing critical social consciousness through collective analysis and action; in contrast to conventional education, it explicitly links the personal and political, theory and practice. There has emerged a feminist popular education, too, that challenges the "rationalist masculinist ideology" underlying much popular education, which sometimes promotes a "gendered division between male public and female private, culture and nature, reason and emotion, mind and body."[3]

I would like to add the "local/global" relationship to this list of dualisms to be challenged. A local/global education honors people's daily lives and personal histories, acknowledging that this is where people act, but it also "recognizes the global in the local, and the world itself as a locality (in the sense of its ecological wholeness)."[4]

In the Canadian context, local/global education draws upon a rich tradition of "development education"[5] through NGOs as well as a more recent development of "global education" within the public schools.[6] In the Mexican context, I have been influenced by the rich theoretical and methodological work of popular educators, who historically have always located their analysis in a global context and more recently have refined notions of "local power" and "citizenship education."[7]

COLLECTIVE ACTION

Popular education processes often lead to collective action; a critical analysis of the impact of global forces can feed joint protests as well as local alternatives. Grassroots initiatives not only respond to physical survival needs but also often represent more democratic practices. In a sense, these activities are the building blocks for creating a more just and sustainable society from the ground up.

We have already seen examples of collective action in the case studies. Human rights and environmental groups in Mexico, for example, are organizing to improve the living and working conditions of Indigenous migrant workers, creating day care programs for Indigenous children as well as workshops for the workers on pesticides and health.[8] In the Canadian context, consumers mobilized outside a Loblaws supermarket to call for the labeling of genetically modified food. Retail unions also engage in collective action through their contract bargaining process, fighting against wage rollbacks and the replacement of full-time with part-time jobs.

This chapter offers examples of collective action that moves beyond the local level but is still grounded in the initiatives of civil society organizations.

TRANSNATIONAL COALITIONS

As Tamara Kay suggests: "although globalization and economic integration disempower social movements relative to capital, social movements can also benefit from the political openings and transnational networks globalization and economic integration create."[9] The globalization of civil society and of social movements is an important reconceptualization of a process that offers hope to the forces working for greater social justice, equity, and sustainability. As a counterpoint to the deepening power of multinational corporations and mergers of economic interests, transnational coalitions represent collective action that has crossed both borders and sectors. The growing protests against increasing corporate power and international financial institutions are inaccurately dubbed "antiglobalization," I think, when these cross-border actions are, in fact, globalizing social movements.

The Tomasita Project itself reflects some of these new efforts to redefine relationships of solidarity and to seek new forms of collaboration.[10] Through cross-border research and educational processes, we have uncovered many examples of new alliances, both among social movements within Canada as well as across geopolitical borders, that are challenging a globalization that deepens inequities and accelerates the degradation of ecosystems.

To bring life to these notions of resistance and the creation of alternatives and alliances, I offer snapshots of the four levels of resistance in both Mexico and Canada.

Mexico: Viva la Resistencia!

INDIVIDUAL THOUGHT AND ACTION: SUSANA'S SUBVERSIVE PHOTOGRAPHY

The possibilities of organizing collectively in the Santa Rosa fields, packing houses, or greenhouses are severely limited. Women working for agribusinesses are often exhausted from the physical work and long hours as well as their double or triple days that include domestic duties and subsistence agricultural activity. Survival itself is a form of resistance under these circumstances, as they are forced to compromise a lot merely to feed their families.

Outside the fields and plants, away from the eyes of company managers, women were more candid in speaking with me about their work, their bosses, and the hardships they must endure. Susana, for example, exhibited a kind of defiance and critical perspective on the greenhouse operation where she worked. When she learned that we were not permitted to photograph within the greenhouse, she offered to take photographs herself. As an employee, she could enter the workplace with a camera and take candid shots of her friends, contributing to the documentation of this kind of work. So I gave Susana a roll of film and left the task to her.

When we returned a few months later, to our surprise and delight, she presented us with her photographs, capturing not only the context and the multiple tasks but also the relationships and playfulness that workers will only share in each other's presence. Susana's photography represents a creative act of resistance, making the invisible visible. Some of her images appear in chapters 6 and 7.

LOCAL/GLOBAL EDUCATION: MEXICAN POPULAR EDUCATION CARTOONS AND VIDEOS

The Mexican Institute for Community Development (IMDEC) has been a beacon and a training ground for popular educators around Mexico for more than forty years. Founded in Guadalajara in 1963, its early work involved intensive community organizing in poor barrios of the city, through which IMDEC developed strengths in the areas of popular education and popular communications.

IMDEC served as an organizational base for the Tomasita Project in Mexico, and staff members collaborated in many aspects of the research. I participated, along with Canadian research assistants, in IMDEC popular communications training workshops, where we developed a strategic plan for the Tomasita Project in 1996.[11] IMDEC's training institutes in popular education methodology and in popular communications have given hundreds of Mexican popular educators conceptual frameworks, techniques, and tools for practicing local/global education in their communities. Through the 1990s, IMDEC's staff of about twenty have grappled with a process of reframing their work within the context of globalization, while also promoting a deeper process of "local power," consistent with the visions of "the other globalization."

Two tools for local/global education were produced by IMDEC in the late 1990s, closely related to the Tomasita Project. The first, a cartoon booklet, "Tomasita Tells All: True Confessions of Tomasita the Abused Tomato," was produced by IMDEC's resident graphic artist, Carlos Leal, based on skits created by North American popular educators. This bilingual cartoon booklet represents popular education in various ways: by starting with northern consumers' interest in healthy food, by unveiling both historical processes of global agriculture as well as the current continental food system, and by calculating at the cash register the "hidden costs" (Indigenous land expropriation, environmental degradation, workers' health, etc.) of the production of the corporate tomato. The local and the global are inextricably linked in the personal stories of northern consumers and southern producers.

IMDEC also produced a video documentary, "Mirando al Sol,"[12] or "Looking toward the Sun," that follows a Mexican campesino north to the U.S. border in what has become the quintessential dynamic in all campesino families and communities—migration *al norte*, seeking work in more prosperous regions or countries. The video locates the increased movement north in the broader processes of neoliberal trade liberalization and globalized food production. It exposes as well the contradictory policies of the United States, eager to exploit the cheap labor of illegal migrants, while treating the border-crossers like criminals. The interrelation of narcotics, corruption, and agroexport is also revealed.

Over the years, IMDEC has welcomed several Canadian graduate students from York University's Faculty of Environmental Studies as interns, resulting in educational tools for use in both Mexico and Canada. Working with IMDEC's videographer Pato Esquivel in 1999, Michele Doncaster produced a bilingual video, "Campo y Ciudad: Somos la Misma Cosa," based on organic agricultural experiments around Guadalajara, and in 2002 Daniel Schami created "Circle of Responsible Production and Consumption," a video on a producer-consumer co-op organized by the Jalisco Ecology Collective.[13] Cindy McCulligh's video, "Semilla de la Esperanza," focusing on a model organic farmer recovering traditional practices, led her to produce other tools on the issue of water; these efforts embody of the growing south-north exchange. She is now working full-time with IMDEC, doing community development work as well as research and advocacy on water privatization and health issues. In the decade since our initial collaboration in the mid-1990s, IMDEC has shifted its emphasis to environmental issues[14] such as maize and water, and moved its participatory research and popular education programming from urban settings to rural municipalities to support grassroots struggles around sustainability and justice issues.

COLLECTIVE ACTION: EL CAMPO NO AGUANTA MÁS

The devastating impact of neoliberal trade policies on Mexican small farmers leading to the disintegration of rural life has mobilized new coalitions of campesino and Indigenous organizations, protesting the North American Free Trade Agreement (NAFTA), the World Trade Organization (WTO), the proposed Free Trade Area of the Americas (FTAA), and the Plan Puebla Panamá (PPP). Twelve farmers' organizations—united under the banner "El Campo No Aguanta Más," or "The Countryside Can't Stand It Anymore!"—organized a series of protests and a culminating march of one hundred thousand farmers and allies in January 2003, on the ninth anniversary of NAFTA. They issued a joint proposal calling for:

- A three-year moratorium and renegotiation of the agricultural chapter of NAFTA (to exempt corn and beans) and a revision of Article 27 to reclaim communal land ownership as a right.
- A revaluing of the Mexican countryside through long-term structural changes.
- A reform of the rural credit system.
- Allocation of 1.5 percent of GDP for productive development and another 1.5 percent for social and environmental development in the rural sector in 2003.
- Food safety and quality for consumers, including a moratorium on the import of genetically engineered seeds and food.
- Recognition of the rights and culture of Indigenous people.[15]

Aimed at stopping "socially and environmentally unsustainable trading practices that pit highly subsidized agribusiness corporations against family farmers,"[16] the coalition entered into public negotiations with the state, resulting in a National Agreement for the Countryside in April 2003. The concessions offered by the government, however, ignored many of the proposals for structural and institutional reforms made by the alliance, and several member groups, including UNORCA, the National Union of Autonomous Regional Farmers' Organizations, refused to sign the agreement. By July 2004, the coalition was split over issues of organizational and political strategy, one side pushing for a consolidated organizational structure to leverage government institutions, the other side advocating a looser movement working from the base and bringing in allies from other sectors.

Member organizations of the Countryside Can't Stand It Anymore movement were also involved in another broader alliance with NGOs—both in Mexico and internationally—to push the World Trade Organization to renegotiate its

Agreement on Agriculture. They mobilized ten thousand farmers from around Mexico to participate in the International Farmers' March for Food Sovereignty in September 2003 to coincide with the International Farmers' Forum, a counter-conference to the meeting of the fifth WTO Ministerial meeting in Cancun, Mexico. They joined forces with the network Our World Is Not for Sale[17] and the sixty delegates of the international network Vía Campesina to develop a double strategy, with meetings and actions outside the official meetings impacting what went on inside. The most dramatic action outside the convention center was the self-immolation of Korean Vía Campesina activist Lee Kyung Hae, garnering world press attention. Adding "We do not want to die anymore!" to their central mantra "We will not negotiate with the WTO!" the alliance declared the "Victory of Cancun" when the ministers declared a stalemate in their negotiations.[18] Clearly there was a growing grassroots movement in Mexico ready to take on the big actors in the neoliberal trade arena.

TRANSNATIONAL ACTIVISM: THE ZAPATISTAS AND LA OTRA CAMPAÑA

There is perhaps no post-NAFTA collective action in Mexico that has inspired more visioning about "the other globalization" than the armed uprising on 1 January 1994 of the Zapatista Army of National Liberation (EZLN) in the southern state of Chiapas. Its timing on the first day of the implementation of NAFTA was a wake-up call not only for peasants and Indigenous peoples but for civil societies and the architects of globalization everywhere. Richard Stahler-Sholk explores the layers of Zapatista discourse and action that link "the rights of indigenous peoples in Chiapas to calls for an insurrection of civil society, for the democratization of Mexico, and for a global struggle against neoliberalism."[19] I have found useful his delineation of the ways in which the Zapatista movement has resisted globalization and what it thus offers other transnational movements for social and environmental justice.

First, the increasing globalization of agriculture that is at the core of the tomato story has had a devastating impact on Chiapas peasant and Indigenous communities. Corn had been central not only to the economic survival of these communities but also to the social, cultural, and spiritual aspects of their lives. With the oil boom and bust of the 1980s, the subsequent structural adjustment programs that cut rural credit and price supports, and the 1992 reform of Article 27 that threatened the ejido system and further commodified the land, a neoliberal offensive not only undermined their traditional production practices but also inspired autonomous peasant organizing initiatives, precursors to the Zapatistas.

The Zapatistas were seen as an obstacle to transnational investment capital in the region, especially after thirty-eight Chiapas municipalities were declared autonomous in early 1995. The Mexican government responded by militarizing the state, then applying a low-intensity warfare strategy of paramilitary repression. The Zapatistas continued to promote autonomy and local control, particularly of the natural resources constituting the region's rich biodiversity, and resisted attempts by multinational corporations to appropriate, modify, and patent Indigenous genetic forms.

Deepening the notions of autonomy and community control, the Zapatistas have modeled participatory democratic practices, challenging the technocratic model of decision making that characterizes neoliberalism. They have promoted democracy not only locally but in their dealings with government negotiators (insisting on consulting remote communities in the midst of negotiations for the San Andres accords in 1996), with other Indigenous groups (creating a National Indigenous Congress of thirty-six ethnic groups in 1996), and with other Mexican civil society groups (founding a civic Zapatista Front for National Liberation in 1997). In 1999, five thousand Zapatistas visited communities around Mexico, involving more than three million Mexicans in more than fifteen thousand roundtables and discussions in a National Consultation. They have redefined the nature of state and civil society relations and have challenged notions of power that have historically driven social movements in countering the state. "Rather than seeking state power, they seek to rediscover the power in society."[20]

It is this vision that has drawn global justice activists in solidarity with the Zapatista cause to ongoing dialogue with the movement—through conferences (such as the July 1996 International Encounter for Humanity and against Neoliberalism and the Intergalactic Encounter in January 2007[21]) and through their imaginative use of the Internet. The International Encounter brought three thousand people from around the world who supported the Zapatista vision: "The universal need for a more just and inclusive world, in opposition to the commodified and exclusionary world of neoliberalism, is the great event of our century; it opens the possibility of joining together local, national, sectoral and class

struggles, in one single struggle for the formation of a Planetary Community, the self-realization of civil society and the construction of a world 'where many worlds fit.'"[22]

In 2001, the Zapatista National Liberation Front[23] focused on the struggle for Indigenous rights, organizing the Zapatour, a "March of Those Who Are the Color of the Earth," from Chiapas to Mexico City, and culminating in a speech to the Mexican Congress by Comandante Ramona, an Indigenous woman leader. This represented one of the last efforts to influence the state directly. While the Fourth Declaration of the Lacandona Jungle proposed in 1996 that "another world is possible" outside of political parties and government,[24] it was the Sixth Declaration, issued in 2005, that outlined a process for developing this "other form of doing politics," called "La Otra Campaña" or "The Other Campaign." Subcomandante Marcos, known on the campaign as Delegate Zero, traveled throughout the country over the course of 2006 listening to communities who were invited to collectively build a new platform, articulating the principles, characteristics, structure, specific spaces, policy for developing alliances, and immediate tasks that they envisioned. These meetings ran parallel to the federal electoral campaign, were aimed at consolidating the anticapitalist left,[25] and were based on a very different dynamic, defined from the bottom up. As Marcos emphasized: "Something that defines traditional politics is that one person speaks and everyone listens. The Other Campaign hopes to invert this relationship, to listen to the other, to hear their history and struggle."[26]

Diversity is the source of the Zapatistas' unity and strength, and in some ways, the "other" campaign was seen as literally a campaign of "others," since it brought together the most marginalized sectors: Indigenous peoples, gays and lesbians, the disabled, punks, and anarchists.[27] Indigenous communities, supported by the National Indigenous Congress, organized their own meetings as part of The Other Campaign, seeing it as a space for defending their autonomy, territories, and ways of life. A gathering in Wixarika in March 2006 poignantly expressed their perspective: "The neoliberals want to privatize and destroy the territories, of the Nation and our peoples, separating each of its parts, things that for us are inseparable: water, air, land, mountains, corn, plants, animals, forests, minerals, coasts and seas, including our traditional knowledges."[28] An Encounter of the Indigenous Peoples of the Americas was planned for October 2007, in Sonora state, hosted by the Yaquí people and geared to consolidate hemispheric efforts to defend Mother Earth, Indigenous territories, and cultures.

For an increasingly globalizing civil society, or "the other globalization," the Zapatista movement offers a redefinition of state–society relations, a bottom-up concept of autonomy based on Indigenous rights and culture, and a new form of "ethnic citizenship" for Indigenous communities. It negotiates the tension between the local and the global in seemingly paradoxical ways, rooted in the local conditions of Indigenous communities in Chiapas and promoting an "autonomy of autonomies," while linking with groups through cyberspace and multisectoral gatherings in the jungle to counter what they see as a common neoliberal threat to this vision.

United States: In the Belly of the Beast

In the first edition of this book, I did not include examples of resistance in the United States, which ironically has gotten short shrift in my treatment of the tomato journey, even though it is also where most of the key decision makers around global food production are based. Of the three corporations we've focused on as case studies, McDonald's is the only one whose headquarters is located in the United States. And in the new millennium it has become a major target not only of anti-globalization activists worldwide (www.mcspotlight.org), but also, as noted in chapter 3, of once-loyal U.S. consumers who are increasingly concerned about the impact of fast food on their own health, and in particular, on child obesity. But how do you broaden the public consciousness from concern about people's own health to concern about the workers who grow the food they eat? To concern about the entire production-distribution-consumption process and its impact on the environment?

A convergence of factors in early 2007 revealed the other side of economic integration of the Americas, and made McDonald's sit up and take notice of the Mexican tomato workers in their midst. First of all, the increased migration of Indigenous campesinos from the south of Mexico (chapter 5) to northern agribusinesses has spilled over into the tomato fields of California, Florida, and points north. An estimated three million undocumented Mexican workers in the United States (150,000 NAFTA refugees enter per year[29]) send remittances home, one of Mexico's major sources of foreign exchange. But these workers have also brought their political consciousness and organizing skills to the fields. In 2005, the Coalition of Immokalee Workers (CIW), a community-based organization in southeastern Florida, succeeded in getting Taco Bell (now owned by Yum Foods) to agree to pay one cent more per pound for tomatoes it bought from growers in the area, having the effect of almost doubling their wages.[30] The four-year campaign had garnered support from a wide range of social, economic, and environmental justice groups: church groups, labor unions, students, artists, and musicians. Having sharpened their teeth on the tacos and buoyed by the precedent-setting agreement, the coalition and its allies moved on to the largest target, Big Mac.[31]

This campaign lasted less than two years, but in the meantime, the coalition both contributed to and benefited from a major new movement of undocumented workers. What is being heralded as a new civil rights movement has some of the energy and momentum of the 1960s, and echoes and revitalizes the United Farm Workers movement of that era in California.[32] The movement represents the growing political force of Hispanics in the United States, almost surpassing African Americans as the largest minority and a significant voting block. The momentum of this broader movement surely fed the CIW's campaign to pressure McDonald's to follow Taco Bell's lead by paying a penny more per pound for the tomatoes picked in southeastern Florida. The food giant resisted initially, claiming that a grower-developed agreement, SAFE, ensured labor standards were being followed. This claim was discredited when CIW won a court case against AgMart, a major grower, resulting in the imprisonment of a crew leader for keeping workers in debt bondage and forced labor.[33]

In 2006, the CIW helped found the Alliance for Fair Food,[34] and mobilized the support of its member groups for this campaign, with a multipronged strategy. Members of national church organizations and trade unions, representing the more privileged sectors in the alliance, became shareholders of McDonald's to push from within for the adoption of a human rights code of conduct. Student groups added migrant farmworkers' issues to their anti-sweatshop organizing and pushed for sustainable and equitable purchasing policies. CIW used popular education strategies (skits, cartoons, fiestas) in its local organizing, drew on cultural practices such as *carnavál* and fiestas to bring new energy to political work, and organized hunger strikes and pilgrimages or long marches with a Latino twist. It adopted as a mascot Rolando the Clown, the long-lost half-brother of Ronald McDonald. In early 2007, it organized for a national demonstration in mid-April near the Illinois-based McDonald's corporate headquarters. Thousands of allies were committed to join forces there, as well as key popular musicians like Rage Against the Machine and Cuban hip-hop groups.

Four days prior to the big gathering, supported by the Carter Center as mediators, McDonald's agreed to CIW's chief demand to pay more for the Florida tomatoes served in U.S. restaurants. As importantly, they agreed to work with their produce suppliers and CIW to develop a new code of conduct for Florida tomato growers as well as increased farmworker participation in ensuring that the increase goes toward workers' wages.[35] It was estimated that if a migrant worker picked tomatoes regularly for both McDonald's and Taco Bell suppliers, his or her wages could almost double, from about U.S. $40 per day to over $70. Of course, it is a big IF, since most are still day laborers who go early every morning to a parking lot, where they may or may not get contracted for a day's work. And they are also likely to follow the seasonal harvests up the east coast, thus working for other employers who don't abide by the same agreement.

While the victory was hailed as a landmark decision and the Chicago protest was transformed into a celebration, the impact on the industry was unclear. First of all, McDonald's garnered excellent public relations points for less than one million dollars, the estimated cost to the company for the increased price of tomatoes, and a very small percentage of its advertising budget. What's more, only grape tomatoes were covered in this deal, not the tomatoes that are sliced and inserted into a Big Mac (which still may be produced in Mexico, where workers earn less than one-quarter the amount that Florida workers earn). Grape tomatoes are key ingredients in McDonald's Premium Salad, a $4 item that appeals to health-conscious consumers who are willing to pay more; in fact, it accounts for 10 percent of total revenue.[36] Thus, indirectly, the company that has been trying to repair its image of promoting unhealthy eating has gotten more attention for its salads, while also scoring points for supporting struggling Mexican farmworkers in Florida. But would Mexican farmworkers in Mexico ever get similar increases?

This story reveals a new kind of coalition, one that is led by the most exploited workers in the NAFTA food chain, a transnational workforce; CIW is really a relatively small group of 2,500–3,500 workers of Mexican, Mayan, Haitian, and African American origin, but with a new strategy of cracking the corporate tomato by targeting the big companies and buyers as well as consumers with a concern for health and, increasingly, for justice. The significance of this campaign is twofold. On the one hand, it has signaled to not only all big fast-food companies but also food retailers that they are going to have to consider codes of conduct around the wages and living conditions of the workers who grow the food they profit from. And, on the other hand, the organizing led by the mainly Latino workers has converged with a growing movement of undocumented workers in the United States, who have been fighting to secure legal status as citizens. CIW tapped the interests of major social, economic, and environmental justice groups, who have formed the Alliance for Fair Food, now ready to take on other food giants. This alliance represents the first major cross-sectoral coalition in the United States to integrate issues of food safety, environmental degradation, and workers' rights; it has the potential to link with other organizations in Canada and Mexico mobilizing cross-sectorally around these related issues.

Canada: Heating Up the North

We now turn to Canada for stories that also reflect the four levels of resistance: individual thought/action, local/global education, collective action, and transnational alliances.

INDIVIDUAL CRITICAL THOUGHTS AND ACTION:
MARISSA—WORKER, LEARNER, TEACHER

> Dear Deborah—
> Thanks for letting me read your article "Whose Choice?" Let me say first after reading the paper I felt an overwhelming sadness and connection to all the women in the "tomato food chain." We all play a seemingly small part but the ramifications of our work are enormous. Individually, the women are trying to cope, they're trying to survive, in Mexico and Canada. As groups, however, I can see we are all entrapped in the corporate workings of flexibilization. However, the dilemma still exists for all of us in the food chain: we're trying to survive.[37]

This was one of several letters I have received over the past ten years from Marissa, the part-time Loblaws cashier featured in chapter 4. From the first interview in 1997, Marissa demonstrated a keen interest in the Tomasita Project, welcoming both the opportunity to reflect on her own work career of over thirty years, as well as the chance to learn about women workers in other links of the chain. She read every article and book I passed her way related to our research and was especially intrigued with the story of Tomasa, the field-worker in Mexico, comparing the pressures of globalization on the two of them in such different contexts: "Tomasa used to make her own tortillas but now she has to go to work, so she buys ready-made tortillas. And she's feeling that pull just like North American women are: Should I stay home with the kids? Should I go to work? She's taking care of the family, that's a priority in her life; I'd like to think that in my life that's a priority."[38]

Marissa was able to meet Irena and other Mexican migrant workers picking Ontario tomatoes two hours west of Toronto. She brought her daughters along on this outing, explaining to them the working conditions of the Mexican women as well as why they left their children at home to come to Canada. A few days after this visit, she wrote me a nine-page letter of her observations. "The highlight for me was sharing this life experience with my 'sisters' from Mexico. . . . I was very interested in the relationship between the workers, government, and 'patrons.' Such a powerful word relegated to a farmer who hires you as a picker."

Particularly moving was how Marissa engaged her daughters in discussions of ethical dilemmas she faced as both a worker and consumer of food:

"I asked Connie about buying a product such as Nescafe on special, knowing that the workers on the coffee plantation were not treated well, or buying a more expensive coffee ('Alternative Grounds' fair trade coffee). She said it would be better to buy Alternative Grounds even if it would mean having less money to spend on other things; at least we knew the workers were being treated/paid fairly and they took care of the environment. It was very rewarding to see my 11-year-old weighing these aspects and to realize that she has a consciousness about the global food system and understands her impact as a consumer."

Marissa also participates in social causes at work by coordinating the food drive for her store. Her ever-present curiosity, deepening social analysis, and willingness to take small actions reflect the power of one individual to respond daily and critically to globalization, even while also working deeply within its structures.

One kind of individual action open to everyone is to buy and eat locally, thus not contributing to the environmental, social, and economic costs created by the processes that bring us food from faraway places, averaging 1,500 miles. Two young Canadians, Alisa Smith and James MacKinnon, took up the challenge of a 100-Mile Diet, launching a one-year experiment on the first day of spring in 2005 to gather food and drink only from within one hundred miles of their Vancouver apartment. They got to know the seasons and preserved food for the winter, admitting that it wasn't easy and took time. "But it also raises interesting questions about how we're spending our time," they wrote on their blog. "What if we spent more time on self-sufficiency and less time at the office?" The story of their adventure was published as a book in 2007 and inspired many other similar actions.[39]

LOCAL/GLOBAL EDUCATION: FOODSHARE TORONTO

The major local base for the Tomasita Project was FoodShare Toronto, the largest food security organization in North America, which works with diverse communities to improve access to nutritious, affordable, and culturally appropriate food. Spawned by the municipal government in 1985, this multiprogram agency has drawn many ideas from experiments in the south,[40] such as community kitchens in Peru and the Municipal Secretariat of Supplies that tackles food issues in Belo Horizonte, Brazil, where nutritious food has been officially declared a basic right.[41] Two programs described here reflect FoodShare's commitment to popular education and research that recognizes the local–global dynamic: the first was part of FoodShare's Focus on Food program and the second was an initiative of its Urban Agriculture program.

Eating Stories, Telling Food

In 1997–1998, the Tomasita Project collaborated with FoodShare on a project that involved eight immigrant women in tracing the journeys and histories behind their favorite recipes. When the women began cooking for each other, the storytelling really began to flow, connect, and deepen—in the kitchen and at the dinner table. Over a period of months, the exchange of recipes, meals, and stories not only created a strong bond among the women, but led to profound insights about the relationship between food and colonialism, immigration, and racism.

We facilitated the telling of the stories and their integration with photos on storyboards that were displayed at an Eco Art and Media Festival in a downtown gallery; the women were both the artists and the cooks, offering their meals along with their stories. The local/global nature of the process, revealing international histories within multicultural meals, represented the best of cultural fusions, a feast for the eyes as well as the palate.[42]

Seeds of Our City

As a pioneer in urban agriculture in Canada, FoodShare realized that Toronto's multicultural population was a rich source of knowledge not only about culinary traditions but also about agricultural practices and products. Between 1999 and 2002, FoodShare partnered with the AfriCan FoodBasket and Greenist City to undertake a participatory research and community development project[42] in eight very different community gardens, involving dedicated gardeners who had come to Canada from many countries, including China, Ghana, Jamaica, Sri Lanka, and Vietnam. The purposes were multiple: to determine how much food could be grown in a community garden plot, to assess its impact on the food security of participants, to identify innovative growing techniques that newcomers have brought in Canada, to contribute to new municipal food policy, and to exchange seeds, stories, and meals among gardener-researchers in eight neighborhoods.

Coordinated by Lauren Baker, then FoodShare's urban agriculture coordinator and a major researcher in the Tomasita Project, the research report documented how gardens are started and maintained, and revealed the incredible breadth of food plants grown in Toronto, as well as the intensive production methods used by urban gardeners. It also made more visible the barriers faced by immigrants trying to participate in the citywide gardening networks, such as transportation, funding, language, and the cultural nature of events. Finally, Baker and her colleagues made policy recommendations to city agencies that more training be offered, that events be more accessible, and that events be more culturally appropriate.[43]

COLLECTIVE ACTION: FOOD SECURE CANADA

Food activists in Canada gathered forces during the 1990s, mobilized by issues such as the depletion of the fisheries and diminishing support for farmers as well as insurgent initiatives across the country nurturing alternative local food systems and promoting sustainable and organic agriculture, farmers' markets, and consumer activism.

After key national gatherings (the Working Together Conference in Toronto in 2001 and the Growing Together Conference in Winnipeg in 2004) declared the need for a national alliance, Food Secure Canada/Sécurité Alimentaire Canada

(FSC-SAC) was formed in 2005 at the Third National Conference on Food Security in Waterloo, Ontario.

FSC-SAC provides a structure for collaborative research, policy advocacy, debate and exchange, and cross-sector grassroots organizing—all aimed at the following interconnected goals:

- **Zero hunger:** that all have the ability to acquire, in a dignified manner, adequate quantity and quality of culturally and personally acceptable food.
- **A sustainable food system** harvested, produced, processed, distributed, and consumed in a way that enhances the quality of land, air, and water for future generations, providing a living wage in a safe and healthy environment for those who harvest, grow, produce, process, handle, retail, and serve food.
- **Healthy and safe food:** nourishing foods uncontaminated by pathogens or industrial chemicals, with new food rigorously and independently tested and tracked to ensure its safety.[45]

A careful reading of these goals reveals a very integrated and interdisciplinary approach to food security guided by principles of economic equality, social justice, and environmental sustainability. A steering committee with members from most provinces and territories named issues of equity in their litany of problems to be addressed: the growing use of food banks, the financial desperation of farmers and fishers, diabetes among aboriginal people, child and adult obesity, and habitat destruction. Food security was also linked to sovereignty issues such as aboriginal relations to traditional lands, farmers' rights to save seeds and protect biodiversity, and workers' rights to fair wages and better working conditions.[46]

Similar to the new Alliance for Fair Food in the United States, Food Secure Canada offers a base for political action across sectors and a coalitional force that can lobby both key corporate players as well as different levels of government around questions of policy, health, and poverty reduction. The cross-sectoral collaboration has challenged historical schisms between constituencies such as labor and environmentalists and a conventional notion of "jobs *versus* the environment"; new "blue-green alliances" have emerged around a shared goal of "prevent(ing) corporate greed from hurting working families and the natural environment."[47]

The Canadian Labour Congress developed a Healthy Food Charter[48] and launched a Healthy Food Campaign in 2005, with a goal of food security for all Canadians, in terms of availability, accessibility, acceptability, and adequacy.[49] These initiatives come from social unionists committed to forging community-labor alliances. As Cliff Stainsby, the B.C. Government and Service Employees' Union representative on the FSC steering committee, articulates: "We got to thinking about environmental issues, social justice, economic issues and how they're all tied together. . . . At some point, it occurred to me, 'Food is a central theme here, a platform from which we can address all these issues.'"[50] The CLC campaign acknowledges how food security ties in with many other concerns of the national labor body: "globalization, cancer prevention, fighting pesticide use, creating sustainable green jobs, promoting zero toxins, support of the Kyoto Accord on climate change, and building a good public health system."[51]

TRANSNATIONAL ACTIVISM: COMMON FRONTIERS AND THE HEMISPHERIC SOCIAL ALLIANCE

Civil society groups in Canada were the first to seriously organize in opposition to free trade, developing a new coalition politics to fight (unsuccessfully) the 1988 election of a conservative government and the signing of the Free Trade Agreement with the United States. Action Canada, the cross-sectoral coalition formed during that period, evolved into Common Frontiers, which since then has been the Canadian partner in cross-border alliances challenging myriad agreements led by governments and driven by corporate interests, all supporting privatization, deregulation, and the reduction of social spending. Victor Osorio of Fronteras Comunes (Common Borders) suggested that early efforts at coalition-building in Canada had, in fact, served as a model for Mexican civil society organizations that formed the Mexican Action Network on Free Trade (RMALC)[52] in the early 1990s.

Common Frontiers now works in solidarity with U.S. and Latin American coalitions to confront and propose alternatives to the social, environmental, and economic effects of the economic integration of the Americas. The network—comprised of seventeen Canadian organizations representing labor, church, environmental, and international development interests—develops strategy and coordinates campaigns with the Reseau Quebeçois sur l'integration Continentale (RQIC) in Quebec and with international partners: RMALC (Mexico), the Al-

liance for Responsible Trade (U.S.),[53] the Brazilian Network for a People's Integration, Alliance Chile for Just and Sustainable Trade, and all members of the Social Hemispheric Alliance.[54]

One critical role of Common Frontiers has been to monitor the impact of the North American Free Trade Agreement (NAFTA) and to push the Canadian government to undertake a review of it. Members argue that free trade has protected the rights of investors while limiting the power of governments, and, contrary to the promises of more and better jobs, has led to more part-time jobs, lower wages, and declining benefits. In Canada, farmers have particularly suffered, earning now about what they did in the 1930s, and all Canadians have experienced the loss of employment insurance benefits, old age security, and health and education spending.[55]

By 2007, the focus shifted from fighting the Free Trade Agreement of the Americas, which was derailed (due in part to the emergence of progressive governments in Bolivia, Venezuela, Argentina, Uruguay, Chile, Brazil, and Nicaragua), to countering provincial "free trade" deals[56] as well as bilateral trade agreements that Canada is pursuing with several Latin American countries, without any human rights considerations. Of greatest concern, however, is the Security and Prosperity Partnership (SPP), a program announced in 2005 by the leaders of Canada, Mexico, and the United States to speed up the process of integration; in 2006, they created the North American Competitiveness Council, made up of ten CEOs from each of the three countries, allowing large companies to bypass legislatures and civil society.[57] The SPP represents yet another entrenchment of neoliberalism under the guise of "national security."

From the start, Common Frontiers has been working within the Hemispheric Social Alliance (HSA), which defines itself as "the voices of the unions, popular and environmental organizations, women's groups, human rights organizations, international solidarity groups, indigenous, peasant and student associations and church groups." The platform of the HSA integrates a critique—"We reject this project of liberalized trade and investment, deregulation, and privatization. We are opposed to a neoliberal, racist, sexist and inequitable project that is destructive of the environment."—with an alternative vision: "We propose to build new modes of continental integration based on democracy, equality, solidarity, respect for human rights and the environment."[58]

Member Organizations of the Hemispheric Social Alliance
Alliance for Responsible Trade (ART—United States)
Brazilian Network for a Peoples' Integration (REBRIP)
Civil Society Initiative on Central American Integration (ICIC)
Common Frontiers—Canada
Inter-America Regional Organization of Workers (ORIT)
Latin American Congress of Rural Organizations (CLOC)
Mexican Action Network on Free Trade (RMALC)
Quebec Network on Continental Integration (RQIC—Quebec)

The Hemispheric Social Alliance has followed all key meetings of free trade architects in the past decade and was present at two major meetings of leaders of the Americas held in Canada in the early 2000s. At the June 2000 meeting of the Organization of American States in Windsor, Ontario, transnational activists joined Canadian women workers in making demands for all women and denounced the corporate control of food, reminding us of the women workers in the south who pick and pack tomatoes for us. The NGO gathering featured a photo exhibit, "Attacking the Corporate Tomato: Turning Globalization on Its Face," which I produced as a synthesis of the stories in this book.

In April 2001, more than sixty thousand protesters converged on Quebec City to denounce the Free Trade Agreement of the Americas being crafted by the thirty-four heads of state at the Summit of the Americas. Most provocative was a $40 million security perimeter erected to keep people out of the official gathering, creating a fortresslike mentality that has become common fare at these meetings. The wall itself was alternately dubbed the "wall of shame," because it shut out democratic dissent and was reinforced by six thousand police, on the one hand, and the "wall of democracy," on the other, because it created a space for popular movements from across the hemisphere to connect and develop alternative proposals. There were many creative street events, among them a rally in front of the Quebec Ministry of Agriculture organized by a Canadian group, "The Belly of Resistance." Billed as "a community picnic against GMOs, patents on life, and neoliberal agricultural policies," the event was peppered with poetry and popular theater of peasants losing land and non-GMO tomatoes, among other playful protests.

While the media were drawn to the confrontations that toppled the chain link fence and blanketed the city in tear gas, they were almost silent in their cov-

erage of a less photogenic gathering: the six-day Peoples' Summit, organized by Common Frontiers and the HSA. More than two thousand delegates of civil society groups hammered out two documents with an alternative vision to the market-driven FTAA; one focused on debt, finance, and investment and the other on social exclusion, jobs, and poverty.

The HSA documents include many recommendations relevant to the issues raised by the stories in this book:

> Any hemispheric trade agreement must include, as a principal objective, the eradication of poverty and inequalities within and among nations, between men and women, and among races. (5)
>
> Government must recognize the particular history and rights of Indigenous peoples and address the particular needs of women in both the national budget and in the use of any foreign aid fund, promoting a new development model, based on popular participation in the planning, decision-making, implementation, and evaluation of development plans. (6, 7)
>
> Governments must include mechanisms for adjustment and the creation of high quality jobs, with special allocations for women (10); they must also acknowledge the needs of women in waged and unwaged work, taking into consideration the unequal share of responsibility assigned to most women for child-rearing, care for family members, and domestic labor, and the lack of value accorded to that work. (11)
>
> In addition, they should analyze the impact of trade liberalization on women . . . and ensure that childcare is affordable, accessible, and of high quality. (11)

In the case of Indigenous migrants within national boundaries, it is important to promote training, improve living and working conditions, provide fair remuneration, and respect native forms of social and economic organization and methods of production. (11)

Charging that the model of development being promoted by the designers of the FTAA, treats food, genetic resources, and other life forms as mere commodities, to be produced and marketed in the cheapest form possible, (12) the document proposes the primacy of international environmental agreements over trade agreements, (13) returning to governments the right to regulate . . . trade so that it benefits rather than harms social and environmental sustainability. (14)

Any hemispheric trade agreement must protect biodiversity by rejecting intellectual property claims over life-forms, protecting the collective rights of local communities in species conservation, recognizing the rights of black and Indigenous communities to full autonomy over traditional habitats, and guarantee the free circulation of knowledge and access to genetic resources. (14)

What's more, it should oppose projects which affect climate change by, among other things, eliminating subsidies for fossil-fuel energy. (14)

Finally, trade agreements must promote the goal of food security by rebuilding local systems of production and supply in order to promote self-reliance in agricultural production, which includes reducing the use of toxic chemicals, offering incentives for the conservation of soil, assuring the traditional rights of Indigenous peoples to live off their ancestral lands, supporting the rural sector, ensuring public and private support for small-scale farming, family enterprises, and cooperatives . . . as well as improvement of food distribution networks, (15) testing new food products in a publicly transparent manner, and eliminating the production and export of genetically altered food.

To emphasize their concern for the undemocratic processes through which these agreements have been forged, the HSA members call for the subordination of corporate rights by human rights, which include civil and political rights; economic, social, and cultural rights; and environmental rights and the rights of people and communities. Individualism, competition, and corporate power are to be replaced by values of solidarity, social justice, and democracy.

While the popular documents were important results of these transnational gatherings, they could not entirely convey the emotion and depth of the experiences of those most affected by the policies driving corporate globalization. At the Peoples' Summit in Quebec City, an Indigenous leader from Mexico denounced neoliberalism's megaprojects that provoke migration, genocide, disintegration of families, and destruction of land and nature. "We have suffered in our flesh and our hearts, and have resisted with dignity attempts to exterminate, immobilize or co-opt us. Governments have responded with the militarization of our regions, the repression of our organizations, the privatization of our natural resources, goods, and services, excluding us from decisions that affect us. We remain alive. We honor the people in our cultures who taught us that we come

from the land, from the corn. Never again a Mexico without us! Never again an America without Indigenous peoples!"

FROM HEMISPHERIC TO GLOBAL ACTIVISM: VÍA CAMPESINA AND THE SLOW FOOD MOVEMENT

Vía Campesina

Transnational activism has not been limited to continents, as neoliberalism's reach is global. Formed in 1993, Vía Campesina, the largest international peasant and farm movement, has been "turning up everywhere, a troublesome and discordant voice amid the chorus extolling the praises of globalization."[59] By 2006, 149 organizations from 56 countries on every continent had joined, almost half from Asia; in the NAFTA context, Mexico was represented by seven key peasant and agricultural worker coalitions, the United States by the National Family Farm Coalition and the Border Farm Workers Project, and Canada by the National Farmers Union (NFU) and the Quebec-based Union Paysanne.

While promoting actions at the local and regional levels, Vía Campesina's efforts internationally have been focused on taking the World Trade Organization (WTO) out of agriculture and ratifying an International Convention on Food Sovereignty. This notion was most hotly debated at the NGO/CSO Forum on Food Sovereignty, coinciding with the World Food Summit organized by the UN's Food and Agricultural Organization in Rome in 2002. Echoing a 2001 campaign for Peoples' Food Sovereignty, peasant organizations argued for policies that "promote sustainable, family-farm based production rather than industry-led, high-input and export-oriented production," offer equitable access to land, seeds and water, ban GMOs and food irradiation, and monitor high environmental. social, and health quality standards.[60] There was resistance on the part of some NGOs to support this vision of a radical transformation, claiming it was not realistic; this represented a split in strategy, as NGOs had been negotiating with the WTO on a lamer "right to food" platform which didn't challenge the deeper structures.[61]

Within the international alliance, there have also been attempts to address issues of gender parity. Since its 2000 conference, Vía Campesina has expanded its international coordinating committee to include one man and one woman from each of its regions. But organizing women at both the local and global level was filled with challenges; national organizations remained male-dominated and there were differences in vision and strategy between the Latin American women and Asian women, for example. But efforts at equity persisted and, prior to the 2004 conference in Brazil, there was both a youth assembly and a women's assembly. Both seemed to inject creative energy into the broader gathering, creating a new sense of community through the integration of theater, dance, and song.[62]

Slow Food Movement

Another transnational coalition that deserves mention is the Slow Food Movement. Founded in Italy in 1989 to counteract both fast food and fast life, the organization now boasts 80,000 members in 850 local chapters and articulates its philosophy in a straightforward manner: "Slow Food is good, clean and fair food. We believe that the food we eat should taste good; that it should be produced in a clean way that does not harm the environment, animal welfare or our health; and that food producers should receive fair compensation for their work."[63] Small-scale projects around the world protect traditional production methods by supporting producers and helping them find markets for traditional foods. Slow Food promotes eco-gastronomy, emphasizing the relationship between the plate and the planet.

Engagement over Cynicism

The examples offered in this chapter of individuals and groups, networks and coalitions, in both Mexico and Canada, challenge the relentless push for globalization of food systems, of women's devalued work, of homogenized production and consumption practices. Wherever people are engaged in challenging unjust and unsustainable practices and in creating alternatives that promote equity and ecological health, there is movement and there is hope. I have been inspired over the years by the commitment and creativity of my graduate students in York University's Faculty of Environmental Studies, many of whom joined the protests in Windsor and Quebec City described above, others who are creating community gardens and organizing food justice organizations, and still others

who are supporting Indigenous struggles in Mexico to maintain biodiversity and cultural identities. Their graduate research has often overlapped with mine, and they have been stimulating collaborators in this decade-long learning journey.[64]

As civil society groups denounce corporate monopolies and the state police forces defending them, we must also challenge resigned indifference or academic cynicism around these issues. Endless critique or despair without exploring

alternatives lead nowhere; a sense that "another world is possible" is awakened only through efforts to transform critical analyses into action—no matter how small. As the Chilean poet Pablo Neruda poignantly declared, "Our guiding stars must be struggle and hope."[65]

Notes

1. Carolyn Sachs, *Gendered Fields: Rural Women, Agriculture, and Environment* (Boulder, Colo.: Westview, 1996), 26.

2. Arcelia, quoted in the video "The Global Food Puzzle: Where Do You Fit into the Picture?" co-produced by Mark Haslam and Anuja Mendiratta with Deborah Barndt for the Tomasita Project, distributed by FoodShare, 239 Queen St. West, Lower Level, Toronto, ON M5V 1Z7 Canada, (416) 392-6653; foodshare@web.net.

3. Carmen Luke, "Feminist Pedagogies in Radical Pedagogy," in *Feminism and Critical Pedagogy*, ed. Carmen Luke and Jennifer Gore (New York: Routledge, 1992), 34.

4. Deborah Barndt, "Crafting a 'Glocal' Education: Focusing on Food, Women, and Globalization," *Atlantis* 22, no. 1 (fall/winter 1997): 43–51.

5. Development education was shaped by Canadians who returned from overseas volunteer activities in the 1960s and 1970s transformed by their experiences and committed to educating Canadians about global issues, and particularly of the complicity of northern countries such as Canada in the underdevelopment of the Third World. See Jean Christie, "Critical History of Development Education in Canada," *Canadian and International Education Journal* 12, no. 3 (1983): 8–20.

6. Graham Pike and David Selby, *Global Teacher, Global Learner* (London: Hodder & Stoughton, 1988); and Tara Goldstein and David Selby, eds., *Weaving Connections: Educating for Peace, Social and Environmental Justice* (Toronto: Sumach, 2000).

7. Carlos Nuñez H., *La Revolución Ética* (Guadalajara: IMDEC, 1998).

8. Since the publication in 1999 of our collective anthology, *Women Working the NAFTA Food Chain: Women, Food, and Globalization*, we have sent royalties from that book to two environmental organizations in Sirena. It has been gratifying to learn that these small donations have funded child-care centers for children of Indigenous migrant workers, pesticide workshops for fumigators, and recycling programs in that tomato-producing area.

9. Tamara Kay, "A Conceptual Framework for Analyzing 'Labor Relations' in a Post-NAFTA Era: The Impact of NAFTA on Transnational Labor Cooperation and Collaboration in North America," presented to the Latin American Studies Association, Miami, March 2000, 3.

10. Drawing on Chandra Mohanty's notion of "imagined communities," Lauren Baker assesses the cross-border collaboration emerging from the Tomasita Project in "A Different Tomato: Creating Vernacular Landscapes," in *Women Working the NAFTA Food Chain: Women, Food, and Globalization*, ed. Deborah Barndt (Toronto: Second Story, 1999), 250–59.

11. I served on the training staff of a Popular Communications workshop in 1997, introducing photography to their repertoire of tools.

12. "Mirando al Sol" can be purchased (in Spanish) from IMDEC; contact imdec@laneta.org.

13. There is a growing network of organic markets or "tianguis" (a Náhuatl word for market) in Mexico, similar to the burgeoning of farmers' markets in North America, both

recognizing the importance of local food production. See http://www.chapingo.mx/ciestaam/to. Many are part of networks of fair trade and responsible consumption, coordinated by Greenpeace: http://www.greenpeace.org/mexico/campaigns/consumidores.

14. Another York University student, Petra Kukacka, worked with IMDEC in 2004 on a needs assessment study that laid the ground for their new environmental programming.

15. http://www.unorca.org.mx/ingles/movementactivities.htm.

16. Ibid.

17. http://www.ourworldisnotforsale.org.

18. http://www.unorca.org.mx/ingles/movementactivities.htm.

19. Richard Stahler-Sholk, "A World in Which Many Worlds Fit: Zapatista Responses to Globalization," paper presented to the Latin American Studies Association, Miami, March 2000, 1.

20. Gustavo Esteva, "The Meaning and Scope of the Struggle for Autonomy," *Latin American Perspectives* 28, no. 2 (March 2001): 120–48.

21. The Intergalactic Encounter, in the autonomous caracol of Oventic in Chiapas, offered opportunities for dialogue within which all groups represented could share what was going on in their particular contexts and what visions and strategies were guiding them. Personal communication with Heather Hermant, 30 May 2007.

22. Ejército Zapatista de Liberación Nacional (EZLN), *Crónicas intergalácticas: Primer Encuentro Intercontinental por la Humanidad y contra el Neoliberalismo* (Chiapas, Mexico: Planeta Tierra, 1996).

23. In 1996, the FZLN or Zapatista National Liberation Front was formed as the political arm, while the EZLN or Zapatista National Liberation Army remained the military arm. "El Ejercito Zapatista celebra el 12 aniversario de su alzamiento con el inicio de 'La Otra Campaña," Encuentre Casa Rural, 28 May 2005, http://www.lukor.com/notpor/0601/01/01171020.htm.

24. Gustavo Esteva, *Celebración del Zapatismo Posdata* (Oaxaca, Mexico: Ediciones ¡Basta¡, 2006), 16.

25. By October 2005, "181 Indigenous associations, 68 left formations, 197 social organizations, 474 NGOs and collectives, and 1,898 individuals and families had subscribed to La Otra Campaña and committed themselves to make it work." John Ross, "The Zapatistas Challenge in Mexico's Presidential Elections," http://www.counterpunch.org/ross11052005.html.

26. Subcomandante Insurgente Marcos, "Aprender a Decir Nosotr@s," *Rebeldía* 44 (junio 2006): 6.

27. John Ross, "The Zapatistas Challenge to Mexico's Presidential Elections."

28. Quoted in Lucio Dias Marielle, "Los Pueblos Indios en la Otra Campaña," *Rebeldía* 44 (junio 2006): 44.

29. "NAFTA: A Flood of Undocumented Mexican Workers: Economic Brutality, Violence, Ethnic Tension," unpublished paper; Sources: U.S. General Accounting Office and BusinessMexico, a Mexico-based English-language trade publication.

30. "Victorious in the Taco Bell Boycott: The Fight for Fair Food Continues," http://www.ciw-online.org, accessed 29 November 2005.

31. "About CIW: Consciousness + Commitment = Change," http://www.ciw-online.org/about.html.

32. The United Farm Workers, led by Chicano leader Cesar Chavez, won a major strike in 1975, after a successful boycott of grapes, one of the first campaigns to engage consumers in a direct way, while raising consciousness about the dangers of pesticides on the

health of both those who pick and those who eat the grapes. David Bacon, "Class War in the Tomatoes and Roses," http://dbacon.igc.org/FarmWork/05tomato.html, accessed 10 April 2007.

33. CIW is a founding member of the national Freedom Network USA to Empower Victims of Slavery and Trafficking and has won several court cases denouncing the indentured servitude of farmworkers. "CIW Anti-Slavery Campaign," http://www.ciw-online.org/slavery/html.

34. The Alliance for Fair Food is a network of human rights, religious, student, labor, and grassroots organizations that work in partnership with CIW. www.allianceforfairfood.org/index.html, accessed 28 May 2007.

35. John Schmeltzer, "Migrants Harvest Tiny Raise, Big Win: McDonald's Case Could Set Standard," *Chicago Tribune*, 10 April 2007. See also "McDonald's USA and Its Produce Suppliers to Work with the Coalition of Immokalee Workers," http://www.mcdonalds.com/usa/news/current/conpr_04092007.html.

36. Melanie Warner, "You Want Any Fruit with That Big Mac?" *New York Times*, 20 February 2005, http://www.nytimes.com/2005/02/30/business/yourmoney/20mac.html.

37. Personal correspondence with Marissa, July 1998.

38. Interview with Marissa, Toronto, October 1997.

39. http://www.100milediet.org/category/about/, accessed 3 June 2007. See also Alisa Smith and J. B. MacKinnon, *The 100-Mile Diet: A Year of Local Eating* (Toronto: Random House Canada, 2007), and Barbara Kingsolver, *Animal, Vegetable, Miracle: A Year of Food Life* (New York: HarperCollins, 2007).

40. Debbie Field, speaking to the "Building Power: Participatory Democracy in Latin America" Conference, Ryerson University, Toronto, April 2007.

41. Allison Gifford, "Food Fighters," *This Magazine* (May/June 2002): 23.

42. The rich process and products of the Roots and Routes project are analyzed in Deborah Barndt and Anuja Mendiratta, "Telling Food and Eating Stories: Immigrant Women Tap the Power of Food," unpublished paper, 1999.

43. Seeds of Our City was funded for three years by the Urban Issues Program of the Samuel and Saidye Bronfman Family Foundation of Montreal, and resulted in a report, "Seeds of Our City: Case Studies from 8 Diverse Gardens in Toronto," which can be ordered from www.foodshare.net.

44. Lauren Baker and Jin Huh, "Rich Harvest," *Alternatives Journal* 29 no. 1: 21–25.

45. http://www.foodsecurecanada.org/about.html.

46. There have been debates internationally between those (primarily in the north) who frame their activism around issues of "food security" and those (primarily in the south) who see their struggles as better defined as the fight for "food sovereignty." In some ways, this debate reflects the distancing perpetuated by a global food system in which production has been relegated to southern lands and labor, driven by the demands and interests of northern consumers and retailers. Food Secure Canada tries to address food sovereignty but could still have better transnational links with peasant, Indigenous, and social justice organizations in the south.

47. Andrew Quinn, quoted by Carole Pearson, "The Future of Food: A Labour Issue," *Our Times*, August/September 2006, 24.

48. http://canadianlabour.ca.

49. http://canadianlabour.ca/index.php/healthy_food_campaign, accessed 27 May 2007.

50. Quoted in Carole Pearson, "The Future of Food," 21.

51. Pearson, "The Future of Food," 22.

52. http://www.laneta.apc.org/rmalc, accessed 27 May 2007.

53. http://www.art-us.org/about_art, accessed 27 May 2007.

54. http://www.commonfrontiers.ca/aboutus.html, accessed 27 May 2007.

55. Common Frontiers, "'Free Trade' at the Crossroads," 1, report can be downloaded from http://www.commonfrontiers.ca.

56. In April 2006, Alberta and British Columbia entered into a "Trade, Investment and Labour Mobility Agreement," prohibiting any restriction on trade and covering municipalities, school boards, and health and social service entities. Ibid., 3.

57. Ibid., 2.

58. Unpublished handout, "Declaration of the Second People's Summit of the Americas," Quebec City, 19 April 2001.

59. Annette Aurélie Desmarais, *La Vía Campesina: Globalization and the Power of Peasants* (Black Point, Nova Scotia: Fernwood Publishing, 2007), 6.

60. http://www.peoplesfoodsovereignty.org/new/statements.container.htm.

61. In defense, NGOs tried to discredit Vía Campesina and other peasant organizations as not being authentic representatives of farmers, as though the NGOs could better represent their interests. Desmarais, *La Vía Campesina*, 133–34.

62. Each day of the conference began with a region representing its history, peasant roots, and current struggles using cultural forms that broke through language barriers, "accentuating the cultural significance of seed and planting ceremonies, a history of oppression and repression, and a determination to survive against enormous odds." Desmarais, *La Vía Campesina*, 188.

63. http://www.slowfood.com/about_us/eng/philosophy.lasso, accessed 3 June 2007.

64. During the period of this study, I have been privileged to supervise the MES major papers of outstanding student activists, who have taught me as much as I have taught them. See Lauren Baker, "Global Food Systems, Local Responses" (1998); Charlie Clarke, "There Is Always This Tension: Stories of and Reflections on Student Activism in the Movement for Global Justice" (2003); Sheelagh Davis, "Popular Education for Sustainable Community Alternatives: The Case of Perempitz, Mexico" (2000); Michele Doncaster, "Linking Urban and Rural Life" (Campo y Ciudad: La Misma Coas) (2001); Erika Fuchs, "Pedagogía de la Terra: Popular Education in the Brazilian Landless Peasant Movement" (2004); Mark Juhasz, "The NAFTA and Environmental Politics in Mexico: The Communicative Process under Agricultural Modernization" (2001); Melanie Kramer, "Garden the City: Interventionist Art" (2003); Leslie Lane, "Maize as Cultural Messenger" (2006); Egla Martinez-Salazar, "Indigenous Women and Men and Development in Post-Conflict Guatemala" (1999); Anuja Mendiratta, "Local Responses to the 'Dominant Global Food System'" (1999); Sally Miller, "Food Fight: Cultivating Democracy through Alternatives to the Food System" (2004); Lisa Mitchell, "The Praxis of Popular Environmental Education" (2004); Danielle Schami, "Building Alternatives to the Dominant Food System in Jalisco, Mexico: The Circle of Responsible Production and Consumption" (2002); and Roberta Stimac, "From Seed to Seed" (2005).

65. Pablo Neruda, 1971 Nobel Prize Acceptance Speech, quoted in Valerie Miller, *Between Struggle and Hope: The Nicaraguan Literacy Crusade* (Boulder, Colo.: Westview, 1985), 1.

In Gratitude

The challenge of producing the second edition of *Tangled Routes* offered me a chance to revisit key collaborators and the people whose stories are featured in these pages. This process reminded me that such research projects are never just about creating knowledge, they are also about relationships. Through the Tomasita Project, I have developed lifelong friendships—which are often reaffirmed around food! On this page, I honor some who were central to this new edition: in Mexico, Gabriel Torres, who for more than ten years has joined me in the hunt for tomato companies; Antonieta Barrón, whose work on women workers inspired me and whose kitchen table and family are my home base in Mexico; Teresa and Pedro Sintero de la Torre who, along with their granddaughter Ana Maria, are now picking cherry tomatoes at a U.S.-owned Mexican greenhouse; Amanda Henderson, my quintessential research assistant; and Wendy Rogers, the featured Loblaws cashier, who has become a researcher, too, in this endless, tangled, and delightful process. My gratitude to them and to others!

Index

319

About the Author

Deborah Barndt is a mother, popular educator, photographer, and professor on the faculty of environmental studies at York University in Toronto. For over forty years she has worked with social justice movements in Canada, the United States, and Central America. Her photographs have been published and exhibited widely, and her extensive publications include *Education and Social Change: A Photographic Study of Peru; To Change This House: Popular Education under the Sandinistas; Naming the Moment: Political Analysis for Action; Women Working the NAFTA Food Chain: Women, Food, and Globalization* (editor); *Just Doing It: Popular Collective Action in the Americas* (co-editor with Gene Desfor and Barbara Rahder) and *Wild Fire: Art as Activism* (editor).